STRATEGY

THE INDIRECT APPROACH

STRATEGY

THE INDIRECT APPROACH

B.H. Liddell Hart

PENTAGON PRESS

Strategy: The Indirect Approach / **B.H. Liddell Hart**

First Indian Edition: 2012

Reprint: 2022

ISBN 978-81-8274-607-7

Indian Edition Published by arrangement.

Published in India by

PENTAGON PRESS
206, Peacock Lane, Shahpur Jat,
New Delhi-110049
Phones: 011-64706243, 26491568
Telefax: 011-26490600
email: rajan@pentagonpress.in
website: www.pentagonpress.in

Printed at New Elegant Printers, New Delhi.

To

IVOR MAXSE

Trainer of Troops for War

CONTENTS

★

CONTENTS

Part III

STRATEGY OF THE SECOND WORLD WAR

Part IV

FUNDAMENTALS OF STRATEGY AND GRAND STRATEGY

MAPS

★

Sketch Maps

MAPS

★

Sketch Maps

'All warfare is based on deception. Hence, when able to attack, we must seem unable; when using our forces, we must seem inactive; when we are near, we must make the enemy believe that we are away; when far away, we must make him believe we are near. Hold out baits to entice the enemy. Feign disorder, and crush him.'

'There is no instance of a country having been benefited from prolonged warfare.'

'It is only one who is thoroughly acquainted with the evils of war that can thoroughly understand the profitable way of carrying it on.'

'Supreme excellence consists in breaking the enemy's resistance without fighting.

Thus the highest form of generalship is to baulk the enemy's plans; the next best is to prevent the junction of the enemy's forces; the next in order is to attack the enemy's army in the field; the worst policy of all is to besiege walled cities.'

'In all fighting, the direct method may be used for joining battle, but indirect methods will be needed in order to secure victory.'

'Appear at points which the enemy must hasten to defend, march swiftly to places where you are not expected.'

'You may advance and be absolutely irresistible, if you make for the enemy's weak points; you may retire and be safe from pursuit if your movements are more rapid than those of the enemy.'

'All men can see these tactics whereby I conquer, but what none can see is the strategy out of which victory is evolved.'

'Military tactics are like unto water; for water in its natural course runs away from high places and hastens downwards. So in war, the way to avoid what is strong is to strike what is weak.

Water shapes its course according to the ground over which it flows; the soldier works out his victory in relation to the foe whom he is facing.'

'Thus, to take a long circuitous route, after enticing the enemy out of the way, and though starting after him, to contrive to reach the goal before him, shows knowledge of the artifice of *deviation*.'

'He will conquer who has learnt the artifice of deviation. Such is the art of manœuvring.'

'To refrain from intercepting an enemy whose banners are in perfect order, to refrain from attacking an army drawn up in calm and confident array—this is the art of studying circumstances.'

'When you surround an army leave an outlet free. Do not press a desperate foe too hard.'

'Rapidity is the essence of war; take advantage of the enemy's unreadiness, make your way by unexpected routes, and attack unguarded spots.'

SUN TZU, *The Art of War*—500 B.C.

'The most complete and happy victory is this: to compel one's enemy to give up his purpose, while suffering no harm oneself.'

BELISARIUS

'By indirections find directions out.'

SHAKESPEARE, *Hamlet*, Act II, Scene I

'The whole art of war consists in a well-reasoned and extremely circumspect defensive, followed by rapid and audacious attack.'

NAPOLEON

'All military action is permeated by intelligent forces and their effects.'

CLAUSEWITZ

'A clever military leader will succeed in many cases in choosing defensive positions of such an offensive nature from the strategic point of view that the enemy is compelled to attack us in them.'

MOLTKE

'Gallant fellows, these soldiers; they always go for the thickest place in the fence.'

ADMIRAL DE ROBECK—
watching the Gallipoli landing, 25th April 1915

PREFACE

★

The appearance of the hydrogen bomb has cast a shadow over the world—and the gloom is deepest in 'the free world'. Those whom the weapon was designed to protect show a much more acute anxiety. Their increased sense of insecurity is an ironical reflection on the hasty and thoughtless way in which their leaders agreed in 1945 to unloose the atomic 'Frankenstein's monster' in order to hasten Japan's collapse. The most startlingly significant revelation in the final volume of Sir Winston Churchill's war memoirs, aptly entitled *Triumph and Tragedy*, is his statement that 'there never was a moment's discussion as to whether the atomic bomb should be used or not.'

The H-bomb might be regarded as retribution for Hiroshima—a 'trigger-release' which looked to the responsible statemen so easy and simple a way of assuring a quickly complete victory and subsequent world peace. Their thought, Sir Winston Churchill says, was that: 'to bring the war to an end, to give peace to the world, to lay healing hands upon its tortured peoples by a manifestation of overwhelming power at the cost of a few explosions, seemed, after all our toils and perils, a miracle of deliverance.' But the tortured anxiety of the peoples of the free world to-day is a manifestation that their leaders failed to think *through* the problem—of attaining peace through such a victory.

They did not look beyond the immediate strategic aim of 'winning the war', and were content to assume that military victory would assure peace—an assumption contrary to the general experience of history. The outcome has been the latest of many lessons that pure military strategy needs to be guided by the longer and wider view from the higher plane of 'grand strategy'.

In the circumstances of World War II, the pursuit of triumph was foredoomed to turn into tragedy, *and* futility. A complete overthrow of Germany's power of resistance was bound to clear the way for Soviet Russia's domination of the Eurasian continent, and for a vast extension of Communist power in all directions. It was equally natural that the striking demonstration of atomic weapons with which the war closed should be followed by Russia's development of similar weapons.

No peace ever brought so little security, and after eight nerve-racking years the production of thermo-nuclear weapons has deepened the 'victorious peoples' sense of insecurity. But that is not the only effect.

The H-bomb, even in its trial explosions, has done more than anything else to make plain the nonsense of 'total war' as a method and 'victory' as a war-aim. Both terms, and the concepts they express, are seen to be totally absurd.

That has come to be recognized by the chief exponents of strategic bombing. Marshal of the R.A.F. Sir John Slessor recently declared his belief that 'total war as we have known it in the past forty years is a thing of the past . . . a world war in this day and age would be general suicide and the end of civilization as we know it.' Marshal of the R.A.F. Lord Tedder earlier emphasized the same point as 'an accurate, cold statement of the actual possibilities', and said: 'A contest using the atomic weapon would be no duel, but rather mutual suicide.'

Less logically, he added: 'that is scarcely a prospect to encourage aggression.' For a cold-blooded aggressor may count on his opponents' natural reluctance to commit suicide—as an immediate response to a threat that is not clearly fatal.

Would any responsible government, when it came to the point, dare to *use* the H-bomb as an answer to indirect aggression, or any aggression of a local and limited kind? It would be lunacy to take the lead in what the air chiefs themselves warn us would be 'suicide'. So it may be assumed that the H-bomb would not be used against any menace less certainly and immediately fatal than itself.

The trust which the statesmen place in such weapons as a deterrent to aggression would seem to rest on illusion. The threat to use this trump-card may be regarded as a bluff. Indeed, it is less likely to be taken seriously in Russia, and the Kremlin in particular, than in countries on the near side of the Iron Curtain whose people are perilously close to Russia and *her* strategic bombing forces. The atomic threat, if exploited for their protection, may only suffice to weaken their resolution in resistance. Its 'backblast' has already been very damaging.

PREFACE

The H-bomb is more handicap than help to the policy of 'containment'. To the extent that it reduces the likelihood of all-out war, it increases the possibilities of 'limited war' pursued by indirect and widespread local aggression. The aggressor can exploit a choice of techniques, differing in pattern but all designed to make headway while causing hesitancy—about employing counter-action with H-bombs, or A-bombs.

For the 'containment' of the menace we now become more dependent on 'conventional weapons'. That conclusion, however, does not mean that we must fall back on conventional methods. It should be an incentive to the development of newer ones.

We have moved into a new era of strategy that is very different to what was assumed by the advocates of air-atomic power—the 'revolutionaries' of the past era. The strategy now being developed by our opponents is inspired by the dual idea of evading and ham-stringing superior air-power. Ironically, the further we have developed the 'massive' effect of the bombing weapon, the more we have helped the progress of this new guerrilla-type strategy.

Our own strategy should be based on a clear grasp of this concept, and our military policy needs re-orientation. There is scope, and we might effectively develop it, for a counter-strategy of corresponding kind. Here one may remark, in parenthesis, that to wipe out cities with H-bombs would be to destroy our potential 'Fifth Column' assets.

The common assumption that atomic power has cancelled out strategy is ill-founded, and misleading. By carrying destructiveness to a 'suicidal' extreme, atomic power is stimulating and accelerating a reversion to the indirect methods that are the essence of strategy—since they endow warfare with intelligent properties that raise it above the brute application of force. Signs of such a reversion to the 'indirect approach' had already become manifest in World War II—where strategy played a greater part than in World War I, although grand strategy was missing. Now, the atomic deterrent to direct action on familiar lines is tending to foster a deeper strategic subtlety on the part of aggressors. It thus becomes all the more important that this development should be matched by a similar understanding of strategical power on our side. The history of strategy is, fundamentally, a record of the application and evolution of the indirect approach.

Twenty-five years have passed since my original study of 'the strategy of indirect approach' was published, under the title *The*

Decisive Wars of History. In 1941 an enlarged edition was brought out, under the theme title. Further editions were published during and immediately after the war, but the book has been out of print in English for a long time. Moreover, the larger book, *The Strategy of Indirect Approach*, was never published in the U.S.A.—only the original 1929 thesis. The growing number of foreign translations since the war has suggested that it might be worth while to bring it out again in English, and take the opportunity of extending its account of the history of strategy and of expanding its discussion of the theory of strategy. In the process, it has become a much bigger book—without, I hope, departing from the original aim of pruning the unessential detail of campaigns so that 'the wood' should not be obscured by 'the trees'.

When, in the course of studying a long series of military campaigns, I first came to perceive the superiority of the indirect over the direct approach, I was looking merely for light upon strategy. With deepening reflection, however, I began to realize that the indirect approach had a much wider application—that it was a law of life in all spheres: a truth of philosophy. Its fulfilment was seen to be the key to practical achievement in dealing with any problem where the human factor predominates, and a conflict of wills tends to spring from an underlying concern for interests. In all such cases, the direct assault of new ideas provokes a stubborn resistance, thus intensifying the difficulty of producing a change of outlook. Conversion is achieved more easily and rapidly by unsuspected infiltration of a different idea or by an argument that turns the flank of instinctive opposition. The indirect approach is as fundamental to the realm of politics as to the realm of sex. In commerce, the suggestion that there is a bargain to be secured is far more potent than any direct appeal to buy. And in any sphere it is proverbial that the surest way of gaining a superior's acceptance of a new idea is to persuade him that it is his idea! As in war, the aim is to weaken resistance before attempting to overcome it; and the effect is best attained by drawing the other party out of his defences.

This idea of the indirect approach is closely related to all problems of the influence of mind upon mind—the most influential factor in human history. Yet it is hard to reconcile with another lesson: that true conclusions can only be reached, or approached, by pursuing the truth without regard to where it may lead or what its effect may be—on different interests.

PREFACE

History bears witness to the vital part that the 'prophets' have played in human progress—which is evidence of the ultimate practical value of expressing unreservedly the truth as one sees it. Yet it also becomes clear that the acceptance and spreading of their vision has always depended on another class of men—'leaders' who had to be philosophical strategists, striking a compromise between truth and men's receptivity to it. Their effect has often depended as much on their own limitations in perceiving the truth as on their practical wisdom in proclaiming it.

The prophets must be stoned; that is their lot, and the test of their self-fulfilment. But a leader who is stoned may merely prove that he has failed in his function through a deficiency of wisdom, or through confusing his function with that of a prophet. Time alone can tell whether the effect of such a sacrifice redeems the apparent failure as a leader that does honour to him as a man. At the least, he avoids the more common fault of leaders—that of sacrificing the truth to expediency without ultimate advantage to the cause. For whoever habitually suppresses the truth in the interests of tact will produce a deformity from the womb of his thought.

Is there a practical way of combining progress towards the attainment of truth with progress towards its acceptance? A possible solution of the problem is suggested by reflection on strategic principles—which point to the importance of maintaining an object consistently and, also, of pursuing it in a way adapted to circumstances. Opposition to the truth is inevitable, especially if it takes the form of a new idea, but the degree of resistance can be diminished—by giving thought not only to the aim but to the method of approach. Avoid a frontal attack on a long established position; instead, seek to turn it by a flank movement, so that a more penetrable side is exposed to the thrust of truth. But, in any such indirect approach, take care not to diverge from the truth—for nothing is more fatal to its real advancement than to lapse into untruth.

The meaning of these reflections may be made clearer by illustration from one's own experience. Looking back on the stages by which various fresh ideas gained acceptance, it can be seen that the process was eased when they could be presented, not as something radically new, but as the revival in modern terms of a time-honoured principle or practice that had been forgotten. This required not deception, but care to trace the connection—since 'there is nothing new under the sun'. A notable example was the way that the opposition to mechanization was diminished by showing that the mobile armoured vehicle—the fast-moving tank—was fundamentally the heir of the armoured horseman, and thus the natural means of reviving the decisive role which cavalry had played in past ages.

B. H. Liddell Hart

PREFACE TO THE ORIGINAL EDITION

★

The first chapter of this book is in a general sense the preface, explaining its purpose, scope, and theme. These have evolved more gradually and less consecutively than is usual in the preparation of a book, and as the guiding idea has been that of an attempt to distil the essence of one's reading and reflection over a number of years, so the historical narrative is a condensed product of the notes made when studying each of the several wars epitomized. It would have been easier to have woven these notes into a narrative of greater length, but the desire that the 'wood' should not be obsucred by the 'trees' has prompted a severe pruning of unessential facts. If the foliage is too bare for the taste of some readers, I would ask their forgiveness on the score that, for the specialized student, this book is intended as a guide in historical study rather than as a compendium of history.

I would also utilize this 'preliminary' preface to acknowledge the kindness of those who have read and criticized the typescript and proofs at various stages. For helpful comments and suggestions my thanks are due, in particular, to my friends, Brigadiers J. G. Dill, B. D. Fisher, J. F. C. Fuller, H. Karslake, Colonel the Viscount Gort, Mr. E. G. Hawke, and T.E.S.

(These were their ranks in 1929 when the original edition was published—but now read: Field-Marshal Sir John Dill, Lieut.-General Sir Bertie Fisher, Major-General J. F. C. Fuller, Lieut.-General Sir Henry Karslake, and Field-Marshal the Viscount Gort. The late T. E. Lawrence was then serving in the ranks of the Royal Air Force under the name of T. E. Shaw, legally assumed for the time, and for reasons of discretion wished only his initials to appear in the acknowledgement.)

PART I

★

STRATEGY FROM FIFTH CENTURY B.C. TO TWENTIETH CENTURY A.D.

CHAPTER I

HISTORY AS PRACTICAL EXPERIENCE

★

'Fools say that they learn by experience. I prefer to profit by others' experience.' This saying, quoted of Bismarck, but by no means original to him, has a special bearing on military questions. Unlike those who follow other professions, the 'regular' soldier cannot regularly practise his profession. Indeed, it might even be argued that in a literal sense the profession of arms is not a profession at all, but merely 'casual employment'—and, paradoxically, that it ceased to be a profession when mercenary troops who were employed and paid for the purpose of a war were replaced by standing armies which continued to be paid when there was no war.

If the argument—that strictly there is no 'profession of arms'—will not hold good in most armies to-day on the score of work, it is inevitably strengthened on the score of practice because wars have become fewer, though bigger, compared with earlier times. For even the best of peace training is more 'theoretical' than 'practical' experience.

But Bismarck's aphorism throws a different and more encouraging light on the problem. It helps us to realize that there are two forms of practical experience, direct and indirect—and that, of the two, indirect practical experience may be the more valuable because infinitely wider. Even in the most active career, especially a soldier's career, the scope and possibilities of direct experience are extremely limited. In contrast to the military, the medical profession has incessant practice. Yet the great advances in medicine and surgery have been due more to the scientific thinker and research worker than to the practitioner.

Direct experience is inherently too limited to form an adequate foundation either for theory or for application. At the best it produces an atmosphere that is of value in drying and hardening the structure of thought. The greater value of indirect experience lies in its greater variety and extent. 'History is universal experience'—the experience not of another, but of many others under manifold conditions.

Here is the rational justification for military history as the basis of military education—its preponderant practical value in the training and mental development of a soldier. But the benefit depends, as with all experience, on its breadth: on how closely it approaches the definition quoted above; and on the method of studying it.

Soldiers universally concede the general truth of Napoleon's much-quoted dictum that in war 'the moral is to the physical as three to one'. The actual arithmetical proportion may be worthless, for morale is apt to decline if weapons are inadequate, and the strongest will is of little use if it is inside a dead body. But although the moral and physical factors are inseparable and indivisible, the saying gains its enduring value because it expresses the idea of the predominance of moral factors in all military decisions. On them constantly turns the issue of war and battle. In the history of war they form the more constant factors, changing only in degree, whereas the physical factors are different in almost every war and every military situation.

This realization affects the whole question of the study of military history for practical use. The method in recent generations has been to select one or two campaigns, and to study them exhaustively as a means of professional training and as the foundation of military theory. But with such a limited basis the continual changes in military means from war to war carry the danger that our outlook will be narrow and the lessons fallacious. In the physical sphere, the one constant factor is that means and conditions are invariably inconstant.

In contrast, human nature varies but slightly in its reaction to danger. Some men by heredity, by environment, or by training may be less sensitive than others, but the difference is one of degree, not fundamental. The more localized the situation, and our study, the more disconcerting and less calculable is such a difference of degree. It may prevent any exact calculation of the resistance which men will offer in any situation, but it does not impair the judgement that they will offer less if taken by surprise than if they are on the alert; less if they are weary and hungry than if they are fresh and well fed. The broader the psychological survey the better foundation it affords for deductions

The predominance of the psychological over the physical, and its greater constancy, point to the conclusion that the foundation of any theory of war should be as broad as possible. An intensive study of one campaign unless based on an extensive knowledge of the whole history of war is likely to lead us into pitfalls. But if a specific effect is seen to follow a specific cause in a score or more cases, in different epochs and diverse conditions, there is ground for regarding this cause as an integral part of any theory of war.

The thesis set forth in this book was the product of such an 'extensive' examination. It might, indeed, be termed the compound effect of certain causes—these being connected with my task as military editor of the *Encyclopaedia Britannica*. For while I had previously delved into various periods of military history according to my inclination, this task compelled a general survey of all periods. A surveyor—even a tourist, if you will—has at least a wide perspective and can take in the general lie of the land, where the miner knows only his own seam.

During this survey one impression became increasingly strong—that, throughout the ages, effective results in war have rarely been attained unless the approach has had such indirectness as to ensure the opponent's unreadiness to meet it. The indirectness has usually been physical, and always psychological. In strategy, the longest way round is often the shortest way home.

More and more clearly has the lesson emerged that a direct approach to one's mental object, or physical objective, along the 'line of natural expectation' for the opponent, tends to produce negative results. The reason has been expressed vividly in Napoleon's dictum that 'the moral is to the physical as three to one'. It may be expressed scientifically by saying that, while the strength of an opposing force or country lies outwardly in its numbers and resources, these are fundamentally dependent upon stability of control, morale, and supply.

To move along the line of natural expectation consolidates the opponent's balance and thus increases his resisting power. In war, as in wrestling, the attempt to throw the opponent without loosening his foothold and upsetting his balance results in self-exhaustion, increasing in disproportionate ratio to the effective strain put upon him. Success by such a method only becomes possible through an immense margin of superior strength in some form—and, even so, tends to lose decisiveness. In most campaigns the dislocation of the enemy's psychological and physical balance has been the vital prelude to a successful attempt at his overthrow.

This dislocation has been produced by a strategic indirect approach, intentional or fortuitous. It may take varied forms, as analysis reveals. For the strategy of indirect approach is inclusive of, but wider than, the *manœuvre sur les derrières* which General Camon's researches showed as being the constant aim and key-method of Napoleon in his conduct of operations. Camon was concerned primarily with the logistical moves—the factors of time, space, and communications. But analysis of the psychological factors has made it clear that there is an underlying relationship between many strategical operations which have no outward resemblance to a manœuvre against the enemy's rear—yet are, none the less definitely, vital examples of the 'strategy of indirect approach'.

To trace this relationship and to determine the character of the operations, it is unnecessary to tabulate the numerical strengths and the details of supply and transport. Our concern is simply with the historical effects in a comprehensive series of cases, and with the logistical or psychological moves which led up to them.

If similar effects follow fundamentally similar moves, in conditions which vary widely in nature, scale, and date, there is clearly an underlying connection from which we can logically deduce a common cause. And the more widely the conditions vary, the firmer is this deduction.

The objective value of a broad survey of war is not limited to the research for new and true doctrine. If a broad survey is an essential foundation for any theory of war, it is equally necessary for the ordinary military student who seeks to develop his own outlook and judgement. Otherwise his knowledge of war will be like an inverted pyramid balanced precariously on a slender apex.

CHAPTER II

GREEK WARS—EPAMINONDAS, PHILIP, AND ALEXANDER

★

The most natural starting-point for a survey is the first 'Great War' in European history—the Great Persian War. We cannot expect much guidance from a period when strategy was in its infancy; but the name of Marathon is too deeply stamped on the mind and imagination of all readers of history to be disregarded. It was still more impressed on the imagination of the Greeks; hence its importance came to be exaggerated by them and, through them, by Europeans in all subsequent ages. Yet by the reduction of its importance to juster proportions, its strategical significance is increased.

The Persian invasion of 490 B.C. was a comparatively small expedition intended to teach Eretria and Athens—petty states in the eyes of Darius—to mind their own business and abstain from encouraging revolt among Persia's Greek subjects in Asia Minor. Eretria was destroyed and its inhabitants deported for resettlement on the Persian Gulf. Next came the turn of Athens, where the ultra-democratic party was known to be waiting to aid the Persian intervention against their own conservative party. The Persians, instead of making a direct advance on Athens, landed at Marathon, twenty-four miles north-east of it. Thereby they could calculate on drawing the Athenian army towards them, thus facilitating the seizure of power in Athens by their adherents, whereas a direct attack on the city would have hampered such a rising, perhaps even have rallied its force against them; and in any case have given them the extra difficulty of a siege.

If this was the Persians' calculation, the bait succeeded. The Athenian army marched out to Marathon to meet them, while they proceeded to execute the next step in their strategical plan. Under the protection of a covering force, they re-embarked the rest of the army in order to move it round to Phalerum, land there, and make a spring at unguarded Athens. The subtlety of the strategic design is notable, even though it miscarried owing to a variety of factors.

Thanks to the energy of Miltiades, the Athenians took their one chance by striking without delay at the covering force. In the Marathon battle, the superior armour and longer spears of the Greeks, always their supreme assets against the Persians, helped to give them the victory—although the fight was harder than patriotic legend suggested, and most of the covering force got safely away on the ships. With still more creditable energy the Athenians countermarched rapidly back to their city, and this rapidity, combined with the dilatoriness of the disaffected party, saved them. For when the Athenian army was back in Athens, and the Persians saw that a siege was unavoidable, they sailed back to Asia—as their merely punitive object did not seem worth purchasing at a heavy price.

Ten years passed before the Persians made another and greater effort. The Greeks had been slow to profit by the warning, and it was not until 487 B.C. that Athens began the expansion of her fleet —which was to be the decisive factor in countering the Persian's superiority in land forces. Thus it can with truth be said that Greece and Europe were saved by a revolt in Egypt—which kept Persia's attention occupied from 486 to 484—as well as by the death of Darius, ablest of the Persian rulers of that epoch.

When the menace developed, in 481, this time on a grand scale, its very magnitude not only consolidated the Greek factions and states against it, but compelled Xerxes to make a direct approach to his goal. For the army was too big to be transported by sea, and so was compelled to take an overland route. And it was too big to supply itself, so that the fleet had to be used for this purpose. The army was tied to the coast, and the navy tied to the army—each tied by the leg. Thus the Greeks could be sure as to the line along which to expect the enemy's approach, and the Persians were unable to depart from it.

The nature of the country afforded the Greeks a series of points at which they could firmly block the line of natural expectation and, as Grundy has remarked, but for the Greeks' own dissensions of interest and counsel 'it is probable that the invaders would never have got south of Thermopylae'. As it was, history gained an immortal story and it was left to the Greek fleet to dislocate the invasion irredeemably by defeating the Persian fleet at Salamis—while Xerxes and the Persian army watched helplessly the destruction of what was not merely their fleet, but, more vitally, their source of supply.

It is worth noting that the opportunity for this decisive naval battle was obtained by a ruse which might be classified as a form of indirect approach—Themistocles' message to Xerxes that the Greek fleet was ripe for treacherous surrender. The deception, which drew the Persian fleet into the narrow straits where their superiority of numbers was discounted, proved all the more effective because past experience endowed the message with plausibility. Indeed, Themistocles' message was inspired by his fear that the allied Peloponnesian commanders would withdraw from Salamis, as they had advocated in the council of war—thus leaving the Athenian fleet to fight alone, or giving the Persians a chance to use their superior numbers in the open sea.

On the other side there was only one voice raised against Xerxes' eager desire for battle. It was that of the sailor-queen, Artemisia, from Halicarnassus, who is recorded as urging the contary plan of abstaining from a direct assault and, instead, co-operating with the Persian land forces in a move against the Peloponnesus. She argued that the Peloponnesian naval contingents would react to such a threat by sailing for home, and thereby cause the disintegration of the Greek fleet. It would seem that her anticipation was as well justified as Themistocles' anxiety, and that such a withdrawal would have been carried out the very next morning but for the fact that the Persian galleys blocked the outlets, preparatory to attack.

But the attack started to take a turn fatally disadvantageous to the attackers through a withdrawal on the part of the defenders which acted like a bait in drawing the heavier side into an unbalanced lunge. For when the attackers advanced through the narrow straits, the Greek galleys backed away. The Persian galleys thereupon quickened their rate of rowing, and as a result became a congested mass, helplessly exposed to the counterstroke which the Greek galleys delivered from either flank.

In the seventy years that followed, one of the chief factors which restrained the Persians from further intervention in Greece would seem to have been the power of indirect approach, to the Persians' own communications, that Athens could wield—this deduction is supported by the prompt revival of such interference after the

GREECE
Miles
10 0 20 40
Land over 3000 ft.
Stanford. London.
Thermopylae
Cytinium
Amphissa
Naupactus
Elatea
Parapotamii
Chaeronea
BOEOTIA
Thebes
Leuctra
Eretria
Marathon
Athens
Salamis
Corinth
Mantinea
Tegea
Caryae
Megalopolis
Mount Ithome
Messene

destruction of the Athenian fleet at Syracuse. Historically, it is worth note that the use of strategic mobility for an indirect approach was realized and exploited much earlier in sea than in land warfare. The natural reason is that only in a late stage of development did *armies* come to depend upon 'lines of communication' for their supply. Fleets, however, were used to operate against the seaborne communications, or means of supply, of opposing *countries*.

With the passing of the Persian menace, the sequel to Salamis was the rise of Athens to the ascendency in Greek affairs. This ascendency was ended by the Peloponnesian War (431–404 B.C.). The extravagant duration of these twenty-seven years of warfare, and their terrible drain—not only on the chief adversaries but on the luckless would-be neutrals—may be traced to the fluctuating and often purposeless strategy into which both sides repeatedly drifted.

In the first phase Sparta and her allies attempted a direct invasion of Attica. They were foiled by Pericles's war policy, of refusing battle on land while using the superior Athenian navy to wear down the enemy's will by devastating raids.

Although the phrase 'Periclean strategy' is almost as familiar as that of 'Fabian strategy' in a later age, such a phrase narrows and confuses the significance of the course that war pursued. Clear-cut nomenclature is essential to clear thought, and the term 'strategy' is best confined to its literal meaning of 'generalship'—the actual direction of military force, as distinct from the policy governing its employment and combining it with other weapons: economic, political, psychological. Such policy is in application a higher-level strategy, for which the term 'grand strategy' has been coined.

In contrast to a strategy of indirect approach which seeks to dislocate the enemy's balance in order to produce a decision, the Periclean plan was a grand strategy with the aim of gradually draining the enemy's endurance in order to convince him that he could not gain a decision. Unluckily for Athens, an importation of plague tipped the scales against her in this moral and economic attrition campaign. Hence in 426 B.C. the Periclean strategy was made to give place to the direct offensive strategy of Cleon and Demosthenes. This cost more, and succeeded no better, despite some brilliant tactical successes. Then, in the early winter of 424 B.C., Brasidas, Sparta's ablest soldier, wiped out all the advantage that Athens had painfully won. He did this by a strategic move directed against the roots, instead of the trunk, of the enemy power. By-passing Athens itself, he marched swiftly north through the length of Greece and struck at the Athenian dominion in Chalcidice—aptly termed the 'Achilles heel of the Athenian empire'. Through a combination of military force with the promise of freedom and protection to all cities which revolted against her, he so shook the hold of Athens in Chalcidice that he drew her main forces thither. At Amphipolis they suffered a disastrous defeat. Although Brasidas himself fell in the moment of victory, Athens was glad to conclude a negative peace with Sparta.

In the succeeding years of pseudo-peace, repeated Athenian expeditions failed to regain the lost footing in Chalcidice. Then, as a last offensive resort, Athens undertook an expedition against Syracuse, the key to Sicily, whence came the overseas food supply of Sparta and the Peloponnese generally. As a grand strategy of indirect approach it had the defect of striking, not at the enemy's actual partners, but rather at his business associates. Thereby, instead of distracting the enemy's forces, it drew fresh forces into opposition.

Nevertheless, the moral and economic results of success might well have changed the whole balance of the war if there had not been an almost unparalleled chain of blunders in execution. Alcibiades, the author of the plan, was recalled from his joint command by the intrigues of his political enemies. Rather than return to be put on trial for sacrilege, and meet a certain death sentence, he fled to Sparta—there to advise the other side how to thwart his own plan. The stubborn opponent of the plan, Nicias, was left in command to carry it out, and by his obstinate stupidity, carried it to ruin.

With her army lost at Syracuse, Athens staved off defeat at home by the use of her fleet, and in the nine years of sea warfare which followed she came within reach not only of an advantageous peace but of the restoration of her empire. Her prospects, however, were dramatically extinguished by the Spartan admiral, Lysander, in 405 B.C. In the words of the *Cambridge Ancient History* 'his plan of campaign . . . was to avoid fighting, and reduce the Athenians to extremities by attacking their empire at its most vulnerable points. . . .' The first clause is hardly accurate, for his plan was not so much an evasion of battle as an indirect approach to it—so that he might obtain the opportunity when, and where, the odds were heavily in his favour. By skilful and mystifying changes of course, he reached the entrance to the Dardanelles and there lay in wait for the Pontic grain-ships on their way to Athens. 'Since the grain supply of Athens was a life interest,' the Athenian commanders 'hurried with their entire fleet of 180 ships to safeguard it. For four successive days they tried in vain to tempt Lysander to battle, while he gave them every encouragement to think they had cornered him. Thus, instead of retiring to revictual in the safe harbour of Sestos, they stayed in the open strait opposite him at Aegospotamoi. On the fifth day, when most of the crews had gone ashore to collect food, he suddenly sallied out, captured almost the whole fleet without a blow, and 'in one single hour brought the longest of wars to an end'.

In this twenty-seven years' struggle, where scores of direct approaches failed, usually to the injury of those who made them, the scales were definitely turned against Athens by Brasidas's move against her Chalcidice 'root'. The best-founded hopes of a recovery came with Alcibiades' indirect approach—on the plane of grand strategy—to Sparta's economic root in Sicily. And the *coup de grâce*, after another ten years' prolongation, was given by a tactical indirect approach at sea, which was itself the sequel to a fresh indirect approach in grand strategy. For it should be noted that the opportunity was created by menacing the Athenians' 'national' lines of communication. By taking an economic objective Lysander could hope at the least to drain their strength; through the exasperation and fear thus generated, he was able to produce conditions favourable to surprise and so obtain a swift military decision.

With the fall of the Athenian empire the next phase in Greek history is the assumption by Sparta of the headship of Greece. Our next question is, therefore—what was the decisive factor in ending Sparta's ascendancy? The answer is—a man, and his contribution to the science and art of warfare. In the years immediately preceding the rise of Epaminondas, Thebes had released herself from Sparta's dominion by the method later christened Fabian, of refusing battle—a grand strategy of indirect approach, but a strategy merely of evasion—while Spartan armies wandered unopposed through Boeotia. This method gained Thebes time to develop a picked professional force, famous as the Sacred Band, which formed the spear-head of her forces subsequently. It also gained time and opportunity for disaffection to spread, and for Athens, thereby relieved of land pressure, to concentrate her energy and man-power on the revival of her fleet.

Thus in 374 B.C. the Athenian confederacy, which included Thebes, found Sparta willing to grant an advantageous peace. Although quickly broken, through an Athenian maritime adventure, a fresh peace congress was convened three years later—by which time the Athenians were tired of war. Here Sparta regained at the council table much that she had lost on the field of war, and succeeded in isolating Thebes from her allies. Thereupon Sparta eagerly turned to crush Thebes. But on advancing into Boeotia in 371 B.C., her army, traditionally superior in quality and actually superior in number (10,000 to 6,000) was decisively defeated at Leuctra by the new model army of Thebes under Epaminondas.

He not only broke away from tactical methods established by the experience of centuries, but in tactics, strategy, and grand strategy alike laid the foundations on which subsequent masters built. Even his structural designs have survived or been revived. For in tactics the 'oblique order' which Frederick made famous was only a slight elaboration of the method of Epaminondas. At Leuctra, reversing custom, Epaminondas placed not only his best men but the most on his left wing, and then, holding back his weak centre and right, developed a crushing superiority against one wing of the enemy—the wing where their leader stood, and thus the key of their will.

A year after Leuctra, Epaminondas led the forces of the newly-formed Arcadian League in a march upon virgin Sparta itself. This march into the heart of the Peloponnesian peninsula, so long Sparta's unchallenged domain, was distinguished by the manifold nature of its indirect approach. It was made in mid-winter and by three separated, but converging, columns—thus distracting the forces and direction of the opposition. For this alone it would be almost unique in ancient, or, indeed, pre-Napoleonic warfare. But with still deeper strategical insight, Epaminondas, after his force had united at Caryae, twenty miles short of Sparta, slipped past the capital and moved up from the rear. This move had the additional and calculated advantage of enabling the invaders to rally to themselves considerable bodies of Helots and other disaffected elements. The Spartans, however, succeeded in checking this dangerous internal movement by an emergency promise of emancipation; and the timely arrival at Sparta of strong reinforcements from her Peloponnesian allies thwarted the chance of the city falling without a set siege.

Epaminondas soon realized that the Spartans would not be lured into the open, and that a prolonged investment meant the dwindling of his own heterogeneous force. He therefore relinquished the blunted strategic weapon for a more subtle weapon—a grand strategy of indirect approach. At Mount Ithome, the natural citadel of Messenia, he founded a city as the capital of a new Messenian state, established there all the insurgent elements that had joined him, and used the booty he had gained during the invasion as an endowment for the new state. This was to be a check and counterpoise to Sparta in southern Greece. By its secure establishment she lost half her territory and more than half her serfs. Through Epaminondas's foundation of Megalopolis, in Arcadia, as a further check, Sparta was hemmed in both politically and by a chain of fortresses, so that the economic roots of her military supremacy were severed. When Epaminondas left the Peloponnese, after only a few months' campaign, he had won no victory in the field, yet his grand strategy had definitely dislocated the foundations of Spartan power.

The politicians at home, however, had desired a destructive military success, and were disappointed at not achieving it. With Epaminondas's subsequent, if temporary, supersession, Theban democracy—by short-sighted policy and blundering diplomacy—forfeited the advantage won for it. Thus it enabled its Arcadian allies, repudiating gratitude in growing conceit and ambition, to dispute Theban leadership. In 362 B.C., Thebes was driven to a choice between the forcible reassertion of her authority and the sacrifice of her prestige. Her move against Arcadia caused the Greek states to divide afresh into two opposing coalitions. Happily for Thebes, not only was Epaminondas at her service, but also the fruits of his grand strategy—for his creations of Messenia and Megalopolis now contributed not merely a check to Sparta but a makeweight to the Theban side.

Marching into the Peloponnese, he joined forces with his Peloponnesian allies at Tegea, thus placing himself between Sparta and the forces of the other anti-Theban states, which had concentrated at Mantinea. The Spartans marched by a roundabout route to join their allies, whereupon Epaminondas made a sudden spring by night with a mobile column at Sparta itself, and was only foiled because a deserter warned the Spartans in time for them to double back to their city. He then determined to seek a decision by battle and advanced from Tegea against Mantinea, some twelve miles distant, along an hour-glass shaped valley. The enemy took up a strong position at the mile-wide 'waist'.

With his advance we are on the borderline between strategy and tactics; but this is a case where arbitrary division is false, all the more because the sources of his victory at Mantinea are to be found in his indirect approach to the actual contact. At first, Epaminondas marched direct towards the enemy camp, causing them to form up in battle order facing his line of approach—the line of natural expectation. But, when several miles distant, he suddenly changed direction to the left, turning in beneath a projecting spur. This surprise manœuvre threatened to take in enfilade the enemy's right wing; and to dislocate still further their battle dispositions, he halted, making his troops ground arms as if about to encamp. The deception succeeded; the enemy were induced to relax their battle order, allowing men to fall out and the horses to be unbridled. Meanwhile, Epaminondas was actually completing his battle dispositions—similar to, but an improvement on, those of Leuctra—behind a screen of light troops. Then, on a signal, the Theban army took up its arms and swept forward—to a victory already assured by the dislocation of the enemy's balance. Epaminondas himself fell in the moment of victory, and in his death contributed not the least of his lessons to subsequent generations—by an exceptionally dramatic and convincing proof that an army and a state succumb quickest to paralysis of the brain.

The next decisive campaign is that which, just over twenty years later, yielded to Macedon the supremacy of Greece. All the more significant because of its momentous results, this campaign of 338 B.C. is an illuminating example of how policy and strategy can assist each other and also of how strategy can turn topographical obstacles from its disadvantage to its advantage. The challenger, though a Greek, was an 'outsider', while Thebes and Athens were united in the effort to form a Pan-Hellenic League to oppose the growing power of Macedon. They found a foreign backer in a Persian king—strange comment upon past history and human nature. Once more it is the challenger who is seen to have grasped the value of the indirect approach. Even the pretext for Philip of Macedon's attempt to secure the supremacy was indirect, for he was merely invited by the Amphictyonic Council to aid in punishing Amphissa, in western Boeotia, for a sacrilegious offence. It is probable that Philip himself prompted this invitation, which rallied Thebes and Athens against him, but at least ensured the benevolent neutrality of other states.

After marching southwards, Philip suddenly diverged at Cytinium from the route to Amphissa—the natural line of expectation—and instead occupied and fortified Elatea. That initial change of direction foreshadowed his wider political aims; at the same time it suggests a strategic motive which events tend to confirm. The allied Thebans and Boeotians barred the passes into Boeotia, both the western route from Cytinium to Amphissa, and the eastern pass of Parapotamii, leading from Elatea to Chaeronea. The first route may be likened to the upper stroke of an L, the route from Cytinium to Elatea as the lower stroke, and the prolongation across the pass to Chaeronea as the upward finish of the lower stroke.

Before initiating a further military move, Philip took fresh steps to weaken his opponents—politically, by forwarding the restoration of Phocian communities earlier dispersed by the Thebans; morally, by getting himself proclaimed as the champion of the God of Delphi.

Then he sprang suddenly, in the spring of 338 B.C., after clearing his path by a stratagem. Having already, by occupying Elatea, distracted the strategic attention of the enemy towards the eastern route—which had now become the line of natural expectation—he distracted the tactical attention of the force barring the western route by arranging that a letter which spoke of his return to Thrace should fall into its hands. Then he moved swiftly from Cytinium, crossed the pass by night and debouched into western Boeotia at Amphissa. Pressing on to Naupactus, he opened up his communications with the sea.

He was now on the rear of, if at a distance from, the defenders of the eastern pass. Thereupon they fell back from Parapotamii—not only because if they stayed their line of retreat might be cut, but also there was no apparent value in staying. Philip, however, once more diverged from the line of expectation, and made yet another indirect approach. For, instead of pressing eastwards from Amphissa through hilly country which would have aided resistance, he switched his army back through Cytinium and Elatea, turned southward through the now unguarded pass of Para-

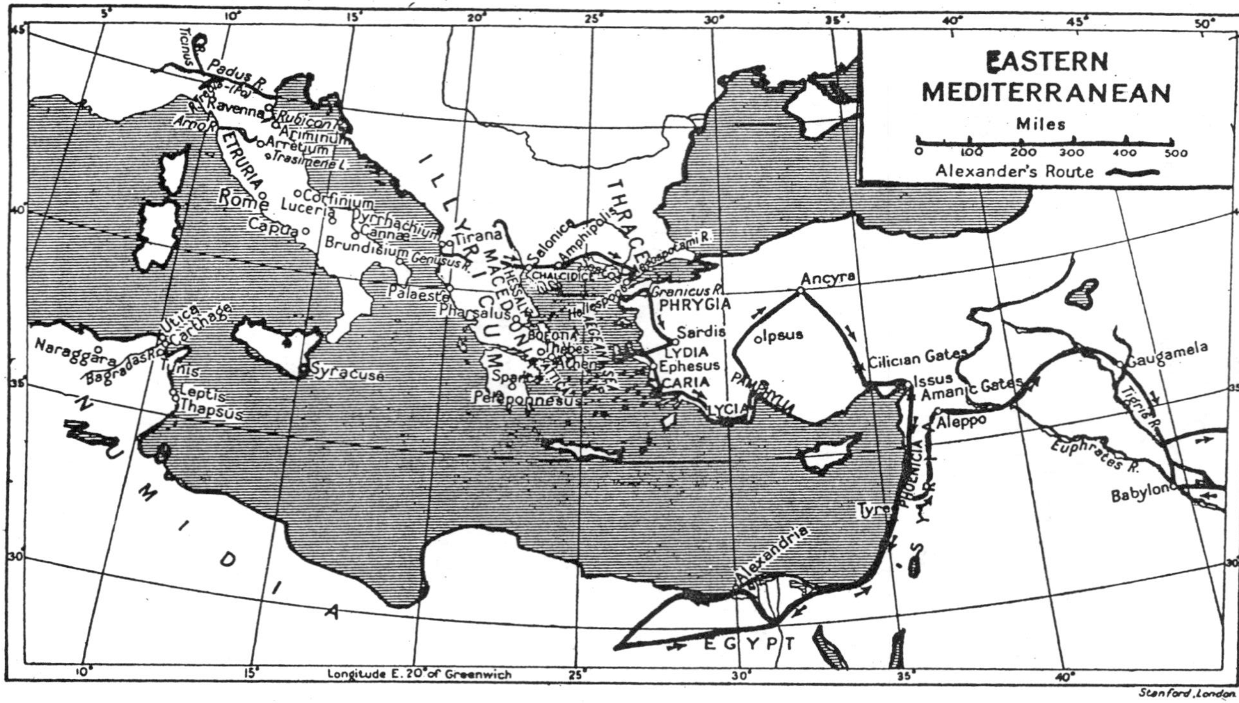
EASTERN MEDITERRANEAN
Miles
0 100 200 300 400 500
Alexander's Route
Ticinus
Padus R.
Ravenna
Rubicon R.
Ariminum
Arno R.
ETRURIA
Arretium
Trasimene L.
Rome
Corfinium
Luceria
Capua
Dyrrhachium
Cannae
Brundisium
Genusus R.
Tirana
Palaeste
Pharsalus
ILLYRICUM
MACEDONIA
THESSALY
CHALCIDICE
Salonica
Amphipolis
THRACE
Aegospotami R.
Hellespont
AEGEAN SEA
BOEOTIA
Thebes
Athens
ATTICA
Sparta
Peloponnesus
Granicus R.
PHRYGIA
Sardis
LYDIA
Ephesus
CARIA
LYCIA
Ancyra
Ipsus
Cilician Gates
Issus
Amanic Gates
Aleppo
PHOENICIA
Tyre
Gaugamela
Tigris R.
Euphrates R.
Babylon
Alexandria
EGYPT
Utica
Carthage
Naraggara
Bagradas R.
Tunis
Leptis
Thapsus
Syracuse
NUMIDIA
Longitude E. 20° of Greenwich
Stanford, London

potamii, and descended upon the enemy's army at Chaeronea. This manœuvre went far towards assuring his victory in the battle that followed. Its effect was completed by his subtle tactics. He lured the Athenians out of position—by giving way before them, and then, when they had pressed forward on to lower ground, breaking their line with a counterstroke. As the result of Chaeronea the Macedonian supremacy was established in Greece.

Fate cut off Philip before he could extend his conquests to Asia, and it was left to his son to conduct the campaign that he had intended. Alexander had as legacy not only a plan and a model instrument—the army which Philip had developed[1]—but a conception of grand strategy. Another heirloom of decided material value was the possession of the Dardanelles bridgeheads, seized under Philip's direction in 336 B.C.

If we study a chart of Alexander's advance we see that it was a series of acute zigzags. A study of its history suggests that the reasons for this indirectness were more political than strategical, although political in the grand strategical sense.

In his earlier campaigns his logistical strategy was direct and devoid of subtlety. The cause would appear to be, first, that in the youthful Alexander, bred to kingship and triumph, there was more of the Homeric hero than in the other great captains of history;[2] and, still more perhaps, that he had such justifiable confidence in the superiority of his instrument and his own battle-handling of it that he felt no need to dislocate preparatorily his adversaries' strategic balance. His lessons for posterity lie at the two poles—grand strategy and tactics.

Starting from the eastern shore of the Dardanelles in the spring of 334 B.C., he first moved southward and defeated the Persian covering force at the Granicus river. Here the enemy were bowled

[1] Philip had spent three years of his youth as a hostage in Thebes when Epaminondas was at his peak—and the impressions Philip then received can be clearly traced in the subsequent tactics of the Macedonian army.

[2] At the start of his invasion of Asia, Alexander romantically re-enacted the Homeric story of the expedition against Troy. While his army was waiting to cross the Dardanelles, Alexander himself with a picked detachment landed near Ilium, at the spot where the Greeks were supposed to have moored their ships in the Trojan War, and then advanced to the site of the original city, where he offered sacrifice in the temple of Athena, staged a mimic battle, and delivered an oration at the reputed burial-mound of Achilles, his traditional ancestor. After these symbolical performances, he rejoined his army, to conduct the real campaign.

over by the weight and impetus of his spear-armed cavalry, but had the shrewdness to appreciate that if they could concentrate against, and kill, the over-bold Alexander himself, they would paralyse the invasion at its birth. They narrowly failed in this purpose.

Alexander next moved south on Sardis, the political and economic key to Lydia, and thence west to Ephesus, restoring to these Greek towns their former democratic government and rights, as a means to secure his own rear in the most economical way.

He had now returned to the Aegean coast, and he pursued his way first south and then eastward along it though Caria, Lycia, and Pamphylia. In this approach his object was to dislocate the Persian command of the sea—by depriving the Persian fleet of freedom to move, through depriving it of its bases. At the same time, by freeing these sea-ports, he deprived the enemy fleet of much of its man-power, which was recruited from them.

Beyond Pamphylia, the coastline of the rest of Asia Minor was practically barren of ports. Hence Alexander now turned north again to Phrygia, and eastwards as far as Ancyra (modern Ankara)—consolidating his hold on, and securing his rear in, central Asia Minor. Then, in 333 B.C., he turned south through the Cilician 'Gates' on the direct route towards Syria, where Darius III was concentrating to oppose him. Here, through the failure of his intelligence service and his own assumption that the Persians would await him in the plains, Alexander was strategically out-manœuvred. While Alexander made a direct approach, Darius made an indirect—and, moving up the higher reaches of the Euphrates, came through the Amanic Gates onto Alexander's rear. He, who had been so careful to secure his chain of bases, now found himself cut off from them. But, turning back, he extricated himself at the battle of Issus by the superiority of his tactics as well as of his tactical instrument—no Great Captain applied this unexpectedness of indirectness more in his tactics.

Thereafter he again took an indirect route, down the coast of Syria instead of pressing on to Babylon, the heart of the Persian power. Grand strategy clearly dictated his course. For although he had dislocated the Persian command of the sea, he had not yet destroyed it. So long as it existed it might be the means of menacing his own rear, and Greece, especially Athens, was unpleasantly restive. His advance into Phoenicia disrupted the Persian fleet, for what remained was mainly Phoenician. Most of it came over to him, and the Tyrian portion fell with the fall of Tyre. Even then he again moved southward, into Egypt, a move more difficult to explain on naval grounds, except as an additional precaution. It is more intelligible, however, in the light of his political purpose of occupying the Persian empire and consolidating his own in substitution. For this purpose Egypt was an immense economic asset.

At last, in 331 B.C., he marched northwards again to Aleppo, then turned eastwards, crossed the Euphrates, and pushed on to the upper reaches of the Tigris. Here near Nineveh (modern Mosul) Darius had assembled a large new army. Alexander was eager for battle, but his approach was indirect. Crossing the Tigris higher up, he came down the east bank, compelling Darius to shift his position. Once again in battle, at Gaugamela (a battle popularly called Arbela—the nearest city, but sixty miles distant) Alexander and his army showed their complete superiority to an army that was the least serious of the obstacles in Alexander's path to his grand-strategic goal. The occupation of Babylon followed.

Alexander's succeeding campaigns, until he reached the borders of India, were militarily a 'mopping up' of the Persian empire, while politically the consolidation of his own. He forced the Uxian defile and the Persian 'Gates' by an indirect approach, and when he was confronted on the Hydaspes by Porus, he produced a masterpiece of indirectness which showed the ripening of his own strategical powers. By laying in stores of corn, and by distributing his army widely along the western bank, he mystified his opponent as to his intentions. Repeated noisy marches and counter-marches of Alexander's cavalry first kept Porus on tenterhooks, and then, through repetition, dulled his reaction. Having thus fixed Porus to a definite and static position, Alexander left the bulk of his army opposite it, and himself with a picked force made a night crossing eighteen miles upstream. By the surprise of this indirect approach he dislocated the mental and moral balance of Porus, as well as the moral and physical balance of his army. In the ensuing battle Alexander, with a fraction of his own army, was enabled to defeat almost the whole of his enemy's. If this preliminary dislocation had not occurred there would have been no justification, either in theory or in fact, for Alexander's exposure of an isolated fraction to the risk of defeat in detail.

In the long wars of the 'Successors' which followed Alexander's death and rent his empire asunder, there are numerous examples of the indirect approach and its value. Alexander's generals were abler men than Napoleon's marshals, and their experience had led them to grasp the deeper meaning of economy of force. While many of their operations are worth study, the present analysis is restricted to the decisive campaigns of ancient history, and in these wars of the Diadochi only the last, in 301 B.C., can be definitely so termed. The claim of this to decisiveness can hardly be challenged, for in the measured words of the *Cambridge Ancient History*, by its issue 'the struggle between the central power and the dynasts was ended' and 'the dismemberment of the Graeco-Macedonian world became inevitable'.

By 302 B.C., Antigonus, who claimed to stand in Alexander's place, was at last within reach of his goal of securing the empire for himself. Expanding from his original Satrapy of Phrygia, he had won control of Asia from the Aegean to the Euphrates. Opposing him, Seleucus had held on to Babylon with difficulty; Ptolemy was left only with Egypt; Lysimachus was more secure in Thrace; but Cassander, the most formidable of the rival generals and the keystone of the resistance to Antigonus's almost realized dream, had been driven from Greece by Antigonus's son Demetrius—who in many characteristics was a second Alexander. Called upon for unconditional surrender, Cassander replied by a stroke of strategic genius. The plan was arranged at a conference with Lysimachus, and Ptolemy's aid towards it was sought, while he in turn got in touch with Seleucus by sending messengers on camels across the Arabian desert.

Cassander kept only some 31,000 men to face Demetrius's invasion of Thessaly—with a reputed 57,000—and lent the rest of his army to Lysimachus. The latter crossed the Dardanelles eastwards, while Seleucus moved westwards towards Asia Minor, his army including five hundred war elephants obtained from India. Ptolemy moved northwards into Syria, but on receiving a false report of Lysimachus's defeat, returned to Egypt. Nevertheless, the convergent advance from both sides on the heart of his empire constrained Antigonus to recall Demetrius urgently from Thessaly, where Cassander had succeeded in keeping him at bay until the indirect move against his strategic rear in Asia Minor called him off—as Scipio's fundamentally similar move later forced Hannibal's return to Africa.

At the battle of Ipsus, in Phrygia, Cassander's strategy was consummated by his partner's decisive tactical victory, which ended in the death of Antigonus and the flight of Demetrius. In this battle, it is worth remark, the war elephants were the decisive instrument, and, fittingly, the tactics of the victors were essentially indirect. After their cavalry had disappeared from the scene with Demetrius in hot pursuit, their elephants cut off his return. Even then, instead of assaulting Antigonus's infantry, Lysimachus demoralized them by threat of attack and arrow fire—until they began to melt. Then Seleucus struck, with a thrust at the point where Antigonus himself stood.

When the campaign had opened the scales were heavily weighted and steeply tilted on the side of Antigonus. Rarely has the balance of fortune so dramatically changed. It would seem clear that Antigonus's balance had been upset by the indirect approach which Cassander planned. This dislocated the mental balance of Antigonus, the moral balance of his troops and his subjects, and the physical balance of his military dispositions.

CHAPTER III

ROMAN WARS—HANNIBAL, SCIPIO, AND CAESAR

★

The next conflict decisive in its results, and in effect on European history, was the struggle between Rome and Carthage—in which the Hannibalic, or Second Punic, War was the determining period. This falls into a series of phases or campaigns, each decisive in turning the current of the war into a fresh course.

The first phase opens with Hannibal's advance from Spain towards the Alps and Italy, in 218 B.C., and the natural closing-point appears to be the annihilating victory of Trasimene the next spring, which left Rome unshielded, save by her walls and garrison, to Hannibal's immediate approach—if he had chosen to make it.

The reason commonly assigned for Hannibal's initial choice of the circuitous and arduous land route in preference to the direct sea route is that of Rome's supposed 'command of the sea'. But it is absurd to apply the modern interpretation of this phrase to an era when ships were so primitive, and their ability to intercept a foe at sea so uncertain. Moreover, apart from such limitations, the Romans' superiority at that time is brought in doubt by a passage of Polybius (iii, 97) when, speaking of the very time of Trasimene, he refers to the Roman Senate's anxiety lest the Carthaginians 'should obtain a more complete mastery of the sea'. Even in the closing stage of the war, after the Romans had won repeated victories at sea, deprived the Carthaginian fleet of all its Spanish bases, and were established in Africa, they were powerless to prevent Mago landing an expeditionary force on the Genoese Riviera, or Hannibal sailing tranquilly back to Africa. It seems more probable that Hannibal's indirect and overland route of invasion was due to the aim of rallying the Celts of Northern Italy against Rome.

Next, we should note the indirectness even of this land march, and the advantage gained thereby. The Romans had dispatched the consul, Publius Scipio (father of Africanus), to Marseilles, with the object of barring Hannibal's path at the Rhône. Hannibal, however, not only crossed this formidable river unexpectedly high up, but then turned still further northward—to take the more devious and difficult route by the Isère valley, instead of the straighter but more easily barred routes near the Riviera. Polybius says that when the elder Scipio arrived at the crossing three days later he was 'astonished to find the enemy gone; for he had persuaded himself that they would never venture to take this [northerly] route into Italy' (Polybius). By prompt decision and speedy movement, leaving part of his army behind, he got back to Italy by sea in time to meet Hannibal on the plains of Lombardy. But here Hannibal had the advantage of suitable ground for his superior cavalry. The victories of the Ticinus and the Trebia were the sequel, and their moral effect brought Hannibal recruits and supplies 'in great abundance'.

Master of the north of Italy, Hannibal wintered there. The following spring, anticipating Hannibal's continued advance, the new consuls took their armies, the one to Ariminum (Rimini) on the Adriatic, the other to Arretium (Arezzo) in Etruria—thereby commanding the eastern and western routes respectively by which Hannibal could advance towards Rome. Hannibal decided on the Etrurian route, but instead of advancing by one of the normal roads, he made thorough inquiries, through which 'he ascertained that the other roads leading into Etruria were long and well known to the enemy, but that one which led through the marshes was short, and would bring them upon Flaminius by surprise. This was what suited his peculiar genius, and he therefore decided to take this route. But when the report was spread in his army that the commander was going to lead them through the marshes, every soldier felt alarmed . . .' (Polybius).

Normal soldiers always prefer the known to the unknown. Hannibal was an abnormal general and hence, like other Great Captains, chose to face the most hazardous *conditions* rather than the certainty of meeting his opponents in a position of their own choosing.

For four days and three nights Hannibal's army marched 'through a route which was under water', suffering terribly from fatigue and enforced want of sleep, while losing many men and more horses. But on emerging he found the Roman army still passively encamped at Arretium. Hannibal attempted no direct attack. Instead, as Polybius tells us, 'he calculated that, if he passed the camp and made a descent into the district beyond, Flaminius—partly for fear of popular reproach and partly from personal irritation—would be unable to endure watching passively the devastation of the country but would spontaneously follow him . . . and give him opportunities for attack.'

This was a mental application of the manœuvre against the enemy's rear, based on searching inquiries about his opponent's character. It was followed by a physical execution. Pressing along the road to Rome, Hannibal laid and achieved the greatest ambush in history. In the misty dawn of the following morning the Roman army, in hot pursuit of Hannibal along the hill-bordered skirts of the Lake of Trasimene, was caught by surprise in a trap front and rear, and annihilated. Readers of history who remember the victory are apt to overlook the mental thrust that made it possible. But Polybius brought out the basic lesson in his reflection —'for as a ship, if you deprive it of its steersman, falls with all its crew into the hands of the enemy; so, with an army in war, if you outwit or out-manœuvre its general, the whole will often fall into your hands'.

Why, after Trasimene, Hannibal did not march on Rome is a mystery of history—and all solutions are but speculation. Lack of an adequate siege-train is an obvious reason, but may not be the complete explanation. All we know for certain is that the succeeding years were spent by Hannibal in trying to break Rome's hold on her Italian allies and to weld them into a coalition against her. Victories were merely a moral impetus towards this end. The tactical advantage would always be assured if he could bring about a battle under conditions favourable for his superior cavalry.

This second phase opened on the Roman side with a form of the indirect approach that was more in accord with Greek than with Roman character—a form which has given to history and to subsequent imitations, many of them bad, the generic title 'Fabian strategy'. The strategy of Fabius was not merely an evasion of battle to gain time, but calculated for its effect on the morale of the enemy—and, still more, for its effect on their potential allies. It was thus primarily a matter of war-policy, or grand strategy. Fabius recognized Hannibal's military superiority too well to risk a military decision. While seeking to avoid this, he aimed by military pin-pricks to wear down the invaders' endurance and, coincidentally, prevent their strength being recruited from the Italian cities or their Carthaginian base. The key condition of the strategy by which this grand strategy was carried out was that the Roman army should keep always to the hills, so as to nullify Hannibal's decisive superiority in cavalry. Thus this phase became a duel between the Hannibalic and the Fabian forms of the indirect approach.

Hovering in the enemy's neighbourhood, cutting off stragglers and foraging parties, preventing them from gaining any permanent base, Fabius remained an elusive shadow on the horizon, dimming the glamour of Hannibal's triumphal progress. Thus Fabius, by his immunity from defeat, thwarted the effect of Hannibal's previous victories upon the minds of Rome's Italian allies and checked them from changing sides. This guerrilla type of campaign also revived the spirit of the Roman troops while depressing the Carthaginians who, having ventured so far from home, were the more conscious of the necessity of gaining an early decision.

But attrition is a two-edged weapon and, even when skilfully wielded, puts a strain on the users. It is especially trying to the mass of the people, eager to see a quick finish—and always inclined to assume that this can only mean the enemy's finish. The more the Roman people recovered from the shock of Hannibal's victory, the more they began to question the wisdom of the Fabian treatment which had given them a chance to recover. Their smouldering doubts were fanned by ambitious hotheads in the army, who criticized Fabius for his 'cowardly and unenterprising spirit'. This led to the unprecedented step of appointing Minucius, who was both Fabius's chief subordinate and his chief critic, as co-dictator. Thereupon Hannibal seized the opportunity to draw Minucius into a trap from which he was barely rescued by Fabius's speedy intervention.

For a time this sequel quieted criticism of Fabius. But when his six months' appointment expired, neither he nor his policy was popular enough to secure an extension. At the consular elections, one of the two chosen was the impetuous and ignorant Varro, who had earlier engineered Minucius's appointment. Moreover, the Senate passed a resolution that they should give battle to Hannibal. There was ground for this decision in the devastation that Italy was suffering, and it was backed up by the practical step of raising for the campaign of 216 B.C. the largest army, eight legions, which Rome had ever placed in the field. But the Romans were to pay dearly for electing a leader whose offensive spirit was not balanced by judgement.

The other consul, Paullus, wished to wait and manœuvre for a favourable opportunity, but such caution did not accord with Varro's ideas—'So much had been said about men taking the field not to set sentinels, but to use their swords.' Varro's conception, and public promise, was to attack the enemy wherever and whenever they found him. As a result, he took the first opportunity of offering battle to Hannibal—in the plain at Cannae. When Paullus argued that they should try to draw Hannibal into country more suitable for infantry action, Varro used his alternate day of command to advance into close contact. When Paullus kept the troops in their entrenched camp next day, calculating that shortage of supplies would soon force Hannibal to move away, Varro 'became more than ever inflamed with the desire for fighting'—according to Polybius's account. And that feeling was shared by most of the troops, who chafed at the delay. 'For there is nothing more intolerable to mankind than suspense; when a thing is once decided, men can but endure whatever out of the catalogue of evils it is their misfortune to undergo.'

Next morning, Varro moved the Roman army out of camp to offer battle—and the kind of battle which Hannibal desired. As was customary, the infantry of both sides were posted in the centre, and the cavalry on the flanks—but Hannibal's detailed disposition was unconventional. For he pushed forward the Gauls and Spaniards, who formed the centre of the infantry line, while holding back his African foot, posted at each end of the line. In that way the Gauls and Spaniards formed a natural magnet for the Roman infantry, and were, as intended, forced back—so that what had been a line bulging outwards became a line sagging inwards. The Roman legionaries, flushed with their apparent success, crowded into the opening—where the press grew ever denser, until they could scarcely use their weapons. While they imagined that they were breaking the Carthaginian front, they were actually pushing themselves into a Carthaginian sack. For at this juncture Hannibal's African veterans wheeled inwards from both sides, thus automatically enveloping the thickly packed Romans.

This manœuvre produced in a more calculated way a situation, and trap, similar to the sea battle of Salamis. It might aptly be termed a collective tactical form of ju-jitsu—which is essentially based on the indirect approach.

Meanwhile, Hannibal's heavy cavalry on the left wing had broken through the opposing cavalry on that flank and, sweeping round the Romans' rear, dispersed their cavalry on the other flank—who had been held in play by the elusive Numidian horse. Leaving the pursuit to the Numidians, the heavy cavalry now delivered the final stroke by bursting into the rear of the Roman infantry, who were already surrounded on three sides and too tightly jammed to offer effective resistance. Thenceforward the battle became a massacre. According to Polybius, out of the 76,000 men in the Roman army, 70,000 fell on the field of battle. Among them was Paullus, whereas Varro, ironically, succeeded in making his own escape from the crash which he had caused.

The disaster at Cannae broke up the Italian confederation for a time, but failed to break Rome itself—where Fabius helped to rally the people for sustained resistance. Rome's recovery owed much to the sober resolution and persistence shown in pursuing the strategy of evasion at any sacrifice, but was helped by Hannibal's lack of adequate siege-equipment and reinforcements, as well as by his situation as the invader of a primitively organized land. (When Scipio later retorted with a counter-invasion of Africa he found the more highly developed economic structure of Carthage an aid to his decisive aim.)

The second phase of the war ended in 207 B.C. with another type of the strategic indirect approach, when Nero, the consul, slipped away from his position facing Hannibal, and concentrated by forced marches against Hannibal's brother, who had just arrived with his army in northern Italy. After destroying this army at the Metaurus, and with it Hannibal's hope of a reinforcement sufficient for victory, Nero was back in his camp opposite Hannibal before the latter realized that it had been empty.

Thereafter stalemate reigned in Italy—the third phase. During five years, Hannibal stood at bay in southern Italy, and a succession of Roman generals retired licking their wounds from their too direct approaches to the lion's lair.

Meantime, Publius Scipio the younger had been sent to Spain in 210 B.C. on a desperate venture to redeem the disaster which had there befallen the armies commanded by his father and uncle, to avenge their deaths, and to maintain, if possible, Rome's slender foothold in the north-east corner of Spain—against the greatly superior Carthaginian forces in that country. By swiftness of movement, superior tactics, and skilful diplomacy he converted this defensive object into an offensive, if indirect, thrust at Carthage and at Hannibal. For Spain was Hannibal's real strategic base; there he had trained his armies, and thither he looked for reinforcements. By a masterly combination of surprise and timing, Scipio had first deprived the Carthaginian armies of Cartagena, their main base in Spain, as a prelude to depriving them of their allies and overthrowing their armies.

Then elected consul on his return to Italy in 205 B.C., he was ready for a second and decisive indirect approach, long conceived by him, against Hannibal's strategic rear. Fabius, now old and set in mind, is reputed to have voiced the orthodox view, urging that Scipio's duty was to attack Hannibal in Italy. 'Why do you not apply yourself to this, and carry the war in a straightforward manner to the place where Hannibal is, rather than pursue that roundabout course according to which you expect that when you have crossed into Africa, Hannibal will follow you thither?'

Scipio gained from the Senate a bare permission to cross into Africa, but was refused leave to levy troops. In consequence he set out on his expedition in the spring of 204 B.C. with a mere 7,000 volunteers and two disgraced legions—which had been relegated to garrison duty in Sicily in penance for their share in the defeat at Cannae. On landing in Africa, he was met by the only cavalry force which Carthage had immediately available. By a cleverly graduated retreat, he lured it into a trap and destroyed it. Thereby he not only gained time to consolidate his position but also created a moral impression which, on the one hand, induced the home authorities to back him more generously and, on the other, shook the hold of Carthage upon her African allies—except for the most powerful, Syphax.

Scipio then tried to secure the port of Utica, to serve as his base, but was baffled in an attempt to take it as swiftly as he earlier succeeded in capturing Cartagena. He was forced to abandon the siege of Utica six weeks later when Syphax brought an army of 60,000 men to reinforce the new Carthaginian forces which Hasdrubal Gisco was raising. On the approach of the combined armies, much superior to his own in numbers if not in quality, Scipio fell back to a small peninsula where he fortified a prototype of Wellington's Lines of Torres Vedras. Here he first lulled the commanders of the investing forces into a feeling of security, then distracted their attention by ostensible preparations for a seaborne thrust against Utica, and finally made a night move upon the enemy's two camps.

The demoralizing and disorganizing effect of the surprise was intensified by Scipio's subtle calculation in first launching an attack on Syphax's less orderly camp, where the swarm of huts overflowed the fortified boundaries and were made of inflammable reeds and matting. In the confusion caused by setting fire to these huts the Romans were able to penetrate into the camp itself, while the blaze drew Hasdrubal's Carthaginians to open their own gates and pour out to the rescue, imagining that the conflagration was accidental—for when darkness fell, all had been quiet and normal in the Roman camp, seven miles distant. When the gates of the Carthaginian camp were thus opened, Scipio launched upon them the second stroke of his attack, so gaining entry without the cost of making a breach. Both the hostile armies were routed, with the reputed loss of half their total strength.

If in tracing that operation we have outwardly crossed the border-line from strategy into tactics, it is in reality a case where strategy not merely paved the way for a victory in battle but produced it. The victory was merely the last act of the strategic approach. For an unresisted massacre is not a battle.

After his bloodless triumph Scipio did not at once move on Carthage. Why? If history does not give a definite answer it affords clearer grounds for a deduction than in the case of Hannibal's neglect of Rome after Trasimene and Cannae. Unless there is opportunity and favourable prospect for a quick surprise assault, a siege is the most uneconomic of all operations of war. When the enemy has still a field army capable of intervening, a siege is also the most dangerous—for until it is crowned by success the assailant is progressively weakening himself out of proportion to his enemy. Scipio had to reckon not only with the walls of Carthage but with the return of Hannibal—a contingency which was, indeed, his calculated aim. If he could compel the capitulation of Carthage before Hannibal could return, it would be a great advantage. But it must be by a moral, and hence inexpensive, dislocation of the city's resistance—not by a heavy physical expenditure of force which might leave him still facing unbreached walls when Hannibal descended on his rear.

Instead of moving on Carthage, Scipio systematically lopped off her supply areas and allies. Above all, the relentless pursuit and overthrow of Syphax was a detachment of force which abundantly justified itself. For by restoring his own ally, Masinissa, to the throne of Numidia he ensured for himself the cavalry resources to counter Hannibal's best weapon.

To reinforce these forms of moral suasion he advanced to Tunis, in sight of Carthage, as 'a most effective means of striking the Carthaginians with terror and dismay'. Coming on top of the other indirect forms of pressure it was sufficient to dislocate the Carthaginians' will to resist, and they sued for peace. But while the terms were awaiting ratification in Rome, the provisional peace was broken when Carthage received news of Hannibal's return, and of his landing at Leptis (202 B.C.).

Scipio was thus placed in a difficult and dangerous position. For although he had not weakened himself by an assault on Carthage, he had let Masinissa go back to Numidia, to consolidate his new kingdom—after Carthage had accepted Scipio's peace terms. In such circumstances, an orthodox general would either have taken the offensive, in order to prevent Hannibal reaching Carthage, or have stood on the defensive to await relief. Instead, Scipio took a course that when plotted geographically looks fantastic. For if Hannibal's direct route from Leptis to Carthage be pictured as travelling up the right-hand stroke of an inverted V (Λ), Scipio, leaving a detachment to hold his camp near Carthage, marched away down the left-hand stroke. A most indirect approach! But this route, the Bagradas valley, took him into the heart of Carthage's main source of supplies from the interior. It also brought him nearer, with every step he marched, to the Numidian reinforcements which Masinissa was bringing in response to an urgent summons.

The move attained its strategic aim. The senate of Carthage, aghast at the news that this vital territory was being progressively devastated, sent messengers urging Hannibal to intervene at once and bring Scipio to battle. Hannibal, although he told them in answer 'to leave such matters to him', was nevertheless drawn by the compulsion of conditions—created by Scipio—to move west by forced marches to meet Scipio, instead of north to Carthage. Thus Scipio had lured him to an area of his own choosing, where Hannibal lacked the material reinforcement, stable pivot, and shelter in case of defeat which he would have enjoyed if the battle had taken place near Carthage.

Scipio had thrust on his enemy the need of seeking battle, and he now exploited this moral advantage to the full. When Masinissa joined him, almost coincidently with Hannibal's arrival on the scene, Scipio fell back instead of going forward, and so drew Hannibal to a camping-ground where the Carthaginians suffered from lack of water—and to a battleground in the plain where Scipio's newly acquired advantage in cavalry could have full play. He had taken the first two tricks; on the battlefield of Zama (more correctly, Naraggara) he was enabled to take the rubber by tactically over-trumping Hannibal's former cavalry trump. And when tactical defeat for the first time overtook Hannibal, the consequences of his preliminary strategic defeat also overtook him—for there was no sheltering fortress at hand where the defeated army could rally before the pursuit annihilated it. The bloodless surrender of Carthage followed.

The campaign of Zama made Rome the dominant power in the Mediterranean world. The subsequent extension of that supremacy, and its translation into suzerainty continued without serious check, if not without recurrent threat. Thus 202 B.C. forms a natural conclusion for a survey of the turning points, and their military causes , in the history of the ancient world. Ultimately the tide of Roman expansion was to ebb, then that universal empire was to fall to pieces, partly under barbarian pressure but still more from internal decay.

During the period of 'the Decline and Fall', during the centuries when Europe was shedding its old single-coloured skin for a new skin of many colours, there is profit to be got from a study of the military leadership—sometimes much profit, as in the case of Belisarius and later generals of the Byzantine empire. But, on the whole, decisiveness is too difficult of definition, turning points too obscure, purposeful strategy too uncertain, and records too unsafe, to provide a basis for scientific deductions.

Before the power of Rome had reached its zenith there was, however, one internal war that calls for examination, both because it was the stage for another Great Captain and because it vitally affected the course of history. For just as the Second Punic War gave the world to Rome, so the Civil War of 50–45 B.C. gave the Roman world to Caesar—and Caesarism.

When Caesar crossed the Rubicon in December of 50 B.C., his power rested only upon Gaul and Illyricum; Pompey was in control of Italy and the rest of Rome's dominions. Caesar had nine legions, but only one was with him at Ravenna; the remainder were far away in Gaul. Pompey had ten legions in Italy, seven in Spain, and many detachments throughout the empire. But those in Italy had only cadres present with the eagles—and a legion in hand was worth more than two unmobilized. Caesar has been criticized for his rashness in moving south with such a fraction of his army. But time and surprise are the two most vital elements in war. And beyond his appreciation of them, Caesar's strategy was essentially guided by his understanding of Pompey's mind.

From Ravenna there were two routes to Rome. Caesar took the longer and less direct—down the Adriatic coast—but he moved fast. As he passed through this populous district many of the levies being assembled for Pompey joined him instead—a parallel with Napoleon's experience in 1815. Morally shaken, the Pompeian party quitted Rome and fell back to Capua—while Caesar, interposing between the enemy's advanced force at Corfinium and their main force under Pompey round Luceria, secured another bloodless transfer of strength to himself. He then continued his advance south towards Luceria, the snowball process likewise continuing. But his advance, which had now become direct, stampeded the enemy into a retreat to the fortified port of Brundisium (Brindisi) on the heel of Italy, and the very vigour of his chase hastened Pompey's decision to retire across the Adriatic to Greece. Thus an excess of directness and a want of art, in the second phase, robbed Caesar of his chance of ending the war in one campaign, and condemned him to four more years of obstinate warfare all round the Mediterranean basin.

The second campaign now opened. Caesar, instead of following Pompey into Greece, turned to deal with the Pompeian front in Spain. For thus concentrating against the 'junior partner' he has been much criticized. But his estimate of Pompey's inactivity was justified by the event. This time Caesar began the campaign too bluntly, and a direct advance on the enemy's main forces at Ilerda (modern Lerida), just across the Pyrenees, enabled them to decline battle. An assault failed, and Caesar only averted disaster by his personal intervention. The morale of his men continued to sink until, just in time, he changed his method of approach.

Instead of making any further attempt to press the siege, Caesar devoted his energies to the creation of an artificial ford which enabled him to command both banks of the river Sicoris, on which Ilerda stood. This threatened tightening of his grip on their sources of supply induced Pompey's lieutenants to retire, while there was time. Caesar allowed them to slip away unpressed, but sent his Gallic cavalry to get on their rear and delay their march.

Then, rather than assault the bridge held by the enemy's rear-guard, he took the risk of leading his legions through the deep ford, which was regarded as only traversable by cavalry and, marching in a wide circuit during the night, placed himself across the enemy's line of retreat. Even then he did not attempt battle, but was content to head off each attempt of the enemy to take a fresh line of retreat—using his cavalry to harass and delay them while his legions marched wide. Firmly holding in check the eagerness of his own men for battle, he at the same time encouraged fraternization with the men of the other side, who were growing more and more weary, hungry and depressed. Finally, when he had shepherded them back in the direction of Ilerda, and forced them to take up a position devoid of water, they capitulated.

It was a strategic victory as bloodless for the defeated as for the victor—and the less men slain on the other side, the more potential adherents and recruits for Caesar. Despite the substitution of manœuvre for direct assaults upon his enemy the campaign had cost him only six weeks of his time.

But in his next campaign, 48 B.C., he changed his strategy—and it lasted eight months before victory crowned his arms, even then not being complete. Instead of advancing into Greece by the indirect land route through Illyricum, Caesar decided on the direct sea route. Thereby he gained time initially but lost it ultimately. Pompey had originally a large fleet, Caesar none—and although he had ordered the construction or collection of ships on a large scale, only part were available. Rather than wait, Caesar sailed from Brindisi with barely half his assembled force. On landing at Palaeste he headed up the coast for the important seaport of Dyrrachium (Durazzo), but Pompey just reached there first. Fortunately for Caesar, Pompey was as slow as ever, and missed the chance of using his superior strength before Antony, with the other half of Caesar's army evaded the opposing fleet and joined Caesar. And even when Antony landed on the other side of Dyrrachium, Pompey, though centrally placed, failed to prevent Caesar and Antony effecting a junction at Tirana. Pompey then fell back, followed by his opponent, who offered battle in vain. Thereafter the two armies lay facing each other on the south bank of the river Genusus, which itself was south of Dyrrachium.

The deadlock was broken by an indirect approach. By a long and difficult circuit of some forty-five miles through the hills, Caesar succeeded in placing himself between Dyrrachium and

Pompey before the latter, who had only a straight twenty-five miles to cover, awoke to the danger and hurried back to save his base. But Caesar did not press his advantage; and as Pompey had the sea for supplies there was no inducement to a man of his temperament to take the lead in attack. Caesar then took the original but singularly profitless course of constructing extensive lines of investment round an army which was not only stronger than his own, but could supply itself easily, or move away, by sea, whenever it wished.

Even Pompey the passive could not forgo the opportunity of striking at weak points of such a thin line, and his success led Caesar into an attempt to redeem it by a concentrated counter-attack which failed disastrously. Only Pompey's inertia saved Caesar's demoralized troops from dissolution.

Caesar's men clamoured to be led afresh against the enemy, but Caesar had learnt his lesson, and after making good his retreat he reverted to a strategy of indirect approach. Pompey had a better opportunity to apply it at this juncture—by recrossing the Adriatic and regaining control of Italy, where his path would have been smoothed by the moral impression of Caesar's defeat. Caesar, however, showed more appreciation of the possibilities of this *westward* move—as a danger to himself. He moved rapidly *eastward* against Pompey's lieutenant, Scipio Nasica, who was in Macedonia. Pompey, thereby mentally dominated, was drawn to follow Caesar; taking a different route, he hurried to Scipio's support. Caesar arrived first, but rather than throw his troops against fortifications, he allowed Pompey to come up. This seeming loss of an opportunity on Caesar's part may also have been due to his view that, after Dyrrachium, a strong inducement would be needed to make Pompey give battle in the open. If so, that idea was correct, for although Pompey had a two to one superiority in numbers, he took the risk of offering battle only under the persuasion of his lieutenants. Just as Caesar had prepared a series of manœuvres to create the opportunity, Pompey advanced and gave it to him—at Pharsalus. For Caesar's interest, the battle was undoubtedly premature—and the closeness of the issue was the measure of its prematurity. Caesar's indirect approach had been made to restore the strategic balance, and a further one was needed to upset Pompey's balance.

After the victory of Pharsalus, Caesar chased Pompey across the Dardanelles, through Asia Minor, and thence across the Mediterranean to Alexandria—where Ptolemy assassinated him, thus saving Caesar much trouble. But Caesar forfeited the advantage by intervening in the quarrel between Ptolemy and his sister Cleopatra over the Egyptian succession, thereby wasting eight months in an unnecessary diversion of effort. It would seem that Caesar's recurrent and deep-rooted fault was his concentration in pursuing the objective immediately in front of his eyes to the neglect of his wider object. Strategically he was an alternating Jekyll and Hyde.

The interval allowed the Pompeian forces to rally, and to obtain a new lease of life in Africa and Spain.

In Africa Caesar's difficulties were increased by the direct action already adopted by his lieutenant, Curio. After landing, and winning an initial victory, Curio had let himself be lured into a trap by King Juba, ally of the Pompeian party, and there exterminated. Caesar opened his own African campaign (46 B.C.) with equal directness, impetuosity, and insufficiency of force as in his Greek campaign, ran his head into a noose, and was extricated from it by his usual combination of luck and tactical skill. After this he settled down in a fortified camp near Ruspina to await the arrival of his other legions, refusing all temptation to battle.

The Jekyll of blood-saving manœuvre then became uppermost in Caesar—and for several months, even after his reinforcements arrived, he pursued a strategy of extreme but narrow indirectness of approach, manœuvring repeatedly to inflict a series of pinpricks whose wearing and depressing effect on the enemy's morale was shown in the swelling stream of desertions. At last, by a somewhat wider indirect approach to the enemy's important base at Thapsus, he created a favourable opportunity for battle, and his troops—taking the bit in their teeth—launched the attack and won the battle without higher direction.

In the Spanish campaign of 45 B.C. which followed, and closed the war, Caesar from the outset strove to avoid loss of life and manœuvred ceaselessly within narrow limits to work his opponents into a position where he could make a battle cast with the dice loaded for him. He gained such an advantage at Munda, and gained the victory, but the closeness of the struggle, and the heavy cost of life therein incurred, point the distinction between economy of force and mere thriftiness of force.

Caesar's indirectness of approach appears narrow and wanting in surprise. In each of his campaigns he strained the enemy's morale, but did not dislocate it. The reason would appear to be that he was more concerned to aim at the mind of the enemy's troops than at the mind of their command. If his campaigns serve to bring out the distinction between the two qualities of indirect approach—to the opposing forces and to the opposing command—they also bring out most forcibly the difference between a direct and an indirect approach. For Caesar met failure each time he relied on the direct, and retrieved it each time he resorted to the indirect.

CHAPTER IV

BYZANTINE WARS—BELISARIUS AND NARSES

★

After Caesar's crowning victory at Munda in 45 B.C., he was granted 'perpetual dictatorship' of Rome, and the Roman world. This decisive step, a contradiction in terms, spelt the sterilization of the constitution. Thereby it paved the way for the conversion of the Republic into the Empire—which carried within its system the germs of its own decay. The process, however, was gradual—if, on a long view, progressive. Five hundred years passed between Caesar's triumph and the final collapse of Rome. And even then a 'Roman Empire' continued for another thousand years in a different location. This was due, first, to Constantine the Great's transfer of the capital from Rome to Byzantium (Constantinople), in 330; second, to the definite division, in 364, of the Roman world into an Eastern and a Western Empire. The former kept its strength better than the latter, which increasingly crumbled under barbarian attacks and barbarian permeation until, near the end of the fifth century A.D., the establishment of an independent kingdom of Italy—following that of similar kingdoms in Gaul, Spain, and Africa—was accompanied by the deposition of the nominal Emperor of the West.

In the middle of the sixth century there was, however, a period when the Roman dominion was revived in the West—from the East. During Justinian's reign in Constantinople, his generals reconquered Africa, Italy, and southern Spain. That achievement, associated mainly with the name of Belisarius, is the more remarkable because of two features—first, the extraordinarily slender resources with which Belisarius undertook these far-reaching campaigns; second, his consistent use of the tactical defensive. There is no parallel in history for such a series of conquests by abstention from attack. They are the more remarkable since they were carried out by an army that was based on the mobile arm—and mainly composed of cavalry. Belisarius had no lack of audacity, but his tactics were to allow—or tempt—the other side to do the attacking. If that choice was, in part, imposed on him by his numerical weakness, it was also a matter of subtle calculation, both tactical and psychological.

His army bore little resemblance to the classical pattern of the legionary army—it was closer to the medieval form, but more highly developed. To a soldier of Caesar's time it would have been unrecognizable as a Roman army, though a soldier who had served with Scipio in Africa might have found the trend of its evolution less surprising. Between Scipio and Caesar, while Rome itself was changing from a city-state into an Empire, the army had been transformed from a short-service citizen force into a long-service professional force. But military organization had not fulfilled the promise of cavalry predominance that was foreshadowed at Zama. The infantry were the staple of the Imperial Roman Army, and the cavalry (though the breed of horses had greatly improved in size and speed) had become as subsidiary as they had been in the earlier stages of the war against Hannibal. As the need for greater mobility in frontier defence became more evident, the proportion of the cavalry was gradually increased, but it was not until the legions were overwhelmed at Adrianople, in 378, by the cavalry of the Goths, that the Roman armies came to be reorganized in accordance with this lesson. In the generations that followed, the pendulum swung to the other extreme. Under Theodosius, the expansion of the mobile arm was hastened by enlisting vast numbers of barbarian horsemen. Later, the recruiting balance was to some extent corrected, while the new type of organization was systematized. By the time of Justinian and Belisarius, the principal arm was formed by the heavy cavalry, who were armed with bow as well as lance, and clad in armour. The underlying idea was evidently to combine the value of mobile fire-power and of mobile shock-power—as separately demonstrated by the Hun or Persian horse-archer and the Gothic lancer—in a single disciplined fighting man. These heavy cavalry were supplemented by lightly equipped horse-archers—a combination which, both in form and tactics, foreshadowed that of modern light and heavy (or medium) tanks. The infantry likewise were of light and heavy types, but the latter, with their heavy spears and close-locked formation, merely served as a stable pivot round which the cavalry could manœuvre in battle.

BYZANTINE WARS

In the early part of the sixth century the East Roman Empire was in a precarious situation. Its forces suffered a number of humiliating defeats on the Persian frontier, and its whole position in Asia Minor seemed in danger. For a time, pressure was relieved by a Hunnish invasion of Persia from the north, but war broke out afresh on the frontier about 525—though in a rather desultory way. It was here that Belisarius first won distinction, by his conduct of several cavalry raids into Persian Armenia, and later by a spirited counter-attack after the Persians had captured a frontier castle. The contrast with the poor performance of other leaders led Justinian to appoint him Commander-in-Chief of the forces in the East—when he was well under thirty.

In 530, a Persian army of some 40,000 men advanced upon the fortress of Daras. To meet them Belisarius had a force of barely half their strength, mostly composed of raw recruits who had recently arrived. Rather than stand a siege, he decided to risk a battle, though on a position he had carefully prepared for defensive-offensive tactics—he could count on the Persians' contempt for the Byzantines, as well as their superiority in numbers, to make them take the lead in attack. A wide and deep ditch was dug in front of Daras, but near enough to the walls to allow the defenders of the ditch to be supported by overhead fire from the battlements. Here Belisarius placed his less reliable infantry. A cross-trench ran forward at right angles from each end, and from the ends of these projecting trenches another straight one stretched outwards to the hills on either side of the valley. Along these flanking extensions, which had wide passages at intervals, bodies of heavy cavalry were posted ready for counter-attack. The Hunnish light cavalry were posted at the two inner corners so that, if the heavy cavalry on the wings were driven back, they might relieve the pressure by making a harassing sally on to the attacker's rear.

The Persians, on arrival, were baffled by these dispositions, and spent the first day in exploratory skirmishing. Next morning, Belisarius sent a letter to the Persian commander suggesting that the points in dispute could be settled better by mutual discussion than by fighting. According to Procopius, he said in the letter: 'The first blessing is peace, as is agreed by all men who have even a small share of reason. . . . The best general, therefore, is that one which is able to bring about peace from war.' These were remarkable words to come from a soldier so young on the eve of his first great victory. But the Persian commander replied that the promises of Romans could never be trusted. In his mind, Belisarius's message and his defensive attitude behind a trench were merely signs of fear. So the attack was launched. The Persians were careful not to push into the obvious trap in the centre, but their care played into the hands of Belisarius. For it meant not only that their effort was split but that the fighting was confined to the cavalry on the wings—to the arm in which Belisarius was least outnumbered and on which he could best rely. At the same time, his infantry were able to contribute by their archery fire. The Byzantine bow outranged the Persian, and the Persian armour was not proof against the Byzantine arrow as the Byzantine was against the Persian.

Against his left wing the Persian cavalry at first made progress, but then a small cavalry detachment which had been hidden behind a hill on the flank suddenly charged them in rear. This unexpected stroke, coupled with the appearance of the Hunnish light cavalry on their other flank, caused the Persians to retreat. Then, on the other flank, the Persian cavalry pressed still deeper, up to the walls of the city, only to produce a gap between their advancing wing and their static centre—a gap into which Belisarius threw all his available cavalry. This counterstroke at the weakened hinge of the Persian line first drove the Persian cavalry wing off the battlefield into a divergent line of flight, and then turned on the exposed flank of the Persian infantry in the centre. This battle of Daras ended in the decisive defeat of the Persians—the first they had suffered at Byzantine hands for several generations.

After some further reverses the Persian king began to discuss terms of peace with Justinian's envoy. The negotiations were still in progress when the King of the Saracens, an ally of the Persians, suggested a new plan of campaign—for an indirect stroke at the Byzantine power. He argued that, instead of attacking where the Byzantine frontier was strongly held and fortified, there would be more profit in the unexpected. A force composed of the most mobile troops available should move west from the Euphrates across the desert—which had long been considered an impassable barrier—and pounce upon Antioch, the wealthiest city of the East Roman Empire. This plan was adopted, and was carried far enough to prove that such a desert crossing was practicable with a suitably constituted type of army. Belisarius, however, had made his own forces so mobile, and developed such an efficient system of communication along the frontier, that he was able to hasten down from the north in time to anticipate the enemy's arrival.

Having frustrated the threat, he was content to shepherd the invaders back on their homeward course. Such restraint did not please his troops. Aware of their murmurs he tried to point out to them that true victory lay in compelling one's opponent to abandon his purpose, with the least possible loss to oneself. If such a result was obtained, there was no real advantage to be gained by winning a battle—'for why should one rout a fugitive?'—while the attempt would incur a needless risk of defeat, and of thereby laying the Empire open to a more dangerous invasion. To leave a retreating army no way of escape was the surest way to infuse it with the courage of desperation.

Such arguments were too reasonable to satisfy the instinctive blood-lust of the soldiery. So to retain his hold on them he gave rein to their desires—and as a result suffered his only defeat, in the process of proving the truth of his warning. But the Persians' victory over their pursuers was purchased at so heavy a price that they were forced to continue their retreat.

After his successful defence of the East, Belisarius was shortly sent on an offensive mission to the West. A century earlier the Vandals, a Germanic people, had ended their southward migration by occupying Roman Africa, and establishing their capital at Carthage. From there they conducted piracy on a great scale and also sent out raiding expeditions to plunder the cities of the Mediterranean seaboard. In 455 they had sacked Rome itself, and subsequently inflicted an overwhelming defeat on a great punitive expedition sent from Constantinople. After some generations, however, luxury and the African sun not merely softened their manners but began to sap their vigour. Then in 531 the Vandal King Hilderic, who had befriended Justinian in his youth, was deposed and imprisoned by a warlike nephew, Gelimer. Justinian thereupon wrote Gelimer asking him to release his uncle; and when this request was rebuffed he decided, in 533, to send an expeditionary force to Africa under Belisarius. For it, however, he provided only 5,000 cavalry and 10,000 infantry. Though they were picked troops the odds seemed heavily against them, since the Vandals were reputed to have nearly 100,000 troops.

When the expedition reached Sicily, Belisarius heard some encouraging news—that some of the best of the Vandal forces had been sent to deal with a revolt in Sardinia, then a Vandal possession, and that Gelimer himself was away from Carthage at the moment. Belisarius lost no time in sailing for Africa, and made a successful landing, at a point some nine days' march from Carthage, in order to avoid the risk of interception by the superior Vandal fleet. On hearing the news, Gelimer hastily ordered the various contingents of the army to converge on a defile near Ad Decimum, the tenth milestone on the main road to Carthage, where he hoped to surround the invaders. But this plan was dislocated because Belisarius's rapid advance, synchronized with a threat to Carthage by his fleet, caught the Vandal troops in the process of assembling; and a confused series of combats produced such disorder among the Vandal forces that they not only forfeited their opportunity of overwhelming Belisarius, but were dispersed in all directions—thus leaving him a clear path into Carthage. By the time Gelimer had reassembled his troops, and, having recalled his expeditionary force from Sardinia, was ready to take the offensive again, Belisarius had restored the defences of Carthage—which the Vandals had allowed to fall into disrepair.

After waiting several months for the Vandals' expected attempt to eject him, Belisarius concluded from their inactivity that their morale was low, and being on his own side now assured of a secure place of retreat in case of defeat, he decided to venture upon the offensive. Pushing his cavalry ahead, he came upon the Vandals in camp at Tricameron, behind a stream, and started the battle without waiting for his infantry to come up. His idea would seem to have been that by his manifest weakness of numbers he might tempt the Vandals into an attack upon him, so that he could counter-attack them as they were crossing the stream. But a 'provocative' attack and simulated retreat failed to draw them farther than the brook in pursuit. Thereupon Belisarius took advantage of their caution to push a much larger force across the stream undisturbed, and then, after developing an attack on their centre, which fixed their attention, he extended the attack along the whole front.

The Vandals' resistance promptly collapsed, and they took refuge in their stockaded camp. During the night Gelimer himself fled, and after his disappearance his army scattered. This victory, followed up by Belisarius's pursuit and ultimate capture of Gelimer, settled the issue of the war. While the reconquest of Roman Africa had looked a desperate venture in prospect, it had proved astoundingly simple in execution.

That easy triumph encouraged Justinian to attempt, 535, the reconquest of Italy and Sicily from the Ostrogoths—and as cheaply if possible. He sent a small army up the Dalmatian coast. He persuaded the Franks, by a promise of subsidies, to attack the Goths in the north. Under cover of these diversions, he dispatched Belisarius to Sicily with an expeditionary force of 12,000 men, instructing him to give out on arrival there that the force was on its way to Carthage. He was then to occupy the island if he found that it could be easily taken; if not, he was to re-embark without showing his hand. In the event, there was no difficulty. Although the Sicilian cities had been well treated by their conquerors, they readily welcomed Belisarius as their deliverer and protector. The small Gothic garrisons offered no serious resistance to him save at Palermo, which he overcame by a stratagem. In contrast to his success, the attempted invasion of Dalmatia ended in disaster. But as soon as this diversionary advance was renewed by a reinforced Byzantine army, Belisarius crossed the Straits of Messina to begin the invasion of Italy.

Dissension among the Goths and the negligence of their King cleared his path through southern Italy, as far as Naples, which was strongly fortified and held by a garrison equal in scale to his own force. Baulked for a time, Belisarius eventually found a way of entry through a disused aqueduct; filtering a picked body of men through the narrow tunnel, he combined a rear attack with a frontal escalade at night, and thereby gained control of the city.

The news of its fall caused such an outcry among the Goths as to produce an uprising against their King, and his replacement on the throne by a vigorous general named Vitiges. But Vitiges took the typical military view that it was necessary to finish the Frankish war before concentrating against the new invader. So, after leaving what he considered an adequate garrison in Rome, he marched north to deal with the Franks. But the people of Rome did not share his view, and since the Gothic garrison felt that it was not adequate to defend the city without their help, Belisarius was able to occupy the city without difficulty—the garrison withdrawing as he approached.

Too late, Vitiges repented his decision, and, after buying off the Franks with gold and territory, gathered an army of 150,000 men to recapture Rome. To defend it, Belisarius had a bare 10,000. But in the three months' grace allowed him before the siege began, he had remodelled the city's defences and built up large stocks of food. His method of defence, moreover, was an active one—with frequent well-judged sorties. In these he exploited the advantage which his cavalry enjoyed through being armed with bows, so that they could harass the enemy's cavalry masses while themselves keeping out of reach, or tease the Gothic lancers into blind charges. Though the strain on the scanty defenders was severe, the strength of the besieger was shrinking much faster, especially through sickness. To accelerate the process Belisarius boldly took the risk of sending two detachments from his slender force to seize by surprise the towns of Tivoli and Terracina, which dominated the roads by which the besiegers received their supplies. And when reinforcements reached him from home, he extended his mobile raids across to and up the Adriatic coast towards the Goths' main base at Ravenna. Finally, after a year's siege, the Goths abandoned the attempt and withdrew northward—their departure being hastened by the news that a Byzantine raiding force had seized Rimini, a town on their communications disturbingly close to Ravenna. As the rear half of the Gothic army was crowding over the Mulvian bridge, it suffered heavily from a parting stroke which Belisarius launched against it.

While Vitiges retreated north-east towards Ravenna, Belisarius dispatched part of his force, with the fleet, up the west coast to capture Pavia and Milan. He himself, with a mere 3,000 men, rode across to the east coast, where he was joined by a newly landed reinforcement of 7,000, under Narses, the eunuch Court Chamberlain. Thence he hastened to the relief of his endangered detachment at Rimini, which had allowed itself to be shut in by Vitiges. Masking the fortress of Osimo, where the Goths had left a force of 25,000, Belisarius slipped past it and advanced on Rimini, in two columns, while another part of his force went by sea. This advance from three directions was intended to give the Goths an exaggerated impression of his strength. To strengthen the impression, a far-stretched chain of camp-fires were lighted by night. The stratagem succeeded, helped by the fear which Belisarius's name now inspired, and the much larger Gothic army bolted in panic on his approach.

Belisarius now, while keeping watch over Vitiges in Ravenna, planned to clear his communications with Rome by reducing the various fortresses that he had slipped past in his rapid advance. With such small numbers as he possessed this was not an easy problem, but his method was to isolate, and concentrate upon particular fortresses while using a far-flung curtain of mobile detachments to keep any potential relieving forces occupied in their own area. Even so, the task took a considerable time, and was the more protracted because some of his generals—who had influence at court to cover their disobedience—were inclined to seek easier and wealthier objectives. Meantime Vitiges was prompted to send embassies to the Franks and the Persians with the tempting suggestion that there was now a great opportunity to turn the tide of Byzantine expansion if they were to join in a concerted attack on the Empire from both sides while its forces were so widely stretched out. The King of the Franks responded by crossing the Alps with a large army.

The first to suffer were their expectant Allies. For after the passage of Po near Pavia had been opened to them by the Goths, who were there faced by a Byzantine force, they attacked both sides impartially, and put them to flight. They then proceeded to eat up the countryside. As their army was almost entirely composed of infantry, their foraging range was narrow, and before long they perished in thousands from the results of the famine they had created. Hamstrung by their own improvident folly they dared not push on in face of a mobile opponent, and were with little difficulty induced by Belisarius to return home. Belisarius was then able to tighten his grip on Ravenna, and bring about the surrender of Vitiges.

At this point, in 540, he was recalled by Justinian, ostensibly to deal with the Persians' renewed threat—which in itself was real. It would seem, however, that jealousy was the deeper motive, since it had come to Justinian's ears that the Goths had made peace proposals to Belisarius on the basis of recognizing him as Emperor of the West.

While Belisarius was on his way home, Chosroes, the new King of Persia, repeated the cross-desert march that had been frustrated the time before, and succeeded in capturing Antioch. Having despoiled this and other Syrian cities of their wealth, he accepted Justinian's offer of a large annual payment in return for a new peace treaty. Justinian saved his own purse by tearing up the treaty as soon as Chosroes had returned to Persia, and Belisarius to Constantinople. Thus only his subjects were the losers—a result which accorded with the normal experience of warfare.

In the next campaign King Chosroes invaded Colchis, on the Black Sea coast, and captured the Byzantine fortress of Petra. At the same time Belisarius arrived on the eastern frontier. Hearing that Chosroes had gone off on a distant expedition, though it was not yet known where, Belisarius immediately seized the opportunity for a surprise inroad into Persian territory. To extend the effect he dispatched his Arab allies on a raid down the Tigris into Assyria. This well-timed thrust proved to be an unconscious demonstration of the value of the indirect approach. For it threatened the base of the Persian army that had invaded Colchis, and thereby brought Chosroes hurrying back to avert the severance of his communications.

Soon afterwards, Belisarius was recalled to Constantinople—this time because of domestic troubles. During his absence from the East, the Persian King launched an invasion of Palestine with the aim of capturing Jerusalem, now the wealthiest city in the East, since the destruction of Antioch. When the news came, Justinian dispatched Belisarius to the rescue. This time Chosroes had brought a very large army, estimated at 200,000 men, and in consequence could not take the desert route: he had to march up the Euphrates into Syria before turning south against Palestine. Thus sure of the route that Chosroes would have to follow, Belisarius concentrated his available troops, few but mobile, at Carshemish, on the upper Euphrates, whence they could threaten the flank of the invader's line of advance near its most vulnerable point—the bend southward. When their presence was reported to Chosroes, he sent an envoy to Belisarius for the nominal purpose of discussing a possible basis of peace and the real purpose of ascertaining the strength and state of Belisarius's force—which, actually, was less than a tenth, perhaps hardly a twentieth, of the scale of the invading army.

Guessing the object of this mission, Belisarius staged a military 'play'. He picked out the best of his own men—including contingents of Goths, Vandals, and Moors who had enlisted in his service after being taken prisoner—and moved out to a point on the Persian envoy's route of approach, so that the latter might imagine that he had been met at what was one of the outposts of a great army. And the soldiers were instructed to spread out over the plain and kept constantly in movement, so as to magnify their apparent numbers. This impression was deepened by Belisarius's air of light-hearted confidence and the carefree behaviour of the troops—as if they had nothing to fear from any possible attack. The envoy's report convinced Chosroes that it was too hazardous to continue his invasion with so formidable a force on the flank of his communications. Then, by further confusing manœuvres of his cavalry along the Euphrates, Belisarius bluffed the Persians into making a hurried retreat across the river, and thence back home. Never was an invasion, potentially irresistible, more economically defeated. And this miraculous result was achieved by an indirect approach which, though profiting by a flanking position, was in itself purely psychological.

Belisarius was once again recalled to Constantinople through Justinian's jealous suspicion of his ever-growing fame. Before long, the mismanagement of affairs in Italy so imperilled the Byzantines' hold upon it that Justinian was forced to send Belisarius back there to restore the situation. Parsimony combined with jealousy led the Emperor, however, to allow his general the meagrest resources for the task, which had grown to vast dimensions by the time Belisarius arrived at Ravenna. For the Goths, under a new king, Totila, had gradually rebuilt their strength, regained all the north-west of Italy, and then overrun the south. Naples had fallen to them and Rome was threatened. Belisarius made a daring but unsuccessful attempt to save Rome by sailing round the coast with a detachment, and forcing a passage up the Tiber. Totila then dismantled the fortifications, left a force of about 15,000 to pin down Belisarius's 7,000 on the coast, and marched north with the aim of capturing Ravenna in Belisarius's absence. But Belisarius outmanœuvred his 'warders', and slipped into Rome. It would serve as a bait that no Goth of spirit could refuse. In the three weeks before Totila returned with his army, Belisarius had repaired the fortifications so well, save for replacing the gates, that he was able to repulse two successive heavy attacks. In these the Goths lost so heavily that their confidence waned, and when they made a third attempt later Belisarius delivered a counterstroke that threw them back in confusion. Next day they abandoned the siege and withdrew to Tivoli.

But despite repeated appeals Justinian only sent reinforcements in driblets, and thus, instead of being able to attempt the reconquest of the country as a whole, Belisarius was reduced to spending several years in a 'tip and run' campaign among the fortresses, and from port to port. At last, seeing that it was hopeless to expect that Justinian would ever trust him with an adequately strong army, he obtained permission in 548 to give up the task and return to Constantinople.

Four years later, repenting of his decision to abandon Italy, Justinian decided to undertake a fresh expedition. Unwilling to put Belisarius in charge, lest he might be creating a rival sovereign, he eventually gave the command to Narses—who had long been a keen theoretical student of war, and who, in the crowning phase of Belisarius's first Italian campaign, had been given a chance to prove his practical skill.

Narses made full use of the greater opportunity now offered him. In the first place, he made it a condition of accepting the offer that he was provided with a really strong and well-equipped force. With this he marched north round the Adriatic shore. His march was assisted by the Goths' belief that his invasion would necessarily come across the sea—since they assumed that the rugged coastal route, with its numerous river-mouths, was too difficult for him to attempt. But by arranging for a large number of boats to keep pace with his overland advance, and using them to form floating bridges, Narses made unexpectedly rapid progress, and reached Ravenna without opposition. Losing no time, he pressed on southward, circling past the various fortresses which barred the way—with the aim of forcing battle on Totila before his forces were fully assembled. Totila held the main pass across the Apennines, but Narses slipped over by a side path and came upon Totila at Taginae.

Here Narses had a superiority of force over the Goths, in contrast to Belisarius's constant inferiority in former campaigns. Nevertheless, having drawn his full profit from the strategic offensive, Narses preferred the tactical defensive on meeting Totila. Counting on the instinctive 'offensiveness' of the Goths to make them take the lead in attack, he prepared a trap for them—on lines which foreshadowed the English tactics at Crécy, against the French chivalry, eight hundred years later. His design was based on an awareness of the Goth's justified contempt for the frailty of the Byzantine infantry in face of a cavalry charge. In the centre of his line he placed a large body of dismounted cavalry, to use their lances on foot, so that they might appear to the enemy like a mass of infantry spearmen. On each flank of this central body he placed his foot-archers, pushed well forward in a crescent from which they could enfilade any assault on the centre, with most of his mounted cavalry close in rear of them. Well out to the left, under a hill, he posted a picked force of cavalry to deliver a surprise stroke upon the Goths' rear as soon as they became deeply engaged.

This cleverly baited trap fulfilled its purpose. The Gothic cavalry were launched against the supposedly unreliable infantry in the enemy's centre. In their charge they suffered badly from the converging hail of arrows on their flanks, and were then checked in front by the firm stand of the dismounted lancers—while increasingly galled by the archers who now closed in on their flanks. As for the Gothic infantry, these hesitated to come up in support for fear of being themselves attacked in rear by the horse-archers whom Narses had posted near the flanking hill. After continuing the vain effort for some time, the disheartened Gothic cavalry began to fall back, whereupon Narses delivered a decisive counterstroke with his own cavalry, hitherto held in reserve. The defeat of the Goths was so complete that Narses met with little further serious resistance in carrying out the second reconquest of Italy.

The final subjugation of the Goths was accomplished just in time to leave Narses free to deal with a new incursion of the Franks, made in response to the Goths' desperate appeal. This time the Franks pushed much deeper than before—down into Campania. It would seem that Narses, profiting by the experience of their first invasion, wished to give them 'rope to hang themselves'—to avoid battle until their huge strength had dwindled under the rigours of the march and the toll of dysentery. They still numbered 80,000, however, when he offered battle to them at Casilinum (553). Here he devised a trap that was shrewdly fitted to their characteristic tactics. An army of foot, they attacked in a deep column, relying on weight and momentum. Their weapons were of a close-range type—the spear, the throwing axe, and the sword.

At Casilinum Narses held his centre with spearmen and bowmen, on foot. The charge of the Franks drove these back, but then Narses wheeled in his cavalry wings against the Franks flanks. This halted them, and they promptly faced outwards ready to meet a charge. But he made no attempt to close with them, knowing that their formation was too solid to be broken by shock. Instead, he checked his cavalry just out of range of the Franks' throwing axes, and ordered them to use their bows—raining arrows on a mass that could not retaliate without disjointing its own close-ranked formation. When, at last, the Franks sought relief by breaking their ranks, and edging away to the rear, he seized the opportunity to charge home. This well-timed stroke shattered them, and scarcely a man escaped.

At first glance the interest of the campaigns of Belisarius and Narses appears to be tactical rather than strategical, since so many of the movements led directly to battle and there are fewer examples of calculated manœuvring against the enemy's communications than in the campaigns of other Great Captains. But closer examination modifies this impression. Belisarius had developed a new-style tactical instrument with which he knew that he might count on beating much superior numbers, provided that he could induce his opponents to attack him under conditions that suited his tactics. For that purpose his lack of numbers, when not too marked, was an asset, especially when coupled with an audaciously direct strategic offensive. His strategy was thus more psychological than logistical. He knew how to provoke the barbarian armies of the West into indulging their natural instinct for direct assault; with the more subtle and skilful Persians he was able at first to take advantage of their feeling of superiority to the Byzantines, and later, when they learnt respect for him, he exploited their wariness as a means of outmanœuvring them psychologically.

He was a master of the art of converting his weakness into strength; and the opponent's strength into a weakness. His tactics, too, had the essential characteristic of the indirect approach—that of getting the opponent off balance, so that a joint becomes exposed and can be dislocated.

When asked privately by friends during his first Italian campaign the grounds of his confidence in tackling such vastly superior forces, he replied that in the first engagement with the Goths he was on the look-out to discover their weaknesses, and had observed that they were unable to bring their numbers concertedly into play. The reason, apart from the embarrassment of excessive bulk, was that while his own cavalry were all good mounted horsemen, the Goths had no practice in this branch; their horsemen were trained to use only lances and swords, while their foot-archers were accustomed to move behind and under shelter of the cavalry. Thus the horsemen were ineffective except in close combat, while having no means of defending themselves against a mounted opponent who kept just out of reach and rained arrows upon them; as for their foot-archers, these would never risk being caught in the open by the enemy's cavalry. The effect was that the Gothic cavalry were always trying to get to close quarters, and could be easily galled into an ill-timed charge, whereas the infantry tended to hang back when the shielding cavalry got far ahead—so that combination broke down, while a gap was created into which flank counterstrokes could be driven.

The tactical system and the defensive-offensive strategy which

Belisarius developed became the foundation of the Byzantine Empire's successful maintenance of its position, and the Roman tradition, during the centuries that followed—while western Europe was passing through the Dark Ages. The subsequent elaboration of these methods, and the army's reorganization, can be followed in the two great Byzantine military textbooks, the *Strategicon* of the Emperor Maurice and the *Tactica* of Leo. This structure proved strong enough to withstand many-sided barbarian pressure, and even the tidal wave of Mohammedan conquest which submerged the Persian Empire. Although outlying territories were lost, the main bastions of the Byzantine Empire were kept intact, and from the reign of Basil I in the ninth century the lost ground was progressively regained. Under Basil II, early in the eleventh century, the Empire reached the highest point of its power since Justinian, five hundred years before, and stood more securely than it had in his time.

Fifty years later its security was dissipated and its prospects forfeited within the space of a few hours. Prolonged immunity from danger had led to ever-increasing cuts in the military budget, and caused the decay as well as the reduction of the army. Then the rising power of the Seljuk Turks under Alp Arslan, from 1063 onwards, brought a belated awakening to the need for rearmament and in 1068 the general Romanus Diogenes was made emperor—as a step towards coping with the danger. Instead of allowing himself time to train the army up to its former pitch of efficiency, he embarked prematurely on an offensive campaign. Encouraged by initial success on the Euphrates, he led his forces deep into Armenia, and near Manzikert met the main Seljuk army. Impressed by the size of the Byzantine army, Alp Arslan offered to open negotiations for a peace settlement, but Romanus insisted that, prior to any discussions, the Turkish Sultan must evacuate his camp and withdraw—which would have meant a loss of 'face' that he could hardly be expected to accept. Following Alp Arslan's refusal, Romanus launched an attack, and, breaking with the Byzantine military tradition, allowed himself to be drawn on further and further in a vain effort to come to close quarters with an evasive and nimble foe, whose clouds of horse-archers continually harassed his advance. By dusk his troops were exhausted, and their formation became disjointed, when at last he ordered a retirement; the Turks now closed in round his flanks, and under this encircling pressure his army broke up.

The defeat was so disastrously complete that the Turks were soon able to overrun the greater part of Asia Minor. Thus through the folly of a single hot-headed general, whose offensive spirit was not balanced by judgement, the Empire suffered a blow from which it never recovered—although it had sufficient power of endurance to survive, in a diminished form, for a further four hundred years.

CHAPTER V

MEDIEVAL WARS

★

This chapter serves merely as a link between the cycles of ancient and modern history, for although several of the medieval campaigns are tempting as illustrations, the sources for knowledge of them are more exiguous and less reliable than in earlier or later times. For scientific truth in the deduction of causes and effects, the safe course is to base our analysis of history on established facts, and to pass over certain periods, even at the sacrifice of valuable confirmatory examples, where it is necessary to choose between conflicting textual or historical criticism of the evidence. It is true that controversy has raged round the tactical rather than the strategical details of medieval military history, but the dust thus raised is apt to envelop both, in the view of the normal student of war, and to make him perhaps excessively dubious of deductions drawn from this period. But, without including it in our specific analysis, certain of its episodes may be worth sketching, not least as a means to suggest their potential interest and profit.

In the West during the Middle Ages the spirit of feudal chivalry was inimical to military art, though the drab stupidity of its military course is lightened by a few bright gleams—no fewer perhaps, in proportion, than at any other period in history.

The Normans provided some of the earliest gleams, and their descendants continued to illuminate the course of medieval warfare. The value they put on Norman blood led them to expend brains in substitution for it, with notable profit.

The date which every schoolboy knows, if he knows no other, 1066, was marked by strategy and tactics as skilful as their result was decisive—decisive not only for the immediate issue but in its effect on the whole course of history. William of Normandy's invasion of England profited from a strategic distraction, and thereby gained at the outset the virtues of an indirect approach. This distraction was the landing of King Harold's rebel brother, Tostig, and his ally, Harold Hardrada, King of Norway, on the Yorkshire coast. This had seemed less immediate a danger than William's invasion. But it matured earlier, and thus gave added effectiveness to William's plans, even though it was promptly defeated. Two days after the annihilation of the Norse invaders at Stamford Bridge, William landed on the Sussex coast.

Instead of advancing northward, he lured Harold into a precipitate dash southwards—with only a fraction of his force—by ravaging the lands of Kent and Sussex. The further south Harold came, and the sooner he gave battle, the further, both in distance and time, would he be separated from his reinforcements. If this was William's calculation, it was justified by events. He brought Harold to battle near Hastings within sight of the Channel coast, and decided the issue by a tactical indirect approach—ordering a feigned flight by part of his force which led his opponents to dislocate their own dispositions. And, in the final phase, the device of high angle archery fire which caused Harold's death might be classified as an indirect fire approach!

William's strategy after this victory is equally significant. Instead of marching direct on London, he first secured Dover, and his own sea communications. On reaching the outskirts of London, he avoided any direct assault, but made a circle, and a circular swathe of devastation, round London to the west and then to the north. Threatened with starvation, the capital surrendered when William had reached Berkhamstead.

The next century witnessed a further proof of Norman genius for war, in one of the most astonishing campaigns in history. This was the conquest of the greater part of Ireland, as well as the repulse of a strong Norse invasion, by Earl 'Strongbow' and a few hundred knights from the Welsh Marches—an achievement remarkable for the extreme slenderness of the means, the extreme difficulty of the forest and bog country, and for the adaptability with which the conquerors recast and reversed the conventional feudal methods of war. They showed their skill and calculation by the way they repeatedly lured their opponents to battle in open ground, where their mounted charges had full effect; by the way they exploited feigned retreats, diversions, rear attacks to break up the opposing formation; by the strategic surprises, night attacks, and use of archery to overcome opposition when they could not lure an enemy from the shelter of his defences.

The thirteenth century, however, was more plentiful still in examples of strategic skill. The first was in 1216, when King John saved his kingdom, after almost losing it, by a campaign in which pure strategy was unmixed with battles. His means were mobility; the strong resisting power then possessed by fortresses; and the psychological power inherent in the dislike of the townsmen for the barons and their foreign ally, Louis of France. When Louis, after landing in east Kent, occupied London and Winchester, John was too weak to oppose him in battle; and most of the country was dominated by the barons. But John still preserved the fortresses of Windsor, Reading, Wallingford, and Oxford—which commanded the line of the Thames and separated the baronial forces north and south of it—while the key stronghold of Dover remained untaken in Louis's rear. John had fallen back to Dorset, but when the situation became clearer he marched north, in July, to Worcester, securing the line of the Severn and thus establishing a barrage to prevent the tide of rebellion flowing further to the west and south-west. Thence he moved east along the already secured line of the Thames as if to relieve Windsor.

To confirm the besiegers in this belief, he sent a detachment of Welsh archers to fire into their camp at night, while he himself swerved north-east and, thanks to this start, won the race to Cambridge. He was now able to establish a further barrage across the routes to the north, while the main French forces were tied to the siege of Dover. His success in circumscribing and contracting the area of opposition and disaffection spelt the failure of the rebels and their ally, even though King John's own reign was ended by his death in October. If he died of a surfeit of peaches and new ale, their hopes died of a surfeit of strategic strongholds.

The next successful baronial insurrection was broken by the masterly strategy of Prince Edward, later Edward I, in 1265. The sequel to King Henry III's defeat at Lewes had been to establish the supremacy of the baronial party throughout most of England, except on the Welsh Marches. Thither Simon de Montfort marched, crossing the Severn and pursuing his triumphant path as far as Newport. Prince Edward, who had escaped from the baronial army to join his adherents in the border counties, upset de Montfort's plans by seizing the Severn bridges behind him, and then moving down on his rear. Edward not only threw him back across the Usk, but, by a raid with three galleys on his ships at Newport, frustrated his new plan of transporting his army back to

England. De Montfort was thus forced to undertake a roundabout and exhausting march north through the barren districts of Wales, while Edward fell back to Worcester to hold the Severn against his arrival. Then, when de Montfort's son marched to his relief with an army from eastern England, Edward utilized his central position to crush each of the de Montforts in turn while they were separated and blindfolded—by march and counter-march on his part which exploited mobility to achieve a couple of shattering surprises, first at Kenilworth and then at Evesham.

Edward, as king, was to make an even greater contribution to military science in his Welsh wars, not only in developing the use of the bow and the combination of cavalry charges with archery fire, but, still more, in his strategic method of conquest. The problem was to subdue a hardy and savage mountain race who could evade battle by retiring to the hills, and then re-occupy the valleys when the invader broke off operations for the winter. If Edward's means were comparatively limited he had an advantage in the fact that the area of the country was also limited. His solution was a combination of mobility and strategic points. By building castles at these points, by connecting them with roads, and by keeping his opponents constantly on the move—so that they had no chance to recuperate physically and psychologically, or recover geographically, during the winter—he split up and wore down their power of resistance.

Edward's strategic gifts did not survive him, however, and in the Hundred Years' War there is nothing to learn, save negatively, from the strategy of his grandson or his great-grandson. Their purposeless parades through France were mostly ineffective; and the few which had greater results were the outcome of their greater folly. For in the campaigns of Crécy and Poitiers, Edward III and the Black Prince respectively got themselves into perilous situations. These had the extremely indirect and unintended merit that the very predicament of the English incited their direct-minded opponents to rush headlong into battle under conditions all to their disadvantage—and thus give the English the chance to rescue themselves from their predicament. For in a defensive battle, on ground chosen by the English, their use of the longbow in face of the futile tactics of the French chivalry gave them an assured tactical superiority.

The severity of these defeats in battle proved, however, of ultimate advantage to the French. For in the next stage of the war they adhered steadfastly to the Fabian policy of the Constable du Guesclin. The strategy by which he carried out this policy was to avoid battle with the main English army, while constantly hampering the movement, and contracting the territory, of his opponents. Far removed from a passive evasion of battle, his strategy exploited mobility and surprise to a degree that few generals have matched—cutting off convoys, cutting up detachments, and capturing isolated garrisons. Always taking the line of least expectation, his surprise attacks on such garrisons, often by night, were helped both by his new and rapid storm methods and by his psychologically calculated choice of objectives where the garrisons were discontented or the population ripe for treachery. So, also, he fanned every flame of local unrest—as an immediate distraction to the enemy's attention and an ultimate subtraction from their territory.

Within less than five years, du Guesclin had reduced the vast English possessions in France to a slender strip of territory between Bordeaux and Bayonne. He had done it without fighting a battle. Indeed, he never pressed the attack on even a small English force if it had gained time to take up defensive dispositions. Other generals have maintained, in common with moneylenders, the principle 'no advance without security'; du Guesclin's principle was: 'No attack without surprise.'

The next serious English attempt at foreign conquest was at least inspired by method, and by a closer calculation of end and means—after a rash beginning. Henry V's first and most famous campaign was his most foolish. In the 'Edwardian' parade of 1415 which culminated at Agincourt, the French had only to block Henry's path to ensure his collapse from hunger; but their leaders had forgotten the lesson of Crécy and the teaching of du Guesclin. They thought that with a four-to-one superiority of force it would be shameful to use this superiority for anything save a direct attack. As a result they provided a more shameful repetition of Crécy and Poitiers. After this lucky escape, Henry V employed what may be called a 'block-system' strategy, seeking permanent conquest by methodical extensions of territory, in which the population was conciliated as a means to secure his tenure. The interest and value of Henry's later campaigns lie in their grand strategy rather than in their strategy.

In the realm of strategy our survey of the Middle Ages may well close with Edward IV, who in 1461 gained his throne, and in 1471 regained it, after being an exile, by his exceptional use of mobility.

In the first campaign the result was mainly due to swiftness of judgement and movement. Edward was engaged against the local Lancastrians in Wales when he got word that the main Lancastrian army was coming down from the north upon London. Turning back, he reached Gloucester on the 20th February—where he learnt of the Lancastrian victory at St. Albans on the 17th February over the Yorkist force under Warwick. St. Albans to London was twenty miles, Gloucester to London more than one hundred miles; and the Lancastrians had three days in hand. But at Burford, on the 22nd, Edward was joined by Warwick, and heard that the Corporation of London was still arguing the terms of surrender—with the city gates shut. Edward left Burford next day, entered London on the 26th, and was there proclaimed king, while the discomfited Lancastrians retired to the north. When he followed them up, he risked much by attacking an army of superior strength in its chosen position at Towton. But the advantage was regained for him by the accident of a snowstorm and its exploitation by his subordinate, Fauconberg, who galled the blinded defenders with arrows until they indulged in the fatal relief of a disordered charge.

In 1471 there was more subtlety and no less mobility in Edward's strategy. He had lost his throne in the interval; but with a loan of 50,000 crowns from his brother-in-law, 1,200 followers, and some promissory notes of assistance from his former supporters in England, he attempted to retrieve his fortune. When he set sail from Flushing, the coasts of England were guarded against him—but, following the line of least expectation, he landed in the Humber on the shrewd calculation that as this district was Lancastrian in sympathy it would be unguarded. Moving swiftly, before the news of his landing could spread and his foes could gather, he reached York. Thence he marched down the London road and neatly swerved past a force blocking the way at Tadcaster. Keeping the lead from this force, which turned to pursue him, his threat to the next opposing force, which awaited him at Newark, induced it to retire eastwards. Thereupon Edward turned south-west to Leicester, where he gathered in more adherents. He then headed for Coventry, where Warwick, now his chief opponent, was assembling his forces. Having drawn both his pursuers thither, and having still further increased his force at the enemy's expense, he turned south-east and marched straight on London, which opened its gates to him. Now feeling strong enough to accept battle, he marched out to greet his long-baffled pursuers on their arrival at Barnet; and here a fog-confused battle ended in his favour.

That same day the Lancastrian Queen, Margaret of Anjou, landed at Weymouth with some French mercenaries. Gathering her adherents in the West, she marched to unite with the army which the Earl of Pembroke had raised in Wales. By swiftness again, Edward reached the edge of the Cotswolds while her army was marching north along the Bristol–Gloucester road in the valley below. Then, in a long day's race—one army in the valley, the other on the heights above—he caught hers in the evening at Tewkesbury, having prevented it crossing the Severn at Gloucester by sending orders ahead to the Constable to close the gates. Nearly forty miles had been covered since daybreak. That night he camped too close to the Lancastrians for them to escape. Their position was strong defensively, but Edward used his bombards as well as archers to gall them into a charge, and thus gained a decisive advantage in the morning's battle.

Edward's strategy was exceptional in its mobility but typical of the age in its lack of subtlety. For medieval strategy had normally the simple and direct aim of seeking immediate battle. If the result was not indecisive it was usually decisive against those who sought it, unless they could induce the defenders to become tactically the assailant.

The best example of strategy in the Middle Ages comes not from the West but from the East. For the thirteenth century, strategically distinguished in the West, was made outstanding by the paralysing lesson in strategy taught by the Mongols to European chivalry. In scale and in quality, in surprise and in mobility, in the strategic and in the tactical indirect approach, their campaigns rival or surpass any in history. In Jenghiz Khan's conquest of China we can trace his use of Taitong-Fu to bait successive traps as Bonaparte later utilized the fortress of Mantua. By far-flung movements with a combination of three armies he finally broke up the moral and military cohesion of the Kin empire. When in 1220 he invaded the Karismian empire, whose centre of power lay in modern Turkestan, one force distracted the enemy's attention to the approach from Kashgar in the south; then the main mass appeared in the north; screened by its operations, he himself with his reserve army swung wider still—and, after disappearing into the Kizyl-Kum desert, debouched by surprise at Bokhara in the rear of the enemy's defensive lines and armies.

In 1241 his general, Sabutai, set out to teach Europe a lesson in a double sense. While one army, as a strategic flank guard, marched through Galicia—engaging the attention of the Polish, German, and Bohemian forces, besides inflicting successive defeats on them—the main army in three widely separated columns swept through Hungary to the Danube. In this advance, the two outer columns formed both a shield and a cloak to the later released move of the central column. Converging on the Danube, near Gran, the Mongols were baulked by the assembly of the Hungarian army on the far bank, but by a skilfully graduated retirement lured their opponents away from the shelter of the river and the reach of reinforcements. Then, by a swift night manœuvre and surprise on the Sajo river, Sabutai dislocated and annihilated the Hungarian army and became master of the central plains of Europe—until he voluntarily relinquished his conquest a year later, to the astonished relief of a Europe which had no power to eject him.[1]

[1] The strategy and tactics of the Mongols are dealt with more fully in the author's earlier book *Great Captains Unveiled*—which was ehosen as textbook for the first experimental Mechanized Force in 1927.

CHAPTER VI

THE SEVENTEENTH CENTURY—GUSTAVUS, CROMWELL, TURENNE

★

We now come to the first 'Great War' of modern history, the Thirty Years' War (1618–48). Significantly, no campaign during its long course proved decisive.

The nearest was the final duel between Gustavus and Wallenstein which, through the former's death in the culminating battle of Lützen, was decisive in quenching the possibility of a great Protestant confederation under Swedish leadership. But for the French intervention, and Wallenstein's murder, it might have been decisive in establishing a united Germany more than three centuries before that unity was achieved.

Such results and possibilities were indirectly gained, for the only pitched battle of the campaign ended in defeat for those in whose favour it tilted the scales of the war. This defeat, partly due to the inferiority of Wallenstein's fighting machine to that of the Swedes, was also partly due to Wallenstein's failure to profit tactically by his strategical opportunity. For he had obtained prior to the battle a very real advantage, and it is worth noting that this had come through three successive but varied applications of the indirect approach—which had changed the whole aspect of the war.

In 1632, called back to command a non-existent army by the abject entreaties of the sovereign who had wronged him, Wallenstein had gathered within three months some 40,000 soldiers of fortune, drawn by the glamour of his name. Despite the urgent appeal for aid from Bavaria, then being overrun by Gustavus's all-conquering army, Wallenstein instead turned north against Gustavus's weaker ally, the Saxons, and after throwing them out of Bohemia, moved on towards Saxony itself. He even compelled the reluctant Elector of Bavaria to bring his army to join him, thus apparently leaving Bavaria more defenceless than ever. But the reality was otherwise, and Wallenstein's calculation justified—for

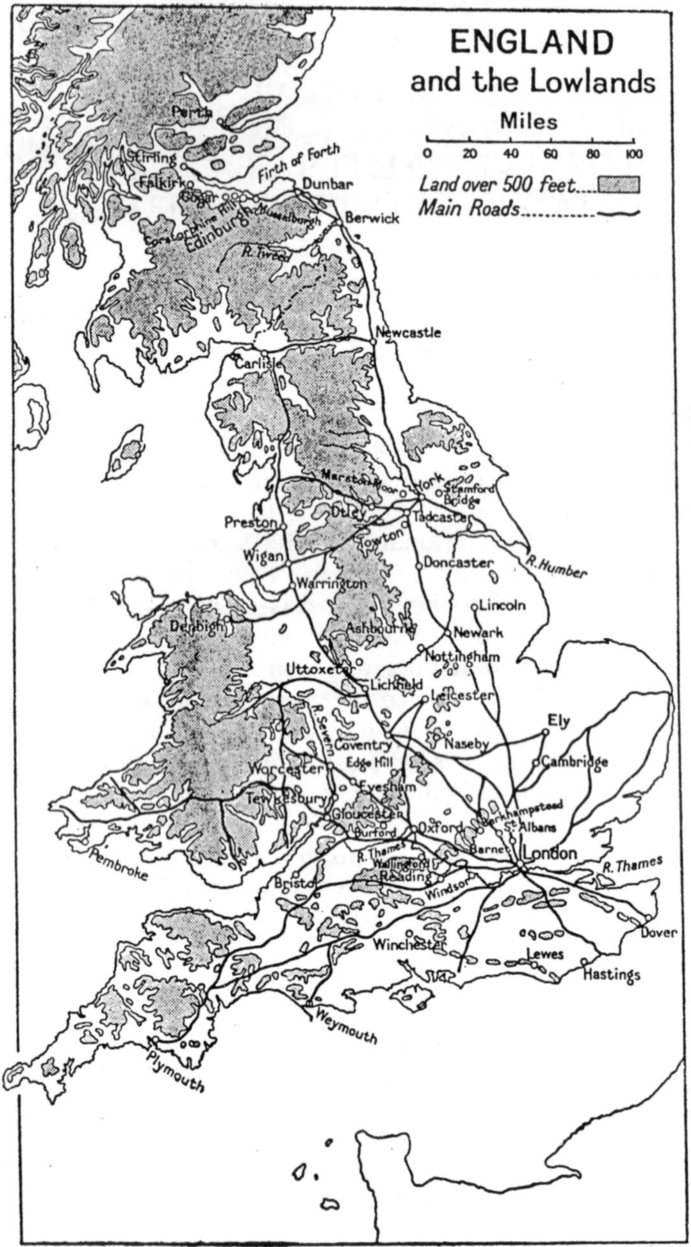

Stanford, London

the threat of losing Saxony, his junior partner, compelled Gustavus to quit Bavaria and hurry to the rescue.

Before he could come up, Wallenstein and the Elector had united. Faced with their combined forces, Gustavus fell back on Nuremberg. Thither Wallenstein followed, but finding the Swedes strongly posted, remarked that 'battles enough had been fought already, and it was time to try another method'. Instead of pitting his new levies against the long-invincible Swedes, he dug himself into a position from which—while his army rested securely, gaining confidence daily—he could command Gustavus's lines of supply with his light horse. He maintained this method and object unswervingly, deaf to all challenges to battle, until the Swedish king, shadowed by the gaunt spectre of famine, attempted a vain assault on his position. The repulse was, militarily, only an unfortunate incident; politically, its echoes resounded throughout Europe. Although it had not dislocated, it had disturbed the moral ascendancy which Gustavus's many victories had gained him, and thereby loosened his hold over the German states. Wallenstein combined a realistic grasp of the limitations of his means with a far-seeing calculation of the higher strategic end.

From Nuremberg, Gustavus marched south against Bavaria once more. Instead of following, Wallenstein turned north against Saxony—a master move. It brought Gustavus to heel as promptly as before. But by superb marching he came up before Wallenstein could intimidate the Saxons into a separate peace. In the desperate battle of Lützen which followed, the Swedish army redeemed its strategic setback by a tactical success; but at the price of its leader's death. This entailed the forfeiture of his project of a great Protestant combination under Swedish direction.

For sixteen years longer the war dragged out its weary and wasteful length, leaving Germany a desert, and yielding to France the predominant place in the polity of Europe.

The outstanding contrast between the civil wars, 1642–52, in Britain, and the wars of the same century on the continent, is that of the decision-seeking spirit which marked the former. It is aptly expressed in Defoe's *Memories of a Cavalier*—'we never encamped or entrenched . . . or lay fenced with rivers or defiles. 'Twas the general maxim of the war—where is the enemy? Let us go and fight him'.

Despite this offensive spirit the First Civil War continued four years, without any battle proving clearly decisive, except tactically—and when it ultimately flickered out in 1646, left the Royalist embers still so numerous and so glowing that, with the aid of discord among the victors, the flames burst out afresh two years later in a greater blaze than before.

In examining the reasons for this indecisiveness where the spirit of decisiveness was so manifest, we may note that the military campaigns took the form of repeated direct advances by one side or the other, interspersed with what in modern language would be called 'mopping up' operations, which had only a local and transient effect—at the price of a drain of strength.

At the outset the royal forces were based on the West and Midlands; the Parliamentary forces, on London. The first Royalist advance on London came to an ignominious end at Turnham Green, often styled the Valmy of the Civil War, a bloodless ending which was the moral sequel to the bloody inconclusiveness of the Battle of Edgehill, fought by the main armies earlier in the advance.

Thenceforward, Oxford and its surrounding towns became the fortified pivot of the Royalists. On the edge of this zone the two main armies long confronted each other ineffectively, while a see-saw struggle between local forces and detachments went on in the west and north. At last, in September 1643, the urgent need of the besieged city of Gloucester compelled the main Parliamentary army under Lord Essex to advance to its relief by a restricted detour past the flank of the Oxford zone. This enabled the Royalists to bar his homeward path; but, again, a direct clash at Newbury yielded an indecisive result.

Natural war-weariness might now have brought the struggle to a negotiated end but for Charles's political blunder in making a truce with the Irish rebels. This, by its appearance of bringing Catholic Irish to subdue Protestant England, brought instead the greater counter-weight of Presbyterian Scotland into the scales against the royal cause. Encouraged by the fact that a Scottish army was advancing to engage the northern Royalists, the Parliamentarians now again concentrated their strength for a direct advance on the Oxford zone—an advance which brought no greater result than the occupation of a few outlying fortresses. The king, indeed, was even able to detach Rupert for a swift concentration with the northern Royalists against the Scots. Unhappily for him, tactical defeat at Marston Moor more than undid the effect of this strategic opportunity. The victors profited little. Once more the ineffectiveness of the direct and main move on Oxford produced loss of heart and desertion and, save for the inflexible purpose of men like Cromwell, might have led to a peace of war-weariness. Fortunately for the Parliament, the royal cause was crumbling even worse, internally—more than from external blows. Thus it was a morally and numerically inferior foe, only preserved so long by faulty Parliamentary strategy, that Fairfax and Cromwell with the New Model army overthrew at Naseby in 1645. Yet even this tactically decisive victory did not prevent the war continuing for another year.

It is a different picture when we come to the Second Civil War, with Cromwell as the ruling mind and the twenty-eight-year-old John Lambert as his brilliant assistant. When it became known, late in April 1648, that the Scots were raising an army to invade England in support of the Royalists, Fairfax prepared to march north to meet them, while Cromwell was sent west to deal with the Royalist risings in South Wales. Then, however, further outbreaks in Kent and East Anglia tied Fairfax to those parts while the invasion of the north was developing. Lambert was left with only a small force to delay the invaders—which he did most effectively by the indirect course of constantly threatening their flank as they marched down the west coast route, while checking any attempt of theirs to cross the Pennines and rally their friends in Yorkshire.

At last, on the fall of Pembroke (the 11th July 1648), Cromwell was able to move north. Instead of advancing direct to meet the Scots, he marched in a sweeping curve by Nottingham and Doncaster—collecting supplies on the way—and then north-westward to join Lambert at Otley on the flank of the Scottish army, which was strung out between Wigan and Preston, with a corps of 3,500 under Langdale covering the left flank. Cromwell had only 8,600 men, including Lambert's horse and the Yorkshire militia, against some 20,000 of the enemy. But his descent on the tail of the Scottish column at Preston dislocated its balance, and caused it to turn and meet him in successive fractions. On Preston Moor, Langdale's corps was overthrown. Then pressing the pursuit fiercely. Cromwell rolled up the Scottish column, driving it through Wigan to Uttoxeter where—checked in front by the Midland militia and pressed in rear by Cromwell's cavalry—it surrendered on the 25th August. This victory was decisive. Not only did it crush the foes of the Parliament, but it enabled the army to 'purge' the Parliament, and to bring the king to trial and execution.

The subsequent invasion of Scotland is really a separate war, waged by the newly established regime, to forestall the plan of the king's son, the future Charles II, to regain the lost throne by Scottish aid. Thus it hardly comes in the category of campaigns which have decisively affected the course of history. At the same time it furnishes remarkable evidence of how strongly Cromwell was imbued with the strategy of indirect approach. When he found the Scottish army, under Leslie, in position across his path to Edinburgh, a mere contact-making engagement satisfied him of the strength of Leslie's situation. Although within sight of his goal, and short of supplies, he had such self-restraint as to abstain from a frontal assault on disadvantageous ground. Despite his innate eagerness for battle he would not venture it unless he could draw the enemy into the open and get a chance to strike at an exposed flank. Hence he fell back on Musselburgh, and then to Dunbar, to re-provision his forces. Within a week he advanced afresh and at Musselburgh issued three days' rations as a preliminary to a wide manœuvre through the hills of Edinburgh and the enemy's rear. And when Leslie succeeded in moving across to bar his path directly at Corstorphine Hill (21st August 1650), Cromwell—though now far from his base—sought yet another approach by a manœuvre to his left, only to be blocked afresh by Leslie at Gogar. Most men would have gambled on a direct battle. But not Cromwell. Cutting his loss—in sick, due to exposure and fatigue—he fell back on Musselburgh and thence to Dunbar, drawing Leslie after him. He would not, however, embark his army, as some of his officers urged, but waited at Dunbar in the hope that the enemy would make a false move that might become his opportunity.

Leslie, however, was a shrewd opponent, and his next move deepened Cromwell's danger. Leaving the main road, Leslie made a circuit round Dunbar during the night of the 1st September, and occupied Doon Hill, overlooking the road to Berwick. He also sent a detachment to seize the pass at Cockburnspath seven miles further south. Thus, next morning, Cromwell found himself cut off from England. His plight was all the worse because his supplies were already short and his sick-list lengthening.

It had been Leslie's plan to wait on the heights in anticipation that the English would try to force their way along the road to Berwick, and then to descend upon them. But the ministers of the

Kirk were eager to see the jaws of 'the Lord's' trap close upon 'the Moabites', and their clamour was reinforced by signs that the invader might be contemplating escape by sea. Moreover, the weather on the 2nd was so tempestuous as almost to drive the Scottish troops off the bare crest of Doon Hill. About 4 p.m. they were seen to be descending the slopes and taking up a position on the lower ground near the Berwick road, where they had more shelter from the rain, while their front was covered by the Brock burn—which ran through a ravine until it neared the sea.

Cromwell and Lambert were together watching the movement, and into their minds, simultaneously, came the thought that: 'it did give us an opportunity and advantage to attempt upon the Enemy.' For the Scots' left wing was wedged between the hill and the steep-sided burn, and would have difficulty in helping the right wing if an attack was concentrated there. At a council of war that evening Lambert put the case for an immediate stroke against the Scots' right wing, to roll up their line, while at the same time concentrating the artillery against their cramped left wing. His arguments carried the council, and in recognition of his initiative Cromwell entrusted him with the conduct of the opening moves. During the night, 'a drakie nicht full of wind and weit', the troops were moved into position along the north side of the burn. After marshalling the guns opposite the Scots' left wing, Lambert rode back to the other flank at daybreak to lead the cavalry's attack near the sea. Helped by surprise, both they and the infantry in the centre were able to cross the burn without difficulty, and although their further advance was temporarily checked the intervention of the English reserves turned the scales on the seaward flank, and enabled Cromwell to roll up the Scottish line from right to left—into a corner, between hill and burn, from which the Scottish troops could only extricate themselves by breaking into flight. Thus by a tactical indirect approach, following instantly upon the over-confident opponent's slip, Cromwell shattered a force twice his own strength—sealing with triumph a campaign in which he had refused all temptation, even to the apparent hazard of his fortunes, to abandon his strategy of indirect approach.

The victory of Dunbar gave Cromwell the control of southern Scotland. It wiped the army of the Kirk, and the Covenanters as a political factor, off the balance-sheet of the war. Only the pure Royalist element of the Highlands was left to oppose Cromwell. The process of settlement was delayed, however, by his grave illness; meantime Leslie had breathing space to organize and train the new Royalist army beyond the Forth.

When, late in June 1651, Cromwell was fit enough to resume operations, he was faced with a difficult problem. His solution, for subtlety and masterly calculation, compares favourably with any strategic combination in the history of war. Although now, for the first time, the superiority in numbers was on his side, he was faced by a canny adversary established in a region of marsh and moorland which afforded every natural advantage to the weaker side in barring the approach to Stirling. Unless Cromwell could overthrow the resistance within a brief time he would be doomed to spend another trying winter in Scotland, with inevitable suffering to his troops and the likelihood of increasing difficulties at home. To dislodge the enemy would not suffice, for a partial success would only disperse the enemy into the Highlands, where they would remain a thorn in his side.

Cromwell's solution of the problem was masterly. First he menaced Leslie in front, storming Callander House, near Falkirk. Then he passed, in stages, his whole army across the Firth of Forth and marched on Perth—thereby not only turning Leslie's defensive barrier across the direct approach to Stirling but gaining possession of the key to Leslie's supply area. By this manœuvre he had, however, uncovered the route to England. Here lay the supreme artistry of Cromwell's plan. He was on the rear of an enemy now threatened with hunger and desertion—and he left a bolt-hole open. As one of his opponents said, 'We must either starve, disband, or go with a handful of men into England. This last seems to be the least ill, yet it seems very desperate.' They naturally chose it, and at the end of July started on the march south into England.

Cromwell, foreseeing this, had prepared their reception—with the aid of the authorities at Westminster. The militia was called out promptly, all suspected Royalists were kept under surveillance, hidden stores of arms were seized. Once more the Scots moved down the west coast route. Cromwell dispatched Lambert's cavalry to follow them, while Harrison moved obliquely across from Newcastle to Warrington, and Fleetwood moved north with the Midland militia. Lambert slipped round the flank of the enemy, and joined Harrison on the 13th August. The two then opposed an elastic delaying resistance to the oncoming invader. Cromwell meantime was marching, twenty miles a day in August heat, down the east coast route and then south-westwards. Thus four forces were converging on the trapped invader. Charles's turn away from the route for London towards the Severn valley only delayed for a few days, and failed to disturb, the closing of the jaws. On the 3rd September, the anniversary of Dunbar, the battlefield of Worcester provided Cromwell with his 'crowning mercy'.

The interminable series of wars between the close of the Thirty Years' War and the opening of the War of the Spanish Succession—in which the armies of Louis XIV faced collectively, or in turn, most of the other armies of Europe—were notably indecisive. Objects were often limited, and objectives followed suit. Two deeper causes of this indecisiveness were, first, that the development of fortification had outpaced the improvement of weapons and given the defensive a preponderance such as was restored to it in the early twentieth century by the development of the machine-gun; second, that armies were not yet organized in permanently self-contained fractions, but usually moved and fought as a single piece, a condition which limited their power of distraction—of deceiving the opponent and cramping his freedom of movement.

In the whole course of the successive wars known as the Fronde, Devolution, Dutch, and Grand Alliance, only one campaign stands out as decisive, even in its particular sphere. This is Turenne's winter campaign of 1674–5, crowned by the victory of Türkheim. It was a critical time for France. Louis XIV's allies had left him one by one, while the Spaniards, Dutch, Danes, Austrians, and most of the German princes had joined the hostile coalition. Turenne had been forced to retire over the Rhine, after laying waste the Palatinate. The Elector of Brandenburg was converging to unite with the imperial army under Bournonville. Turenne imposed a check at Enzheim, in October 1674, on Bournonville—before the Elector came up. But he was forced to withdraw to Dettweiler, while the Germans spread into Alsace and took up winter quarters in the towns between Strasbourg and Belfort.

The stage was set for Turenne's masterpiece. The initial surprise lay in his decision to undertake a mid-winter campaign. To deceive the enemy, he placed the fortresses of middle Alsace in a state of defence. Then he withdrew the whole field army quietly into Lorraine. Next he marched swiftly southward, behind the screening heights of the Vosges, gathering on his way such reinforcements as were available. In the last stages of the move he even split his forces into numerous small bodies in order to mislead the enemy's spies. After a severe march through hilly country and through snow-storms, he reunited his army near Belfort, and, without any pause, invaded Alsace from the south—having left it from the north.

Bournonville, with such forces as he had at hand, tried to stop Turenne at Mulhausen (29th December), but was swept away. Thence the French torrent swept up the trough between the Vosges and the Rhine, driving the scattered Imperialists north towards Strasbourg, cutting off each body which tried to resist. At Colmar, half-way to Strasbourg, the Elector of Brandenburg, now in command of the Germans, had established a dam that was buttressed by a force equal to Turenne's. But the momentum, both physical and moral, was with Turenne, and was skilfully maintained by a tactical indirect approach on the battlefield of Türkheim. Here Turenne sought less to destroy the opposing army than to liquidate the hardening resistance, leaving natural consequences to complete the enemy's dissolution. He succeeded so well that a few days later he was able to report that not a soldier of the enemy was left in Alsace.

The French then recuperated in winter quarters at Strasbourg, drawing supplies freely from the German bank of the Rhine, and even as far as the Neckar. The Elector had retired, with what remained of his forces, to Brandenburg; and Turenne's old rival, Montecuculi, was called back in the spring to command the Imperial armies. He, too, was manœuvred into a position where Turenne had him at a disadvantage, on the Sasbach; but at the outset of the action Turenne was killed by a cannon-shot—and with his fall the balance of the war changed again.

Why is the decisiveness of this winter campaign of Turenne's in such startling contrast with the rest of the campaigns of the seventeenth century in Europe? It was an age when generals, however limited their horizon, were at least supremely skilful in manœuvre. But in this art they were so well matched that even flank moves which in other ages might have succeeded were adroitly parried. A real dislocation of the opponent's system was only this once achieved. Turenne is famous as the one Great Captain who improved continuously with age, and there is thus a special significance in the way in which, after commanding in more campaigns than any other general in all history, he reached in his last campaign a solution of the problem of achieving a decision in seventeenth-century warfare. For he did it without departing from the golden rule of those times—that highly trained soldiers were too costly to be squandered.

It would seem that his experience had taught him that under such conditions a decisive result could only be gained by a strategic plan in which the approach was radically more indirect than any yet conceived. At a time when all manœuvres were based on fortress pivots—which formed the protected supply depots for the maintenance of the field armies—he cut loose from such a base of operations, and sought in the combination of surprise and mobility not only a decision but his security. It was a just calculation, not a gamble. For the dislocation—mental, moral, and logistical—created among the enemy afforded him throughout an ample margin of security.

CHAPTER VII

THE EIGHTEENTH CENTURY—MARLBOROUGH AND FREDERICK

★

The War of the Spanish Succession (1701–13) is remarkable for its curiously dual nature. In policy it was both an extreme case of war with a limited aim, and a decisive struggle to enforce or break the predominant power of France under Louis XIV. In strategy it mainly comprised a futile series of direct approaches or scarcely more purposeful indirect moves, yet was punctuated by a number of brilliant indirect approaches mainly associated with the illustrious name of Marlborough. The significant interest of these lies in the way that they mark the several turning-points of the war.

The coalition against France comprised Austria, Great Britain, several of the German states, Holland, Denmark and Portugal. Louis XIV's main support came from Spain, Bavaria, and at the outset, Savoy.

It was in northern Italy that the war opened, while the other armies were preparing. The Austrians, under Prince Eugène, assembled in Tyrol, and made ostentatious preparations for a direct advance. Thereupon, the opposing army, under Catinat, placed itself to block their path at the Rivoli defile. But Eugène, having secretly reconnoitred a difficult passage through the mountains long unused by troops, came down to the plains by a wide circuit to the east. Pressing his advantage by subsequent manœuvres which repeatedly deluded his opponents as to his intentions, he finally drew them into a disastrous attack upon him at Chiari, and established his position firmly in northern Italy. The result of this indirect approach, and baited gambit, not only gave the Allies a valuable moral tonic at the outset of their struggle with the reputedly invincible armies of the *Grand Monarque*, but dealt a crippling blow to the French and Spanish power in Italy. One important sequel was that the Duke of Savoy, an instinctive adherent of the stronger party, changed sides.

In 1702 the main struggle began. The largest French army was assembled in Flanders, where the French had fortified the sixty-mile long Lines of Brabant from Antwerp to Huy on the Meuse, to secure the rear of their proposed advance. At the threat of invasion, the instinct of the Dutch was to sit tight within their fortresses. Marlborough had a different conception of war. But he did not exchange this passive defensive for a direct offensive against the French army, under Boufflers, then marching towards the Rhine. Instead, uncovering the precious fortresses, he moved swiftly towards the Lines of Brabant, and the French line of retreat. Boufflers, at once feeling the pull of this moral 'lassoo', hurried back. Physically tired and morally dislocated, the French army might have been an easy victim for Marlborough, who was waiting ready to embrace it; but the Dutch deputies, content to see the invasion called off, opposed the consummation by battle. Twice more that year Boufflers was drawn into a trap by Marlborough, and each time the hesitations of the Dutch helped to extricate him.

The next year Marlborough planned a subtle manœuvre to gain possession of Antwerp and thereby penetrate the fortified breakwater. By a direct advance westward from Maastricht he hoped to rivet the French main army, under Villeroi, to the southern end of the Lines. Next, a Dutch force under Cohorn was to attack Ostend, assisted by the fleet, while another Dutch force, under Spaar, moved on Antwerp from the north-west—these moves from the seaboard being intended to make the French commander at Antwerp look over his shoulder, and draw away part of the forces holding the northern end of the Lines. Four days later, a third Dutch force under Opdam would strike at them from the north-east, while Marlborough would give Villeroi the slip and race northward to join in the converging stroke at Antwerp.

The first phase opened promisingly; Marlborough's threat drew Villeroi's army down towards the Meuse. Then, however, Cohorn dropped the Ostend move in favour of a narrower move near Antwerp in conjunction with Spaar—which did not have the same distracting effect. And Opdam, to his danger, moved prematurely. Moreover, when Marlborough started on his switch-march to the north, he did not succeed in giving Villeroi the slip; in fact, Villeroi beat him in the race—by sending Boufflers ahead with thirty of his cavalry squadrons and 3,000 grenadiers holding on to their stirrup-leathers. This mobile force covered nearly forty miles in twenty-four hours, and on the 1st July, together with the Antwerp garrison, fell upon Opdam, whose force was badly mauled before it made good its escape. What Marlborough had proudly christened 'the Great Design' was completely wrecked.

Following this disappointment, Marlborough proposed a direct assault upon the Lines just south of Antwerp. The Dutch commanders rejected his proposal, with good reason—since it would have meant a frontal attack upon a fortified position held by nearly equal forces. Along with his brilliance in manœuvre, Marlborough showed at times, especially times of disappointment, a touch of the reckless gambler. British writers of history, dazzled by his exploits as well as his personal charm, are apt to be unjust to the Dutch—who had more at stake than Marlborough. Danger was too close to their country for them to regard war as a fascinating game or a great adventure. They were acutely aware, like Admiral Jellicoe two centuries later, that they 'could lose the war in an afternoon' —if they courted a battle in circumstances that carried a serious risk of decisive defeat.

In face of the unanimous judgement of the Dutch generals, Marlborough gave up the idea of assaulting the Antwerp sector, and turned back to the Meuse, where he covered the siege of Huy. While there he again urged, late in August, an attack on the Lines, with somewhat better justification—since the southern sector was more favourable. But his arguments failed to convince the Dutch.

Marlborough's intense disgust with the Dutch made him the more susceptible to the arguments that Wratislaw, the Imperial envoy, now skilfully urged in favour of switching his forces to the Danube. The conjunction of these two influences produced in 1704, with the aid of Marlborough's broad strategic outlook, one of the most striking examples in history of the indirect approach. Of the main hostile armies, one under Villeroi was in Flanders; one under Tallard lay on the upper Rhine between Mannheim and Strasbourg, with smaller linking forces; and a combined army of Bavarians and French, under the Elector of Bavaria and Marsin, was near Ulm and the Danube. This last was pushing menacingly forward from Bavaria towards Vienna. Marlborough planned to switch the English part of his army from the Meuse to the Danube, and then to strike decisively at the Bavarians, the junior partner of the enemy firm. This long-range move to a point so far from his base, and from the direct interests which he was shielding in the north, was audacious by any standard, but much more so by that of the cautious strategy of his time. Its security lay in the dislocating effect of its surprise. This was contained in the 'variable' direction of his march, which at each stage threatened alternative objectives, and left the enemy in doubt as to his actual aim.

When he moved south up the Rhine it first appeared that he might be taking the Moselle route into France. Then, when he pressed on beyond Coblenz, it looked as if he might be aiming at the French forces in Alsace—and by making visible preparations to bridge the Rhine at Philipsburg, he reinforced this natural delusion. But on reaching the neighbourhood of Mannheim, whence his obvious direction was south-west, he turned south-east instead, vanished into the wooded hills bordering the valley of the Neckar, and thence marched across the base of the Rhine-Danube triangle towards Ulm. The mask of strategic ambiguity which had covered his march helped to compensate its rather slow pace—averaging about ten miles a day for some six weeks. After meeting Eugène and the Margrave of Baden at Gross Heppach, Marlborough moved on with the forces of the latter, while the former went back to detain, or at least to delay, the French armies on the Rhine—whither Villeroi had belatedly followed Marlborough from Flanders.[1]

But although Marlborough had placed himself on the rear of the Franco-Bavarian army in relation to France, he was still on their front in relation to Bavaria. This geographical juxtaposition combined with other conditions to hinder the exploitation of his strategic advantage. Of these conditions, one was general to the age; the rigidity of the tactical organization of armies, which made difficult the completion of a strategic manœuvre. A general could draw the enemy to 'water', but could not make him drink—could not make him accept battle against his inclination. A more particular handicap was that Marlborough had to share the command with the cautious Margrave of Baden.

The combined armies of the Elector of Bavaria and Marshal Marsin occupied a fortified position on the Danube at Dillingen, east of Ulm and midway between there and Donauwörth. As Marshal Tallard's army might move eastward from the Rhine, Ulm was a precarious place at which to seek an entry into Bavaria.

[1] Until Marlborough definitely quitted the Rhine valley he had always the power of making a swift return down the river to Flanders by embarking his troops in the boats that had been collected. This was a further cause of distraction to the French commanders.

Marlborough decided that he must gain a crossing at Donauworth, the natural terminus of his new line of communications—which had been changed, for greater security, to the easterly route through Nuremberg. With Donauwörth in his possession, he would have safe passage into Bavaria and could manœuvre securely on either bank of the Danube.

Unfortunately, the flank move across the face of the enemy's position at Dillingen was rather too obvious in purpose and slow in pace, so that the Elector was able to dispatch a strong detachment to defend Donauwörth. Although Marlborough made greater haste in the last stage of the march, the enemy were able to extend the entrenchments of the Schellenberg, the hill covering Donauwörth, by the time Marlborough arrived on the 2nd July. Rather than allow the enemy time to complete the defences, he delivered his attack the same evening. The first assault was bloodily repulsed, with the loss of more than half the troops engaged, and it was only when the bulk of the allied armies arrived, giving them a superiority of more than four to one, that weight of numbers began to turn the scales. Even then, the issue was decided through a flanking movement which found and penetrated a weakly held sector of the entrenchments. Marlborough admitted, in a letter, that the capture of Donauwörth '*a coûté un peu cher*'. Criticism of his tactics here was all the more general since the decisive manœuvre had been conducted by the Margrave.

The enemy's main forces now withdrew to Augsburg. Thereupon Marlborough, pressing south into Bavaria, devastated the countryside, burning hundreds of villages and all the crops—as a lever to force the Elector of Bavaria to terms or to accept battle at a disadvantage. The purport of this brutal expedient, of which he was privately ashamed, was nullified by another condition of the time—that, war being the affair of rulers rather than of their peoples, the Elector was slow to be affected by inconveniences at second hand. Thus Tallard had time to come up from the Rhine, and he arrived at Augsburg on the 5th August.

Fortunately, Tallard's appearance on the scene was offset by that of Eugène, who took the bold course of slipping away from before Villeroi in order to join Marlborough. Just previously it had been arranged that, under cover of the forces of Marlborough and Eugène, the Margrave should move further down the Danube to besiege the enemy held fortress of Ingolstadt. Then, on the 9th, news came that the combining enemy armies were moving north, towards the Danube. It looked as if their aim was to strike at Marlborough's communications. Nevertheless, Marlborough and Eugène allowed the Margrave to continue his divergent march towards Ingolstadt—thereby reducing their combined forces to 56,000 men in face of the enemy's total of some 60,000, which might be increased. Their willingness to dispense with the Margrave was understandable in view of their distaste for his caution, but their readiness to release his forces was remarkable because of their decision to seek battle at the first opportunity. It showed great confidence in their own qualitative superiority over the enemy——almost over-confidence in view of the closeness of the battle which followed.

Fortunately for them, there was quite as much confidence on the other side. The Elector of Bavaria was eager to take the offensive, although most of his own troops had not yet arrived. When Tallard argued that it would be wiser to wait for them, and meantime entrench, the Elector scoffed at such caution. Tallard sarcastically retorted: 'If I were not so convinced of your Highness's integrity, I should imagine that you wished to gamble with the King of France's forces without having any of your own, to see at no risk what would happen.' It was then agreed, as a compromise, that the French forces should make a preliminary bound to a position near Blenheim, behind the little river Nebel, on the way to Donauwörth.

Here the next morning, the 13th August, they were caught by the sudden advance of the Allies along the north bank of the Danube. Marlborough struck direct at the French right, near the Danube, while Eugène swung inland against the French left—the narrow space between the river and the hills allowed little room for manœuvre. The Allies' only advantage, apart from their spirit and training, lay in the unexpectedness of their action in seeking battle under such circumstances. This partial measure of surprise hindered the two French armies from making properly co-ordinated dispositions, so that they fought in order of encampment rather than in order of battle. This was in itself an unbalancing effect. It resulted in a scarcity of infantry in the wide central sector. But the disadvantage did not become apparent until late in the day, and might never have become important but for other slips.

The first stage of the battle went adversely for the Allies. The attack of Marlborough's left wing on Blenheim failed with heavy loss, and the attack of his right wing on Oberglau also failed. Eugène's attack further to the right was twice repulsed. And when Marlborough's troops in the centre were in process of crossing the Nebel, their head was smitten by a French cavalry charge that was barely repelled. Owing to a misunderstanding that was lucky for them, this counterstroke was carried out by fewer squadrons than Tallard intended. But it was followed by another counterstroke, on their exposed flank, from Marsin's cavalry—which was interrupted in the nick of time by a counter-stroke from part of Eugène's cavalry, unhesitatingly released by him in response to Marlborough's appeal.

While disaster had been averted, nothing more than a precarious equilibrium had been achieved, and unless Marlborough could push on he would be in a bad hole—with the marshy Nebel at his back. But Tallard was now to pay dearly for his miscalculation in allowing Marlborough to cross the river unopposed—or rather, for the ineffective execution of his design. For once Tallard's cavalry counterstrokes had failed in their purpose of overwhelming the van of Marlborough's centre, the remainder of it was able to form up across the river during the ensuing lull. And although Tallard had 50 battalions of infantry altogether to Marlborough's 48, he had only 9 in the central sector to oppose 23—owing to the fault in the initial dispositions, which he had not readjusted while there was time. When these few squares of infantry were eventually overwhelmed by weight of numbers and close-quarter artillery fire, Marlborough was able to push through an open gap, thereby cutting off the congested mass of the French infantry near the Danube at Blenheim, and also laying bare Marsin's flank. The latter was able to disengage himself from Eugène and withdraw without being seriously pressed, but a large part of Tallard's army was penned against the Danube and forced to surrender.

Blenheim was a victory gained at heavy cost, and at still heavier risk. In dispassionate analysis it becomes clear that the scales were turned more by the stoutness of the rank and file, together with the miscalculations of the French command, than by Marlborough's skill. But the ultimate fact of victory sufficed to make the world overlook what a gamble the battle had been. And the shattered 'invincibility' of French arms changed the whole outlook of Europe.

The Allied armies, following up the French retreat, advanced to the Rhine and crossed it at Philipsburg. But the cost of victory at

Blenheim now became apparent in the general disinclination to further exertions—save on Marlborough's own part—and the campaign petered out.

For 1705 Marlborough devised a plan for the invasion of France by which he would avoid the entangling network of the Flanders fortresses. While Eugène engaged the French forces in northern Italy, and the Dutch stood on the defensive in Flanders, the main Allied army, under Marlborough, would advance up the Moselle on Thionville, and the Margrave's army would make a converging advance across the Saar. But the design was marred by a series of hitches. Supplies were not delivered as promised, transport was lacking, Allied reinforcements fell much below expectation, and the Margrave showed a reluctance to co-operate —which has been ascribed to jealousy, but had a better justification in an inflamed wound from which he subsequently died.

Nevertheless, Marlborough persisted in his plan when every condition of success had faded—and it had become a direct approach in the narrowest sense. He pushed up the Moselle, apparently in the hope that his very weakness would tempt the French to battle. But Marshal Villars preferred to see Marlborough become weaker still through shortage of food, and Villeroi took the offensive in Flanders with such effect as to make the Dutch urgently call for aid. This dual pressure led Marlborough to break off the venture—though in the bitterness of his disappointment he made the Margrave his scapegoat. He even sent to Villars a letter of apology for his retreat, in which he placed the entire responsibility on the Margrave's shoulders.

Marlborough's swift march back to Flanders promptly relieved the situation there. On his approach Villeroi gave up the siege of Liége and retired within the Lines of Brabant. Marlborough then devoted his mind to the elaboration of a scheme for piercing this barrier. By a feint at a weakly fortified sector near the Meuse he drew the French southward, and then, doubling back, broke through a strongly fortified but weakly held sector near Tirlemont. He failed, however, to exploit the opportunity by a prompt advance on Louvain and over the Dyle. That failure, it would seem, was due partly to the fact that he had deceived his Allies even more thoroughly than the enemy, but still more to a momentary exhaustion of his own energy. None the less, the famous Lines were no longer a barrier.

A few weeks later he formed a fresh design which bore evidence of evolution in his generalship. Although it was not crowned by greater success, it revealed a greater Marlborough. His previous manœuvre in Flanders had been based on pure deception, and for success had required a speed of execution which was difficult to attain with his Dutch clogs. This time he tried an indirect approach by a route that offered alternative objectives—thus producing a wide distraction of the opposing forces which diminished the need for superior speed.

Swinging south of Villeroi's position near Louvain, he advanced on a line which kept the enemy in doubt as to his aim, since it threatened any of the fortresses in that area—Namur, Charleroi, Mons, and Ath. Then, on reaching Genappe, he wheeled north up the road through Waterloo towards Brussels. Villeroi hurriedly decided to march back to the rescue of the city. Just as the French were about to move, Marlborough, who had made a fresh swerve back eastwards during the night, appeared on the new front they had taken up. Owing to his distracting move it was an ill-knit front, if less vulnerable than their marching flank would have been. He had arrived just too soon for his own advantage, and the wary Dutch generals thus found reason for resisting his desire to deliver an immediate attack—arguing that, whatever the confusion on the other side, the enemy's actual position behind the Ysche was stronger than at Blenheim.

In the next year's campaign Marlborough conceived the idea of carrying out an indirect approach of far wider scope—by crossing the Alps to join Eugène. He might thus drive the French out of Italy and gain a back entrance to France, combining his land approach with amphibious operations against Toulon and with Peterborough's operations in Spain. The Dutch, departing from their usual caution, agreed to take the risk of letting him go. The project was forestalled by Villars's defeat of the Margrave of Baden and Villeroi's advance in Flanders. This venturesome French move was due to Louis XIV's belief that to take the offensive 'everywhere' would create such an impression of strength as to give him the best chance of securing on favourable terms the peace that he now needed and desired. To take the offensive in the theatre where Marlborough lay proved for the French a short cut, not to peace, but to a defeat that would spoil their aim. Marlborough lost no time in seizing his opportunity—it was, in his judgement, the second time that the French had redeemed his prospects by their reluctance to stay quietly within their lines when the game was in their hands. He met them at Ramillies, where they had occupied a concave position. He exploited his position on the chord of the arc to execute a tactical indirect approach. Following an attack on the French left, which drew their reserves thither, he skilfully disengaged his own troops on that wing and switched them across to press home the advantage gained on his own left wing, where the Danish cavalry had penetrated a gap. This menace in rear coupled with the pressure in front caused the collapse of the French. Marlborough exploited the victory by a pursuit so effective that all Flanders and Brabant fell into his hands.

That same year the war in Italy was virtually ended by another example of the strategic indirect approach. At the outset Eugène had been forced back as far east as Lake Garda and then into the mountains, while his ally, the Duke of Savoy, was besieged in Turin. Instead of trying to fight his way forward, Eugène outmanœuvred and slipped his opponents, cut himself adrift from his base, pressed on through Lombardy into Piedmont—and at Turin inflicted a decisive defeat on his numerically superior but unbalanced enemy.

The tide of war had now ebbed to the frontiers of France, both north and and south. In 1707, however, disunity of purpose among the allies gave her time to rally, and the next year she concentrated her main forces against Marlborough. Tied by the leg to Flanders, and heavily outnumbered, he turned the balance by a repetition of the Danube move in reverse—whereby Eugène brought his army from the Rhine to join Marlborough. But the French were now under the able Vendôme, and they advanced before Eugène could arrive. Having induced Marlborough to fall back to Louvain by this direct menace, Vendôme scored the first trick by suddenly turning westwards—thereby regaining Ghent, Bruges, and practically all Flanders west of the Scheldt without cost. But instead of marching to oppose him directly, Marlborough audaciously thrust south-westwards, to interpose between him and the French frontier. At Oudenarde, the initial advantage gained by a strategic dislocation was pressed home by a tactical dislocation.

If Marlborough could have carried out his own wish for a prompt move on Paris it is possible that the war might have been ended. Even without that exploiting thrust, Louis was driven to seek peace that winter, offering terms that amply met the Allies' objects. But they rejected the substance for the shadow of his complete humiliation—a failure, and folly, in grand strategy. Marlborough himself was not blind to the value of the offer, but he was better, and keener, at making war than at making peace.

Thus the war had a fresh lease of life in 1709. Marlborough's project now was for an indirect military approach to a key political objective—his idea being to slip past the enemy's forces, mask their fortresses and aim at Paris. But this was too bold even for Eugene's stomach. Hence it was modified to a plan which avoided a direct attack on the entrenched Lines covering the frontier between Douai and Bethune, but instead was aimed to secure the flanking fortresses of Tournai and Mons as a preliminary to an advance into France down a route east of the fortified zone.

Once again Marlborough succeeded in deceiving his opponents. His menace of a direct attack on the barrier-line led them to draw off most of the garrison of Tournai to reinforce it, whereupon Marlborough doubled back and closed upon Tournai. But this place resisted so stubbornly as to cost him two months' delay. However, a fresh threat to the lines of La Bassée enabled him to pounce upon Mons and invest it unchecked. But the French moved across rapidly enough to block his onward path and the further development of his design. This frustration led him to revert to a direct approach in which he showed too little calculation of the consequences in relation to the circumstances—less wise than Cromwell before Dunbar. Although the assault on the well-entrenched and prepared enemy holding the Malplaquet 'gateway' ended in a victory, it was at such a disproportionate cost that Villars, the defeated commander, was justified in writing to Louis, 'If God gives us another defeat like this, your Majesty's enemies will be destroyed.' His judgement was prophetic in so far as this victory in battle proved to have cost the Allies their hopes of victory in the war.

In 1710 stalemate reigned, with Marlborough caged behind the bars of the *Ne Plus Ultra* lines, which the French had constructed from Valenciennes to the sea, while his political opponents were given fresh leverage to loosen his position at home. Fortune, too, turned against those who had forfeited her favours, for in 1711 Eugène's army was called away by the political situation, and Marlborough was left to face a greatly superior foe. Too weak to attempt or achieve any decisive operation, he could at least assert his own mastery by exploding the French boast in naming their lines *Ne Plus Ultra*. This he did by the most uncannily indirect of all his approaches—deceiving, distracting, doubling successively, until he was able to slip through the lines without firing a shot. But two months later he was recalled home to meet disgrace, and in 1712 a war-weary England left her Allies to fight alone.

The Austrians and Dutch, now under Eugène, still held their own for a time, and both sides were growing equally exhausted. But in 1712 Villars produced a compound manœuvre that for deceptiveness, secrecy, and rapidity was worthy of Marlborough, and in consequence gained a cheap and decisive victory over the Allies at Denain. This completed the disintegration of the coalition, and Louis was able to gain a peace very different from what would have been his lot before Malplaquet. One direct approach had, by its vain cost, done much to undo the aggregate advantage which indirect approaches alone had built up. And it is not the least significant feature that the issue was finally settled, in the reverse way, by yet another example of the indirect approach.

Although the Allies had forfeited their primary object of preventing Louis XIV's practical union of France and Spain, England came out of the war with a territorial profit. This owed much to the fact that Marlborough's vision stretched beyond the limits of his own theatre of war. As a military distraction and a political asset, he had combined long-range operations in the Mediterranean with his own in Flanders. The expeditions of 1702 and 1703 helped to subtract Portugal and Savoy from the enemy's balance and paved the way for a move against their greater asset, Spain. The next move, in 1704, gained Gibraltar. Then Peterborough in Spain ably fulfilled a distracting role, and in 1708 another expedition took Minorca. Although later operations in Spain were mishandled, and less fortunate in result, England came out of the war in possession of Gibraltar and Minorca, two keys to the command of the Mediterranean, as well as of Nova Scotia and Newfoundland in the North Atlantic.

Frederick's Wars

The indecisive results of the war of the Austrian Succession, 1740–8, cannot be better illustrated than in the fact that the most militarily successful nation, the French, merely gleaned from it the phrase 'you are as stupid as the Peace' to hurl at fellow-citizens who were objects of dislike. Frederick the Great was the one ruler to profit, or profiteer. He gained Silesia early and then retired from the competition. Although he came in again later, he risked much without gaining more, except the right to embroider some illustrious victories on his colours. The war, however, established the prestige of Prussia as a great power.

The events which decided the cession of Silesia to Prussia, by the early peace of Breslau in 1742, deserve notice. At the opening of that year, the prospect seemed to be fading. A combined advance by the French and Prussians upon the Austrian main army had been arranged. But the French were soon brought to a standstill. Then Frederick, instead of continuing westwards to unite with his ally, suddenly turned southwards towards Vienna. Although his advanced troops appeared before the enemy capital, he quickly fell back—for the enemy army was marching to cut him off from his base. This advance of Frederick's has usually been denounced as a mere and rash demonstration; yet in view of its sequel the charge may perhaps be harsh. For his rapid retreat, an apparent *sauve qui peut*, acted as a bait and drew the Austrians in pursuit of him far into Silesia—where, turning at bay near Chotusitz, he inflicted a sharp reverse, exploiting it by a vigorous pursuit. Only three weeks later, Austria made a separate peace with Frederick, by which Silesia was ceded. It may be unwise to draw strong deductions from this event, yet it is at least significant that this sudden disposition to a peace of sacrifice should have followed the one indirect approach of the war in this theatre—even though it comprised but a mere appearance before Vienna and a small tactical victory, wrested apparently from the jaws of defeat and far less spectacular than many of Frederick's other victories.

While the war of the Austrian Succession was indecisive in its general results, the other and succeeding major war of the mid-eighteenth was no better—from the standpoint of European policy. The one country that achieved results which decisively affected the course of European history was England, and she was not only an indirect participant in the Seven Years' War (1756–63), but made her contribution and took her profits indirectly. While the armies of Europe were exhausting themselves and their states in direct action, small detachments from England were turning this weakness to advantage by acquiring the British Empire. Moreover, the fact that Prussia, when on the verge of exhaustion, obtained a peace of indecision instead of humiliation, was as much due to the indirect dislocation of the offensive power of France through her colonial disasters, as it was to the abandonment of Russia's intended *coup de grâce* to Prussia through the death of the Tsaritsa. Fate was merciful to Frederick the Great: by 1762 his long string of brilliant victories in battle had left him almost stripped of resources and incapable of further resistance.

Only one campaign between European forces in this long series can truly be termed decisive either in its military or political results—the campaign which ended in the English capture of Quebec. That was not only the briefest, but waged in a secondary theatre. As the capture of Quebec and the overthrow of the French dominion in Canada was made possible by the capacity for grand-strategic indirect approach contained in sea-power, so the actual military course of the campaign was decided by a strategic indirect approach. The result is the more suggestive because this apparently hazardous move was only undertaken after the direct approach on the line of the Montmorency had failed with serious loss of lives and, still more, of morale. In justice to Wolfe, it must be pointed out that he only resigned himself to this direct approach after various baits—the bombardment of Quebec, as well as the exposure of isolated detachments at Point Levis and near the Montmorency Falls—had failed to lure the French from their strong position. But in the failure of these, compared with the success of his final hazardous landing on the French rear above Quebec, there is a lesson. To *entice* the enemy out was not enough; it was necessary to *draw* him out. So also there is a lesson in the failure of the feints by which Wolfe tried to prepare his direct approach. To *mystify* the enemy was not enough; he must be *distracted*—a term which implies combining deception of the enemy's mind with deprivation of his freedom to move for counter-action, and with the distension of his forces.

Gambler's last throw as Wolfe's ultimate move seemed on the surface, all these conditions were fulfilled—and the result was victory. Even so, to those who habitually study military history purely in terms of armed force, the degree of dislocation caused in the French *forces* does not seem to warrant the measure of their collapse. Numerous theses have been written to show what the French might have done, and how they might well have repaired their situation. But Quebec is an illuminating example of the truth that a decision is produced even more by the mental and moral dislocation of the command than by the physical dislocation of its forces. And these effects transcend the geographical and statistical calculations which fill nine-tenths of the normal book on military history.

If, as history shows, the main European channel of the Seven Years' War was so indeterminate in its course, despite so many tactical victories, it is worth while to inquire into the cause. While the number of Frederick's foes is the usual explanation, the sum of his advantages is a counterbalance so strong as to make the explanation not altogether adequate. We need to probe deeper.

Like Alexander and Napoleon, and unlike Marlborough, Frederick was free from the responsibility and limitations which are imposed on a strategist in the strict sense of the word. He combined in his person the functions of strategy and grand strategy. Moreover, the permanent associations between him, as king, and his army enabled him to prepare and develop his means for the end which he chose. The comparative scarcity of fortresses in his theatres of war was another advantage.

Although faced by the coalition of Austria, France, Russia, Sweden, and Saxony, with England as his only ally, Frederick had at the outset, and until midway through the second campaign, a superiority in the actual forces available. In addition, he had the two great assets of a tactical instrument superior to any of his enemies, and of a central position.

This enabled him to practise what is commonly called the strategy of 'interior lines'—striking outwards from his central pivot against one of the forces on the circumference, and utilizing the shorter distance he had thus to travel to concentrate against one of the enemy forces before it could be supported by the others.

Ostensibly, it would seem that the further apart these enemy forces, the easier it must be to achieve a decisive success. In terms of time, space, and number, this is undoubtedly true. But once more the moral element intrudes. When the enemy forces are widely separated each is self-contained and tends to be consolidated by pressure. When they are close together they tend to coalesce and 'become members one of another', mutually dependent in mind, morale, and matter. The minds of the commanders affect each other, moral impressions are quickly transfused, and even the movements of each force easily hinder or disorganize those of the others. Thus while the antagonist has less time and space for his action, the dislocating results of it take effect more quickly and easily. Further, when forces are close together the enemy's mere divergence from his approach to one of them may become an unexpected, and therefore truly indirect approach to another. In contrast, when forces are widely separated there is more time to prepare to meet, or avoid, the second blow of the army which is exploiting its central position.

The use of 'interior lines' as Marlborough used them in his march to the Danube is a form of the indirect approach. But although it is an indirect approach in relation to the enemy forces as a whole, it is not so in relation to the force that is the actual target, unless this is taken unaware. Otherwise the move needs to be completed by a further indirect approach—to the objective itself.

Frederick consistently used his central position to concentrate against one fraction of the enemy, and he always employed tactics of indirect approach. Thereby he gained many victories. But his tactical indirect approach was geometrical rather than psychological—unprepared by the subtler forms of surprise favoured by Scipio—and for all their executive skill, these manœuvres were narrow. The opponent might be unable to meet the following blow, owing to the inflexibility of his mind or his formations, but the blow itself did not fall unexpectedly.

The war opened at the end of August 1756 with Frederick's invasion of Saxony to forestall the plans of the Coalition. Profiting by initial surprise, Frederick entered Dresden almost unopposed. When an Austrian army came belatedly to the rescue, he advanced up the Elbe to meet it and, repulsing it in a battle at Lobositz near Leitmeritz, assured his occupation of Saxony. In April 1757, he crossed the mountains into Bohemia and marched on Prague. On arrival, he found the Austrian army posted in a strong position on the heights behind the river. Thereupon, leaving a detachment to mask his movement and watch the fords, he marched upstream during the night, crossed the river, and advanced against the enemy's right. Although his approach began in an indirect way, it became direct before the manœuvre was complete—for the Austrian army had time to change front, so that the Prussian infantry found themselves attempting a frontal assault across a fire-swept glacis. They fell in thousands. Only the unexpected arrival of Zeiten's cavalry, which had been sent on a wide detour, turned the scales of battle at Prague and produced the retreat of the Austrians.

The subsequent siege of Prague was interrupted by the advance, to the city's relief, of a fresh Austrian army under Daun. When word came of its approach, Frederick took as much of his force as he could spare from the siege and moved to meet Daun. When he encountered the Austrian army at Kolin on the 18th June, he found it strongly entrenched, and also nearly twice as strong as his own. Once more, he attempted a move past its right flank, but the manœuvre was so narrow that his columns, galled by the fire of the enemy's light troops, were drawn off their course into a direct and disjointed attack—which ended in disastrous defeat. Frederick was forced to give up the siege of Prague, and then to evacuate Bohemia.

Meantime the Russians had invaded East Prussia, and a French army had overrun Hanover, while a mixed army of the Allies, under Hildburghausen, was threatening to march on Berlin from the west. To prevent the junction of the last two armies, Frederick made a hurried march back through Leipzig, and succeeded in checking the menace. But he was then called away by fresh danger in Silesia, and while he was on his way thither an Austrian raiding force entered and sacked Berlin. This force had hardly been chased away before Hildburghausen again began to advance, and Frederick raced to meet him.

In the battle of Rossbach that followed, the Allied army, twice Frederick's strength, tried to copy Frederick's characteristic manœuvre and turn it against him. Not only did the narrowness of the manœuvre give him ample warning, but the Allies' hasty assumption that he was retreating led them to 'distract' their own forces in order to catch him up—so that when he counter-manœuvred, not to face them, but to fall on their far flank, they were almost instantaneously dislocated. Thus here, through his opponents' bungling, Frederick achieved a real indirect approach of surprise, not merely of mobility. Rossbach was by far the most economical of all his victories, for at the price of only 500 casualties he inflicted 7,700 and dispersed an army of 64,000.

Unhappily for him, he had drained his strength too low in the previous battles to reap the full benefit. He had still to deal with the Austrian army that he had failed to break up at Prague and Kolin, and although he succeeded at Leuthen, the victory there won by his famous oblique advance—a brilliantly executed if rather obvious indirect approach—cost him more than he could afford.

Thus the war continued, with the prospect dimmer, in 1758. Frederick began by a real indirect approach against the Austrians, marching right across their front and past their flank to Olmütz, twenty miles into enemy territory. Even when he lost an important convoy of supplies, he did not fall back, but instead continued his march through Bohemia right round the Austrian rear and into their entrenched base at Königgrätz. But he had now once more to pay forfeit for the opportunities lost at Prague and Kolin, for the Russian 'steam-roller' had at last got up steam and had rolled forward to Posen, on the road to Berlin. Frederick decided that he must forgo the completion of his Bohemian campaign and march north to stop the Russians. He succeeded, but the battle of Zorndorf was another Prague. Once again Frederick circumvented the obstacle offered by the Russians' strong position, marching right round their eastern flank in order to strike them from the rear. But once again the defender was able to achieve a change of front, and convert Frederick's indirect approach into a frontal attack. This had brought him into grave difficulties before his brilliant cavalry commander, Seydlitz, intervened by a circling stroke against the enemy's new flank across ground that had been deemed impassable—thus giving his manœuvre an unexpectedness which made it, in effect, a truly indirect approach. But Frederick's losses, if somewhat lighter than the Russians', were the heavier in comparison with his resources.

With his human capital still more reduced, he had to leave the Russians to recuperate and move back against the Austrians—to suffer at Höchkirch, not only a further reduction but a defeat, through undue confidence that his old Austrian opponent, Daun, would never take the initiative. Thus Frederick was surprised in a double sense; surrounded by night, he was only saved from destruction through Zeiten's cavalry keeping a passage open for his retreat. So, on the war went in 1759, with Frederick's strength declining. At Kunersdorf he suffered the worst defeat of his career, from the Russians, and at Maxen another from Daun—again due to misplaced confidence. Henceforth he could do no more than passively block the enemy.

But while the fortunes of Prussia were sinking into twilight the sun was shining in Canada. Wolfe's progress there encouraged England to send troops directly to Germany, and by a victory over the French at Minden, these offset Frederick's own disasters.

Nevertheless, his weakness was more marked than ever in 1760.

He gained a respite from the pressure in the east by the ruse of letting the Russians capture a dispatch worded 'Austrians totally defeated to-day, now for the Russians. Do what we agreed upon'. But although the Russians promptly acted upon this gentle hint, and retired, the 'posthumous' defeat of the Austrians at Torgau subsequently was another Pyrrhic victory for Frederick. Paralysed by his own losses, with only 60,000 men left in all, he could not venture another battle and was even shut up in Silesia, cut off from Prussia. Fortunately, the Austrian army's strategy was as nerveless as ever, while the Russian army's rear services broke down with the consistency that always marked them. And at this lingering crisis the Tsaritsa died. Her successor not only made peace, but began to contemplate aiding Frederick. For a few months, France and Austria continued a desultory war, but the former's strength was undermined by her colonial disasters, and, with Austria now not only inert but weary, peace was soon arranged—leaving all the warring countries exhausted, and none, except England, better off for the seven years' exuberant bloodshed.

While many lessons can be found in Frederick's campaigns, the main one would appear to be that his indirectness was too direct. To express this in another way, he regarded the indirect approach as a matter of pure manœuvre with mobility, instead of a combination of manœuvre with mobility and surprise. Thus, despite all his brilliance, his economy of force broke down.

CHAPTER VIII

THE FRENCH REVOLUTION AND NAPOLEON BONAPARTE

★

Thirty years pass and the curtain rises on 'The Great War' that was illumined by the genius of Napoleon Bonaparte. As had been the case a century before, France was the menace against which the powers of Europe banded themselves. But this time the course of the struggle was different. Revolutionary France had many sympathizers, but they did not form the governments of the nations, nor did they control the armed forces of their states. Yet, beginning the war alone, forcibly isolated as if infected by the plague, she not only repulsed the combined effort to smother her, but, changing in nature, became an expanding military menace to the rest of Europe, and ultimately, the military master of most of it. The clue to her achievement of such power is to be found in a combination of favourable conditions and impelling factors.

The revolutionary spirit which inspired the citizen armies of France created such a condition and impulse simultaneously. In compensation for the precise drill which it made impossible, it gave rein instead to the tactical sense and initiative of the individual. These new tactics of fluidity had for their simple, yet vital pivot, the fact that the French now marched and fought at a quick step of 120 paces to the minute, while their opponents adhered to the orthodox 70 paces. This elementary difference, in days before mechanical science endowed armies with means of movement swifter than the human leg, went far to make possible the rapid transference and reshuffled concentrations of striking power whereby the French could, in Napoleon's phrase, multiply 'mass by velocity' both strategically and tactically.

Another favourable condition was the organization of the army into permanent divisions—the fractioning of the army into self-contained parts which, while operating separately, could co-operate to a common goal. This organic change had been initiated by Bourcet in theory, and to some extent applied in practice, during the 1740s. It was officially accepted by Marshal de Broglie when he was made commander-in-chief in 1759. It was more fully developed by another fresh-minded thinker, Guibert, and incorporated by him in the army reforms of 1887—on the eve of the Revolution.

A third condition, linked with this, was that the chaotic supply system and the undisciplined nature of the Revolutionary armies compelled a reversion to the old practice of 'living on the country'. The distribution of the army in divisions meant that this practice detracted less from the army's effectiveness than in old days. Where, formerly, the fractions had to be collected before they could carry out an operation, now they could be serving a military purpose while feeding themselves.

Moreover the effect of 'moving light' was to accelerate their mobility, and enable them to move freely in mountainous or forest country. Similarly, the very fact that they were unable to depend on magazines and supply-trains for food and equipment lent impetus to hungry and ill-clad troops in descending upon the rear of an enemy who had, and depended on, such direct forms of supply.

Beyond these conditions was a decisive personal factor—a leader, Napoleon Bonaparte, whose military ability was stimulated by study of military history and, even more, by the food for thought provided in the theories of Bourcet and Guibert, the two most outstanding and original military writers of the eighteenth century.

From Bourcet he learnt the principle of calculated dispersion to induce the enemy to disperse their own concentration preparatory to the swift reuniting of his own forces. Also, the value of a 'plan with several branches', and of operating in a line which threatened alternative objectives. Moreover, the very plan which Napoleon executed in his first campaign was based on one that Bourcet had designed half a century earlier.

From Guibert he acquired an idea of the supreme value of mobility and fluidity of force, and of the potentialities inherent in the new distribution of an army in self-contained divisions. Guibert had defined the Napoleonic method when he wrote, a generation earlier: 'The art is to extend forces without exposing them, to embrace the enemy without being disunited, to link up the moves or the attacks to take the enemy in flank without exposing one's own flank.' And Guibert's prescription for the rear attack, as the means of upsetting the enemy's balance, became Napoleon's practice. To the same source can be traced Napoleon's method of concentrating his mobile artillery to shatter, and make a breach at, a key point in the enemy's front. Moreover, it was the practical reforms achieved by Guibert in the French army shortly before the Revolution which fashioned the instrument that Napleon applied. Above all, it was Guibert's vision of a coming revolution in warfare, carried out by a man who would arise from a revolutionary state, that kindled the youthful Napoleon's imagination and ambition.

While Napoleon added little to the ideas he had imbibed, he gave them fulfilment. Without his dynamic application the new mobility might have remained merely a theory. Because his education coincided with his instincts, and because these in turn were given scope by his circumstances, he was able to exploit the full possibilities of the new 'divisional' system. In developing the wider range of strategic combinations thus possible Napoleon made his chief contribution to strategy.

The amazement caused by the discomfiture, at Valmy and Jemappes, of the first partial invasion of 1792 has tended to obscure the fact that France and the Revolution were subsequently in far greater danger. For it was only after the execution of Louis XVI that the First Coalition was formed—by England, Holland, Austria, Prussia, Spain, and Sardinia—and only then that determination of spirit and resources of men and material were thrown into the scales. Although the conduct of the war by the invaders lacked purposeful and skilful direction, the situation of the French grew more and more precarious until fortune changed dramatically in 1794 and the tide of invasion flowed back. Henceforth France, from being the resisting party, became the aggressor. What caused this ebb? Certainly no strategic master-stroke; but though the aim was vague and limited, the significance of the event is that the decision sprang from a strategic approach that was definitely indirect.

While the main armies were pitting themselves against each other near Lille, with much bloodshed but no finality, Jourdan's far-distant army of the Moselle was ordered to assemble a striking force on its left for an advance westwards through the Ardennes, to operate towards Liége and Namur. Reaching Namur after a hungry march, during which his troops had lived on such supplies as they could pick up from the countryside, Jourdan heard—by message and the distant sound of gun-fire—that the right wing of the main army was engaged unsuccessfully in front of Charleroi. So, instead of laying formal siege to Namur, he moved south-westwards towards Charleroi and the rear flank of the enemy. His arrival intimidated the fortress into surrender.

Jourdan seems to have had no wider object in view, but the innate psychological 'pull' of such a move on to the enemy's rear gave him what Napoleon and other great captains sought as a calculated result. Coburg, the enemy commander-in-chief, hurried back eastwards, collecting such troops as he could on his way. He threw them into an attack upon Jourdan, who was entrenched to cover Charleroi. Although the struggle, famous as the battle of Fleurus, was severe, the French had the inestimable advantage of having strategically unbalanced the enemy, and of having drawn him to attack with a fraction of his strength. The defeat of this fraction was followed by the general retreat of the Allies.

When the French, in turn, assumed the role of invaders, they failed, despite their superior numbers, to achieve any decisive results in the main campaign across the Rhine. Indeed the campaign was, in the end, not merely blank, but blasted—and by an indirect approach. In July 1796, the Archduke Charles, faced by the renewed advance of the two superior armies of Jourdan and Moreau, decided, in his own words, 'to retire both armies [his own and Wartensleben's] step by step without committing himself to a battle, and to seize the first opportunity to unite them, so as to throw himself with superior, or at least equal, strength on one of the two hostile armies'. But the enemy's pressure gave him no chance to practise this 'interior lines' strategy—direct in aim, save for the idea of yielding ground to gain an opportunity—until a French change of direction suggested a more audacious stroke. It was due to the initiative of a cavalry brigadier, Nauendorff, whose wide reconnaissance showed him that the French were diverging from the Archduke's front to converge on and destroy Wartensleben. He sent the inspired message: 'If your Royal Highness will or can advance 12,000 men against Jourdan's rear, he is lost.' Although the Archduke's execution was not as bold as his subordinate's conception, it was sufficient to bring about the collapse of the French offensive. The disorderly retreat of Jourdan's shattered army back to and over the Rhine, compelled Moreau to relinquish his successful progress in Bavaria and fall back similarly.

But while the main French effort on the Rhine failed, and failed afresh later, the decision came from a secondary theatre, Italy—where Bonaparte succeeded in converting a precarious defensive into a decisive indirect approach to a victorious issue. The plan was already in his mind two years before, when he had been a staff officer in this zone, and subsequently in Paris it had taken definite form. Just as the plan itself was a reproduction of the 1745 plan, improved by application of the lessons of that campaign, so Bonaparte's key ideas had been moulded by the masters who had guided his military studies during his most impressionable years. That period of study was brief—he was only twenty-four when, as Captain Bonaparte, he was given command of the artillery at the siege of Toulon, and only twenty-six when he was made commander-in-chief of the 'Army of Italy'. While he had packed much reading and thinking into a few years, he had little leisure for reflection thereafter. Dynamic rather than deep-thinking, he did not evolve any clear philosophy of war. And his working theory, so far as it found expression in his writings, was rather a patch-work quilt—lending itself to misinterpretation by subsequent generations of soldiers who have hung upon his words.

This tendency, as well as the natural effect of his early experience, is illustrated in one of the most significant and oft-quoted of his sayings—'The principles of war are the same as those of a siege. Fire must be concentrated on one point, and as soon as the breach is made, the equilibrium is broken and the rest is nothing.' Subsequent military theory has put the accent on the first clause instead of on the last: in particular, on the words 'one point' instead of on the word 'equilibrium'. The former is but a physical metaphor, whereas the latter expresses the actual psychological result which ensures 'that the rest is nothing'. His own emphasis can be traced in the strategic course of his campaigns.

The word 'point' even has been the source of much confusion, and more controversy. One school has argued that Napoleon meant that the concentrated blow must be aimed at the enemy's strongest point, on the ground that this, and this only, ensures decisive results. For if the enemy's main resistance be broken, its rupture will involve that of any lesser opposition. This argument ignores the factor of cost, and the fact that the victor may be too exhausted to exploit his success—so that even a weaker opponent may acquire a relatively higher resisting power than the original. The other school—better imbued with the idea of economy of force, but only in the limited sense of first costs—has contended that the offensive should be aimed at the enemy's weakest point. But where a point is obviously weak this is usually because it is remote from any vital artery or nerve centre, or because it is deliberately left weak to draw the assailant into a trap.

Here, again, illumination comes from the actual campaign in which Bonaparte put this maxim into execution. It clearly suggests that what he really meant was not 'point', but 'joint'—and that at this stage of his career he was too firmly imbued with the idea of economy of force to waste his limited strength in battering at the enemy's strong point. A joint, however, is both vital and vulnerable.

It was at this time, too, that Bonaparte used another phrase that has subsequently been quoted to justify the most foolhardy concentrations of effort against the main armed forces of the enemy. 'Austria is our most determined enemy. . . . Austria overthrown, Spain and Italy fall of themselves. We must not disperse our attacks but concentrate them.' But the full text of the memorandum containing this phrase shows that he was arguing, not in support of the direct attack upon Austria, but for using the army on the frontier of Piedmont for an indirect approach to Austria. In his conception, northern Italy was to be the corridor to Austria. And in this secondary theatre, his aim—following Bourcet's guidance—was to knock out the junior partner, Piedmont, before dealing with the senior partner. In execution, his approach became still more indirect, and acquired a subtler form. For contact with reality shattered the dream which, after his initial success, he communicated to his government—'In less than a month I hope to be on the mountains of Tyrol, there to meet the army of the Rhine, and with it to carry the war into Bavaria.' It was through the frustration of this project that his real opportunity developed. By drawing Austria's forces into successive offensives against him in Italy, and defeating them there, he gained, twelve months later, an open road into Austria.

When Bonaparte assumed command of the 'Army of Italy', in March 1796, its troops were spread out along the Genoese Riviera, while the allied Austrian and Piedmont forces held the mountain passes into the plains beyond. Bonaparte's plan was to make two converging thrusts across the mountains at the fortress of Ceva, and having gained this gateway into Piedmont, to frighten her government into a separate peace by the threat of his advance on Turin. He hoped that the Austrian forces would be still in their winter quarters—although if they should move to join their Allies he had in mind a feint towards Acqui to make them withdraw in a divergent, north-easterly direction.

But in the event it was by fortune rather than design that Bonaparte gained the initial advantage of separating the two armies. The opportunity was created by an offensive move on the part of the Austrians—who made a bound forward to threaten Bonaparte's right flank and forestall any French advance on Genoa. Bonaparte countered this threat by a short-arm jab towards the joint of the Austrian advance—though two more jabs at a neighbouring point were needed before the Austrians accepted the repulse and fell back on Acqui.

Meantime, the bulk of the French army was advancing on Ceva. Bonaparte's rash attempt, on the 16th April, to take the position by direct assault was a failure. He then planned an encircling manœuvre for the 18th, and also changed his line of communications to a route further removed from possible Austrian interference. The Piedmontese, however, withdrew from the fortress before the new attack developed. In following them up, Bonaparte suffered another expensive repulse when he tried another direct assault, on a position where the Piedmontese had chosen to make a stand. But in his next move both their flanks were turned and they were hustled back into the plains.

In the eyes of the Piedmontese government, the threat to Turin from the oncoming French now loomed much larger than the Austrians' belated promise to march to their aid, by a necessarily roundabout route. The 'equilibrium was broken', and its psychological effect dispensed with any need for physical defeat to make the Piedmontese appeal for an armistice. This removed them from the scales of the war.

No commander's first campaign could have been better suited to impress him with the vital importance of the time factor—all the more because it would seem that if the Piedmontese had held out even a few days longer Bonaparte might, for want of supplies, have been obliged to retreat back to the Riviera. Whether this reported admission of his be true or not, the impression made on him is shown in his remark at the time—'It may be that in future I may lose a battle, but I shall never lose a minute.'

He was now superior to the Austrians alone (35,000 to 25,000), but he still took care not to advance directly upon them. The day after the armistice with Piedmont had been settled, he took Milan as his objective; but Tortona to Piacenza was his indirect way thither—or, rather, onto its rear. After deceiving the Austrians into a concentration at Valenza to oppose his expected north-eastward advance, he marched east instead, along the south bank of the Po, and so, on reaching Piacenza, he had turned all the Austrians' possible lines of resistance.

To gain this advantage he had not scrupled to violate the neutrality of the Duchy of Parma, in whose territory Piacenza lay, calculating that he might there find boats and a ferry—to compensate his lack of a proper bridging train. But this disregard for neutral rights had an ironically retributive effect. For when Bonaparte swung north against the Austrians' rear flank the latter decided to retire without loss of time through an intervening strip of Venetian territory—thus saving themselves by following his example of disrespect for the rules of war. Before he could use the Adda as a river-barrier across their line of retreat, the Austrians had slipped out of his reach, to gain the shelter of Mantua and the famous Quadrilateral of fortresses.

In face of these stubborn realities, Bonaparte's vision of invading Austria within a month became a distant vista. And increasingly distant because the Directory, growing anxious over the risks of the move and its own straitened resources, ordered him to march down to Leghorn, and 'evacuate' the four neutral states on the way—which meant, in the language of the time, to plunder their resources. In that process Italy was despoiled to such an extent that it never recovered its former state of prosperity.

From a military point of view, however, this restriction of Bonaparte's freedom of action proved the proverbial 'blessing in disguise'. For by compelling him to delay the pursuit of his dreams, it enabled him, with the enemy's assistance, to adjust his end to his means—until the balance of forces had turned far enough to bring his original end within practicable reach. To quote the judgement of Ferrero, the great Italian historian:

'For a century the first campaign in Italy has been described—I am almost tempted to say, sung—as a triumphant epic of offensive movements, according to which Bonaparte conquered Italy so easily because he followed up attack with attack, with a boldness that was equal to his good luck. But when the history of the campaign is studied impartially, it is clear that the two enemies attacked, or were attacked alternately, and that in the majority of cases the attacker failed.'

More by force of circumstances than by Bonaparte's design, Mantua became a bait to draw successive Austrian relieving forces far from their bases, and into his jaws. It is significant, however, that he did not entrench himself in a covering position after the custom of the traditional general, but kept his forces mobile, disposed in a loose and wide-flung grouping which could be concentrated in any direction.

In face of the first Austrian attempt at relief, Bonaparte's method was imperilled by his own reluctance to give up the investment of Mantua, and only when he cut loose from this anchor was he able to use his mobility to overthrow the Austrians, at Castiglione.

He was now ordered by the Directory to advance through the Tyrol and co-operate with the main Rhine army. The Austrians profited by this direct advance on his part to slip away eastwards with the bulk of their force, through the Val Sugana, down into the Venetian plain, and then westwards to relieve Mantua. But Bonaparte, instead of pursuing his advance north, or falling back to guard Mantua, turned in hot chase of their tail through the mountains, thereby retorting to the enemy's indirect approach with one of his own—but with a more decisive aim than theirs. At Bassano, he caught and crushed the rear half of their army. And when he emerged into the Venetian plain in pursuit of the other half, he directed the pursuers to cut the enemy off from Trieste and their line of retreat to Austria, not to head them off from Mantua. Thus they became a fresh addition to his Mantuan safe-deposit.

The locking up of so much of her military capital drove Austria to a fresh expenditure. This time, and not for the last time, the directness of Bonaparte's tactics imperilled the successful indirectness of his strategy. When the converging armies of Alvintzi and Davidovich drew near to Verona, his pivot for the guarding of Mantua, Bonaparte hurled himself at the former, the stronger, and suffered a severe repulse—at Caldiero. But instead of retreating, he chose the daring course of a wide manœuvre round the southern flank of Alvintzi's army and on to its rear. How desperate he felt was shown in the letter he wrote to warn the Directory—'The weakness and exhaustion of the army cause me to fear the worst. We are perhaps on the eve of losing Italy.' The delays caused by marshes and water-courses increased the hazard of his manœuvre, but it upset the enemy's plan of closing their jaws on his army, supposed to be at Verona. While Alvintzi wheeled to meet him, Davidovich remained inactive. Even so, Bonaparte found it hard to overcome Alvintzi's superior numbers. But when the scales of battle were hanging in the balance at Arcola, Bonaparte resorted to a tactical ruse, a device rare for him—sending a few trumpeters on to the Austrian rear to sound the charge. Within a few minutes the Austrian troops were streaming away in flight.

Two months later, in January 1797, the Austrians made a fourth and last attempt to save Mantua, but this was shattered at Rivoli —where Bonaparte's loose group formation functioned almost perfectly. Like a widespread net whose corners are weighted with stones, when one of the enemy's columns impinged on it the net closed in round the point of pressure and the stones crashed together on the intruder.

This self-protective formation which thus, on impact, became a concentrated offensive formation, was Bonaparte's development of the new divisional system—by which an army was permanently subdivided into independently moving fractions, instead of, as formerly, constituting a single body from which only temporary detachments were made. The group formation of Bonaparte's Italian campaigns became the more highly developed *bataillon carré*, with army corps replacing divisions, of his later wars.

Although at Rivoli this loaded net was the means of crushing the Austrians' manœuvring wing, it is significant that the collapse of their main resistance came from Bonaparte's audacity in sending a single regiment of 2,000 men across Lake Garda, in boats, to place themselves on the line of retreat of a whole army. Mantua then surrendered, and the Austrians—who had lost their armies in the effort to save this outer gate to their country—had now to watch, helplessly, Bonaparte's swift approach to the defenceless inner gate. This threat wrung peace from Austria while the main French armies were still but a few miles beyond the Rhine.

In the autumn of 1798, the Second Coalition was formed by Russia, Austria, England, Turkey, Portugal, Naples, and the Papacy—to cast off the shackles of this peace treaty. Bonaparte was away in Egypt, and when he returned the fortunes of France had sunk low. The field armies were greatly depleted, the treasury was empty, and the conscript levies were falling off.

Bonaparte—who on his return had overthrown the Directory and become First Consul—ordered the formation at Dijon of an Army of Reserve, composed of all the home troops that could be scraped together. But he did not use it to reinforce the main theatre of war, and the main army on the Rhine. Instead, he planned the boldest of all his indirect approaches—a swoop along an immense arc onto the rear of the Austrian army in Italy. This had driven the small French 'Army of Italy' back almost to the French frontier and penned it into the north-west corner of Italy. Bonaparte had intended to move through Switzerland, to Lucerne or Zurich, and then to descend into Italy as far east as the Saint Gothard pass, or even the Tyrol. But the news that the Army of Italy was hard pressed led him to take the shorter route by the Saint Bernard pass. Thus, when he debouched from the Alps at Ivrea, in the last week of May 1800, he was still on the right front of the Austrian army. Instead of pressing south-east direct to the aid of Masséna, who was shut up in Genoa, Bonaparte sent his advanced guard due south to Cherasco, while under cover of this distraction, he slipped eastward to Milan with the main body.

Thus, instead of advancing to meet the enemy in what he termed 'their natural position', facing west of Alessandria, he gained a 'natural position' across the Austrians' rear—forming that strategic back-stop, or barrage, which was the initial objective of his deadliest manœuvres against the enemy's rear. For such a position, offering natural obstacles, afforded him a secure pivot from which to prepare a stranglehold for the enemy, whose instinctive tendency, when cut off from their line of retreat and supply, was to turn and flow back, usually in driblets, towards him. This conception of a strategic barrage was Bonaparte's chief contribution to the strategy of indirect approach.

At Milan he had barred one of the two Austrian routes of retreat, and now, extending his barrage south of the Po to the Stradella defile, he also blocked the other. But here, for the moment, his conception had somewhat outranged his means—for he had only 34,000 men, and owing to Moreau's reluctance, the corps of 15,000 that Bonaparte had ordered the Army of the Rhine to send over the Saint Gothard pass was late in arriving. Concern over the thinness of his barrage became accentuated. And at this juncture Genoa capitulated, thereby removing his 'fixative' agent.

Uncertainty as to the route the Austrians might now take, and the fear that they might retire to Genoa, where the British navy could revictual them, led him to forfeit much of the advantage he had gained. For, crediting his opponents with more initiative than they possessed, he quitted his 'natural position' at the Stradella and pushed westward to reconnoitre them, sending Desaix with a division to cut the road from Alessandria to Genoa. Thus he was caught at a disadvantage, with only part of his army at hand, when the Austrian army suddenly emerged from Alessandria and advanced to meet him on the plains of Marengo (the 14th June 1800). The battle was long in doubt, and even when Desaix's detachment returned the Austrians were only driven back. But then Bonaparte's strategic position became the lever which enabled him to wring from the demoralized Austrian commander an agreement that the Austrians were to evacuate Lombardy and retire behind the Mincio.

Although the war was resumed in a desultory fashion beyond the Mincio, the moral repercussion of Marengo was manifested in the armistice which closed the war of the Second Coalition six months later.

After several years of uneasy peace, the curtain that had fallen on the French Revolutionary Wars rose on a new act—the Napoleonic wars. In 1805, Napoleon's army of 200,000 men was assembled at Boulogne, menacing a descent on the English coast, when it was suddenly directed by forced marches to the Rhine. It is still uncertain whether Napoleon seriously intended a direct invasion of England, or whether his threat was merely the first move in his indirect approach to Austria. Probably, he was acting on Bourcet's principle of 'a plan with branches'. When he decided to take the eastward branch, he calculated that the Austrians would, as usual, send an army into Bavaria to block the exits of the Black Forest. On this basis he planned his wide manœuvre round their northern flank, across the Danube, and on to the Lech—his intended strategic barrage across their rear. It was a repetition, on a grander scale, of the Stradella manœuvre—and Napoleon himself emphasized the parallel to his troops. Moreover, his superiority of force enabled him, once the barrage was established, to convert it into a moving barrage. This, closing down on the rear of the Austrian army, led to its almost bloodless surrender at Ulm.

Having wiped out the weaker partner, Napoleon had now to deal with the Russian army, under Kutosov—which, after traversing Austria and gathering smaller Austrian contingents, had just reached the Inn. A less immediate threat was the return of the other Austrian armies from Italy and the Tyrol. The size of his forces was now, for the first time but not the last, an inconvenience to Napoleon. With such large armies, the space between the Danube and the mountains to the south-west was too cramped for any local indirect approach to the enemy, and there was not time for a wide movement of the range of the Ulm manœuvre. So long, however, as the Russians remained on the Inn, they were in a 'natural position'—forming not only a shield to Austrian territory, but a shield under cover of which the other Austrian armies could come up from the south, through Carinthia, and join them in presenting Napoleon with a solid wall of resistance.

Faced with this problem, Napoleon used a most subtle series of variations of the indirect approach. His first aim was to push the Russians as far east as possible, thus separating them from the Austrian armies now returning from Italy. So, while advancing directly east towards Kutosov and Vienna, he sent Mortier's corps along the north bank of the Danube. This threat to Kutosov's communications with Russia was sufficient to induce him to fall back obliquely north-eastwards, to Krems on the Danube. Napoleon thereupon dispatched Murat on a dash across Kutosov's new front, with Vienna as his goal. From Vienna, Murat was directed northwards on Hollabrunn. Thus, after first threatening the Russians' right flank, Napoleon now menaced their left rear.

Owing to Murat's mistaken agreement to a temporary truce, this move failed to cut off the Russians, but it at least drove them into a hurried retreat still further north-east to Olmütz, within close reach of their own frontier. Although they were now separated from the Austrian reinforcements, they were nearer to their own, and at Olmütz they actually received a large instalment. To press them further back would only consolidate their strength. Besides, time pressed, and the entry of Prussia into the war was imminent.

Hence Napoleon resorted to the psychological indirect approach of tempting the Russians into taking the offensive by a subtle display of his own apparent weakness. To face the 80,000 men of the enemy army, he concentrated only 50,000 at Brünn, and from there pushed out isolated detachments towards Olmütz. This impression of weakness he supplemented by 'doves of peace' to the Tsar and the Austrian emperor. When the enemy swallowed the bait, Napoleon recoiled before them to a position at Austerlitz designed by nature to fit his trap. In the battle which followed he used one of his rare examples of the tactical indirect approach to offset his equally rare inferiority of numbers on the battlefield. Luring the enemy to stretch their left in an attack on his line of retreat, he swung round his centre against the weakened 'joint' and thereby obtained a victory so decisive that within twenty-four hours the Emperor of Austria asked for peace.

When, a few months later, Napoleon turned to deal with Prussia, he had a superiority of almost two to one available; an army that was 'grand' both in quantity and quality against one that was defective in training and obsolete in outlook. The effect of this assured superiority on Napoleon's strategy was marked, and had a growing influence on the conduct of his later campaigns. In 1806, he still sought, and gained, the advantage of initial surprise. To this end he had cantoned his troops near the Danube, and thence swiftly concentrated to the north behind the natural screen formed by the Thüringian forest. Next, debouching suddenly from the wooded range into the open country beyond, his *bataillon carré* drove straight ahead towards the heart of the enemy country. Thus Napoleon found himself, rather than placed himself, on the rear of the Prussian forces; and in swinging round to crush them at Jena, he seems to have relied primarily on sheer weight—the moral effect of his position being incidental, although important.

So also in the campaign against the Russians which followed, in Poland and East Prussia, Napoleon seems concerned mainly with the single end of bringing his enemy to battle—confident that, when this happened, his machine would overpower the enemy. He still used the manœuvre onto the enemy's rear, but it was more as a means of gripping them firmly, so that they could be drawn into his jaws, than as a means of liquefying their morale to make mastication easier.

The indirect approach as seen here was a means of distraction and physical 'traction' rather than of distraction and moral dislocation.

Thus in the Pultusk manœuvre he aimed to draw the Russians westwards so that when he advanced north from Poland, he might cut them off from Russia. The Russians slipped out of his jaws. In January 1807 the Russians moved westwards on their own volition, towards the remnant of their Prussian allies at Danzig, and Napoleon was quick to seize the opportunity to cut their communications with Prussia. His instructions, however, fell into the hands of the Cossacks, and the Russian army fell back just in time. Napoleon, thereupon, followed them up directly; and, finding them in a frontal position at Eylau, ready to accept battle, he relied on a purely tactical manœuvre against their rear. Its working suffered from the interference of snowstorms, and the Russians, though mauled, were not masticated.

Four months later, both sides had recuperated, and the Russians suddenly moved south against Heilsburg, whereupon Napoleon wheeled his *bataillon carré* east to cut them off from Königsberg, their immediate base. But this time he was, apparently, so obsessed with the idea of battle that when his cavalry, reconnoitring to the flank of his route, reported the presence of the Russians in a strong position at Friedland, he swung his forces straight at the target. The tactical victory was won, not by surprise or mobility, but by pure offensive power—here expressed in Napoleon's new artillery tactics, the massed concentration of guns at a selected point. This was to become more and more the driving-shaft of his tactical mechanism. Although at Friedland, as often later, it ensured victory, it did little to save lives.

It is curious how the possession of a blank cheque on the bank of man-power had so analogous an effect in 1807–14 and in 1914–18. And curious, also, that in each case it was associated with the method of intense artillery bombardments. The explanation may be that lavish expenditure breeds extravagance, the mental antithesis of economy of force—to which surprise and mobility are the means. This hypothesis is strengthened by the similarity of effect seen in Napoleon's policy.

Napoleon was able to use the glamour of his victory at Friedland to reinforce the glamour of his personality in seducing the Tsar from his partners in the Fourth Coalition. But he then risked his advantage, and ultimately his empire, by excess in exploiting it. The severity of his terms to Prussia undermined the security of the peace, his policy towards England contemplated nothing short of her ruin, and his aggression raised Spain and Portugal as fresh enemies. These were basic errors in grand strategy.

Here it is apt to note that it was an indirect approach—Sir John Moore's brief 'in and out' thrust against Burgos and the communications of the French forces in Spain—which dislocated Napoleon's plans in Spain, gave the national rising time and space to gather strength, and thus ensured that the Iberian peninsula should henceforth be a running sore in Napoleon's side. Above all, the moral influence of this first check to Napoleon's irresistible progress gives it a decisive significance.

Napoleon had no chance to redeem it, for he was called back by the threatened uprising of Prussia and the fresh intervention of Austria. The latter threat matured, and in the campaign of 1809 Napoleon is again seen trying, at Landshut and Vienna, to manœuvre on to the enemy's rear. But when hitches occurred in the execution of these manœuvres, Napoleon's impatience led him to gamble on a direct approach and battle, and at Aspern-Essling he suffered in consequence his first great defeat. Although he retrieved it by the victory of Wagram at the same point, six weeks later, the price was high and the peace thereby gained was unstable.

The Peninsular War

Napoleon had two years' grace, however, in which to operate on and cure the 'Spanish ulcer'. As Moore's intervention had thwarted Napoleon's attempt to check the inflammatory condition in its early stages, so in the years that followed Wellington was to hinder all remedial measures and enable the wound to fester, the poison to spread, through the Napoleonic system. The French had beaten, and continued to beat any regular Spanish forces, but the thoroughness of these defeats was of the greatest benefit to the defeated. For it ensured that the main effort of the Spanish was thrown into guerrilla warfare. An intangible web of guerrilla bands replaced a vulnerable military target, while enterprising and unconventional guerrilla leaders, instead of hide-bound Spanish generals, conducted operations.

The worst misfortune for Spain, and hence for England, was the temporary success of attempts to form fresh regular forces. Fortunately there were soon beaten, and as the French dispersed them so, coincidently, did they disperse their own good fortune. The poison spread again instead of coming to a head.

In this curious warfare, England's most profound influence was in aggravating the trouble and encouraging the sources of it. Rarely has she caused a greater distraction to her opponents at the price of so small a military effort. The effect produced in Spain was in significant contrast with the slight results, indeed the unhappy results, produced on the one hand by her attempts at direct co-operation with her Continental allies during these wars, and on the other by her expeditions to trans-oceanic points too remote, geographically and psychologically, to affect her opponent. From the standpoint of national policy and prosperity the second class of expedition, however, had its justification in adding Cape Colony, Mauritius, Ceylon, British Guiana, and several West Indian islands to the British Empire.

But the real effect of England's grand-strategic indirect approach in Spain has been obscured by the traditional tendency of historians to become obsessed with battles. Indeed, by treating the Peninsular War as a chronicle of Wellington's battles and sieges it becomes meaningless. Sir John Fortescue did much to correct this tendency and fallacy, despite the fact that he was primarily concerned with the localized 'History of the British Army'. It is significant that as his own researches deepened he gave more and more emphasis to the predominant influence of the Spanish guerrillas on the issue of the struggle.

While the presence of the British Expeditionary Force was an essential foundation for this influence, Wellington's battles were materially the least effective part of his operations. By them he inflicted a total loss of some 45,000 men only—counting killed, wounded and prisoners—on the French during the five years' campaign until they were driven out of Spain, whereas Marbot reckoned that the number of French deaths alone during this period averaged a hundred a day. Hence it is a clear deduction that the overwhelming majority of the losses which drained the French strength, and their morale still more, was due to the operations of the guerrillas, and of Wellington himself, in harrying the French and in making the country a desert where the French stayed only to starve.

Not the least significant feature is that Wellington fought so few battles in so long a series of campaigns. Was this due to that essentially practical 'common-sense' which biographers have declared to be the key to his character and outlook? In the words of one recent biographer—'direct and narrow realism was the essence of Wellington's character. It was responsible for his limitations and defects, but in the larger stage of his public career it amounted to genins.' This diagnosis is borne out by Wellington's strategy in the peniusula.

The expedition which was to have such momentous consequences was itself a subtraction of force from the main and abor-

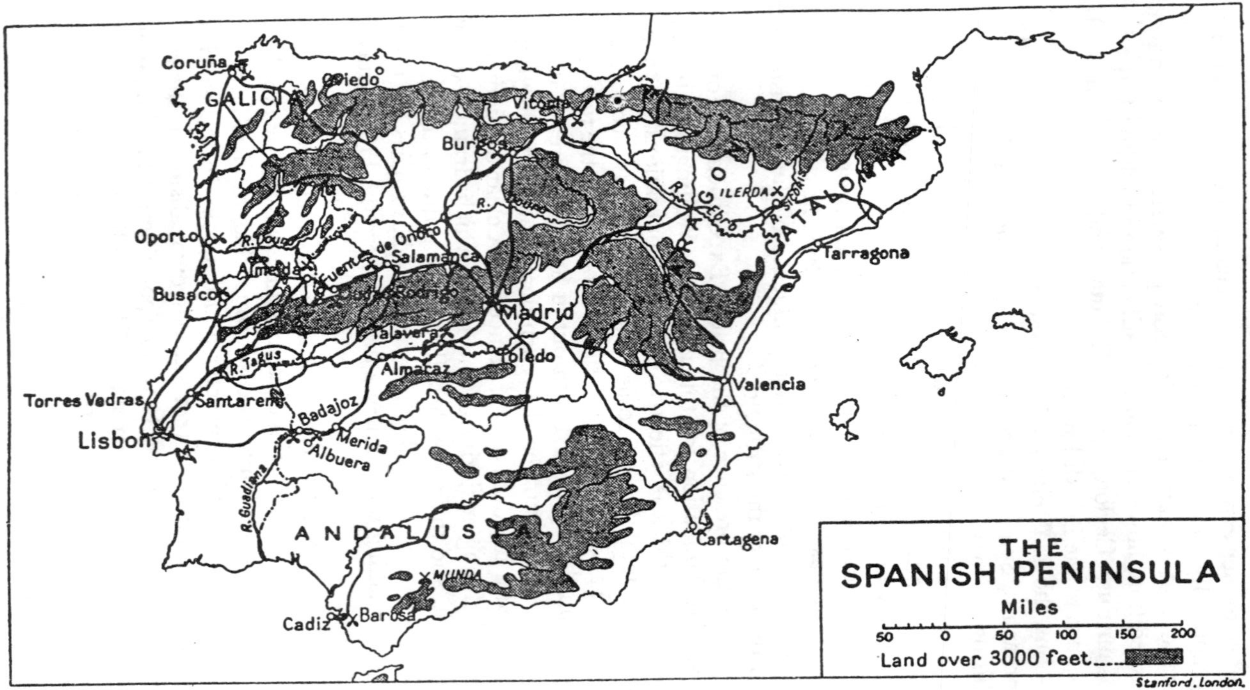
THE
SPANISH PENINSULA
Miles
50 0 50 100 150 200
Land over 3000 feet
Coruña
Oviedo
GALICIA
Vitoria
Burgos
Oporto
R. Douro
Almeida
Fuentes de Onoro
Salamanca
Ciudad Rodrigo
Busaco
Madrid
Talavera
R. Tagus
Almaraz
Toledo
Torres Vedras
Santarem
Lisbon
Badajoz
Merida
Albuera
R. Guadiana
ANDALUSIA
MUNDA
Cadiz
Barosa
Cartagena
Valencia
Tarragona
ARAGON
CATALONIA
ILERDA
R. Sicoris
R. Ebro
Stanford, London.

tive effort on the Scheldt, and was undertaken by the British government more from the hope of saving Portugal than from any deep appreciation of its grand-strategic potentialities in aggravating the 'Spanish ulcer'. Castlereagh's uphill advocacy, however, was aided by the expressed opinion of Sir Arthur Wellesley (the future Duke of Wellington) that, if the Portuguese army and militia were reinforced by 20,000 British troops, the French would need 100,000 to conquer Portugal, a quantity they could not spare if the Spanish still continued to resist. Expressed in a different way, this might mean that 20,000 British would suffice to cause the 'distraction' of nearly 100,000 French, part at least from the main theatre of war in Austria.

As an aid to Austria the expedition was to prove of no avail, and as a shield to Portugal not altogether satisfactory from a Portuguese standpoint. But as a strain on Napoleon and an advantage to England it bore fruit tenfold.

Wellesley was given 26,000 men, and in April 1809 he arrived at Lisbon. Partly as a result of the Spanish insurrection, and partly as a sequel to Moore's thrust at Burgos and retreat to Corunna, the French were widely scattered over the peninsula. Ney was vainly trying to subdue Galicia in the extreme north-western corner. South of him, but in the north of Portugal, Soult lay at Oporto, with his army itself dispersed in detachments. Victor lay round Merida, facing the southern route to Portugal.

Profiting by his central position, his unexpected appearance, and the enemy's dispersion, Wellesley moved north against Soult. Although he failed to cut off Soult's most southerly detachments as he had planned, he surprised Soult himself before the latter could assemble his force, upset his dispositions by a crossing higher up the Douro, and developed this incipient dislocation by heading Soult off from his natural line of retreat. Like Turenne in 1675, Wellesley mopped up the resistance without it ever having had the chance to coagulate. At the end of Soult's enforced retreat through the bleak mountains northward into Galicia, his army had suffered loss and exhaustion out of all proportion to the fighting.

Wellesley's second operation, however, was neither so profitable nor so well-conceived in its adjustment of end and means. Victor, who had remained passively at Merida, was recalled, after Soult's 'disappearance', to Talavera, where he could cover the direct approach to Madrid. A month later Wellesley decided to march by this route on Madrid, pushing into the heart of Spain—and into the lion's jaws. For he offered a target on which all the French armies in Spain could concentrate by the easiest routes. Moreover, by thus rallying on their central pivot they had the chance of knitting together the communications between them—when the armies were scattered these communications were their greatest source of weakness.

Wellesley advanced with only 23,000 men, supported by a similar number of Spanish troops under the feeble Cuesta, whereas Victor in falling back had brought himself within close reach of support from two other French forces near Madrid. The hostile concentration was likely to total over 100,000, since 'through accident rather than design'—as Fortescue remarks—the forces of Ney, Soult, and Mortier had drifted Madrid-wards from the north. Hampered by Cuesta's irresolution and his own supplies, Wellesley did not succeed in joining issue with Victor until the latter was reinforced by Joseph Bonaparte from Madrid. Constrained to fall back in his turn, Wellesley emerged somewhat luckily from a defensive battle at Talavera, but would have advanced again if Cuesta had not refused. This was fortunate for Wellesley, as Soult was descending upon his rear. Cut off from the route by which he had come, Wellesley escaped by slipping south of the Tagus; but only after a costly, demoralizing and exhausting retreat did he regain the shelter of the Portuguese frontier. Want of food hampered the French pursuit. This closed the campaign of 1809 and taught Wellesley the worthlessness of Spanish regular forces—a lesson already brought out in Moore's experience. As a reward for his efforts he was created Viscount Wellington, and did more to deserve this the next year.

For in 1810, with Austria driven to peace, Napoleon was free to concentrate his attention on Spain and Portugal—until 1812. These two years were the critical period of the Peninsular War. The inability of the French to accomplish their purpose then is of greater historical significance than their subsequent defeats, or Wellington's victories, in 1812 and 1813. The foundation of the British success lay in Wellington's shrewd calculation of the military economic factor—the limited French means of subsistence—and his construction of the Lines of Torres Vedras. His strategy was essentially that of indirect approach to a military economic object and objective.

Before the main campaign opened he was aided by the Spanish regular forces in their customary way. They embarked on a winter campaign in which they were so thoroughly crushed and dispersed that the French, deprived of any target, were induced to stretch themselves more widely still over Spain—invading the rich province of Andalusia in the south.

Napoleon now took control, from a distance, and by the end of February 1810 had concentrated nearly 300,000 men in Spain—with more to come. Of this total, 65,000 were assigned to Masséna for the task of driving the British out of Portugal. While the number was large, its small proportion to the whole is illuminating evidence of the growing strain of the guerrilla war in Spain. Wellington, by the inclusion of British-trained Portuguese troops, had made up his total to 50,000.

Masséna's invasion came by the north, past Ciudad Rodrigo, and thus gave Wellington the longest time and space for his strategy to take effect. His precautions in stripping the country of provisions formed a 'transmission-brake' on Masséna's advance, while his half-way stand at Bussaco served as a 'foot-brake'—which was strengthened by Masséna's folly in committing his troops to a needless direct assault. Then Wellington fell back to the Lines of Torres Vedras which he had constructed, across the mountainous peninsula formed by the Tagus and the sea, to cover Lisbon. On the 14th October, four months and barely two hundred miles from his start, Masséna came within sight of the Lines—a sight which struck him with the full shock of surprise. Unable to force them, he hung on for a month until compelled by starvation to retreat to Santarem, thirty miles back, on the Tagus. Wellington, shrewdly, made no attempt to press his retreat or bring on a battle, but set himself to confine Masséna within the smallest possible area so that the latter might have the greatest possible difficulty in feeding his men. The French, now and later, had to pay dearly for their faith in the optimistic illusions fostered by Napoleon's sweeping rebuke to cautious strategists: 'Supplies?—don't talk to me about them. Twenty thousand men can live in a desert.'

Wellington maintained this strategy resolutely, despite the indirect risk of a change of policy at home, and the direct risk caused by Soult's advance in the south, by way of Badajoz, which was made as a diversion to relieve the constriction of Masséna. Wellington withstood every effort of Masséna to draw him into an attack. He was both justified and rewarded, for at last, in March, Masséna had to go—and when the starving wreckage of his army re-crossed the frontier he had lost 25,000 men, of whom only 2,000 had fallen in action.

Meantime the Spanish guerrillas had been growing ever more active and numerous. In Aragon and Catalonia alone, two French corps (totalling nearly 60,000 men), instead of helping Masséna's Army of Portugal, had been practically paralysed during several months by a few thousand guerrillas and troops used guerrilla-wise. In the south, too, where the French were besieging Cadiz, the very failure of the Allies to exploit their victory at Barrosa and raise the siege proved of advantage to them by retaining the besieging troops there on a vain task. Another distracting influence during these years was the constant threat and frequent fact of British landings, at points along the immense coastline, made possible by sea power.

Henceforth Wellington's greatest influence came through his threats rather than his blows. For, whenever he threatened a point, the French were forced to draw off troops thither, and thus give the guerrillas greater scope in other districts.

Wellington, however, was not content with threats. Following up Masséna's retreat on Salamanca, he used his army to cover the blockade of the frontier fortress of Almeida in the north, while he directed Beresford to invest Badajoz in the south. Thereby he tied up his own power of mobility, and divided his force—into two nearly equal parts. But fortune favoured his course. Masséna, having rallied and slightly reinforced his army, came back to the rescue of Almeida; and at Fuentes de Onoro Wellington was caught in a bad position and seriously imperilled. But he managed to beat off the attack—although he admitted, 'If Boney had been there, we should have been beat'. Near Badajoz, too, Beresford marched out to meet Soult's relieving force; after mishandling the fight and admitting defeat at Albuera, the situation was saved for him by his subordinates and troops—if at an exorbitant cost.

Wellington now concentrated his efforts on the siege of Badajoz, but without a siege-train, until he had to raise the siege as a result of the unfettered move southwards of Marmont—who had taken over Masséna's army—to join Soult. The two now planned a united advance on Wellington. Fortunately, fusion brought friction. And Soult, alarmed by the fresh blaze-up of guerrilla war in Andalusia, returned thither with part of his army, leaving Marmont in control. Thanks to Marmont's extreme caution, the campaign of 1811 petered out quietly.

By his battles Wellington had risked much, and it would be hard to argue that they had gained much advantage beyond that already produced and promised by his earlier strategy. In view of his slender margin of strength, they were not a profitable investment, for while his loss in them was less than the French, it was proportionately much greater. But he had tided over the most critical period. And now Napoleon unwittingly came to his aid—to make his advantage secure. For Napoleon was preparing his invasion of Russia. Thither his attention and his strength were henceforth turned. This development and the trying guerrilla situation caused a change of plan in Spain, where the main French line of effort was altered to an attempt to subdue Valencia and Andalusia thoroughly before concentrating afresh against Portugal.

Compared with 1810, the French troops were reduced by 70,000: and of those who remained, no less than 90,000 were employed—from Tarragona on the Mediterranean coast to Oviedo on the Atlantic coast—in guarding the communications with France against the guerrillas.

Thus given free scope and weakened opposition, Wellington sprang suddenly on Ciudad Rodrigo and stormed it, while a detachment under Hill stood guard over his strategic flank and rear. Marmont was unable to intervene, unable to retake the fortress because his siege-train had been captured there, and unable also to follow Wellington across the food-stripped country between them.

Under cover of this hunger-screen, Wellington slipped south and stormed Badajoz in turn—if at a far greater cost, and by a narrower margin of time. At Badajoz he captured the French pontoon train. As he promptly followed up this gain by destroying the French bridge of boats across the Tagus at Almaraz, he had now achieved a definite strategic separation of the two armies of Marmont and Soult, whose nearest way of communication was now by the bridge at Toledo, over three hundred miles from the mouth of the Tagus.

Apart from this, Soult was tied fast to Andalusia by a want of supplies and a surfeit of guerrillas, while Wellington, now able to operate secure from interference, concentrated two-thirds of his strength for an advance on Marmont at Salamanca. But the directness of his approach propelled Marmont back towards his source of reinforcement.

The balance of numbers thus being restored, Marmont manœuvred against Wellington's communications, with all the more advantage because he had none of his own to worry about. On several occasions the two armies raced alongside each other in parallel columns, only a few hundred yards apart, each seeking a favourable chance to strike. The French, by their capacity to outmarch the British, tended to outmanœuvre them. But on the 22nd July over-confidence led Marmont into a slip which momentarily unbalanced his own forces. He allowed his left wing to become too far separated from his right wing and Wellington instantly exploited the opportunity by a swift pounce upon the exposed wing. This produced the defeat of the French army—before further reinforcements reached it.

Wellington did not, however, achieve its real disruption in this battle of Salamanca; and he was still heavily inferior to the French in the peninsula as a whole. He has been blamed for not following up the defeated French forces, now under Clausel. But having lost the immediate chance of dispersing them, it is unlikely that he could have regained it before they reached the shelter of Burgos, and such a pursuit would have exposed him to the risk that King Joseph from Madrid might have descended at any moment on his own rear and communications.

Instead, he decided to make a move on Madrid—for its moral and political effect. His entry into the capital was a symbol and a tonic to the Spanish, while Joseph made a fugitive exit. But the defect of this coup was that Wellington's stay could only be fleeting if the French gathered in force; and nothing was more likely than the loss of Madrid to make their armies, scattered on the circumference, rally on the centre. Wellington cut his stay short without compulsion and marched on Burgos. But the French system of 'living on the country' deprived such a stroke at their communications with France of anything like a normal influence on their situation. Even the limited influence was forfeited by the ineffectiveness of Wellington's siege methods and means, whereby time dribbled away that he could not afford to lose. For his very success at, and after, the battle of Salamanca had induced the French to abandon their tasks and territory in Spain in order to concentrate from all quarters against him. In relation to their armies Wellington was more dangerously placed than Moore before him, but he fell back just in time. When Hill joined him, he felt secure enough to offer battle to the united French armies at Salamanca—once again. Their numerical advantage was slight compared with earlier days, 90,000 to 68,000, and they did not care to accept the challenge on a battlefield chosen by Wellington. Hence Wellington continued his retreat to Ciudad Rodrigo. With his arrival there, the curtain came down on the campaign of 1812.

Although he was back once more on the Portuguese frontier, and thus, superficially, no further forward, actually the issue of the Peninsular War was decided. For by abandoning the greater part of Spain to concentrate against him, the French had abandoned it to the Spanish guerrillas—and lost the chance of shaking their grip. On top of this disaster came the news of Napoleon's retreat from Moscow, which led to the withdrawal of more French troops from Spain. Thus when the next campaign opened the situation had completely changed.

Wellington, now reinforced to 100,000 men—less than half of whom were British—was the aggressor and the superior, while the French, demoralized more by the strain of the incessant guerrilla war than by military defeats, were almost at once compelled to fall back behind the Ebro, and reduced to the role of trying to hold on to the northern fringe of Spain. Even there, the scales were turned against them by the pressure of guerrillas in their rear, in Biscay and the Pyrenean districts—which forced the French to take away four divisions from their slender strength to withstand this back pressure. Wellington's gradual advance to the Pyrenees and into France—though flecked by occasional misadventures, successfully retrieved—is no more than a strategic epilogue to the story of the Peninsular War.

This happy conclusion could hardly have come but for the moral and physical support of Wellington's presence in the peninsula; and his activities, by distracting the attention of the French in part to him, repeatedly facilitated the spread of the guerrilla war.

Yet it is a question, and an interesting speculation, whether his victories in 1812, by stirring the French to cut their loss and contract their zone, did not improve their prospects and make his own advance harder in 1813. For the wider and the longer the French were dispersed throughout Spain, the more sure and more complete would be their ultimate collapse. The Peninsular War was an outstanding historical example, achieved by instinctive common sense even more than by intention, of the type of strategy which a century later Lawrence evolved into a reasoned theory, and applied in practice—although without so definite a fulfilment.

From observing the 'Spanish ulcer' we have now to turn back to examine another type of strategical growth, which was insidiously affecting Napoleon's own mind.

Napoleon from Vilna to Waterloo

The Russian campaign of 1812 was the natural climax to the tendencies already seen to be growing in Napoleon's strategy—that of relying more on mass than on mobility, and on strategic formation rather than on surprise. The geographical conditions merely served to accentuate its weaknesses.

The very scale of Napoleon's forces—450,000 men—induced him to adopt an almost linear distribution, which in turn entailed a direct approach along the line of natural expectation. It is true that, like the Germans in 1914, he 'loaded' one end—the left—of his line, and sought to swing it round in a vast sweep upon the Russians at Vilna. But even allowing for his brother Jerome's inertia in the role of fixing the enemy, this manœuvre was too cumbersome and too direct to be an effective means of distracting and dislocating the enemy, unless they had been of abnormal stupidity. In the event, the manœuvre's limitations were exposed by the Russians' deliberate adoption of a strategy of evasion.

As Napoleon pressed into Russia, after his first blows 'in the air' he contracted his line into his customary *bataillon carré*, and tried to swing it tactically on to the enemy's rear. But when the Russians, changing to a 'battle' policy, were so foolish as to push their heads towards Napoleon's open jaws, these jaws closed so obviously at Smolensk, that the Russians slipped out; while at Borodino the jaws broke off their own teeth. No example could have better demonstrated the drawbacks of a convergent approach as compared with a true indirect approach. The disastrous results of the subsequent retreat from Moscow were due less to the severe weather—the frost actually was later than usual that year—than to the demoralization of the French army. This was caused through the frustration of its direct battle-aimed strategy by the Russian strategy of evasion—which in turn was the strategic method here used to carry out what may be classified as a war policy or grand strategy of indirect approach.

Moreover, the harm done to Napoleon's fortunes by his defeat in Russia was immensely increased by the moral and material effects of the ill-success of his armies in Spain. It is significant to note in assessing the deadly effect of England's action here that, in this campaign, England was following her traditional war policy of 'severing the roots'.

When, in 1813, Napoleon, with fresh forces more massive and less mobile than ever, was confronted with the uprising of Prussia and with the invading armies of Russia, he sought to crush them in his now habitual way by the converging weight of his *bataillon carré*. But neither the battle of Lützen nor the battle of Bautzen was decisive, and thereafter the Allies, by an ever-lengthening retirement, thwarted Napoleon's further attempts to bring them to battle. Their evasiveness induced Napoleon to ask for a six weeks' suspension of hostilities; and when it terminated Austria, also, was arrayed with his enemies.

The autumn campaign which followed throws a curious light on Napoleon's changed mentality. He had 400,000 men, a total nearly equal to that of his opponents. He used 100,000 for a convergent advance against Berlin, but this direct pressure merely consolidated the resistance of Bernadotte's forces in that area, and the French were thrown back. Meantime Napoleon himself, with the main army, had taken up a central position covering Dresden in Saxony. But his impatience overcame him, and he suddenly began to advance directly east upon Blücher's 95,000. Blücher fell back to lure him into Silesia, while Schwarzenberg, with 185,000, began to move northward down the Elbe from Bohemia, and across the Bohemian mountains into Saxony—onto Napoleon's rear at Dresden.

Leaving a detachment behind, Napoleon hurried back, intending to counter this indirect approach with a still more deadly one. His plan was to move south-west, cross the Bohemian mountains, and place himself across Schwarzenberg's line of retreat through the mountains. The position he had in mind was ideal for a strategic barrage. But the news of the enemy's close approach made him lose his nerve, and at the last moment he decided instead on a direct approach to Dresden, and to Schwarzenberg. This resulted in another victorious battle; but it was only tactically decisive, and Schwarzenberg retreated safely southward through the mountains.

A month later, the three Allied armies began to close in upon Napoleon who, weakened by his battles, had fallen back from Dresden to Düben, near Leipzig. Schwarzenberg lay to the south, Blücher to the north and, unknown to Napoleon, Bernadotte was almost round and behind his northern flank. Napoleon decided on a direct, followed by an indirect, approach—first, to crush Blücher and then to cut Schwarzenberg's communications with Bohemia. In the light of historical experience as set forth in earlier pages, it would seem that the sequence was at fault. Napoleon's direct move on Blücher did not bring the latter to battle. Yet it had one curious result, all the more significant because it was unpremeditated. The direct move upon Blücher was, quite unrealized, an indirect move upon Bernadotte's rear. By unnerving Bernadotte, it led him to fall back hurriedly northward, and so removed him from Napoleon's line of retreat. Thereby this 'blow in the air' at Blücher saved Napoleon from utter disaster a few days later. For when Blücher and Schwarzenberg closed in upon him at Leipzig, Napoleon accepted the gage of battle and suffered defeat—but, in his extremity, still had a path by which he could extricate himself, and withdraw safely to France.

In 1814, the Allies, now vastly superior in numbers, made their converging invasion of France. Napoleon was driven, for want of the numbers he had expended—through his imperial faith in the power of mass—to resharpen his old weapons of surprise and mobility. Nevertheless, brilliant as was his handling of them, he was too impatient, and too obsessed with the idea of battle, to use them with the artistic subtlety of a Hannibal or a Scipio, a Cromwell or a Marlborough.

By their use, however, he long postponed his fate. And he made a discerning adjustment between his end and his means. Realizing that his means were too reduced to obtain him a military decision, he aimed to dislocate the co-operation between the Allied armies; and he exploited mobility more astonishingly than ever to this end. Even so, remarkable as was his success in retarding the enemy's advance, it might have been more effective and enduring if his ability to continue this strategy had not been diminished by his inherent tendency to consummate every strategic by a tactical success. By repeated concentrations—five of them marked by manœuvres which *struck* the target in rear—against the separated fractions of enemy, he inflicted a series of defeats on them; until he was rash enough to make a direct approach and attack on Blücher at Laon, and suffered a defeat that he could not afford.

With only 30,000 men left, he decided, as a last throw, to move eastward to Saint Dizier, rally such garrisons as he could find, and raise the countryside against the invaders. By this move he would be across Schwarzenberg's communications. He had, however, not only to place himself on the enemy's rear but to raise an army there before he could act. The problem was complicated not only by lack of time and lack of force, but by the peculiar moral sensitiveness of the base he thereby uncovered. For Paris was not like an ordinary base of supply. As a crowning mishap, his orders fell into the enemy's hands, so that both surprise and time were forfeited. Even then, so potent was the strategic 'pull' of his manœuvre, it was only after heated debate that the Allies resolved to move into Paris, instead of turning back to counter his move. Their move proved to be a moral 'knock-out' for Napoleon's cause. It has been said that the factor which most influenced their decision was the fear that Wellington, moving up from the Spanish frontier, would reach Paris first. If this be true, it forms an ironical final triumph for the strategy of indirect approach and its decisive 'pull'.

In 1815, after his return from Elba, the size of Napoleon's forces seems to have sent the blood to his head again. Nevertheless, in his own fashion he used both surprise and mobility, and in consequence came within reach of a decisive result. While his approach to the armies of Blücher and Wellington was geographically direct, its timing was a surprise and its direction dislocated the enemy's 'joint'. But, at Ligny, Ney failed to carry out the manœuvre role allotted to him—the tactical indirect approach—so that the Prussians escaped decisive defeat. And when Napoleon turned on Wellington at Waterloo his approach was purely direct, thus entailing a loss of time, and of men, which accentuated the greater trouble caused by Gouchy's failure to keep Blücher 'distracted' well away from the battlefield. Thus Blücher's appearance, even though he merely arrived on Napoleon's flank, was by its unexpectedness a psychological indirect approach—and as such was decisive.

CHAPTER IX

1854-1914

★

When the great 'Peace' Exhibition of 1851 ushered in a fresh era of bellicosity, the first war of the new series was as indecisive in its military course as in its political end. Yet from the squalor and stupidity of the Crimean War we can at least cull negative lessons. Chief among them is the barrenness of the direct approach. When the generals wore the blinkers it was natural that an aide-de-camp should launch the Light Brigade straight at the Russians' guns. In the British army, the directness which permeated every sphere of action was so extremely precise and rigidly formal that it perplexed the French commander, Canrobert—until some years later he attended a court ball. Then light came to him, and he exclaimed: 'The British fight as Victoria dances.' But the Russians were no less deeply imbued with the instinct of directness—so that even when a spasmodic manœuvre was attempted, a regiment, after marching all day, finally found itself back facing Sebastopol as at daybreak.

In studying the depressing evidence of the Crimea we cannot overlook, although we should not exaggerate, the fact that in the forty years which had elapsed since Waterloo the armies of Europe had become more strictly professionalized. Its significance is not as an argument against professional armies, but as an illustration of the latent dangers of a professional environment. These dangers are inevitably accentuated on the higher levels, and with length of service, unless counteracted by revivifying touch with the outer world of affairs and thought. On the other hand, the early stages of the American Civil War were to reveal the weaknesses of an unprofessional army. Training is essential to forge an effective instrument for the general to handle. A long war or a short peace afford the most favourable conditions for the production of such an instrument. But there is a defect in the system if the instrument is superior to the artist.

In this, as in other aspects, the American Civil War of 1861–5 offers an illuminating contrast. The military leaders, especially in the South, were mainly drawn from those who had made arms their profession, but the pursuit of this profession had in many cases been varied with civil employment or leisure for individual study. The parade ground had not been either the breeding ground or the boundary of their strategical ideas. Nevertheless, despite a refreshing breadth of view and fertility of resource in what may be termed local strategy, the conventional aim at first ruled the major operations.

The tendency was increased by the development of railways. These provided strategy with a new speed of movement, but without an accompanying flexibility—the other essential constituent of true mobility. The American Civil War was the first war in which rail transportation played a major part, and by the fixed form of its own routes it naturally tended to make strategy run on strait and straight-forward lines.

Moreover, in this and subsequent wars, armies came to depend on the railway for their maintenance without realizing how dependent they had become. Increased ease of supply encouraged the commanders to swell their numbers—at the end of the railway line—without asking themselves what effects such numbers would have on their power of action. The result of the new means of movement was, paradoxically, to reduce mobility rather than increase it. The railway fostered the expansion of armies—it could forward more men, and feed them, than could fight effectively. It fostered their wants, and they became tied to the railhead. At the same time their sustenance 'hung on a thread'—the long stretch of the rail-line behind, which was very vulnerable.

These effects were seen early in the American Civil War, and became very marked by 1864. The Union armies being accustomed to ampler feeding, were more susceptible to paralysis than their opponents. In the Western theatre, especially, the dangers of a rail-fed mass were exposed by the mobile raids of such brilliant Confederate cavalry leaders as Forrest and Morgan. (It was a foreshadowing of the future—when the communications of mass armies could be reached by air and tank forces.) Eventually, the North found in Sherman a strategist who diagnosed the sources of trouble more clearly than any other of his time, or later—until the new school of thought after World War I who became the pioneers of mechanized mobile warfare. The enemy had struck at Sherman

Stanford, London

through his railways; he would strike at them through theirs, after immunizing himself. To regain an adequate power of strategic manoeuvre, and exercise it without danger of a sudden paralytic stroke, he saw that he must free himself from a fixed line of supply, which meant that he must move self-contained, and this in turn meant that he must reduce 'requirements' to the barest necessities, In other words, the way to avoid being trapped by the tail was to coil up his tail and carry it under his arm while making each long bound. So, having cut down impedimenta to the minimum, he cut loose from his own rail communications, and marched through the 'back door of the Confederacy' to cut the lines which fed its main army and wreck its supply system at the source. The effect was dramatically decisive.

The American Civil War

In the opening campaign the opposing armies sought each other in a direct advance. The result was indecisive alike in Virginia and in Missouri. Then McClellan, appointed to the command-in-chief of the North, in 1862 conceived the plan of utilizing sea-power to transfer his army on to the enemy's strategic flank. This had richer prospects than a direct overland advance, but seems to have been conceived more as the means of a shorter direct approach to Richmond, the enemy's capital, than as an indirect approach in the true sense. Its prospects were nullified by President Lincoln's reluctance to accept a calculated risk—in consequence of which he kept back McDowell's corps for the direct protection of Washington. This deprived McClellan not only of part of his strength but of the element of distraction essential to the success of his plan.

Hence, on landing, McClellan lost a month in front of Yorktown, and the plan had to be altered to a convergent or semi-direct approach in conjunction with McDowell, who was only allowed to advance overland along the direct approach from Washington to Richmond. 'Stonewall' Jackson's indirect operations in the Shenandoah Valley then exerted such a moral influence on the Washington Government as again to suspend McDowell's share in the main advance. Even so, McClellan's advanced troops were within four miles of Richmond, ready for the final spring, before Lee was sufficiently strong to intervene. And even after McClellan's tactical setback in the Seven Days' Battles, he had the strategical advantage—perhaps a greater one than in the previous phase. For the interruption of his flank march had not prevented him switching his base southwards to the James River, whereby he had not only secured his own communications but placed himself dangerously close to the enemy's communications running southward from Richmond.

The advantage was forfeited by a change of strategy. Halleck, placed over McClellan's head from political motives as general-in-chief, ordered McClellan's army to be re-embarked and withdrawn northward to unite with Pope's army in a direct overland advance. As so often in history, a direct doubling of strength meant not a doubling but a halving of the effect—through simplifying the enemy's 'lines of expectation'. Yet Halleck's strategy fulfilled the obvious interpretation of the principle of concentration—thereby revealing the pitfalls which underlie this conventional path to the military goal. The ineffectiveness of the strategy of direct approach which ruled throughout the second half of 1862 was appropriately sealed by the bloody repulse at Fredericksburg on the 13th December. And the continuance of this strategy in 1863 led, not to a closer approach to Richmond, but to a Confederate invasion of Northern territory—following the collapse of the Union army's offensive.

Initially this invasion had a strategical indirectness, physically and psychologically, but lost this effect when Lee became drawn into an increasingly direct assault on Meade's position at Gettysburg—an assault in which he persisted until, by the third day, he had lost nearly half his strength. The close of the year saw both armies back in their original positions, both too drained of blood to do more than bare their teeth at each other across the Rapidan and Rappahannock.

It is significant that in these campaigns of mutual direct approach, such advantage as there was inclined in turn to the side which stood on the defensive, content to counter the other's advance. For in such strategical conditions the defensive, by its mere avoidance of vain effort, is inherently the less direct form of two direct strategies.

The repulse of Lee's invasion at Gettysburg has commonly been acclaimed the turning-point of the war, but the claim is only justified in a dramatic sense. The sober verdict of historical opinion has more and more emphasized that the decisive effects came from the West.

The first was as early as April 1862, when Farragut's squadron ran past the forts guarding the mouth of the Mississippi, and thereby gained the bloodless surrender of New Orleans. It was the thin end of a strategical wedge which split the Confederacy up the vital line of this great river.

The second decisive effect was achieved higher up the Mississippi on the same day (the 4th July) as Lee began his retreat from the battlefield of Gettysburg. This was the capture of Vicksburg by Grant, which gave the Union complete control of this vital artery. Thereby the Confederacy was deprived permanently of the nourishment of reinforcements and supplies from the Trans-Mississippi states. But the grand-strategic effect of this concentration against the junior partner should not be allowed to overshadow the strategic means by which it was achieved. The first advance on Vicksburg—in December 1862—had been made by an overland route down the railway, combined with a waterborne expedition under Sherman down the Mississippi. When Grant's advance was hamstrung by Confederate cavalry raids on his communications, the Confederate forces were able to concentrate against Sherman's move, which thus became an essentially direct approach—and was repulsed without difficulty when he tried to make a landing close to Vicksburg.

In February and March 1863, four unsuccessful attempts were made to reach the goal by narrow outflanking manœuvres. Then, in April, Grant resorted to a truly indirect approach which had a likeness, not merely in its audacity, to Wolfe's final bid for Quebec. Part of the Union fleet and transports ran southward past the Vicksburg batteries, by night, to a point thirty miles below the fortress. The bulk of the army moved thither overland, by the west bank of the Mississippi; and, under cover of Sherman's distracting movements towards the north-east of Vicksburg, it was transported to the east bank in face of weak opposition. Then, when Sherman rejoined him, Grant took the calculated risk of cutting himself loose from his new temporary base and moving north-eastward into the enemy's territory to place himself on the rear of Vicksburg, and astride its communications with the main Eastern states of the Confederacy. In this manœuvre he made almost a complete circuit from his starting-point. He thus appeared to put himself midway between the enemy's upper and lower jaws —their two forces which were concentrating, respectively, at Vicksburg and at Jackson, forty miles to the east (Jackson was the junction of a lateral north and south railway with the main east and west line). But in reality he dislocated the action of these jaws.

It is worth while to note that, on arriving at this railway, he found it advisable first to move his whole army eastward to compel the enemy to evacuate Jackson. This illustrated the change in strategical conditions brought about by the development of railways. For while Napoleon had used the line of a river or a range of hills as his strategic barrage, Grant's strategic barrage was constituted by the possession of a single point—a railway junction. Once this was secured, he turned about and moved on Vicksburg, which was now isolated, and remained isolated long enough to ensure its capitulation seven weeks later. The strategic sequel was the opening of the Chattanooga gateway into Georgia, the granary of the Confederacy, and thence into the Eastern states as a whole.

Defeat was now hardly avoidable by the Confederacy. Yet the Union almost forfeited the victory already ensured. For in 1864, with the North growing weary under the strain, the moral element became preponderant. The peace party was daily swelled from the ranks of the war-weary, the presidential election was due in November, and unless Lincoln was to be supplanted by a president pledged to seek a compromise peace, a solid guarantee of early victory must be forthcoming. To this end, Grant was summoned from the west to take over the supreme command. How did he seek to gain the required early victory? By reverting to the strategy which good orthodox soldiers always adopt—that of using his immensely superior weight to smash the opposing army, or at least to wear it down by a 'continuous hammering'. We have seen that in the Vicksburg campaign he had only adopted the true indirect approach after repeated direct approaches had failed. He had then brought it off with masterly skill—but the underlying lesson had not impressed itself sufficiently on his mind.

Now, in supreme command, he was true to his nature. He decided on the old and direct overland approach southward from the Rappahannock, towards Richmond. But with a certain difference of aim—for the enemy's army rather than the enemy's capital was his real objective. He directed his subordinate, Meade, that 'wherever Lee goes, there you will go too'. In justice to Grant, it should also be noted that if his approach was direct in the broad sense, it was in no sense a mere frontal push. Indeed, he continuously sought to turn his enemy's flanks by manœuvre, if manœuvre of a narrow radius. Further, he fulfilled all the military precepts about keeping his army well concentrated and maintaining his objective undeterred by alarms elsewhere. Even a Foch could not have surpassed his 'will to victory'. And those who practised a similar method in 1914–18 might have felt envy of him for the generous support given, and unfailing confidence shown, by his political chief. It would be hard to find conditions more ideal for the orthodox strategy of direct approach in its best manner.

Yet by the end of the summer of 1864 the ripe fruit of victory had withered in his hands. The Union forces had almost reached the end of their endurance, and Lincoln despaired of re-election—a sorry repayment for the blank cheque he had given his military executant. It is an ironical reflection that the determination with which Grant had wielded his superior masses, now fearfully shrunk after the fierce battles of the Wilderness and Cold Harbor, had utterly failed to crush the enemy's army, while the chief result—the geographical advantage of having worked round close to the rear of Richmond—was gained by the bloodless manœuvres which had punctuated his advance. He had thus the modified satisfaction of being back, after immense loss, in the position which McClellan had occupied in 1862.

But when the sky looked blackest it suddenly lightened. At the November elections, Lincoln was returned to power. What factor came to the rescue, and averted the probability that McClellan, the nominee of the peace-desiring Democratic party, would replace him? Not Grant's campaign, which made practically no progress between July and December, and definitely petered out with a costly double failure in mid-October. By the verdict of historians, Sherman's capture of Atlanta in September was the instrument of salvation.

When Grant had been called to the supreme command, Sherman, who had played no small part in his Vicksburg success, had succeeded him in the chief command in the west. Between the two there was a contrast of outlook. While Grant took the opposing army as his primary objective, Sherman's method was to threaten strategic points in such a way as to make the opposing army uncover itself in trying to cover them, or else abandon them in order to keep its own balance. Thus he always had an alternative aim, although in the outcome it was the second which he achieved—with far-reaching effect. Atlanta, the base of the army opposing him, was not only the junction of four important railways, but the source of vital supplies. As Sherman pointed out, it was 'full of foundries, arsenals and machine shops', besides being a moral symbol; he argued that 'its capture would be the death-knell of the Confederacy'.

Whatever divergence of opinion may exist as to the respective merits of Grant's objective and Sherman's, it is obvious that the latter is better suited to the psychology of a democracy. Perhaps only an absolute ruler, firmly in the saddle, can hope to maintain unswervingly the military ideal of the 'armed forces' objective—even he would be wise to adjust it to the realities of the situation, and to weigh the prospects of fulfilling it. But the strategist who is the servant of a democratic government has less rein. Dependent on the support and confidence of his employers, he has to work with a narrower margin of time and cost than the 'absolute' strategist, and is more pressed for quick profits. Whatever the ultimate prospects he cannot afford to postpone dividends too long. Hence it may be necessary for him to swerve aside temporarily from his objective, or at least to give it a new guise by changing his line of operations. Faced with these inevitable handicaps, it is fitting to ask whether military theory should not be more ready to reconcile its ideals with the inconvenient reality that its military effort rests on a popular foundation—that for the supply of men and munitions, and even for the chance of continuing to fight at all, it depends on the consent of the 'man in the street'. He who pays the piper calls the tune, and strategists might be better paid in kind if they attuned their strategy, so far as is rightly possible, to the popular ear.

Sherman's economy of force by manœuvre is the more notable because, compared with Grant in Virginia, he was practically tied to one line of railway for his supplies. Yet, rather than commit his troops to a direct attack, he cut loose temporarily even from this line of supply. Only once in all these weeks of manœuvre did he attempt a frontal attack, at Kenesaw Mountain; and it is as significant that he did it to save his troops from the strain of a further flank march over rain-swamped roads as that it suffered a repulse—which was mitigated because this attack was stopped immediately after the first check. This, indeed, was the only occasion during the whole 130-mile advance through mountainous and river-intersected country that Sherman committed his troops to an offensive battle. Instead, he manœuvred so skilfully as to lure the Confederates time after time into vain attacks upon him—attacks that were foiled by the way that his offensive moves were combined with a highly developed technique of quick entrenching and breast-work building. From each enemy failure to pierce his mobile shield he drew the strategic advantage of a fresh vantage point gained. To force an opponent acting on the strategic defensive into such a succession of costly tactical offensives was an example of strategic artistry rarely seen in history. It was all the more remarkable because of the way Sherman was tied to a single line of communications. Even from the narrowest military criterion, ignoring its immense moral and economic effect, it was a great feat; for Sherman inflicted more casualties than he suffered, not merely relatively but actually—in striking comparison with Grant in Virginia.

After gaining Atlanta, Sherman took a risk greater than ever before, and for which he has been much criticized by military commentators. He was convinced that if he could march through, and ruin the railway system of, Georgia—the 'granary of the South'—and then march through the Carolinas—the heart of the South—the moral impression of this invasion, and the stoppage of supplies going north to Richmond and Lee's army, would cause the collapse of the Confederates' resistance.

Hence, ignoring Hood's army, which he had forced to evacuate Atlanta, he began his famous 'march to the sea' through Georgia, living on the country while he destroyed the railways. On the 15th November 1864, he left Atlanta; on the 10th December he reached the outskirts of Savannah, and there reopened his communications—this time, by sea. To cite the verdict of the Confederate general, and historian, Alexander—'There is no question that the moral effect of this march upon the country at large . . . was greater than would have been the most decided victory.' Sherman then moved northwards through the Carolinas towards Lee's rear, depriving the South of its chief remaining ports.

Sherman's operational methods deserve more detailed examination. For the march through Georgia he had not only cut loose from his communications but had cut down all impedimenta so drastically that his army became a huge 'flying column' of light troops, sixty thousand strong. Each of his four corps was self-contained, and the foraging parties acted as a wide-flung screen across the front and flanks of the marching columns.

Moreover, in this march Sherman developed a new strategic practice. In the Atlanta campaign he had been handicapped, as he realized, by having a single geographical objective, thus simplifying the opponent's task in trying to parry his thrusts. This limitation Sherman now ingeniously planned to avoid by placing the opponent repeatedly 'on the horns of a dilemma'—the phrase he used to express his aim. He took a line of advance which kept the Confederates in doubt, first, whether Macon or Augusta, and then whether Augusta or Savannah was his objective. And while Sherman had his preference, he was ready to take the alternative objective if conditions favoured the change. The need did not arise, thanks to the uncertainty caused by his deceptive direction.

Having proved in the march through Georgia how light an army could move, Sherman now proved that it could move lighter still. Prior to starting northward, through the Carolinas, he sought to convert his army 'into a mobile machine willing and able to start at a moment's notice and to subsist on the scantiest of food'. Although it was winter, even the officers were now made to bivouac in pairs under a strip of canvas stretched over sticks or boughs; all tents and camp furniture were discarded.

Once more Sherman took a deceptive line between alternative objectives, so that his opponents could not decide whether to cover Augusta or Charleston, and their forces became divided. Then, after he had ignored both points and swept between them to gain Columbia—the capital of South Carolina and the centre of Lee's best source of supply—the Confederates were kept in uncertainty as to whether Sherman was aiming for Charlotte or Fayetteville. And when in turn he advanced from Fayetteville they could not tell whether Raleigh or Goldsborough was his next, and final, objective. He himself had not been certain whether it would be Goldsborough or Wilmington!

In the physical and moral effect of this deceptive direction lies the only reasonable explanation of his unchecked progress across 425 miles of country strewn with obstacles—rivers, creeks and swamps—and in face of an enemy whose numerical strength was ample for effective resistance. To the irresistibility of this progress Sherman's flexibility contributed almost as much as his variability of direction. Moving on a wide and irregular front—with four, five, or six columns, each covered by a cloud of foragers—if one was blocked, others would be pushing on. In effect, as in method, they were the forerunners of the panzer forces which swept through France in 1940. The opposing troops became so 'jumpy' that they repeatedly gave way to this moral pressure, and fell back before they felt any serious physical pressure—their minds so saturated with the impression of Sherman's manœuvring power that whenever they took up a position of resistance they were thinking about their way of retreat. It is even recorded that the shout, 'We're Bill Sherman's raiders—you'd better git', sufficed as a hint on occasions. If confidence be half the battle, then to undermine the opponent's confidence is more than half—because it gains the fruits without a fight. Sherman might claim, as truly as Napoleon in Austria—'I have destroyed the enemy merely by marches'.

On the 22nd March Sherman reached Goldsborough, where he was met by supplies and by Schofield's force, and refitted in readiness for the final stage of closing in on Lee, who still clung to Richmond.

Not until the beginning of April did Grant resume his advance. This obtained a dramatic success, and the surrender of Richmond was followed within a week by the surrender of Lee's army. Superficially, it was a triumphant vindication of Grant's direct strategy and 'battle' objective. But, for a serious judgement, the time factor is all important. The collapse of the Confederate resistance was due to the emptiness of its stomach reacting on its morale and to 'news from home'. Before Sherman had even reached Goldsborough Grant was able to write: 'Lee's army is now demoralized and deserting very fast'.

Man has two supreme loyalties—to country and to family. And with most men the second, being more personal, is the stronger. So long as their families are safe they will defend their country, believing that by their sacrifice they are safeguarding their families also. But even the bonds of patriotism, discipline, and comradeship are loosened when the family is itself menaced. It was the supreme deadliness of Sherman's rear attack—against the rear of a people, not merely of an army—that it set the two loyalties in opposition, and so imposed a breaking strain on the will of the soldier.

The indirect approach to the enemy's economic and moral rear had proved as decisive in the ultimate phase as it had been in the successive steps by which that decision was prepared in the west. The truth comes home to anyone who undertakes a careful and comprehensive study of the war. It was appreciated more than thirty years ago by the future British official historian of the First World War, General Edmonds, who in his history of the American Civil War reached the conclusion that:

'The military genius of the great confederate leaders, Lee and Jackson, the unrivalled fighting capacity of the Army of Northern Virginia, and the close proximity of the rival capitals, have caused a disproportionate attention to be concentrated upon the eastern theatre of war. It was in the west that the decisive blows were struck. The capture of Vicksburg and Port Hudson in July 1863 was the real turning point of the war, and it was the operations of Sherman's Grand Army of the West which really led to the collapse of the Confederacy at Appomattox Court House'—the site of Lee's surrender in the east.

The disproportionate attention may be traced partly to the glamour of battle which hypnotizes most students of military history, and partly to the spell cast by Henderson's epic biography of Stonewall Jackson—more epic than history. The distinctive military value of this book is scarcely reduced, and even enriched, through embodying more of Henderson's conception of war than of Jackson's execution. But by the interest it created in the American Civil War it focused the attentions of British military students on the campaigns in Virginia, to the neglect of the western theatres—where the decisive acts took place. A modern historian might render a service to future generations if he were to analyse the effect of this 'disproportionate attention', not merely one-sided but fallacious, upon British military thought before 1914, and British strategy in 1914–18.

Moltke's Campaigns

When the analyst passes from the American Civil War to the wars in Europe which followed on its heels, he is likely to be impressed above all by the sharpness of its contrasts.

The first contrast is that in 1866 and 1870 both sides were, nominally at least, prepared for the conflict. The second, that the contestants were professional armies. The third, that the higher commands made more flagrant mistakes and miscalculations than either side in the American Civil War. The fourth, that the strategy adopted by the Germans in both wars was lacking in art and subtlety. The fifth, that, despite the deficiency, the issue was quickly decided.

Moltke's strategy was, in design, that of a direct approach with little trace of guile, relying on the sheer smashing power of a superior concentration of force. Are we to conclude that these two wars are the proverbial exceptions which prove the rule? They are certainly exceptional, but hardly exceptions to the rule that has emerged from the long list of cases already examined. For in none of them were inferiority of force and stupidity of mind so markedly combined in the scale of the defeated side, weighing it down from the outset.

In 1866, the Austrians' inferiority of force rested primarily in the fact of having an inferior weapon. For the Prussians' breech-loading rifle gave them an advantage over the Austrians' muzzle-loader which the battlefield amply proved, even if academic military thought in the next generation tended to overlook it. In 1870, the French inferiority of force lay partly in their inferior numbers and partly, as with the Austrians of 1866, in their inferior training.

These conditions are more than adequate to explain the decisiveness of the Austrian defeat in 1866 and, still more, the French defeat in 1870. In preparation for war, any strategist would be rash to base his plans on the supposition that his enemy would be as weak in brain and body as the Austrians of 1866 and the French in 1870.

At the same time, it is significant that the German strategy, in both cases, was less direct in execution than in conception. Moreover, it had a most notable flexibility.

In 1866, the need to save time by using all available railways led Moltke to detrain the Prussian forces on a widely extended front of over 250 miles. His intention was, by a rapid advance, converging inward through the frontier mountain belt, to unite his armies in northern Bohemia. But the loss of time due to the King of Prussia's reluctance to appear the aggressor frustrated this intention—and thereby endowed Moltke's strategy with an indirectness of effect that he had not planned. For the Austrian army concentrated and pushed forward in the interval, thus depriving Moltke of his desired concentration area. And the Prussian Crown Prince, believing that the projecting province of Silesia was menaced, wrung from Moltke a reluctant sanction to move his army south-eastwards to safeguard Silesia. Thereby he separated himself further from the other armies; and thereby also he put himself in a position to menace the flank and rear of the Austrian mass. Pedants have spilled much ink in condemning Moltke for sanctioning this wide extension; in reality, it scattered the seeds of a decisive victory, even though he had not sown them deliberately.

These dispositions so disturbed the mental balance of the

CENTRAL EUROPE
Miles
0 20 40 60 80 100 200
Bremen
Rotterdam
R. Rhine
Antwerp
Bruges
Ghent
Brussels
Oudenarde
Louvain
Maastricht
Tournai
Waterloo
Ramillies
Bethune
La Bassée
Liége
Agincourt
Huy
Douai
Namur
Mons
Coblenz
Crecy
Valenciennes
Denain
Amiens
ARDENNES
R. Moselle
Sedan
Rouen
Laon
Mannheim
Thionville
R. Saar
Reims
Philippsburg
Paris
Gravelotte
Metz
Weissenburg
Vionville
St. Dizier
Meuse
Dettweiler
Sasbach
Strassburg
R. Seine
BLACK FOREST
R. Neckar
Turkheim
Colmar
Enzheim
Loire
Mülhausen
Tours
VOSGES
Belfort
Zurich
Lucerne
Limoges
ST. BERNARD
Lyons
Ivrea
Milan
Turin
Valenza
Rivoli
Alessandria
Tortona
PIEDMONT
Marengo
R. Rhone
Cherasco
Genoa
GULF OF GENOA
Nimes
Longitude E 10

Lubeck
Hamburg
R. Elbe
Berlin
Zorndorf
Kunersdorf
Posen
R. Oder
Düben
Torgau
SAXONY
Leipzig
Lützen
Dresden
Maxen
Bautzen
Leuthen
SILESIA
Jena
Leitmeritz
Königgratz
Prague
Kolin
BOHEMIA
Olmütz
Nüremberg
Brunn
Austerlitz
BAVARIA
Ingolstadt
Blenheim
Augsburg
Dilligen
R. Danube
Krems
Hollabrunn
Vienna
Buda-Pest
R. Lech
R. Inn
TYROL
R. Adige
Trent
Bassano
Trieste
Arcola
Verona
Mantua
Venice
R. Po
ADRIATIC SEA
of Greenwich
Stanford, London

Austrian command that the Prussians, despite a prodigal series of blunders, were able, first to get through the mountains on both sides, and then to reap the harvest at Königgrätz—where more blunders contributed to the indirectness, and hence the decisiveness of their approach. The Austrian commander, indeed, was beaten before the battle opened: he had telegraphed to his Emperor urging an immediate peace.

It is worth note that Moltke's far-stretched assembly of his forces proved to have more flexibility than the Austrians' concentration on a front of forty miles—which gave them the apparent advantage of being able to operate on 'interior lines'. It should also be mentioned that, although Moltke's intention had been to concentrate his forces before the enemy was met, this was not with the aim of delivering a direct attack. His original plan had two branches. If exploration were to show that the Austrians' supposed position behind the Elbe at Josefstadt was insecure, the Crown Prince's army was to side-step eastwards and take it in flank, while the other two armies pinned it in front. If an attack seemed impracticable, all three armies were to circle westward, cross the Elbe at Pardubitz, and then, swinging east, menace the enemy's communications with the south. In the event, however, the Austrians were found to be on the near side of the Elbe, having concentrated further forward than Moltke expected—so that the Crown Prince's direction of advance automatically turned their flank, and brought about their envelopment.

In 1870, Moltke had intended to bring about a decisive battle on the Saar, in which all his three armies would concentrate on and pulverize the French. This plan was upset—not by the enemy's action, but by their paralysis. This paralysis was caused by the mere news that the German Third Army, on the extreme left, had crossed the frontier far to the east and won a minor tactical success over a French detachment at Weissenburg. Pressing ahead, it then enveloped and routed—in a confused battle at Woerth—the flank corps of the French right wing, before the rest came on the scene. In the outcome, the indirect effect of this partial and detached engagement was more decisive than the intended great battle would probably have been. For, instead of being wheeled inwards to augment the main mass, the Third Army was allowed to pursue its course along an open path well outside the zone of the main opposing armies. Thus it took no part in the blundering battles of

Vionville and Gravelotte—the position of the French was such that it could hardly have taken an effective part if it had been nearer. And it thereby became the vital factor in the next, and decisive, phase.

For when the French main army—stimulated rather than depressed by the result of the battle of Gravelotte—fell back to a flank, into Metz, it might easily have slipped away from the exhausted German First and Second armies. But the likelihood of interception by the Third Army was an inducement to Bazaine to stay securely in Metz. Thus the Germans had time to recover cohesion; the French, time to lose it, in the inactivity which followed their abandonment of the open field. In consequence, MacMahon was enticed—or, rather, politically pressed—into his ill-advised and worse-conducted move to the relief of Metz.

Thus, unintended and unforeseen, was created the opportunity for the German Third Army, still marching free towards Paris, to make an indirect approach to MacMahon's army. Making a complete change of direction from westward to northward, it moved round the flank and rear of MacMahon. That move resulted in his army being trapped and forced to surrender at Sedan.

There was more indirectness in the decisive phase than a superficial view would suggest. But it was the superficial, not the underlying deduction, that influenced the mass of military theorizing which followed 1870. This influence dominated the next large-scale war—between Russia and Japan in 1904-5.

The Russo-Japanese War

The Japanese strategy, following its German mentors, was essentially that of a direct approach. There was no real attempt to take advantage of the unusually advantageous condition that the Russian war-effort was entirely dependent on a single line of railway—the Trans-Siberian. Never in all history has an army drawn breath through so long and narrow a windpipe, and the very size of its body made its breathing more difficult. But all that Japan's strategists contemplated was a direct blow at, and into, the teeth of the Russian army. And they held their own forces more closely grouped than those of Moltke in 1870. It is true that they attempted a certain convergence of approach before Liao-Yang, and subsequently, on making contact, sought repeatedly to outflank their opponent; but if these outflanking movements look comparatively wide on the map they were extremely narrow in proportion to the scale of the forces. Although they had no 'free' army as it was Moltke's good fortune to have, no unintended bait such as Metz, and no MacMahon to swallow it—for they had swallowed their own bait in taking Port Arthur—they hoped for a Sedan. Instead, there was an abundance of indecisive bloodshed. As a result, they were so exhausted after the final indecisive battle of Mukden that they were glad, and lucky, to make peace with a foe who had no heart in the struggle, and had not yet put one-tenth of his available forces into it.

This survey and analysis of history is concerned with facts and not with conjectures—with what was done, and its result, not with what might have been done. The theory of the indirect approach which has evolved from it must rest on the concrete evidence of actual experience that the direct approach tends to be indecisive. It is not affected by arguments for or against the difficulties of making an indirect approach in a particular case. From the standpoint of the basic thesis it is irrelevant whether a general could have taken, or could have done better by taking, a different course.

For the general service of military knowledge, however, speculation is always of interest, and often of value. So, diverging from the direct path of this study, one may point out the potential parallel between Port Arthur and Mantua—while taking account of the handicaps which the Japanese suffered in the scanty communications and difficult country of Korea and Manchuria. If conditions were harder in some ways, they were more advantageous in others—and the instrument better. Thus reflection prompts the question whether, in the earlier phase of the war, Japanese strategy might not with any advantage have exploited the bait of Port Arthur in the way that Bonaparte exploited Mantua. And, in the later phase, there would seem to have been scope for using at least a proportion of the Japanese forces against the slender Russian windpipe between Harbin and Mukden.

CHAPTER X

CONCLUSIONS FROM TWENTY-FIVE CENTURIES

★

This survey has covered twelve wars which decisively affected the course of European history in ancient times, and the eighteen major wars of modern history up to 1914—counting as one the struggle against Napoleon which, temporarily damped down in one place, burst out afresh in another with no real intermission. These thirty conflicts embraced more than two hundred and eighty campaigns. In only six of these campaigns—those which culminated at Issus, Gaugamela, Friedland, Wagram, Sadowa, and Sedan—did a decisive result follow a plan of direct strategic approach to the main army of the enemy.

In the first two of these, Alexander's advance was prepared by a grand-strategy of indirect approach, which had seriously shaken the Persian empire and its adherents' confidence. Moreover, his success in any battlefield test was virtually guaranteed by the possession of a tactical instrument of greatly superior quality, applied in a technique of tactical indirect approach.

In the next two cases, Napoleon had each time begun by attempting an indirect approach, while his resort to direct attack was due in part to his impatience, and in part to his confidence in the superiority of his instrument. This superiority was based on his use of massed artillery against a key point, and at both Friedland and Wagram the decision was primarily due to this new tactical method. But the price paid for these successes, and its ultimate effect on Napoleon's own fortunes, do not encourage a resort to similar directness even with a similar tactical superiority.

As for 1866 and 1870, we have seen that although both campaigns were conceived as direct approaches, they acquired an unintended indirectness—which was reinforced by the Germans' tactical superiority in each case; a superiority assured by the breech-loader in 1866, and by superior artillery in 1870.

These six campaigns, when analysed, provide little justification for the adoption of direct methods in strategy. Throughout history, however, the direct approach has been normal, and a purposeful indirect approach the exception. It is significant, too, how often generals have adopted the latter, not as their initial strategy, but as a last resource. Yet it has brought them a decision where the direct approach had brought them failure—and thereby left them in a weakened condition to attempt the indirect. A decisive success obtained in such deteriorated conditions acquires all the greater significance.

The survey has revealed a large number of campaigns in which the indirectness of approach is as manifest as the decisiveness of the issue—among them those of Lysander in the Aegean, 405 B.C.; Epaminondas in the Peloponnese, 362 B.C.; Philip in Boeotia, 338 B.C.; Alexander on the Hydaspes; Cassander and Lysimachus in the Near East, 302 B.C.; Hannibal's Trasimene campaign in Etruria; Scipio's Utica and Zama campaigns in Africa; Caesar's Ilerda campaign in Spain; and, in modern history, Cromwell's Preston, Dunbar, and Worcester campaigns; Turenne's Alsace campaign of 1674–5; Eugène's Italian campaign of 1701; Marlborough's Flanders campaign of 1708, and Villars's of 1712; Wolfe's Quebec campaign; Jourdan's Moselle-Meuse campaigns of 1794; the Archduke Charles's Rhine-Danube campaigns of 1796; Bonaparte's Italian campaigns of 1796, 1797, and 1800; his Ulm and Austerlitz campaigns of 1805; Grant's Vicksburg and Sherman's Atlanta campaigns. In addition, the survey has brought out numerous border-line examples in which either the indirectness or its effect are less clearly established.

This high proportion of history's decisive campaigns, the significance of which is enhanced by the comparative rarity of the direct approach, enforces the conclusion that the indirect is by far the most hopeful and economic form of strategy.

Can we draw even more specific deductions from history? Yes. With the exception of Alexander, the most consistently successful commanders when faced by an enemy in a position that was strong naturally or materially, have hardly ever tackled it in a direct way. And when, under pressure of circumstances, they have risked a direct attack, the result has commonly been to blot their record with a failure.

Further, history shows that rather than resign himself to a direct approach, a Great Captain will take even the most hazardous indirect approach—if necessary over mountains, deserts or swamps, with only a fraction of force, even cutting himself loose from his communications. He prefers to face any unfavourable condition rather than accept the risk of frustration inherent in a direct approach.

Natural hazards, however formidable, are inherently less dangerous and less uncertain than fighting hazards. All conditions are more calculable, all obstacles more surmountable, than those of human resistance. By reasoned calculation and preparation they can be overcome almost to timetable. While Napoleon was able to cross the Alps in 1800 'according to plan', the little fort of Bard could interfere so seriously with the movement of his army as to endanger his whole plan.

Turning now to reverse the sequence of our examination, and surveying in turn, the decisive battles of history, we find that in almost all the victor had his opponent at a psychological disadvantage before the clash took place. Examples are Marathon, Salamis, Aegospotamoi, Mantinea, Chaeronea, Gaugamela (through grand strategy), the Hydaspes, Ipsus, Trasimene, Cannae, Metaurus, Zama, Tricameron, Taginae, Hastings, Preston, Dunbar, Worcester, Blenheim, Oudenarde, Denain, Quebec, Fleurus, Rivoli, Austerlitz, Jena, Vicksburg, Königgrätz, Sedan.

Combining the strategical and the tactical examination, we find that most of the examples fall into one of two categories. They were produced either by a strategy of elastic defence—calculated withdrawal—that was capped by a tactical offensive, or by a strategy of offence, aimed to place oneself in a position 'upsetting' to the opponent, and capped by a tactical defensive: with a sting in the tail. Either compound forms an indirect approach, and the psychological basis of both can be expressed in the words 'lure' and 'trap'.

Indeed, it might even be said, in a deeper and wider sense than Clausewitz implied, that the defensive is the stronger form of strategy as well as the more economical. For the second compound, although superficially and logistically an offensive move, has for its underlying motive to draw the opponent into an 'unbalanced' advance. The most effective indirect approach is one that lures or startles the opponent into a false move—so that, as in ju-jitsu, his own effort is turned into the lever of his overthrow.

In offensive strategy, the indirect approach has normally comprised a logistical military move directed against an economic target—the source of supply of either the opposing state or army. Occasionally, however, the move has been purely psychological in aim, as in some of the operations of Belisarius. Whatever the *form*, the *effect* to be sought is the dislocation of the opponent's mind and dispositions—such an effect is the true gauge of an indirect approach.

A further deduction, perhaps not positive but at least suggestive, from our survey, is that in a campaign against more than one state or army it is more fruitful to concentrate first against the weaker partner, than to attempt the overthrow of the stronger in the belief that the latter's defeat will automatically involve the collapse of the others.

In the two outstanding struggles of the ancient world, the overthrow of Persia by Alexander and of Carthage by Scipio both followed upon the severing of the roots. This grand strategy of indirect approach created not only the Macedonian and Roman empires, but the greatest of their successors, the British Empire. On it, too, was founded the fortunes and imperial power of Napoleon Bonaparte. Later still, on this foundation arose the great and solid structure of the United States.

The art of the indirect approach can only be mastered, and its full scope appreciated, by study of and reflection upon the whole history of war. But we can at least crystallize the lessons into two simple maxims—one negative, the other positive. The first is that, in face of the overwhelming evidence of history, no general is justified in launching his troops to a direct attack upon an enemy firmly in position. The second, that instead of seeking to upset the enemy's equilibrium by one's attack, it must be upset before a real attack is, or can be successfully launched.

Lenin had a vision of fundamental truth when he said that 'the soundest strategy in war is to postpone operations until the moral disintegration of the enemy renders the delivery of the mortal blow both possible and easy'. This is not always practicable, nor his methods of propaganda always fruitful. But it will bear adaptation—'The soundest strategy in any campaign is to postpone battle and the soundest tactics to postpone attack, until the moral dislocation of the enemy renders the delivery of a decisive blow practicable.'

PART II

★

STRATEGY OF THE FIRST WORLD WAR

CHAPTER XI

THE PLANS AND THEIR ISSUE IN THE WESTERN THEATRE, 1914

★

The starting-point of a survey of the Western Front campaign in World War I must be the pre-war plans. The Franco-German frontier was narrow, only some 150 miles long, and so afforded little room for the manœuvre of the masses which the conscriptive system had created and developed. At the south-eastern end the frontier abutted on Switzerland, and, after a short stretch of flat country near Belfort, ran for 70 miles along the Vosges mountains. Thence the line was prolonged by an almost continuous fortress chain based on Epinal, Toul, and Verdun; and just beyond the last-named lay the frontiers of Luxembourg and Belgium. In the resurrection and reconstruction period which followed the disasters of 1870, the French plan was that of an initial defensive, based on the frontier fortresses, to be followed by a decisive counterstroke. To this end the great fortress system along the Alsace-Lorraine frontier had been created, and gaps such as the Trouée de Charmes between Epinal and Toul had been left to canalize the expected German invasion so that the counter might be delivered with more assurance and effectiveness.

This plan was marked by a certain indirectness of approach, perhaps as much as was possible in view of the restricted frontier—without violating neutral territory.

But in the decade before 1914 a new school of thought arose, with Colonel de Grandmaison as its prophet, which denounced this plan as contrary to the French spirit and as 'an almost complete atrophy of the idea of the offensive'. The advocates of the *offensive à outrance* found in Joffre, who was appointed Chief of the General Staff in 1912, a lever for their intentions. Grasping it, they gained control of the French military machine, and, throwing over the old plan, formulated the now notorious Plan XVII. This was purely a direct approach in the form of a headlong offensive against the German centre 'with all forces united'. Yet, for this frontal and whole-front offensive, the French plan counted upon having a bare equality of strength against an enemy who would have the support of his own fortified frontier zone—while, by rushing forward, the French forswore any advantage from their own. The one concession to historical experience, and common sense, in this plan was that the fortress of Metz should be masked, not directly assaulted—the attack passing south of it into Lorraine, and north of it also. The left wing would extend the offensive into Belgian Luxembourg if the Germans violated neutral territory. By an historical paradox, the French plan drew its inspiration from a German, Clausewitz, while the German plan was far closer to the Napoleonic in origin—if still more Hannibalic.

Britain's contingent share in the French plan was settled less by calculation than by the 'Europeanization' of her military organization and thought during the previous decade. This continental influence drew her insensibly into a tacit acceptance of the role of an appendix to the French left wing, and away from her historic exploitation of the mobility given by sea-power. At the council of war on the outbreak, Sir John French, who was to command the British Expeditionary Force, expressed a doubt of 'the prearranged plan'; as an alternative, he suggested that the force should be sent to Antwerp—where it would have stiffened the Belgians' resistance and, by its mere situation, have threatened the rear flank of the German armies as they advanced through Belgium into France. But Major-General Henry Wilson, when Director of Military Operations, had virtually pledged the General Staff to act in direct conjunction with the French. The informal staff negotiations between 1905 and 1914 had paved the way for a reversal of England's centuries-old war policy.

This *fait accompli* overbore not only French's strategical idea but Haig's desire to wait until the situation was clearer and the army could be enlarged, and also Kitchener's more limited objection to assembling the expeditionary force so close to the frontier.

The final French plan was the one thing needed to make the original German plan—framed by Graf von Schlieffen in 1905—a true indirect approach. Faced by the blank wall which the French fortified frontier presented, the logical military course was to go round it—through Belgium. Schlieffen decided on this course, and to move as widely as possible. Strangely, even when the invasion of Belgium began, the French command assumed that the Germans would confine their advance to a narrower front, east of the Meuse.

Schlieffen's plan concentrated the bulk of the German forces on the right wing for this gigantic wheel. The right wing was to sweep through Belgium and northern France, and then, continuing to traverse a vast arc, would wheel gradually to the left or east. With its extreme right passing south of Paris, and crossing the Seine near Rouen, it would thus press the French back towards the Moselle, where they would be hammered in rear on the anvil formed by the Lorraine fortresses and the Swiss frontier.

The real subtlety and indirectness of the plan lay, not in this geographical detour, but in the distribution of force and in the idea which guided it. An initial surprise was sought by incorporating reserve corps with active corps at the outset in the offensive mass. Of the 72 divisions which would thus be available, 53 were allotted to the swinging mass, 10 were to form a pivot facing Verdun, and a mere 9 were to form the left wing along the French frontier. This reduction of the left wing to the slenderest possible size was shrewdly calculated to increase the effect of the swinging mass by its very weakness. For if the French should attack in Lorraine and press the left wing back towards the Rhine, it would be difficult for them to parry the German attack through Belgium, and the further they went the more difficult it would be. As with a revolving door, if the French pressed heavily on one side, the other side would swing round and strike them in the back—and the more heavily they pressed the severer would be the blow.

Geographically, Schlieffen's move through Belgium was a strategic approach of very limited indirectness—because of the density of force in relation to space. Psychologically, his design for, and distribution of force on, the left wing made it a definitely indirect approach. And the French plan made it perfect. If a ghost can chuckle, how the departed Schlieffen must have chuckled when he saw that the French did not even have to be enticed into his trap. But his chuckle must soon have changed into chagrin. For his successor, Moltke—'the younger' in family order but the older in caution—abandoned Schlieffen's plan in execution, after having already modified and marred it in pre-war preparation.

Between 1905 and 1914, as more troops became available, he increased the strength of the left wing disproportionately to the right. By making this wing safer, he made the plan unsafe, and began a continuous sapping of its foundations which ended in its collapse.

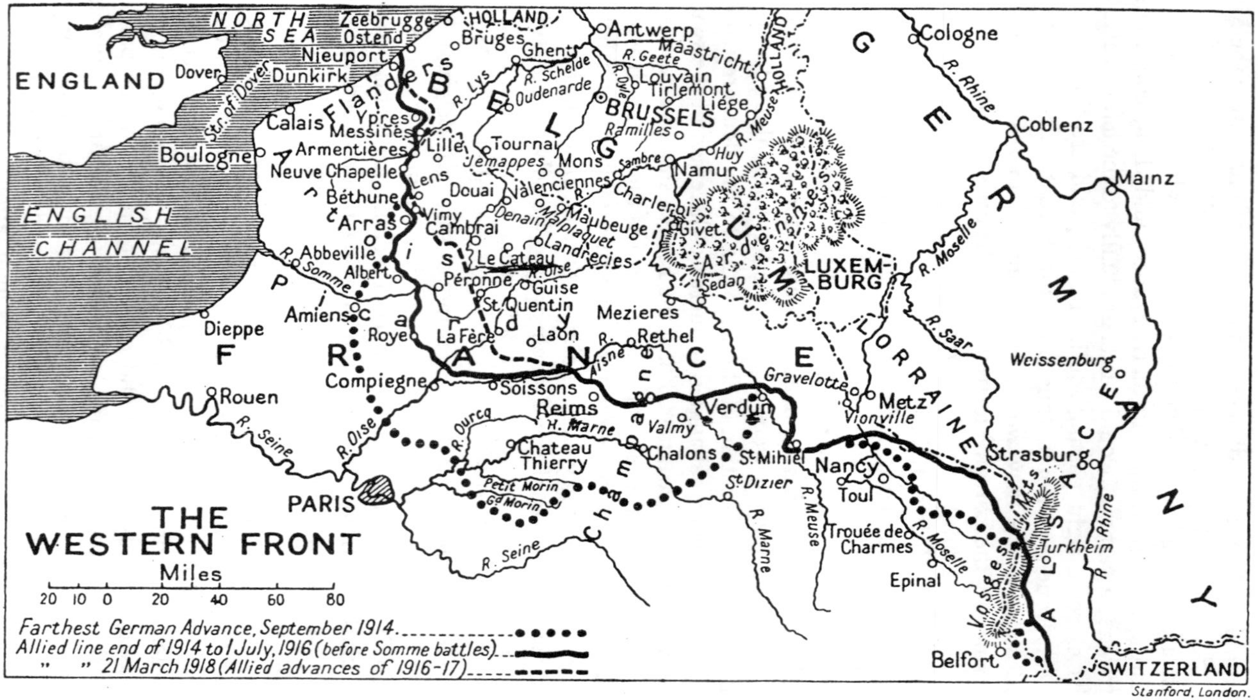

THE WESTERN FRONT

When the French offensive developed in August 1914, Moltke was tempted to accept the challenge in a direct manner, and to seek a decision in Lorraine, postponing the right wing's sweep. The impulse was only a momentary one, but in that brief lapse he had diverted to Lorraine the six newly formed Ersatz divisions which should have gone to increase the strength of his right wing. Moreover, this fresh accession of strength made the German commanders in Lorraine more loath to fulfil their self-suppressing role. Prince Rupprecht of Bavaria, instead of continuing to fall back and lure on the French, halted his army, ready to accept battle. Finding the French attack slow to develop, he arranged with his neighbour to forestall it by a German attack. The two armies had now 25 divisions against 19, but lacked the superiority, as well as the strategic position, to make the counterstroke decisive. The result was merely to throw back the French on to their fortified barrier—and so not only restored and augmented their power of resistance but enabled them to dispatch troops westwards for the battle of the Marne.

The German action in Lorraine undermined Schlieffen's plan even more gravely, if less obviously, than the progressive reduction of the weight and role of the right wing—although it was here that the collapse came, after this wing had been seriously weakened in various ways.

Besides the diversion to Lorraine of the six reinforcing divisions, the seven divisions of the right wing were detached to invest or stand guard over Antwerp, Givet, and Maubauge; then four were withdrawn by Moltke to reinforce the East Prussian front. When Kluck's army on the extreme right wheeled in prematurely—on his neighbour's request and with Moltke's approval—and thereby presented a chance for the Paris garrison to catch him in flank, only 13 German divisions were available against 27 Franco-British divisions on this decisive flank. That fact brings out the extent to which Schlieffen's 'decisive wing' had been weakened—directly and indirectly. While the German inferiority was due to subtraction of force from the right wing, the French superiority was due to the misguided action of the German left wing.

The switching of French divisions from left to right would not have been possible if the French left wing had been allowed to push on deeper into Lorraine. But it is doubtful whether the strength of the German right wing could have been maintained, even apart from the diversions and subtractions. For, as a result of the Belgians' destruction of the bridges over the Meuse, the Germans could run no trains past Liége until the 24th August, and then only by an awkward deviation. This block made it impossible for them to reinforce their right wing as originally planned. Moreover the supplies of all their three right wing armies had to pass through this one half-strangled artery. The demolitions carried out by the French and British in their retreat also hindered the maintenance of supplies. By the time the Germans reached the Marne they bore the air of beaten troops—beaten by hard marching on an empty stomach. If Moltke had avoided his much condemned subtractions, and used larger numbers on this far-advancing right wing, their state would have been still worse. The long-overlooked lesson of the American Civil War was repeated—that the development of railways, and armies' dependence on such communications, both fixed and fragile, fostered the deployment of larger numbers than could be maintained in long-range operations without risk of breakdown.

Although with the battle of the Marne we cross the shadowy border-line between strategy and tactics, this battle, which turned the tide of the war, yields so many sidelights on the problem of the 'approach' that it deserves examination. For these sidelights to be reflected, a background of events is necessary.

The repulse of Joffre's right wing in Lorraine had been followed by the throwing back of his centre in a head-on crash in the Ardennes, and by the narrow escape of his left wing, belatedly extended, from a disastrous encirclement between the Sambre and the Meuse. With Plan XVII shattered to pieces, Joffre formed a new plan out of the wreckage. He decided to swing back his left and centre, with Verdun as the pivot, while drawing troops from his now firmly buttressed right wing to form a fresh 6th Army on his left.

On the German side, the first highly coloured reports from the army commanders in the battles of the Frontiers had given the German Supreme Command the impression of a decisive victory. Then the comparatively small totals of prisoners raised doubts in Moltke's mind, and led him to a more sober estimate of the situation. The new pessimism of Moltke's combined with the renewed optimism of his army commanders to produce a fresh change of plan, which contained the seeds of disaster.

When, on the 26th August, the British left wing fell back southwards from Le Cateau, badly mauled, the German 1st Army, under Kluck, turned south-westwards again. If this direction was partly due to a misconception of the line of retreat taken by the British, it was also in accordance with Kluck's original role of a wide circling sweep. By carrying him into the Amiens-Péronne area, where the first elements of the newly formed French 6th Army were just detraining after being switched from Lorraine, it compelled a hurried withdrawal of the 6th Army—and thus had the effect of dislocating Joffre's design for an early return to the offensive.

But Kluck had hardly swung out to the south-west before he was induced to swing in again. For, to ease the pressure on the British, Joffre had ordered the neighbouring army (Lanrezac) to halt and strike back at the pursuing German 2nd Army (Bülow), which, shaken by the threat, called on Kluck for aid. Lanrezac's attack, on the 29th August, was stopped before this aid was needed; but Bülow asked Kluck to wheel inwards nevertheless, in order to cut off Lanrezac's retreat. Before acceding, Kluck referred to Moltke. The request came at a moment when Moltke was becoming perturbed, in general, over the way the French were slipping away from his embrace, and, in particular, over a gap which had opened between his 2nd and 3rd Armies. Hence Moltke approved Kluck's change of direction, which meant the abandonment of the original wide sweep round the far side of Paris. Now, the flank of the wheeling German line would pass the near side of Paris, and across the face of the Paris defences. By this contraction of his frontage and greater directness of approach, for the sake of security, Moltke sacrificed the wider prospects inherent in the wide sweep of the Schlieffen plan. As it proved, instead of contracting the risk he invited a fatal counterstroke.

The decision to abandon the original plan was definitely taken on the 4th September, and in place of it Moltke substituted a narrower envelopment, of the French centre and right. His own centre (4th and 5th Armies) was to press south-east, while his left (6th and 7th Armies), striking south-westwards, sought to break through the fortified barrier between Toul and Epinal, the 'jaws' thus closing inwards on either side of Verdun. Meantime his right (1st and 2nd Armies) was to turn outwards, and, facing west, hold off any countermove which the French attempted from the neighbourhood of Paris.

But such a French countermove had begun before the newer plan could take effect.

The opportunity was less quickly appreciated by Joffre, who had ordered a continuance of the retreat, than by Galliéni, the Military Governor of Paris. On the 3rd September, Galliéni realized the meaning of Kluck's wheel inwards, and directed Maunoury's 6th Army to be ready to strike at the exposed German right flank. All the next day an argument raged at Joffre's headquarters, the case for an immediate counter-offensive being pressed by Major Gamelin, his military secretary, but stoutly opposed by General Berthelot, the most powerful voice on the general staff. The issue was only settled, and Joffre's sanction gained, when Galliéni came through on the telephone that evening. Once convinced, Joffre acted with decision. The whole left wing was ordered to turn about, and return to a general offensive beginning on the 6th September.

Maunoury was quick off the mark, on the 5th, and as his pressure developed on the Germans' sensitive flank, Kluck was constrained to draw off first one part, and then the remaining part of his army to support his threatened flank guard. Thereby a thirty-mile gap was created between the 1st and 2nd German armies, a gap covered only by a screen of cavalry. Kluck was emboldened to take the risk because of the rapid retreat of the British opposite to that gaping sector. Even on the 5th, instead of turning about, the British had continued a further day's march to the south. But in this 'disappearance' lay the indirect and unintentional cause of victory. For, when the British retraced their steps, it was the report that their columns were advancing into the gap which, on the 9th September, led Bülow to order the retreat of his 2nd Army. The temporary advantage which the 1st Army, already isolated by its own act, had gained over Maunoury was thereby nullified, and it fell back the same day.

By the 11th the retreat had extended, independently or under orders from Moltke, to all the German armies. The attempt at a partial envelopment, pivoting on Verdun, had already failed—the jaw formed by the 6th and 7th Armies merely breaking its teeth on the defences of the French eastern frontier. It is difficult to see how the German command could reasonably have pinned their faith on achieving as an improvised expedient the frontal assault that, in cool calculation before the war, had appeared so hopeless as to lead them to take the momentous decision to advance through Belgium, violating her neutrality, as the only feasible alternative.

Thus, in sum, the battle of the Marne was decided by a jar and a crack. The jar administered by Maunoury's attack on the German right flank caused a crack in a weak joint of the German line, and this physical crack in turn produced a moral crack in the German command.

Against this background it can be seen that Kluck's indirect move, his wheel outward after Le Cateau, was as valuable in upsetting Joffre's second plan—for an early return to the offensive—and in accelerating the dangerous momentum of the Franco-British retreat, as his subsequent wheel inward, directly towards the opponent, was fatal to the German plan. We may note, too, that Moltke's strategic approach became increasingly direct, and that the frontal assault of the German left wing proved not only a costly failure but brought no strategic return to compensate its cost.

It would be far-fetched to characterize Joffre's retreat as an indirect approach. The opportunity on the Marne was presented, not created—nor even sought. Galliéni's thrust was in the nick of time, before the German 1st and 2nd Armies could take up their new flank guard dispositions. But it was too direct to produce decisive results, and would have been more direct still if he had made it south of the Marne as Joffre first instructed. Finally, it can be seen that the actual decision, the move which compelled the Germans to retreat, was due to an indirect approach so unintentional as to form an act of historical comedy. This was the disappearance of the British Expeditionary Force, and its happily belated reappearance opposite the strained and weakened joint of the German right wing. French critics have reproached it for this slowness, not realizing that it contributed a new, if somewhat different point to the fable of the hare and the tortoise. If the B.E.F. had returned sooner the joint would hardly have been so weakened. Maunoury's attack could not have produced a decision—for he had already been brought to a halt while the two German corps taken from the joint were still on the march and contributing nothing to the issue.

In analysing the cause of the German retreat, however, we must take account of a factor customarily overlooked. This was the sensitiveness of the Supreme Command to reports of landings on the Belgian coast which might menace their rear and communications. It led them to contemplate a withdrawal before the battle of the Marne even began. On the 3rd September Lieut.-Colonel Hentsch, the representative of the Supreme Command, came to the 1st Army with the latest precautionary order and informed it that—'The news is bad: the 7th and 6th Armies are blocked before Nancy-Epinal. The 4th and 5th are meeting strong resistance. The French are railing forces from their right towards Paris. The English are disembarking fresh troops continuously on the Belgian coast. There are rumours of a Russian expeditionary force in the same parts. A withdrawal is becoming inevitable.'

The sensitiveness of the German command had enlarged three battalions of marines which landed at Ostend, for forty-eight hours, into a corps of 40,000 men. The Russians are said to have sprung from the heated imagination of an English railway porter —there should be a statue in Whitehall dedicated 'To the Unknown Porter'. Historians may well conclude that this party of temporary visitors to Ostend, together with the Russian myth, were the primary cause of the victory of the Marne.

When the moral effect of these phantom forces is weighed with the material detention of German forces in Belgium, owing to fears of a Belgian sortie from Antwerp—which developed on the 9th September—the balance of judgement would seem to turn heavily in favour of the strategy which Sir John French had suggested at the outset. By it the British Expeditionary Force might have had a positively, not merely negatively, decisive influence on the struggle.

The latent menace of the Belgian coast to the German rear had throughout been appreciated by Falkenhayn, who now replaced Moltke. His first step was to undertake the reduction of Antwerp, and from this grew the germ of a manœuvre which savoured of the indirect approach. Its execution fell short of, and became more direct than, its conception, yet it sufficed to bring the Allies afresh to the verge of disaster.

The Allied frontal pursuit had been definitely checked on the Aisne before Joffre, on the 17th September, seeing that Maunoury's attempts to overlap the German flank were ineffectual, decided to form a fresh army under de Castelnau for an outflanking move. By then the German armies had recovered cohesion, and the German command was ready to meet such limited manœuvre —now the natural line of expectation.

The next month was occupied by the extremely obvious and abortive series of attempts by either side to overlap the other's western flank—a phase popularly, if inaccurately, styled 'the race to the sea'. Falkenhayn tired of the game long before Joffre, and on the 14th October planned a strategic trap for the next Allied attempt which he foresaw would follow. His latest-formed flank army was to parry the attempt, while another—composed of the forces released by the fall of Antwerp and of four newly raised corps—was to sweep down the Belgian coast, crush in the flank, and crash upon the rear, of the attacking Allies. He even held back, momentarily, the troops pursuing the Belgian field army from Antwerp in order to avoid prematurely alarming the Allied command.

Fortunately for the Allies, King Albert, from caution or realism, refused Foch's invitation to join in this outflanking effort, and declined to quit the coastal district. Thereby the Belgian army was in position to withstand, and eventually, by flooding the low coastal strip, frustrate the German sweep from the north. This compelled Falkenhayn to make a more direct approach to the Allied flank—which had just been extended to Ypres by the arrival of Haig's corps from the Aisne.

Although the attempted advance of the earlier-coming British right and centre corps had already been held up, Sir John French ordered his left wing under Haig to attempt the realization of Joffre's outflanking dream. Fortunately again, the attempt coincided with the premature opening of the German attack, and thus was stillborn—although for a day or two French, under Foch's influence, persisted in believing that this British 'attack' was going on, whereas actually Haig's troops were struggling hard even to hold their ground. The delusion of the French and British chiefs as to the reality of the situation was partly responsible for the fact that Ypres, like Inkerman, was essentially a 'soldiers' battle'. Falkenhayn, too, once his hope of sweeping down the coast had faded, persisted for a month in trying to force a decision by a direct approach. When the direct defence, despite weakness of strength, triumphed as usual over the direct attack, the trench barrier became consolidated from the Swiss frontier to the sea—and stalemate ensued.

The Western Theatre, 1915–17

The military record of the Franco-British alliance during the next four years is a story of the attempt to break this deadlock, either by forcing the barrier or by haphazardly seeking a way round.

On the Western Front, with its interminable parallel lines of entrenchments, strategy became the handmaiden of tactics, while tactics became a cripple. The strategical side of the years 1915–17 does not call for much examination. On the Allied side the strategy was purely that of direct approach, and it was ineffectual to break the deadlock. Whatever be our opinion of the merits of attrition, and of the argument that the whole period should be regarded as one continuous battle, a method which requires four years to produce a decision is not to be regarded as a model for imitation.

At Neuve Chapelle, the first attempt at the offensive in 1915, the approach was direct, but tactical surprise at least was sought and gained. Thereafter, with the adoption of prolonged 'warning' bombardments, all the attempts became barefaced frontal assaults. Of this nature were the French offensive near Arras in May 1915; the Franco-British offensives of September 1915 in Champagne and north of Arras; of July to November 1916 on the Somme; of April 1917 on the Aisne and at Arras; and lastly the British offensive at Ypres from July to October 1917 which, like King Charles II, took so long in dying—in the swamps of Passchendaele. On the 20th November 1917, at Cambrai, tactical surprise was revived by the use of massed tanks, suddenly unleashed, in place of a long preliminary bombardment. But strategically this small-scale attack—so happy in its opening, so unhappy in its end—could hardly be termed an indirect approach.

On the German side, the strategy was strictly defensive except for the Verdun offensive interlude in 1916. This, again, was essentially a direct approach—unless the idea of bleeding one's enemy to death by an illimitable series of limited leech-bites can be termed indirect. But the expenditure in leeches caused its bankruptcy.

More akin to the nature of the indirect approach, but purely defensive in aim, was Ludendorff's ably conceived and prepared withdrawal of part of the German forces to the Hindenburg line in the spring of 1917. To anticipate the renewal of the Franco-British offensive on the Somme, a new trench line of great artificial strength was built across the chord of the arc Lens–Noyon–Reims. Then, after devastating the whole area inside the arc, the Germans withdrew by methodical stages to the new and shorter line. This manœuvre, distinguished by its moral courage in yielding ground, dislocated the whole plan of the Allies' spring offensive. Thereby it helped to gain the Germans a year's respite from serious danger and from any combined offensive of the Allies, allowed time for Russia's disintegration to become complete, and enabled Ludendorff to make his supreme bid for victory, with superiority of force, in 1918.

CHAPTER XII

THE NORTH-EASTERN THEATRE

★

On the Eastern Front the plans of campaign were more fluid, less elaborately worked out and formulated—although they were to be as kaleidoscopic in their changes of fortune as in the western theatre. The calculable condition was geographical; the main incalculable, Russia's rate of concentration.

Russian Poland was a vast tongue of country projecting from Russia proper, and flanked on three sides by German or Austrian territory. On its northern flank lay East Prussia, with the Baltic Sea beyond. On its southern flank lay the Austrian province of Galicia, with the Carpathian mountains beyond, guarding the approaches to the plain of Hungary. On the west lay Silesia.

The Germanic border provinces were provided with a network of strategic railways, whilst Poland, as well as Russia itself, had only a sparse system of communications. Thus the German alliance had a vital advantage, in power of concentration, for countering a Russian advance. But if its armies took the offensive, the further they progressed into Poland or Russia proper the more would they lose this advantage. Hence the experience of history suggested that their most profitable strategy was to lure the Russians forward into position for a counter-stroke, rather than to inaugurate an offensive themselves. The one drawback was that such a Punic strategy gave the Russians time to concentrate, and to set in motion their cumbrous and rusty machine.

From this arose an initial cleavage between German and Austrian opinion. Both agreed that the problem was to hold the Russians in check during the six weeks before the Germans, it was hoped, would have crushed France, and could switch their forces eastwards to join the Austrians in a decisive blow against the Russians. The difference of opinion was on the method. The Germans, intent on a decision against France, wished to leave a minimum force in the East. Only a political dislike of exposing national territory to invasion prevented them evacuating East Prussia, and standing on the Vistula line. But the Austrians, under the influence of Conrad von Hötzendorf, Chief of their General Staff, were anxious to throw the Russian machine out of gear by an immediate offensive. As this promised to keep the Russians fully occupied while the campaign in France was being decided, Moltke fell in with this strategy. Conrad's plan was that of an offensive north-eastwards into Poland by two armies, protected by two more on their right, further east.

On the opposing side, also, the desires of one ally vitally affected the strategy of the other. The Russian command, both for military and for racial motives, wished to concentrate first against Austria, while she was unsupported, and to leave Germany alone until later, when the full strength of the Russian army would be mobilized. But the French, anxious to relieve the German pressure against themselves, urged the Russians to deliver a simultaneous attack against Germany. The outcome was that the Russians consented to undertake an extra offensive for which they were neither ready, in numbers, nor organized. On the south-western front, two pairs of armies were to converge on the Austrian forces in Galicia; on the north-western front, two armies were to converge on the German forces in East Prussia. Russia, whose proverbial slowness and crude organization dictated a cautious strategy, was about to break with tradition and launch out on a hasty and double direct approach.

On the outbreak of war the Russian Commander-in-Chief, the Grand Duke Nicholas, accelerated the invasion of East Prussia in order to ease the pressure on his French allies. On the 17th August Rennenkampf's army crossed the east frontier of East Prussia, and on the 19th to 20th August it met and threw back the bulk of Prittwitz's German 8th Army at Gumbinnen. On the 21st August, Prittwitz heard that Samsonov's Army had crossed the southern frontier of East Prussia in his rear, which was guarded by only three divisions—while ten faced them. In panic, Prittwitz momentarily spoke of falling back behind the Vistula, whereupon Moltke superseded him by a retired general, Hindenburg, with Ludendorff as Chief of Staff.

Developing a plan which, with the necessary movements, had been already initiated by Colonel Hoffmann of the 8th Army staff, Ludendorff concentrated some six divisions against Samsonov's left wing. This force, inferior in strength to the Russians, could not have been decisive; but Ludendorff, finding that Rennenkampf was still near Gumbinnen, took the calculated risk of withdrawing the rest of the German troops, except the cavalry screen, from that front and rushing them back against Samsonov's right wing. This daring move was aided by the absence of communication between the two Russian commanders and the ease with which the Germans deciphered the Russian wireless orders. Under converging blows, Samsonov's flanks were crushed, his centre surrounded, and his army practically destroyed. If the opportunity was presented rather than created, this brief Tannenberg campaign forms an almost perfect example of the 'interior lines' form of the indirect approach.

Then, receiving two fresh army corps from the front in France, the German commander turned on the slowly advancing Rennenkampf—whose lack of energy was partly due to his losses at Gumbinnen and subsequent lack of information—and drove him out of East Prussia. As a result of these battles, Russia had lost a quarter of a million men and, what she could afford still less, much war material. The invasion of East Prussia, however, had at least helped to make possible the French revival on the Marne—by causing the dispatch of two corps from the West.

But the effect of Tannenberg was diminished because, away on the Galician front, the scales had tilted against the Central Powers. The offensive of the Austrian 1st and 4th Armies into Poland had at first made progress, but this was nullified by the onslaught of the Russian 3rd and 8th Armies upon the weaker 2nd and 3rd Armies which were guarding the Austrian right flank. These armies were heavily defeated (the 26th to 30th August), and driven back through Lemberg. The advance of the Russian left wing thus threatened the rear of the victorious Austrian left wing. Conrad tried to swing part of his left wing round against the Russian flank, but this blow was parried. And then, caught with his forces disorganized by the renewed advance of the Russian right wing, he was forced, on the 11th September, to extricate himself by a general retreat—falling back almost to Cracow by the end of September.

Austria's plight compelled the Germans to send aid. The bulk of the German force in East Prussia was formed into a new 9th Army, and switched south to the south-west corner of Poland, whence it advanced on Warsaw in combination with a renewed Austrian offensive. But the Russians were now approaching the full tide of their mobilized strength; regrouping their forces and counter-attacking, they drove back the advance and followed it up by a powerful effort to invade Silesia.

The Grand Duke Nicholas formed a huge phalanx of seven armies—three in the van and two protecting either flank. A further army, the 10th, had invaded the eastern corner of East Prussia and was engaging the weak German forces there.

To counter the danger, the German Eastern Front was placed under the firm of Hindenburg-Ludendorff-Hoffmann, which devised yet another master-stroke, based on the system of lateral railways inside the German frontier. The 9th Army, falling back before the Russian advance, slowed it down by a systematic destruction of the scanty communications in Poland. On reaching the Silesian frontier, unpressed, it was first switched northward to the Posen-Thorn area, and then thrust south-east on the 11th November up the west bank of the Vistula, against the joint between the two armies guarding the Russian right flank. The wedge, as if driven in by a mallet, split the two armies, forced the 1st back on Warsaw and almost achieved another Tannenberg against the 2nd—which was nearly surrounded at Lodz, when the 5th Army from the van turned back to its rescue. As a result, part of the German enveloping force almost suffered the fate planned for the Russians, but managed to cut its way through to the main body. If the Germans were baulked of decisive tactical success, this manœuvre had been a classic example of how a relatively small force, by using its mobility for indirect approach to a vital point, can paralyse the advance of an enemy several times its strength. The Russian 'steam-roller' was thrown out of gear, and never again did it threaten German soil.

Within a week, four new German army corps arrived from the Western Front, where the Ypres attack had now ended in failure. Although they came too late to clinch the missed chance of a decisive victory, Ludendorff was able to use them in pressing the Russians back to the Bzura-Ravka river line in front of Warsaw. There, on the East as on the West, the trench stalemate settled in. But the crust was less firm, and the Russians had drained their stock of munitions to an extent that their poorly industrialized country could not make good.

The real story of 1915 on the Eastern Front is that of the tussle of wills between Ludendorff, who desired to reach a decision by a strategy that was at least geographically an indirect approach, and Falkenhayn, who considered that he could both limit his expenditure of force and cripple Russia's offensive power by a strategy of direct approach. Holding the superior appointment, Falkenhayn succeeded in gaining his way, but his strategy did not succeed in fulfilling either object.

Ludendorff perceived that the Russians' autumn advance towards Silesia and Cracow had enmeshed the body of their army deeply in the Polish salient. In the south-western corner they had even poked their head through the meshes, into Austrian territory, when Ludendorff's Lodz blow fell and temporarily paralysed the body; by the time feeling and strength came back, the jagged edges of the net had been re-knit and reinforced. From January to April the Russian body wriggled furiously but ineffectively on the Carpathian side; its struggles merely wrapped its cumbrous mass more firmly in the net.

Ludendorff wished to seize the opportunity for a wide indirect approach round the northern flank near the Baltic, through Vilna, towards the Russian rear and astride their sparse rail communications with the Polish salient. Falkenhayn, however, shrank both from its boldness and its demand upon his reserves—although he was to expend far more in his own way. Reluctantly dissuaded from a fresh attempt to storm the trench-barrier in the West, and compelled to dole out reserves to strengthen his Austrian allies, he decided to employ them in a strategically limited, if tactically unlimited, attempt to lame Russia—so that he might return to renew his offensive in the west undisturbed.

The plan in the East, suggested by Conrad and adopted by Falkenhayn, was to break through the Russian centre in the Dunajec sector between the Carpathians and the Vistula. On the 2nd May the blow fell. The surprise was complete, the exploitation rapid, and by the 14th the whole line along the Carpathians had been rolled back eighty miles to the San.

Here we can see an illuminating example of the difference between the indirect approach and what is commonly called surprise. Surprise of time, place, and force was achieved; but the Russians were merely rolled back in snowball fashion. Although they lost heavily, they were rolled back towards their reserves, supplies and railways. Thereby the Germans consolidated the snowball, and enabled Russian accretions to make good the pieces that fell off. Moreover, while the pressure of this direct approach was a dangerous strain on the Russian command, it was not a dislocating shock.

Falkenhayn now realized that he had committed himself too far in Galicia to draw back. His partial offensive had gained no secure halting-place, and only by bringing more troops from France could he hope to fulfil his aim of transferring troops back there. But once more he chose an almost direct approach. He changed the direction of the offensive from eastward to north-eastward and in conjunction ordered Ludendorff—all this time fretting impatiently in East Prussia—to strike south-eastward. Ludendorff contended that this plan, if convergent, was too much of a frontal attack, and that while the two wings might squeeze the Russians they would do no more. He again urged, and Falkenhayn again rejected, the Vilna manœuvre.

The outcome proved Ludendorff correct. Falkenhayn's shears, as they closed, merely pushed the Russians back out of the now shallow space between them. By the end of September the Russians were back on a long straight line between Riga on the Baltic and Czernowitz on the Rumanian frontier. If never again a direct menace to Germany, they imposed on her an irremediable strain, by detaining large German forces and keeping Austria morally and physically on the rack.

When Falkenhayn broke off large-scale operations, he gave Ludendorff a belated and half-hearted sanction to try the Vilna manœuvre with his own meagre resources. This light and isolated thrust cut the Vilna-Dvinsk railway and almost reached the Minsk railway, the central line of Russian communications—despite the Russians being free to concentrate all their reserves to resist it. These results were a suggestive testimony to its potentialities if attempted earlier, and in strong force, when the Russian body was firmly entangled in the Polish net.

Their offensive in the East being terminated, and their defensive in the West being unshaken, the Central Powers utilized the autumn to carry through a campaign in Serbia. This campaign, from the view point of the war as a whole, was an indirect approach with limited aim, but in its own sphere was decisive in aim. Its course, too, if helped by the geographical and political situation, sheds light on the effect of this method. The plan was based on Bulgaria's intervention in the war on the side of the Central Powers. The direct Austro-German invasion was being held in check when the Bulgarians moved westward into Serbia. Even then, helped by the mountainous country, the Serbians' resistance remained firm until the Bulgar left wing worked round into southern Serbia across their rear, cutting them off from the Franco-British reinforcements which were being sent up from Salonika. Thereupon the Serbian collapse was swift, and only a tattered remnant survived the mid-winter retreat westwards through Albania to the Adriatic coast. This quick concentration against a junior partner relieved Austria of danger on this side while giving Germany free communication through, and control of, Central Europe.

The operations of 1916 and 1917 on the Russian front call for little comment, being essentially defensive on the Austro-German side, and essentially direct on the Russian side. The significance of the Russian operations is that they throw into clear relief not only the barrenness of a strategy which relies on the application of mere weight in a direct approach, but its 'boomerang' moral effect. When the Revolution presaged the complete collapse of Russia's military effort, in 1917, the Russian forces were actually better armed and better equipped than at any previous time. But the immense, and visibly abortive, losses had undermined the fighting will of the most patiently self-sacrificing troops in Europe. A similar effect was seen in the mutinies in the French army after the spring offensive in 1917. Most of the outbreaks there occurred when slaughter-wearied troops were ordered to return to the trenches.

The one Russian operation which had some indirectness of approach was Brusilov's offensive near Luck, in June 1916, and it had this quality because the offensive had no serious intention. It was conceived merely as a diversion, and released prematurely owing to Italy's appeal. No preparation nor concentration of troops had been made, and the unexpectedness of this almost casual advance brought about such a collapse of the somnolent Austrian defence that within three days 200,000 prisoners were netted.

Rarely has a surprise shock been so manifold in its strategic results. It stopped the Austrian attack on Italy. It compelled Falkenhayn to withdraw troops from the Western Front, and so to abandon his attrition campaign round Verdun. It spurred Rumania to enter the war against the Central Powers. It caused the downfall of Falkenhayn and his replacement by Hindenburg and Ludendorff (Hoffmann, to 'the firm's' loss, was left in the east). Although Rumania's entry was the pretext for Falkenhayn's supersession, the real reason was that his direct strategy in 1915, narrow both in purpose and direction, had made possible the Russian revival which completed the ruin of the 1916 strategy.

But the indirectness and the good effect of Brusilov's offensive were short-lived. It led the Russian command, too late, to throw the weight of their forces in this direction. And, in accord with the natural laws of war, the prolongation of the effort along the line of hardening resistance used up the Russian reserves without compensating effect. Brusilov's ultimate loss of 1,000,000 casualties, though terrible, could be made good; but, by revealing to the survivors the mental bankruptcy of the Russian command, it caused the moral bankruptcy of Russia's military power.

The Russians' obsessed concentration on this effort enabled Hindenburg and Ludendorff to carry through another quick-change indirect approach—as against Serbia in 1915. Partly from force of circumstances, it became more truly a strategic indirect approach. Rumania was the target. At the outset she had 23 divisions, indifferently equipped, against 7 opposing her; and she hoped that the pressure of Brusilov, of the British on the Somme, and of the Allied force now at Salonika would prevent these being reinforced. But these pressures were all direct, and they did not prevent the withdrawal of sufficient troops to crush Rumania.

Rumania's territory, sandwiched between Transylvania and Bulgaria, had strong natural ramparts on either side of the Carpathians and the Danube—but by its situation lent itself to a strategy of indirect approach. Further, her Dobruja 'back-yard' strip near the Black Sea formed a bait which a skilful opponent could attach to his hook.

Her desire and decision to take the offensive westwards into Transylvania made her opponents' counter-action more subtly indirect than they intended.

The Rumanian advance began on the 27th August 1916. Three main columns, each of about 4 divisions, moved north-west through the Carpathian passes in a direct approach towards the Hungarian plain. To guard the Danube, 3 divisions were left, and 3 more in the Dobruja—whither the Russians had promised to send reinforcements. But the slow and cautious advance of the Rumanian columns into Transylvania, hampered by the enemy's destruction of bridges but not by resistance, did not seriously menace the 5 weak Austrian divisions which covered the frontier until they had been reinforced by 5 German and 2 Austrian divisions. In fulfilment of the other half of the plan, adopted by Falkenhayn before his downfall, 4 Bulgarian divisions with a German stiffening, and an Austrian bridging train, were placed under Mackensen for the invasion of the Dobruja.

While the Rumanian columns were crawling westward into Transylvania, Mackensen stormed the Turtucaia bridgehead on the 5th September, destroying the 3 Rumanian divisions which guarded the Danube front. Then, with his Danube flank secure, he moved eastwards, deeper into the Dobruja—if away from Bucharest, the natural line of expectation. It was a shrewd moral thrust, for the automatic strategic effect was to draw away the Rumanian reserves intended to support the Transylvania offensive—which lost such impetus as it had.

Falkenhayn, now given the executive command here, launched a counter-offensive—perhaps too eagerly and directly. For although he skilfully concentrated against the southern and centre columns in turn, using smaller if not minimum forces to hold off the other opponents—who hardly needed holding off—the result was to throw the Rumanians back, but not to cut them off from the mountains. The mischance jeopardized the whole German plan. For, with all the passes still in their hands, the Rumanians sturdily repulsed the German efforts to press through on their heels. Falkenhayn's first attempt to get through further west was foiled; but a renewed effort broke through just before the coming of the winter snows. By swinging westward he had now, however, entered Rumania by the front door, and the consequent direct approach had to cross a series of river lines. Fortunately for him, when he had been checked along the Alt, Mackensen intervened.

Mackensen had switched the bulk of his force back from the Dobruja, past Turtucaia, to Sistovo—where, on the 23rd November, he forced the crossing of the Danube. It is a moot point whether this abandonment of his potential position on the Rumanian rear for a convergent advance of their main army towards Bucharest was the most profitable strategy. It enabled Falkenhayn to cross the Alt, but it enabled the Rumanians to use their 'close' central position for a dangerous counter-stroke at Mackensen's flank. This was almost enveloped. Once the danger was averted, however, the combined pressure of Falkenhayn and Mackensen pressed the Rumanian army back through Bucharest, whence it withdrew to the Sereth-Black Sea line.

The Germans had gained possession of most of Rumania, with its wheat and oil, but they had not cut off or destroyed the Rumanian army, whose moral and mental strength had been consolidated in resisting the last stage of the enemy's advance. The next summer its sturdy resistance foiled the German attempt to drive it behind the Prut and thus complete the occupation of Rumania. Only in December 1917, when Bolshevik Russia signed an armistice with Germany, was Rumania, thereby isolated, forced to follow suit.

CHAPTER XIII

THE SOUTH-EASTERN OR MEDITERRANEAN THEATRE

★

The Italian Theatre

In 1917, Italy was the scene and object of the German command's autumn repertory performance. Here again the configuration of the frontier gave the Germans scope for a geographical, or physical, indirect approach which was denied to their opponents. And the latter showed no inclination to try the psychological indirect approach.

The Italian frontier province of Venezia formed a salient pointing to Austria, flanked on the north by the Austrian Tyrol and Trentino, on the south by the Adriatic. Bordering on the Adriatic was a stretch of relatively low ground on the Isonzo front: but the frontier then followed the Julian and Carnic Alps in a wide sweep round to the north-west, the arc continuing south-westward to Lake Garda. The great breadth of the Alpine masses on the north, and the absence of any vital objective, did not encourage Italy to take the offensive in that direction. She was thus restricted, for an offensive, to a direct advance eastwards towards Austria. It inevitably suffered the potential and perpetual menace of an Austrian descent from the Trentino on its rear. But with her choice so restricted she chose this course.

For two and a half years she persevered with the direct approach. By that time the 'eleventh battle' of the Isonzo had been fought in vain, the Italian armies had scarcely advanced beyond their starting-point, and their casualties totalled some 1,100,000—while the Austrians had lost some 650,000. During that period, Austria had only once taken the offensive. This was in 1916, when Conrad had sought to obtain Falkenhayn's support for an attempt to overthrow Italy by a thrust southwards from the Trentino against the rear of the Italian armies then engaged on the Isonzo. But Falkenhayn, distrustful of the plan as well as of 'decisive' strokes, and intent on his Verdun attrition process, declined even to lend the minimum of 9 German divisions for which Conrad asked—to relieve Austrian divisions on the Eastern Front. In default of this aid, Conrad decided to make the attempt single-handed, taking some of his best divisions from the East—and thereby exposing the Eastern Front to Brusilov's subsequent advance, without obtaining adequate force to achieve his Italian plan.

Nevertheless, the attack came close to success. If it could not be said to avoid the natural line of expectation, it had a measure of unexpectedness—because the Italian command did not believe that Conrad had the force or the facilities for a large-scale attack. It was a large-scale attack, but not quite large enough. The attack, when launched, gained rapid success in the first days. Although Cadorna was able, and prompt, to withdraw reserves from the Isonzo sector—besides preparing the evacuation thence of his stores and heavy artillery—it was a race, with the odds even. The Austrian attack was within reach of a break-through into the plain, but had lost its momentum for want of reserves when Brusilov's advance on the Eastern Front caused its suspension.

When Ludendorff, seventeen months later, took up the idea of a combined blow at Italy—because of the serious condition of Austria—the prospects were less favourable. He could only spare his slender general reserve of 6 divisions, while his ally was suffering, morally and materially, from exhaustion. And, for lack of means, the plan was limited to a narrower and more direct approach—a thrust at the north-eastern corner of the Isonzo sector, where it bent round towards the Alpine mass. The choice of the actual sector, however, was chosen on a principle new to this front—that of seeking the line of least tactical resistance.

Originally, the plan was for a break-through at Caporetto, followed merely by rolling up the Isonzo front. It was subsequently expanded into a more ambitious design—without an increase of means. Ludendorff, at Caporetto, like the British that same autumn at Cambrai, provided an example of the profound strategic error of not 'cutting your coat according to your cloth'. He went to the other extreme from Falkenhayn—who had always ordered too little cloth, underestimating the measurements of the coat, and then had to order more, to enlarge the coat: into an unsatisfactory patchwork.

On the 24th October the attack was launched—having been skilfully prepared and concealed—and drove a wedge deep between the Italian armies. A week later, it had reached the Tagliamento. But once the Italians had extricated their severed forces—if with the loss of a large part—the continuation of the advance became a purely direct approach westwards, pressing the Italians back to the Piave river. That was a stout barricade behind which to shelter. Too late, Ludendorff thought of switching reserves round to the Trentino, but was foiled by the inadequacy of the rail communications. The Trentino army made an ineffective attempt to advance with its own slight resources; and this belated stroke had lost the effect of a rear thrust, for the whole Italian front and reserves had been pushed almost as far back.

The initial surprise having passed, the Austro-German attack was now a purely direct convergence, which pressed the Italians back towards their reserves, supplies, homeland, and Allied reinforcements. It had the natural negative result. But the measure of success attained with such slender resources casts an ironical reflection on Falkenhayn's refusal to listen to Conrad's more promising plan early in 1916.

The Balkan Theatre

Before we turn to consider Ludendorff's plan for 1918, it is necessary to survey the action taken or attempted by his opponents, during the previous three years, beyond the bounds of the French and Russian fronts.

While the French and British headquarters in France preserved an unquenchable faith in the power of a direct approach, not only to break through the trench-barrier but to gain a decisive victory, strong doubt of its prospects was felt (from October 1914 onwards) in quarters either further from or closer to the locked front. Those who had this view, from the perspective which distance enables, were not all political leaders; they included Galliéni in France and Kitchener in England. On the 7th January 1915, Kitchener wrote to Sir John French: 'The German lines in France may be looked upon as a fortress that cannot be carried by assault and also that cannot be completely invested, with the result that the lines may be held by an investing force while operations proceed elsewhere.'

It was argued, notably by Winston Churchill, that the enemy alliance should be viewed as a whole, and that modern developments had so changed conceptions of distance and powers of mobility that a blow in some other theatre of war would correspond to the classic attack on an enemy's strategic flank. (In this connection the example of Napoleon, so often quoted to support the case for persevering on the Western front, appears rather to lend its weight to the alternative design.) Further, it was agreed that such an operation would be in accordance with the traditional amphibious strategy of Britain, and would enable her to exploit the military advantage, hitherto neglected, of sea-power. In January 1915, Lord Kitchener advocated a plan for severing Turkey's main line of eastward communication by a landing in the Gulf of Alexandretta. The post-war evidence of Hindenburg and Enver Pasha showed how this would have paralysed Turkey; but it could hardly have exercised a wider influence, or been an indirect approach to the Central Alliance as a whole.

Lloyd George advocated the transfer of the bulk of the British forces to the Balkans as a way to the enemy's 'back-door'. But the French and British commands, confident of an early decision in France, argued vehemently against any alternative strategy—stressing the difficulties of transport and supply, and the ease with which Germany, in their opinion, could switch troops to meet the threat. If there was substance in the argument, their fervour led them to exaggerate their case. Their objections, too, were less relevant when applied to Galliéni's Balkan scheme. He proposed a landing at Salonika as a starting-point for a march on Constantinople with an army strong enough to encourage Greece and Bulgaria to join forces. The capture of Constantinople was to be followed by an advance up the Danube into Austria-Hungary, in conjunction with the Rumanians. This had a fundamental resemblance to the course actually taken in the last months of the war. In September 1918 German military opinion tended to regard such a contingency as 'decisive'. And in the first week of November the threat, though not yet close, was an important factor in hastening Germany's capitulation.

In January 1915, however, the weight of military opinion bore down all counter-proposals to the plan of concentration of effort on the Western Front. But misgivings were not silenced, and at this juncture a situation arose which revived the Near-Eastern scheme in a new, if attenuated form.

On the 2nd January 1915, Kitchener received an appeal from the Grand Duke Nicholas for a diversion which would relieve the Turkish pressure on Russia's forces in the Caucasus. Kitchener felt unable to provide the troops and suggested a naval demonstration against the Dardanelles. Churchill's imagination seized upon the wider strategic possibilities, and he proposed, in default of military aid, to convert the demonstration into an attempt to force the passage. His naval advisers, if not enthusiastic, did not oppose the project; and the admiral on the spot, Carden, drew up a plan. A naval force, mainly of obsolete vessels, was got together with French aid, and after preliminary bombardment, entered the straits on the 18th March. But a newly laid row of mines, in an unsuspected spot, caused the sinking of several ships; and the attempt was abandoned.

It is a moot question whether a prompt renewal of the advance would have succeeded, for the Turkish ammunition was exhausted, and in such conditions the mine obstacle might have been overcome. But the new naval commander, Admiral de Robeck, decided against it unless military aid were forthcoming. Already, a month before, the War Council had determined on a joint attack, and begun the dispatch of a military force under Sir Ian Hamilton. But the authorities, slow in accepting the new scheme, were equally slow in releasing the necessary troops for its execution. Even when these were sent, in inadequate numbers, several more weeks' delay had to be incurred—at Alexandria—in order to redistribute the force in its transports suitably for tactical action. Worst of all, this fumbling policy had thrown away the chance of surprise. When the preliminary bombardment took place in February, only 2 Turkish divisions were at the Straits; this was increased to 4 by the date of the naval attack; and to 6 when Hamilton was at last able to attempt his landing. For this he had only 4 British divisions and 1 French division—actually inferior in strength to the enemy in a situation where the inherent preponderance of defensive over offensive power was multiplied by the natural difficulties of the terrain. His weakness of numbers, and his restricted mission of aiding the passage of the fleet, compelled him to choose a landing on the Gallipoli peninsula in preference to one on the mainland or on the Asiatic shore.

On the 25th April he made his spring, at the southern tip of the peninsula near Cape Helles and also near Gaba Tepe some fifteen miles up the Aegean coast. The French, as a diversion, made a temporary landing at Kum Kale on the Asiatic shore. But once the momentary asset of tactical surprise had passed, and the Turks were able to bring up their reserves, the invaders could not expand their two precarious footholds.

Ultimately, in July, the British Government decided to send a further 5 divisions to reinforce the 7 now on the peninsula. By the time they arrived the Turkish strength in the region had also risen, to 15 divisions. Hamilton decided on a double stroke—a reinforced blow from Gaba Tepe and a new landing at Suvla Bay, a few miles north—to sever the middle of the peninsula and secure the heights commanding the Narrows. If this thrust appears more direct than a landing at Bulair or on the Asiatic shore, its justification is that it was on a line not expected by the enemy command, whose reserves were concentrated at the other points. Only 1½ Turkish battalions barred the way during the thirty-six hours before reserves arrived. Time and opportunity were forfeited by the inexperience of the landing troops and the inertia of the commanders on the spot. The deadlock, the disappointment, and the opposition of those who had always disliked the project, soon brought about the evacuation of the peninsula.

Yet the verdict of Falkenhayn on the Dardanelles scheme was: 'If the straits between the Mediterranean and the Black Sea were not permanently closed to Entente traffic, all hope of a successful course of the war would be very considerably diminished. Russia would have been freed from her significant isolation . . . which offered a safer guarantee than military successes that sooner or later a crippling of the forces of this Titan must take place automatically.'

The fault was not in the conception but in the execution. If the British had used at the outset even a fair proportion of the forces they ultimately expended in driblets, it is clear from the evidence of the opposing commanders that success would probably have crowned their undertaking. While the Dardanelles move was a direct approach to Turkey, it was an indirect approach to the main Turkish armies then engaged in the Caucasus, and, on the higher level, an indirect approach to the Central Powers as a whole. Viewed against the gloomy background of the Western Front, where the density of force in relation to space offered no prospect of a decisive penetration, the Dardanelles conception appears to have fulfilled the principle of adjusting the end to the means as thoroughly as its execution violated this principle.

The Palestine and Mesopotamia Theatres

The Middle East expeditions hardly come within the scope of

this survey. Strategically they were too remote to have any hope of exercising a decisive effect; and, considered as means of strategic distraction, each of them absorbed far greater forces of the British than they diverted of the enemy.

In the sphere of policy, however, a case can be made out for them. Britain, in the past, had often redeemed the forfeits of her Allies on the Continent by seizing the overseas possessions of the enemy. In the event of an unfavourable or indecisive issue to the main struggle such counter-gains are an asset in negotiating a favourable peace settlement. They are also a tonic during the struggle.[1]

The local strategy of the Palestine expedition deserves study. At the outset it combined the disadvantages of both the direct and indirect approach. It took the line of natural expectation, which was also the longest and most difficult way round to any vital point of the Turkish power. After the first two failures (in March and April 1917) at Gaza, which guarded the direct coast approach from Egypt to Palestine, the larger force available in the autumn was used for a less direct attempt.

The plan—designed by Chetwode and adopted by Allenby on relieving Murray in command—was as geographically indirect as the water supply and the narrow width of the tract between the sea and the desert allowed. The Turkish defences stretched some twenty miles inland from Gaza, while Beersheba, ten miles further inland, formed an outlying post guarding the eastern margin of the area of possible approach. Secrecy and ruses drew the Turkish attention Gaza-wards; then Beersheba with its water supply was seized by a wide and swift swoop on its unprotected side. Next in the plan, preceded by a distracting attack on Gaza, was a blow at the flank of the Turkish main position while the cavalry from Beersheba swept round the Turks' rear. But difficulties in the

[1] Those who later opposed any idea of returning some of Germany's confiscated colonies, from concern that they might become a source of danger, failed to take account of the indirect value to Britain, in case of war, of having places where she might score an early success—to offset the depressing effect of enemy successes in the European theatre and help to balance the loss of prestige these might cause. The psychological importance of such counterpoises should never be overlooked, especially by a sea power.

Moreover, a continental power's possession of oversea territories that are liable to be cut off tends to be a curb on her aggressive inclinations. That was manifest in Italy's prolonged hesitation to enter the war that started in 1939—until her ally's victory seemed certain. An entanglement of bases is a restraint even though it may not be a preventative.

water supply and a Turkish counterstroke north of Beersheba hamstrung this manœuvre. Although the Turkish front was pierced, decisive results were missed. The Turkish forces were rolled back, ultimately beyond Jerusalem, but they were not rolled up and cut off as intended.

A decision, and the attempt to reach it, were postponed a year—until September 1918. Meantime, in the desert to the east and south, a curious campaign was not only helping to weaken the fighting strength of Turkey but shedding some new light on strategy—and, in particular, on the indirect approach. This campaign was the Arab Revolt, with Lawrence as its guiding brain. While it comes into the category of guerrilla warfare, which is by its very nature indirect, its strategy had such a scientifically calculated basis that we should not miss its reflection on normal warfare. Admittedly an extreme form of the indirect approach, it was most economically effective within the limits of the instrument. The Arabs were both more mobile and less able to bear casualties than orthodox armies. The Turks were almost insusceptible to loss of men, but not to loss of material—of which they suffered a scarcity. Superb in sitting tight in a trench, firing at a directly oncoming target, they were neither adaptable to, nor able to endure the strain of, fluid operations. They were trying to hold down a vast area of country with a quantity of men which was not large enough to spread itself in a network of posts over the area. Also, they depended on a long and frail line of communications.

From these premisses was evolved a strategy which was the antithesis of orthodox doctrine. Whereas normal armies seek to preserve contact, the Arabs sought to avoid it. Whereas normal armies seek to destroy the opposing forces, the Arabs sought purely to destroy material—and to seek it at points where there was no force. But Lawrence's strategy went further. Instead of trying to drive the enemy away by cutting off their supplies, he aimed to keep them there, by allowing short rations to reach them, so that the longer they stayed the weaker and more depressed they became. Blows might induce them to concentrate, and simplify both their supply and security problems. Pin-pricks kept them spread out. Yet for all its unconventionality this strategy merely carried to its logical conclusion that of following the line of least resistance. As its author has said: 'The Arab army never tried to maintain or improve an advantage, but to move off and strike again somewhere else. It used the smallest force in the quickest time at the farthest place. To continue the action till the enemy had changed his dispositions to resist it, would have been to break the fundamental rule of denying him targets.'

What was this but the strategy evolved in 1918 on the Western Front? Fundamentally the same, but carried to a further degree.

Its application to the problem of normal warfare is conditioned by the factors of time, space, and force. While it is a quickened and active form of blockade it is inherently slower to take effect than a strategy of dislocation. Hence, if national conditions make a quick issue imperative the latter appears preferable. But unless the end is sought by an indirect approach, the 'short-cut' is likely to prove slower, more costly, and more dangerous than the 'Lawrence' strategy. Lack of room and density of force are also handicaps, if rarely insuperable. A reasoned verdict is that in normal warfare the choice should fall on the form of indirect approach which aims at a quick decision, by 'trapping' the opponent—if there is a good prospect of its success. Otherwise, or after it has failed, the choice should fall on that form of indirect approach which aims at an eventual decision by sapping the opponent's strength and will. Anything is preferable to the direct approach.

The opportunity of carrying the strategy of the Arab revolt to completion was not vouchsafed, for in September 1918—when it had reduced the Turkish forces on the Hejaz railway to a state of paralytic helplessness—the main Turkish forces in Palestine were overthrown by a single decisive stroke. In this stroke of Allenby's, however, the Arab forces played a significant part.

Whether these final operations in Palestine should be classified as a campaign or as a battle completed by a pursuit is difficult to determine. For they opened with the forces in contact and the victory was complete before that contact was broken, so that they would seem to fall into the battle category. But victory was achieved mainly by strategic means, and the share of fighting was insignificant.

This has led to a depreciation of the result, especially among those whose scale of values is governed by the dogma of Clausewitz that blood is the price of victory. Though Allenby had a superiority of more than two to one in numbers, perhaps three to one, the balance was not so heavily in his favour as in the original British advance into Palestine, which had ended in failure. And many other offensives had failed, both in the World War and earlier, with similar superiority of force.

A more serious 'depreciation' is on the score of the decaying morale of the Turks. But when full deduction is made for the advantageous conditions of September 1918, the operations deserve to rank among history's masterpieces for their breadth of vision and treatment. While the subject was not a difficult one, the picture is almost unique as a perfect conception perfectly executed —in its broad lines at least.

The plan abundantly fulfilled Willisen's definition of strategy as 'the study of communication', and also Napoleon's maxim that 'the whole secret of the art of war lies in making oneself master of the communications'. For it aimed to make the British the masters of all, and all forms of, the Turkish communications. To cut an army's lines of communication is to paralyse its physical organization. To close its line of retreat is to paralyse its moral organization. And to destroy its lines of intercommunication—by which orders and reports pass—is to paralyse its sensory organization, the essential connection between brain and body. The third effect was here sought and secured by the air force. This drove the enemy aircraft out of the air, making the enemy's command blind; and then, by bombing the main telegraph and telephone exchange of Afule, made it also deaf and dumb. The second phase of this action aptly followed the cutting of the main railway at Deraa by the Arabs, which had the physical effect of shutting off the flow of Turkish supplies temporarily—and temporarily was all that mattered here —and the mental effect of inducing the Turkish command to send part of its scanty reserves thither, just before it was deprived of its power of control.

The three so-called Turkish 'armies' depended on a single artery of railway communication from Damascus which branched at Deraa—one line continuing south to the Hejaz; the other turning west across the Jordan to Afule, where it sent out one shoot towards the sea at Haifa and the other southwards again to the railheads of the 7th and 8th Turkish armies. The 4th Army, east of the Jordan, depended on the Hejaz branch. To get a grip on Afule and the Jordan crossing near Beisan would sever the communications of the 7th and 8th armies, and also close their lines of retreat except for the difficult outlet to the desolate region east of the Jordan. To get a grip on Deraa would sever the communications of all three armies, and the best line of retreat of the 4th.

Deraa was too far to be reached from the British front in a time short enough to exert a prompt influence on the issue. Fortunately, the Arabs were available to emerge like phantoms from the desert and cut all three of its railway 'spokes'. But neither the nature of the Arab tactics nor the nature of the country lent itself to the formation of a strategic barrage across the Turkish rear. As Allenby sought a quick and complete decision he had to seek a closer site for such a barrage—one where the Jordan and the ranges west of it could be utilized to bar the enemy's exit. The railway junction of Afule and the Jordan bridge near Beisan lay within a sixty-mile radius of his front, and hence within the range of a strategic 'bound' by armoured cars and cavalry, provided that these vital points could be reached without check. The problem was to find a line of approach difficult for the Turks to obstruct in time, and to ensure that they did not block it.

How was the problem solved? The flat coastal plain of Sharon afforded a corridor to the Plain of Esdraelon and Valley of Jezreel, where Afule and Beisan lay. This corridor was interrupted by only a single door—so far back that it was unguarded—formed by the narrow mountain belt which separates the coastal Plain of Sharon from the inland Plain of Esdraelon. But the entrance to the corridor was bolted and barred by the trenches of the Turkish front.

By a long-continued psychological preparation, in which ruses were substitutes for shells, Allenby diverted the enemy's attention away from the coast to the Jordan flank. The success of the distraction was helped by the very failure of two attempted advances east of the Jordan during the spring.

In September, while the Turks' attention was still being drawn east, Allenby's troops were moving secretly west—until in the sector near the coast their two-to-one superiority had developed into five to one. On the 19th September, after a quarter of an hour's intense bombardment, the infantry advanced, swept over the two shallow Turkish trench systems, and then wheeled inland—like a huge door swinging on its hinges. The cavalry pressed through the opened door and, riding up the corridor with their armoured cars ahead, gained the passes into the Plain of Esdraelon. This successful passage owed much to the fact that the Air Force had rendered the enemy command deaf, dumb, and blind.

Next day the strategic barrage was established across the Turks' rear. Their one remaining bolt-hole was eastwards over the Jordan. They might have reached this but for the air force—since the direct infantry advance was making slow progress in face of stubborn Turkish rearguards. Early in the morning of the 21st

September, the British aircraft spotted a large column—practically all that survived of the two Turkish armies—winding down the steep gorge from Nablus to the Jordan. Four hours' air attack turned the column into a rabble. From this moment may be timed the extinction of the 7th and 8th 'armies'. The rest was but a rounding-up of cattle.

East of the Jordan, where no strategic barrage was feasible, the fate of the 4th 'army' became a rapid attrition under constant pin-pricks rather than a neat dispatch. The capture of Damascus followed. The victory was then exploited by an advance to Aleppo—200 miles beyond Damascus, and 350 miles from the front from which the British had started thirty-eight days before. During this advance they had taken 75,000 prisoners at a cost of less than 5,000 casualties.

Aleppo had just been reached when Turkey—menaced more imminently by Bulgaria's collapse and Milne's approach from Salonika on Constantinople and her rear—surrendered on the 31st October.

In analysing the decisive victory in Palestine it is to be noted that the Turks were still capable of holding up the British infantry until the strategic barrage across their rear became known and produced its inevitable, and invariable, moral effect. Further, that because a preliminary condition of trench warfare existed the infantry were necessary to break the lock. But once the normal condition of warfare was thus restored the victory was achieved by the mobile elements, which formed only a fraction of the total force. The subtlety of this particular example of indirect approach was limited to the preparation. Its execution depended purely on the dislocating and demoralizing application of mobility which, by its extreme degree, was a sustained surprise.

One other south-eastern theatre requires incidental note—Salonika. The dispatch of Allied troops thither arose out of a belated and ineffectual attempt to send succour to the Serbs in the autumn of 1915. Three years later it was the springboard of an offensive which had vital consequences. But while the retention of a foothold in the Balkans was necessary during the interval for reasons of policy, and of potental strategy, the wisdom and necessity of locking up so many troops, ultimately half a million, in what the Germans ironically called their 'largest internment camp', are open to doubt.

CHAPTER XIV

THE STRATEGY OF 1918

★

Any study of the military course of the final year is dependent upon, and inseparable from, an understanding of the naval situation preceding it. For, in default of an early military decision, the naval blockade had tended more and more to govern the military situation.

Indeed, if the historian was asked what was the day most decisive for the outcome of the World War I he might well choose the 2nd August 1914—before the war, for England, had yet begun—when Winston Churchill, then First Lord of the Admiralty, sent at 1.25 a.m. the order to mobilize the British navy. That navy was to win no Trafalgar, but it was to do more than any other factor towards winning the war for the Allies. For the navy was the instrument of the blockade, and as the fog of war dispersed in the clearer light of the post-war years that blockade was seen to assume larger and larger proportions; to be, more and more clearly, the decisive agency in the struggle. Like those 'jackets' which used to be applied in American jails to refractory prisoners, as the blockade was progressively tightened so did it first cramp the prisoner's movement and then stifle his breathing, while the tighter it became and the longer it continued the less became the prisoner's power of resistance, and the more demoralizing the sense of constriction.

Helplessness induces hopelessness, and history attests that loss of hope, not loss of lives, is what decides the issue of war. No historian would underrate the direct effect of the semi-starvation of the German people in causing the final collapse of the 'home-front'. But leaving aside the question of how far the revolution caused the military defeat, instead of vice versa, the intangible all-pervading factor of the blockade intrudes into every consideration of the military situation.

For it was the fact and the potential menace, if not perhaps the effect, of the blockade which impelled Germany to undertake her first submarine campaign in February 1915. This gave Britain a lever to loosen the Declaration of London and tighten the blockade —by claiming the right to intercept and search all ships suspected of carrying goods to Germany. Moreover, the German action in torpedoing the *Lusitania* gave the United States a vital if delayed propulsion towards entering the war, besides serving to counteract the friction between Britain and the United States caused by the tightened blockade.

Two years later, the economic strain caused by the blockade led the German military leaders to sanction an intensive renewal of the 'unlimited' submarine campaign. Britain's dependence on sea-borne supplies for the sustenance of her people and the maintenance of her armies was a weak point in her armour, and the inherently quicker effect of the submarine form of blockade lent force to the argument that this grand-strategical form of indirect approach would inflict a mortal blow. Although the calculation proved faulty, the case of Britain came critically close to establishing its correctness. The loss of shipping rose from 500,000 tons in February to 875,000 in April. By the time counter-measures combined with Germany's insufficient submarine resources to cause a progressive decline Britain had only food enough to sustain her people for another six weeks.

The German leaders' hopes of an economic decision had reacted on their fears of an economic collapse and led them to initiate the submarine campaign, fully realizing, and accepting as almost certain, the risk that it would bring the United States into the war against them. This risk became fact on the 6th April 1917. But although, as Germany calculated, America's military strength required a long time to develop, her entry into the war had a prompt effect in tightening the grip of the naval blockade. As a party to the war, the United States wielded this economic weapon with a determination, regardless of the remaining neutrals, far exceeding Britain's boldest claims in the past years of controversy over neutral rights. No longer was the blockade hindered by neutral objections. Instead, America's co-operation converted it into a stranglehold under which Germany gradually became limp, since military power is based on economic endurance—a truth too often overlooked.

The blockade may be classified as a grand strategy of indirect approach to which no effective resistance was possible and of a type which incurred no risk except in its slowness of effect. The effect, true to the law of momentum, tended to gather speed as it continued, and at the end of 1917 the Central Powers were feeling it severely. It was this economic pressure which not only lured but constrained Germany into the military offensive of 1918, which, once it failed, became *felo de se*. In default of a timely peace move on her part she had no choice between this offensive gamble and slow enfeeblement ending in eventual collapse.

If, after the Marne in 1914, or even later, she had adopted a war policy of defence in the West, offence in the East, the issue of the war might well have been different. For, on the one hand, she could unquestionably have consummated the dream of *Mittel-Europa*, while, on the other, the blockade was still a loose grip, and could hardly have been tightened effectively so long as the United States remained outside the conflict. With the whole belt of central Europe under her control, with Russia out of the war, even in economic vassalage, there is flimsy ground for any belief that the efforts of Britain, France, and Italy could have done any more, if as much as, to induce Germany to relinquish the bargaining counters of Belgium and northern France in return for the undisputed retention of her gains in the east. A greater Germany, greater too in potential strength and resources, could well have afforded to forgo the desire for a military victory over the Western Allies. Indeed, to forgo aims which are not 'worth the candle' is the difference between grand strategy and grandiose stupidity.

But in 1918 the chance had passed. Her economic endurance had been severely reduced, and the tightening blockade was reducing it faster than any late-hour infusion of the economic resources of conquered Rumania and the Ukraine could restore it.

These were the conditions under which the final German offensive, the bid for a saving military decision, was made. The release of troops from the Russian front gave her superiority of force, though considerably less than the Allies had enjoyed during their offensive campaigns. In March 1917, a total of 178 French, British, and Belgian divisions were marshalled against 129 German divisions. In March 1918, a total of 192 German divisions were available against 173 Allied divisions—counting proportionately the double-sized American divisions, of which 4½ had arrived. While the Germans were able to bring a few more divisions from the East, the American inflow developed from a trickle to a torrent under pressure of the emergency. Of the German total, 85, known as 'storm divisions', were in reserve, and of the Allied total 62—but under no centralized control; for the scheme of a general reserve of 30 divisions under the Versailles military executive committee had broken down when Haig declared that he was unable to contribute his quota of 7. When the test came, the agreement for mutual support made between the French and British commanders also broke down. Disaster hastened an overdue step, and on Haig's initiative Foch was appointed, first to co-ordinate, and then to command, the Allied armies.

The German plan was distinguished by a research for tactical surprise more thorough and far-reaching than in any of the earlier operations of the war. It is to the credit of the German command and staff that they realized how rarely the possession of superior force offsets the disadvantage of attacking in the obvious way. Also, that effective surprise can only be attained by a subtle compound of many deceptive elements. And that only by such a compound key could a gate be opened in the long-locked front.

A brief but intense bombardment with gas-shell was to be the main element—Ludendorff had failed to grasp the significance of the tank and to develop it in time. But, in addition, the infantry were trained in new infiltration tactics—of which the guiding idea was that the leading troops should probe and penetrate the weak points of the defence, while the reserves were directed to back up success, not to redeem failure. The assaulting divisions were brought up by night marches; the masses of artillery were brought close to the front line in concealment, and opened fire without preliminary 'registration'. Further, the preparations made for successive attacks at other points helped to mystify the defender, while being in readiness for the future.

This was not all. From the experience of the vain Allied offensives Ludendorff had drawn the deduction that 'tactics have to be considered before purely strategical objects which it is futile to pursue unless tactical success is possible'. In default of a strategical indirect approach, this was undoubtedly true. Hence in the German design the new tactics were to be accompanied by a new strategy. One was the corollary of the other, both based on a new or resurrected principle—that of following the line of least resistance. The conditions of 1918 in France limited the scope for taking, and Ludendorff did not attempt to take, the line of least expectation. But with the opposing armies spread out in contact along the far-flung line of entrenchments, a quick break-through fol-

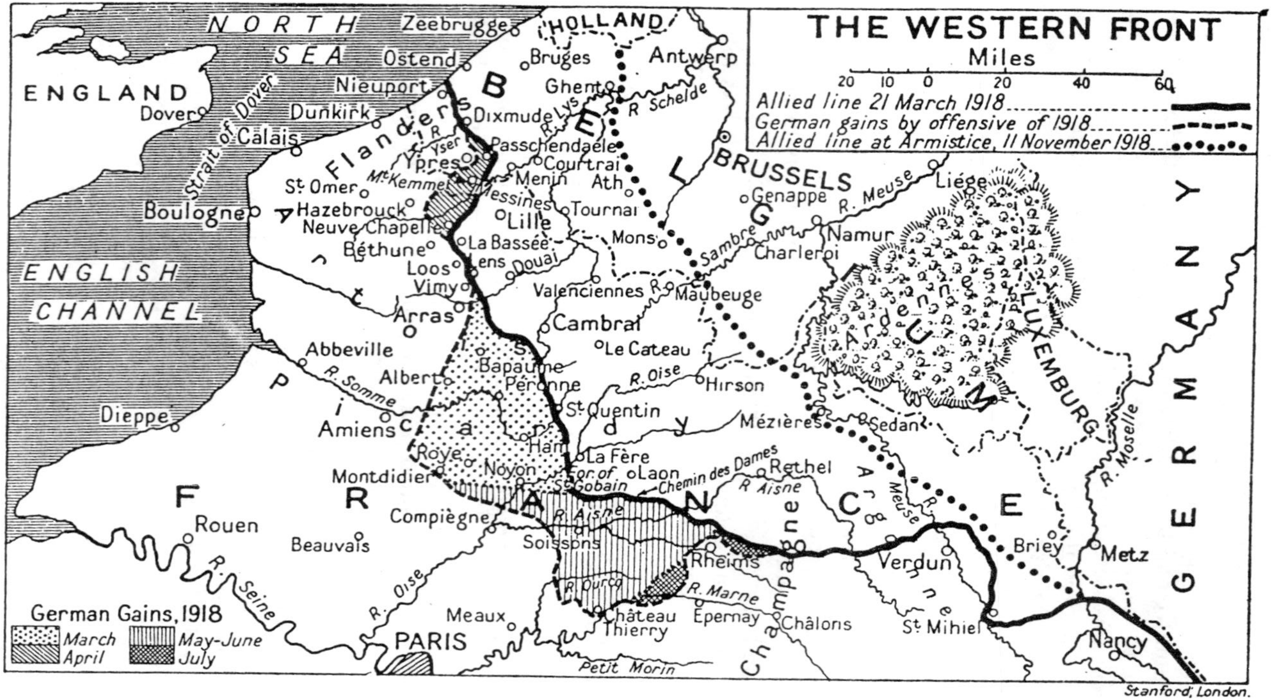
THE WESTERN FRONT
Miles
20 10 0 20 40 60
Allied line 21 March 1918
German gains by offensive of 1918
Allied line at Armistice, 11 November 1918
German Gains, 1918
March
April
May-June
July
ENGLAND
Dover
NORTH SEA
Strait of Dover
ENGLISH CHANNEL
HOLLAND
BELGIUM
LUXEMBURG
GERMANY
FRANCE
Flanders
Artois
Picardy
Champagne
Ardennes
Zeebrugge
Ostend
Nieuport
Dunkirk
Calais
Boulogne
St. Omer
Hazebrouck
Neuve Chapelle
Béthune
Loos
Vimy
Arras
Abbeville
Albert
Amiens
Dieppe
Rouen
Beauvais
Montdidier
Roye
Noyon
Compiègne
Soissons
Meaux
PARIS
Château Thierry
Epernay
Châlons
Rheims
Bruges
Ghent
Antwerp
BRUSSELS
Dixmude
Passchendaele
Ypres
Mt. Kemmel
Messines
Courtrai
Menin
Ath
Tournai
Lille
La Bassée
Lens
Douai
Mons
Valenciennes
Maubeuge
Cambrai
Le Cateau
Bapaume
Péronne
St. Quentin
Ham
La Fère
For. of St. Gobain
Laon
Chemin des Dames
Rethel
Hirson
Mézières
Sedan
Genappe
Charleroi
Namur
Liége
Verdun
St. Mihiel
Briey
Metz
Nancy
R. Yser
R. Lys
R. Scheldt
R. Sambre
R. Meuse
R. Somme
R. Oise
R. Aisne
R. Ourcq
R. Marne
R. Seine
R. Moselle
Petit Morin
Stanford, London.

lowed by a rapid exploitation along the line of least resistance might come within reach of a goal which normally has been only attainable by taking the line of least expectation.

The break-through proved quick, the exploitation rapid. Yet the plan failed. Where did the fault lie? The general criticism subsequent to the event, and to the war, was that the tactical bias had led Ludendorff to change direction and dissipate his strength—to concentrate on tactical success at the expense of the strategical goal. It seemed, and was said, that the principle was false. But a closer examination of the German documents since available, and of Ludendorff's own orders and instructions, throws a different light on the question. It would seem that the real fault lay in Ludendorff's failure to carry out in practice the new principle he had adopted in theory—that he either did not grasp or shrank from the full implications of this new strategic theory. For, in fact, he dissipated too large a part of his reserves in trying to redeem tactical failure, and hesitated too long over decisions to exploit his tactical successes.

The trouble began even in his choice of the point of attack. It was to be made by the 17th, 2nd, and 18th Armies on a sixty-mile front between Arras and La Fère. Two alternative proposals had been considered. One, for an attack on the flanks of the Verdun salient, had been rejected on the score that the ground was unfavourable; that a break-through could hardly lead to a decisive result; and that the French army had recuperated too well after nearly a year's undisturbed convalescence. The other, for an attack between Ypres and Lens—although favoured by Ludendorff's strategical adviser, Wetzell, and espoused by Prince Rupprecht, commanding the front between St. Quentin and the sea—was rejected on the score that it would meet the main mass of the British army and that the low-lying ground would be late in drying.

The choice fell on the Arras-La Fère sector for the reason that, apart from the ground being favourable, this sector was the weakest in defences, defenders, and reserves. Moreover, it was close to the joint between the French and British armies. Ludendorff hoped to separate the two, and then pulverize the British army, which he estimated to be weakened seriously by its prolonged efforts at Ypres. But although the comparative weakness of this sector was true as a generalization, in detail his judgement was badly at fault. The northerly third of it was strong and strongly held, by the

British 3rd Army, with 14 divisions (of which 4 were in reserve), while the bulk of the British reserves were on this flank—which could, and did, receive support more quickly from the other British armies, further north. The remaining two-thirds of the front upon which the German blow fell was held by the British 5th Army. The central sector facing the German 2nd Army was held by 5 divisions. The southern, and longer, part facing the Germany 18th Army, was held by 7 divisions (of which one was in reserve).

Ludendorff gave his 17th Army, near Arras, 19 divisions for the initial attack, by its left wing only, on a fourteen-mile front. As the British salient towards Cambrai was not to be attacked directly, but pinched out, this five-mile stretch was adequately occupied by 2 German divisions of the German 2nd Army. This army concentrated 18 divisions against the left wing of the British 5th Army (5 divisions), on a fourteen-mile front. On the extreme south, either side of Saint Quentin, came the 18th Army. Ludendorff gave it only 24 divisions to attack on a twenty-seven-mile frontage. Despite his new principle, he was distributing his strength according to the enemy's strength, and not concentrating against the weakest resistance.

The direction given in his orders emphasized this tendency still more. The main effort was to be exerted north of the Somme. After breaking through, the 17th and 2nd Armies were to wheel north-west, pressing the British back towards the coast, while the river and the 18th Army guarded their flank. The 18th Army was merely an offensive flank-guard. As it turned out, this plan was radically changed, and had the appearance of following the line of least resistance, because Ludendorff gained rapid success where he desired it little, and failed to gain success where he wanted it most.

The attack was launched on the 21st March, and the surprise was helped by an early morning mist. While the thrust broke through completely south of the Somme, where the defence—but also the attacking force—was thinnest, it was held up near Arras, a check which reacted on all the attack north of the river. Such a result was a calculable certainty. But Ludendorff, still violating his new principle, spent the following days in trying to revive his attack against the strong and firmly held bastion of Arras—maintaining this direction as his principal line of effort. Meantime he kept a tight rein on the 18th Army, which was advancing in the south without serious check from its opponents. As late as the 26th March he issued orders which restrained it from crossing the Avre, and tied it to the pace of its neighbour, the 2nd—which, in turn, was held back by the very limited success of the 17th Army, near Arras. Thus we see that in reality Ludendorff was bent on breaking the British army by breaking down its strongest sector of resistance in a direct assault. Because of this obsession he failed, until too late, to throw the weight of his reserves along the line of least resistance south of the Somme.

The intended wheel to the north-west might have been fulfilled if it had been made after passing the flank, and thus been directed against the rear, of the Arras bastion. On the 26th March the attack north of the Somme (by the left wing of the 17th Army and the right of the 2nd Army) was visibly weakening—the price of its hard-earned gains. South of the Somme the left of the 2nd Army reached, and was now to be embarrassed by, the desert of the old Somme battlefields—a brake on movement and supply. The 18th Army alone was advancing with unslackened impetus.

This situation led Ludendorff to adopt a new plan, but without relinquishing his old. He ordered for the 28th March a fresh and direct attack on the high ground near Arras—by the right of the 17th Army, and to be followed by a 6th Army attack just to the north, between Vimy and La Bassée. But the promising situation south of the Somme led him to indicate Amiens as the principal goal for the 2nd Army. Even so, he restrained the 18th Army from pushing on, to turn the flank of the Amiens resistance, without fresh orders. Amiens, having been recognized as an additional main objective, was to be gained by a direct approach across bad ground.

On the 28th March the Arras attack was launched, unshielded by mist or surprise, and failed completely in face of the well-prepared resistance of Byng's 3rd Army. Only then did Ludendorff abandon his original idea, and direct his main effort, and some of his remaining reserves, towards Amiens. Meantime he ordered the 18th Army to mark time for two days. When the attack was renewed on the 30th March it had little force, and made little progress in face of a resistance that had been allowed time to harden—helped by the cement of French reserves which were now being poured into the sagging wall. That day was the first on which the French artillery, arriving later than the infantry, had come into action in force. A further German effort was made by 15 divisions, of which only 4 were fresh, on the 4th of April, and had still less success.

Rather than be drawn into an attrition struggle, Ludendorff then suspended the attack towards Amiens. At no time had he thrown his weight along the line of fracture between the British and French armies. Yet on the 24th March, Pétain had intimated to Haig that if the German progress continued along his line he would have to draw back the French reserves south-westwards to cover Paris. Only a little more German pressure would have been needed to turn the crack into a yawning chasm.

The knowledge brings confirmation of two historical lessons—that a joint is the most sensitive and profitable point of attack, and that a penetration between two forces or units is more dangerous if they are assembled shoulder to shoulder than if they are widely separated and organically separate.

With a large part of his reserves holding the vast bulge south of Arras, Ludendorff turned, without much confidence, to release a fresh attack further north. On the 25th March he had ordered a small scale attack to be prepared between La Bassée and Armentières as a step towards expanding the width of his break-through. After the failure of his Arras attack on the 28th March, he had extended the scheme. The attack south of Armentières was to be followed twenty-four hours later by an attack north of it, pinching out the town.

Arranged late, the attack was not ready for launching until the 9th April, and, even so, was conceived merely as a diversion. But its astonishing early success—helped again by an early morning fog—against a weakened sector, led Ludendorff to convert it bit by bit into a major effort. Along an eleven-mile front south of Armentières, 9 German divisions, with 5 more in the second wave, fell on 1 Portuguese and 2 British divisions (behind which were 2 more in close reserve). Next day 4 divisions, with 2 more in the second line, attacked north of Armentières on a seven-mile front—again helped by a thick mist. As the resistance began to harden, fresh divisions were thrown in by driblets, until by the end of the first week in May more than 40 had been used. Ludendorff had thus drifted into an attrition campaign.

The British were desperately close to their bases, and the sea, but their resistance had stopped the German tide, after a ten-mile invasion, just short of the important railway junction of Hazebrouck. Then, on the 17th April, Ludendorff attempted a convergent blow on either side of Ypres—but it was forestalled, and almost nullified, by Haig's indirect action in swinging back his line here during the previous forty-eight hours. This project having been deflated, Ludendorff returned to a purely direct attack south of Ypres, where French reserves had arrived to take over part of the line. The attack on the 25th April, falling on the joint, cracked it at Kemmel Hill; but Ludendorff stopped the exploitation for fear of a counter-stroke. Throughout he had doled out reserves sparingly, too late and too few for real success. After the failure of his first offensive he seems to have had little faith in the second, and after a final effort on the 29th he stopped it. But he intended only a temporary suspension until he could draw off the French reserves to their own front—planning then to strike a final and decisive blow at the British in Flanders.

Already, he had ordered preparations for an attack on the Chemin-des-Dames sector between Soissons and Reims. This was intended for the 17th April, but was not ready until the 27th May—largely owing to Ludendorff's prolongation of the Flanders offensive, with its consequent drain on his reserves. The intelligence branch of the American G.H.Q. had predicted the site and approximate date of the attack, but their warnings were only heeded at a late hour when confirmed by a prisoner's report on the 26th May. It was then too late to strengthen the defence, beyond putting the troops on the alert, but the warning enabled reserves to get on the move. Next morning the blow was delivered by 15 divisions, with 7 more close behind—along a twenty-four-mile front held by 5 divisions, French and British (with 4 in reserve behind them). Covered at the start by a cloak of mist and smoke, the attack swept the defenders off the Chemin-des-Dames, and then over the Aisne. It reached the Marne by the 30th May. But once again Ludendorff had obtained a measure of success for which he was neither prepared nor desirous. The surpriser was himself surprised. The opening success not only attracted thither too large a proportion of his own reserves, but forfeited their effect—because they had no start over the Allied reserves in the race.

The extent of the opening success offers scope for analysis. It would seem to have been due in part to the distraction of the Allies' attention and reserves elsewhere, in part to pursuing more assiduously the line of least resistance, and in part to the folly of the local French army commander. He insisted on the infantry being massed in the forward positions, there to be compressed cannon-fodder for the German guns. The artillery, local reserves and command posts of the defence were similarly close to the front—and in consequence the quicker and greater was the collapse that followed the German break-through. Thereby the attack regained the tactical surprise effect which it had partly lost the day before it was launched. For, as the object of all surprise is dislocation, the effect is similar whether the opponent be caught napping by deception or allows himself to be trapped with his eyes open.

Ludendorff had now created two huge bulges, and another smaller one, in the Allied front. His next attempt was to pinch out the Compiègne buttress which lay between the Somme and Marne bulges. But this time there was no surprise, and the blow on the west side of the buttress, on the 9th June, was too late to coincide with the pressure on the east.

A month's pause followed. Ludendorff was anxious to fulfil his long-cherished idea of a decisive blow against the British in Belgium, but he considered that their reserves there were still too strong, and so again decided on a diversion—hoping that a heavy blow in the south would draw off the British reserves. He had failed to pinch out the Compiègne buttress on the west of his Marne salient; he was now about to attempt the same thing on the east, by attacking on either side of Reims. But he needed an interval for rest and preparation, and the delay was fatal—giving the British and French time to recuperate, and the Americans time to gather strength.

The tactical success of his own blows had been Ludendorff's undoing—in the sense that, yielding to their influence, he had pressed each too far and too long, thus using up his own reserves, and causing an undue interval between each blow. He had followed, not the line of least resistance, but the line of hardening resistance. After the initial break-through, each attack had become strategically a pure direct approach. He had driven in three great wedges, but none had penetrated far enough to sever a vital artery; and this strategic failure left the Germans with an indented front which invited flanking counter-strokes.

On the 15th July Ludendorff launched his new attack, but its coming was no secret. East of Reims it was foiled by an elastic defence, and west of Reims the German penetration across the Marne merely enmeshed them more deeply to their downfall—for on the 18th July Foch launched a long-prepared stroke against the other flank of the Marne salient. Here Pétain, who directed the operation, employed the key which Ludendorff lacked, using masses of light tanks to lead a surprise attack—on the Cambrai model. The Germans managed to hold the gates of the salient open long enough to draw their forces back into safety, and straighten their line. But their reserves were depleted. Ludendorff was forced, first to postpone, and then to abandon the offensive in Flanders, so that the initiative definitely and finally passed to the Allies.

The nature of the Allied counter-stroke on the Marne requires examination. Pétain had asked Foch to assemble two groups of reserves at Beauvais and Epernay respectively, with a view to a counter-stroke against the flank of, and subsequent to, any fresh German attack. The first group, under Mangin, was used to break the German attack of the 9th June, and was then switched to a position on the west face of the Marne salient. Foch planned to use it for the direct purpose of an attack against the rail centre of Soissons. While this was being prepared the intelligence service obtained definite news of the forthcoming German attack near Reims. Foch thereupon determined to anticipate it, not retort to it, by launching his stroke on the 12th July. Pétain, however, had the contrary idea of letting the Germans come on and entangle themselves, and then of striking at their rear flank. And, somewhat curiously, the French troops were not ready on the 12th—so that the battle was fought more according to Pétain's than to Foch's conception. More, but not wholly. For Pétain's plan had been, first, to yield his forward position to the attackers, by holding it lightly, and bring them to a halt in face of the intact rear position; then to launch local counter-attacks so that the enemy might be drawn to engage their reserves in the new pockets that their attacks on either side of Reims would make; finally, to unleash Mangin to the real counter-offensive eastward along the base-line of the main Marne salient. Thereby he might close the neck of the vast sack in which the German forces south of the Aisne would be enclosed.

Events and Foch combined to modify this conception. East of Reims the German attack was nullified by the elastic defence—a form of tactical indirect approach. But west of Reims the commanders persisted in the old rigid method of defence, and had their line broken. The Germans penetrated beyond the Marne; to avert the danger, Pétain was driven to throw in most of the reserves he had intended for use in his second phase. To replace them, he decided to draw from Mangin and to postpone the latter's counter-stroke, already ordered by Foch for the 18th July. When Foch heard of this order, he promptly countermanded it. Hence the second phase had to be dropped out, so that the German reserves were available to hold Mangin back, and hold open the neck of the sack. The counter-stroke soon became a purely direct pressure converging, like Falkenhayn's of 1915 in Poland, on the whole sack and pressing the Germans back out of it.

Foch's governing idea henceforth was simply to keep the initiative and to give the enemy no rest while his own reserves were accumulating. His first step was to free his own lateral railways by a series of local offensives. The first was made by Haig on the 8th August in front of Amiens. By skilful precautions and deceptions, Rawlinson's 4th Army was doubled, and the attack—led by 450 tanks—was, in its opening, perhaps the most complete surprise of the war. Although it soon came to a halt—the directness of its pressure was a natural reason—its initial shock of surprise sufficed to dislocate the moral balance of the German Supreme Command, and by convincing Ludendorff of the moral bankruptcy of his troops led him to declare that peace must be sought by negotiation. Meantime, he said, 'the object of our strategy must be to paralyse the enemy's war-will gradually by a strategic defensive'.

Meantime, however, the Allies evolved a new strategic method. Foch gave the first impulse by ordering a succession of attacks at different points. Haig completed its evolution by refusing to agree to Foch's instructions for a continuance of the 4th Army's frontal pressure. Its advance was only resumed after the 3rd and 1st Armies in turn had struck. Hence the Allied offensive—although only in the sphere of Haig's and Pétain's control—became a series of rapid blows at different points, each broken off as soon as its initial impetus waned, each so aimed as to pave the way for the next, and all close enough in time and space to react on one another. Thus a check was placed on Ludendorff's power of switching reserves to anticipate the blows, and a progressive tax placed upon his reserve balance—at an economical cost to the Allied resources. This method, if not a true indirect approach, appears at least a border-line case. If it did not take the line of least expectation, it avoided the line of natural expectation. If it did not take the line of least resistance, it never continued along the line of hardening resistance. In effect, it was a negative form of the indirect approach.

In view of the moral and numerical decline of the German

forces, this method sufficed, for a time at any rate, to ensure a continuous advance and gradual weakening of the German resistance. The clear evidence of this decline and Haig's consequent assurance that he could break the Hindenburg Line, where the German reserves were strongest, caused Foch to relinquish the method in favour of a general and simultaneous offensive at the end of September.

The plan was for a directly convergent pressure upon the vast salient formed by the German front in France. It was hoped that the two Allied wings—formed by the British and Americans respectively—would, as they closed in, cut off a large part of the German armies in the salient. This hope was based on the idea that the Ardennes formed an almost impassable back wall with narrow exits on the flanks. One may add, incidentally, that this idea of the Ardennes must have arisen from a lack of knowledge of the district—for it is well-roaded, and most of it is rolling rather than mountainous country.[1]

Originally, on Pershing's suggestion, the plan had contained a certain degree of indirectness of approach. His proposal was that the American army should exploit its local success in erasing the Saint Mihiel salient by an advance towards Briey, and past Metz, with the aim of getting astride the German communications in Lorraine and menacing their western line of retreat to the Rhine. But Haig objected to this move as divergent from, instead of convergent with, the other Allied attacks. And Foch changed his plan accordingly, discarding Pershing's project. The American army, in consequence, had to transfer its effort westwards and hastily mount an attack, with a bare week's preparation, in the Meuse-Argonne sector. Here the prolonged pressure along the line of hardening resistance resulted in high cost and profound confusion, besides proving unnecessary to ease Haig's advance through the Hindenburg Line.

There, the course of events tended to demonstrate that a direct approach, given overwhelming fire superiority and a morally decaying opponent, can break into the enemy's position—but cannot break him up. By the 11th November, the date of the Armistice, the German forces, at the sacrifice of their rearguards, were safely out of the salient and back on a shortened and straightened line.

[1] A similar misjudgement led the Allied Command in May 1940 to discount the possibility that the German mechanized forces would attempt that route of invasion.

The Allied advance had practically come to a standstill—less because of German resistance than because of the difficulty of its own maintenance and supply across the devastated areas. Under these conditions, a direct approach had merely helped the Germans to slip away faster than they could be followed.

Fortunately, the last phase of the military offensive mattered little. The moral blow which the initial surprise of the 8th August had given to the German Command was completed, and made mortal, by an indirect approach in a far-distant theatre. This was the Allied offensive on the Salonika front. Aimed at a sector where the terrain was so difficult that the defenders were few, it soon broke through. Once this had happened, the difficult mountain country hindered the defenders switching their reserves laterally to block the progress of the advance down the line of least resistance. With their army split in two, the war-weary Bulgarians craved an armistice. This achievement not only knocked away the first prop of the Central Alliance but opened the way for an advance upon Austria's rear.

The menace became closer when an Italian offensive fell on, and broke through, Austria's morally shaken and physically exhausted front; for with Austria's prompt capitulation her territory and railways were available to the Allies as a base of operations against Germany's back door. In September, General von Gallwitz had told the German Chancellor that such a contingency would be 'decisive'.

This menace, together with the heightened moral effect of the blockade—that other, grand-strategical, indirect approach—on a people now hunger-stricken and hopeless, constituted a pair of spurs by which in the last days the German Government was urged towards surrender. They were spurs applied to a bolting steed, but a crack of the whip had made it bolt—the news of the collapse of Bulgaria, reinforced by the first reports of the renewal of the frontal attack in France.

The Supreme Command lost its nerve—only for a matter of days, but that was sufficient, and recovery too late. On the 29th September, Hindenburg and Ludendorff took the precipitate decision to appeal for an armistice, saying that the collapse of the Bulgarian front had upset all their dispositions—'troops destined for the Western Front had had to be dispatched there'. This had 'fundamentally changed' the situation in view of the attacks then being launched on the Western Front; for although these 'had so far been beaten off, their continuance must be reckoned with'.

This clause refers to Foch's general offensive. The American attack in the Meuse-Argonne had begun on the 26th September, but had come practically to a standstill by the 28th. A Franco-Belgo-British attack had opened in Flanders on the 28th; if unpleasant, it did not look really menacing. But on the morning of the 29th Haig's main blow was falling on the Hindenburg Line, and the early news was disquieting.

In this emergency, Prince Max of Baden was called to be Chancellor—to negotiate for peace, with his international reputation for moderation and honour as a covering pledge. To bargain effectively, and without confession of defeat, he needed, and asked, a breathing space 'of ten, eight, even four days, before I have to appeal to the enemy'. But Hindenburg merely reiterated that 'the gravity of the military situation admits of no delay', and insisted that 'a peace offer to our enemies be issued at once'.

Hence, on the 3rd October, the appeal for an immediate armistice went out to President Wilson. It was an open confession of defeat to the world. Even before this—on the 1st October—the Supreme Command had undermined their own home front by communicating the same impression to a meeting of the leaders of all political parties.

Men who had so long been kept in the dark were blinded by the sudden light. All the forces of discord and weakness received an immense impulse.

Within a few days the Supreme Command became more cheerful, even optimistic, when it saw that the British success in breaking into the Hindenburg Line had not been followed by an actual break-through of the fighting front. More encouragement came from reports of a slackening in the force of the Allies' attacks, particularly in the exploitation of opportunities. Ludendorff still wanted an armistice, but only to give his troops a rest as a prelude to further resistance, and to ensure a secure withdrawal to a shortened defensive line on the frontier. By the 17th October he even felt he could do it without a rest. It was less that the situation had changed than that his impression of it had been revised. The situation had never been quite so bad as he had pictured it on the 29th September. But his first impression had now spread throughout the political circles and public of Germany—as the ripples spread when a pebble has been dropped in a pool. The 'home-front' began to crumble later, but it crumbled quicker than the battle-front.

On the 23rd October, President Wilson replied to the German requests by a note which virtually required an unconditional surrender. Ludendorff wished to carry on the struggle in the hope that a successful defence of the German frontier might damp the determination of the Allies. But the situation had passed beyond his control, the nation's will-power was broken, and his advice was in discredit. On the 26th October he was forced to resign.

Then for thirty-six hours the Chancellor lay in coma from an overdose of sleeping draught. When he returned to his office on the evening of the 3rd November, not only Turkey but Austria had capitulated. The back door was open. Next day revolution broke out in Germany, and swept rapidly over the country, fanned, as peace negotiations were delayed, by the Kaiser's reluctance to abdicate. Compromise with the revolutionaries was the only chance, and on the 9th Prince Max handed over to the Socialist Ebert. The German armistice plenipotentiaries were already with Foch. At 5 a.m., on the 11th November, they signed the terms: at 11 a.m. the war was over.

The issue of the war had been finally decided on the 29th September—decided in the mind of the German Command. Ludendorff and his associates had then 'cracked', and the sound went echoing backwards until it had resounded throughout the whole of Germany. Nothing could catch it or stop it. The Command might recover its nerve, the actual military position might improve, but the moral impression—as ever in war—was decisive.

Among the causes of Germany's surrender the blockade is seen to be the most fundamental. Its existence is the surest answer to the question whether but for the revolution the German armies could have stood firm on their own frontiers. For even if the German people, roused to a supreme effort in visible defence of their own soil, could have held the Allied armies at bay, the end could only have been postponed—because of the grip of sea-power, Britain's historic weapon.

But in hastening the surrender, in preventing a continuance of the war into 1919, military action ranks foremost. This conclusion does not imply that, at the moment of the Armistice, Germany's military power was broken or her armies decisively beaten, nor that the Armistice was a mistaken concession. Rather does the record of the last 'hundred days', when sifted, confirm the immemorial lesson that the true aim in war is the mind of the hostile rulers, not the bodies of their troops; that the balance between victory and defeat turns on mental impressions and only indirectly on physical blows. It was the shock of being surprised, and the feeling that he was powerless to counter potential strategic moves, that shook Ludendorff's nerve more than the loss of prisoners, guns, and acreage.

PART III

★

STRATEGY OF THE SECOND WORLD WAR

CHAPTER XV

HITLER'S STRATEGY

★

The course of Hitler's campaigns, before and after the outbreak of actual war in 1939, provided a most striking demonstration of the method traced in the earlier part of this book. In his first period he gave the strategy of indirect approach a new extension, logistically and psychologically, both in the field and in the forum. Later, he gave his opponents ample opportunity to exploit the indirect approach against him.

It is wise in war not to underrate your opponents. It is equally important to understand his methods, and how his mind works. Such understanding is the necessary foundation of a successful effort to foresee and forestall his moves. The peaceful Powers suffered a lot from 'missing the bus' through their slowness to gauge what Hitler would next attempt. A nation might profit a lot if the advisory organs of government included an 'enemy department', covering all spheres of war and studying the problems of the war from the enemy's point of view—so that, in this state of detachment, it might succeed in predicting what he was likely to do next.

Nothing may seem more strange to the future historian than the way that the governments of the democracies failed to anticipate the course which Hitler would pursue. For never has a man of such immense ambition so clearly disclosed beforehand both the general process and particular methods by which he was seeking to fulfil it. *Mein Kampf*, together with his speeches and other utterances, provided abundant clues to his direction and sequence of action. If this amazingly clear self-revelation of how his mind worked is the best evidence that what he achieved was not a matter of accident, nor of mere opportunism, it is also the clearest confirmation of the proverbial saying—'What fools men are'. Even Napoleon did not show such contemptuous disregard for his opponents, and for the risks of unveiling his intentions. Hitler's apparent carelessness in this respect showed a realization that men easily miss what is right under their eye, that concealment can often be found in the obvious, and that in some cases the most direct approach can become the least expected—just as the art of secrecy lies in being so open about most things that the few things that matter are not even suspected to exist.

Lawrence of Arabia remarked of Lenin that he was the only man who had thought out a revolution, carried it out, and consolidated it. That observation can be applied also to Hitler—with the addition that he had 'written it out'. It is clear, too, that he had profited by studying the methods of the Bolshevik revolution, not only in gaining power, but in extending it. It was Lenin who enunciated the axiom that 'the soundest strategy in war is to postpone operations until the moral disintegration of the enemy renders the delivery of the mortal blow both possible and easy'. There is a marked resemblance between this and Hitler's saying that 'our real wars will in fact all be fought before military operations begin'. In Rauschning's account of a discussion on the subject, in *Hitler Speaks*, he declared—'How to achieve the moral breakdown of the enemy before the war has started—that is the problem that interests me. Whoever has experienced war at the front will want to refrain from all avoidable bloodshed.'

In concentrating on that problem Hitler diverged from the orthodox trend of German military thought which, for a century, had concentrated on battle—and had led most of the other nations along the same narrow path of military theory. Accepting the Prussian philosopher of war, Clausewitz, as their master, they blindly swallowed his undigested aphorisms. Such as—'The bloody solution of the crisis, the effort for the destruction of the enemy's forces, is the first-born son of war.' 'Only great and general battles can produce great results.' 'Blood is the price of victory.' 'Let us not hear of generals who conquer without bloodshed.' Clausewitz rejected the idea that 'there is a skilful method of disarming and overcoming an enemy without great bloodshed, and that this is the proper tendency of the Art of War'. He dismissed it as a notion born in the imagination of 'philanthropists'. He took no account of the fact that it might be dictated by enlightened self-interest, by the desire for an issue profitable to the nation; not merely a gladiatorial decision. The outcome of his teaching, applied by unthinking disciples, was to incite generals to seek battle at the *first* opportunity, instead of creating an *advan-*

tageous opportunity. Thereby the art of war was reduced in 1914–18 to a process of mutual mass-slaughter.

Whatever the limit of his lights, Hitler at least transcended these conventional bounds. Rauschning quotes him as saying—'People have killed only when they could not achieve their aim in other ways. . . . There is a broadened strategy, with intellectual weapons. . . . Why should I demoralize the enemy by military means if I can do so better and more cheaply in other ways?' 'Our strategy is to destroy the enemy from within, to conquer him through himself.'

The extent to which Hitler gave a new direction and wider meaning to the German doctrine of war may best be seen by comparing his theory with that of General Ludendorff—the director of Germany's war-effort in the last war, and Hitler's former associate in the abortive 1923 project to seize control of Germany by a 'march on Berlin'.

After the establishment of the totalitarian state, and after he had had nearly twenty years for reflection on the lessons of the last war, Ludendorff set forth his conclusions as to future 'totalitarian warfare'. He opened with a heavy attack on the theories of Clausewitz which had been the foundation of the German doctrine in 1914. To Ludendorff, their fault was not that they went too far in the way of unlimited violence, regardless of cost, but that they did not go far enough. He criticized Clausewitz for allowing policy too much importance, not too little. As typical of Clausewitz, he cited a passage concluding—'The political goal is the *end*, and warfare is a means leading to it, and a means can never be thought of without a certain end.' In Ludendorff's view, this was out of date. The totalitarian principle demanded that in war a nation should place everything at its service; and, in peace, at the service of the next war. War was the highest expression of the national 'will to live', and politics must therefore be subservient to the conduct of war.

Reading Ludendorff's book, it became clear that the main difference between his theory and Clausewitz's was that the former had come to think of war as a means without an end—unless making the nation into an army be considered an end in itself. This was hardly so new as Ludendorff appeared to imagine. Sparta tried it, and in the end succumbed to self-inflicted paralysis. With the aim of developing the nation for war, of creating a super-Sparta, Ludendorff's primary concern was to ensure 'the psychical unity of the people'. Towards this, he sought to cultivate a religion of nationalism through which all women would accept that their noblest role was to bear sons to 'bear the burden of the totalitarian war', and all men would develop their powers for that purpose—in short, to breed, and be bred, for slaughter. The other positive suggestions which Ludendorff offered towards achieving 'psychical unity' amounted to little more than the age-old prescription of suppressing everyone who might express, or even entertain, views contrary to those of the High Command.

Another condition on which Ludendorff insisted was the need for a self-sufficient national economic system suited to the demands of totalitarian war. From this, he appeared to realize that military power rests on an economic foundation. Yet, curiously, when he dwelt on the crippling difficulties caused in the last war by the Allied blockade, he did not see how this admission reflected on his belief that wars are decided by battle between the armies. On this score, he considered that Germany's old master deserved praise—'Clausewitz only thinks of the annihilation of the hostile armies in battle'. In Ludendorff's view this remained an 'immutable principle'—whereas in Hitler's original view the true aim of a war leader should be to produce the capitulation of the hostile armies without a battle.

Ludendorff's picture of the way that the next war would be waged was merely an intensified reproduction of the offensives he had carried out in 1918—which had been brilliant in their opening but barren in their issue. For him the offensive was still a battle-process in which the infantry would be helped forward by artillery, machine-guns, mortars, and tanks until it 'overwhelms the enemy in a man-to-man fight'. All movements should lead to battle; mechanization would merely quicken the rush to battle.

It was not that Ludendorff had any moral or even soldierly objection to the more widely spread forms of warfare. He remarked that the requirements of totalitarian warfare 'will ever ignore the cheap theoretical desire to abolish unrestricted U-boat warfare', while aircraft would in future combine with submarines at sinking every ship which tried to reach the enemy's ports—'even vessels sailing under neutral flags'. And in regard to the question of striking direct at the civil population, he emphasized that a time would come when 'bombing squadrons must inexorably and without pity be sent against them'. But on military grounds, which for him were paramount, the air force must first be used to help in beating the opposing army. Only then should it be unleashed against the interior of the opposing country.

While welcoming every new weapon and instrument, he added them to his armoury rather than fitted them into any grand strategic pattern. He conveyed no clear idea, and seemed to have none, of the relationship between the different elements in war. His message was, in brief—multiply every kind of force as much as you can, and you will get somewhere—but where, he neither wondered nor worried. The one point on which he was really clear was that 'the military Commander-in-Chief must lay down his instructions for the political leaders, and the latter must follow and fulfil them in the service of war'. In other words, those who are responsible for national policy must give him a blank cheque drawn on the present resources of, and future prosperity of, the nation.

Much as there was in common between Ludendorff and Hitler in their conception of the race, the state, and the German people's right to dominate, their differences were quite as great—especially in regard to method.

While Ludendorff demanded the absurdity that strategy should control policy—which is like saying the tool should decide its own task—Hitler solved that problem by combining the two functions in one person. Thus he enjoyed the same advantage as Alexander and Caesar in the ancient world, or Frederick the Great and Napoleon in later times. This gave him an unlimited opportunity, such as no pure strategist would enjoy, to prepare and develop his means for the end he had in view. At the same time he had early grasped what the soldier, by his very profession, is less ready to recognize—that the military weapon is but one of the means that serve the purposes of war: one out of the assortment which grand strategy can employ.

While there are many causes for which a state goes to war, its fundamental object can be epitomized as that of ensuring the continuance of its policy—in face of the determination of the opposing state to pursue a contrary policy. In the human will lies the source and mainspring of conflict. For a state to gain its object in war it has to change this adverse will into compliance with its own policy. Once this is realized, the military principle of 'destroying the main armed forces on the battlefield', which Clausewitz's disciples exalted to a paramount position, fits into its proper place along with the other instruments of grand strategy—which include the more oblique kinds of military action as well as economic pressure, propaganda, and diplomacy. Instead of giving excessive emphasis to one means, which circumstances may render ineffective, it is wiser to choose and combine whichever are the most suitable, most penetrative, and most conservative of effort—i.e. which will subdue the opposing will at the lowest war-cost and minimum injury to the post-war prospect. For the most decisive victory is of no value if a nation be bled white in gaining it.

It should be the aim of grand strategy to discover and pierce the Achilles' heel of the opposing government's power to make war. And strategy, in turn, should seek to penetrate a joint in the harness of the opposing forces. To apply one's strength where the opponent is strong weakens oneself disproportionately to the effect attained. To strike with strong effect, one must strike at weakness.

It is thus more potent, as well as more economical, to disarm the enemy than to attempt his destruction by hard fighting. For the 'mauling' method entails not only a dangerous cost in exhaustion but the risk that chance may determine the issue. A strategist should think in terms of paralysing, not of killing. Even on the lower plane of warfare, a man killed is merely one man less, whereas a man unnerved is a highly infectious carrier of fear, capable of spreading an epidemic of panic. On a higher plane of warfare, the impression made on the mind of the opposing commander can nullify the whole fighting power that his troops possess. And on a still higher plane, psychological pressure on the government of a country may suffice to cancel all the resources at its command—so that the sword drops from a paralysed hand.

To repeat the keynote of the initial chapter: the analysis of war shows that while the nominal strength of a country is represented by its numbers and resources, this muscular development is dependent on the state of its internal organs and nerve-system—upon its stability of control, morale, and supply. Direct pressure always tends to harden and consolidate the resistance of an opponent—like snow which is squeezed into a snowball, the more compact it becomes, the slower it is to melt. Alike in policy and in strategy—or to put it another way, in the strategy of both the diplomatic and the military spheres—the indirect approach is the most effective way to upset the opponent's balance, psychological and physical, thereby making possible his overthrow.

The true purpose of strategy is to diminish the possibility of resistance. And from this follows another axiom—that to ensure attaining *an* objective one should have alternative objectives. An attack that converges on one point should threaten, and be able to diverge against another. Only by this flexibility of aim can strategy be attuned to the uncertainty of war.

Whether by instinct or reflection, Hitler acquired an acute grasp of these strategic truths which few soldiers had recognized. He applied this psychological strategy in the political campaign by which he gained control of Germany—exploiting the weak points of the Weimar Republic, playing on human weakness, alternatively playing off capitalist and socialist interests against each other, appearing to turn first in one direction and then in another, so that by successive indirect steps he approached his goal.

Once his control of Germany was achieved, in 1933, the same compound process was given a wider extension. Having negotiated, the next year, a ten-year peace pact with Poland to cover his eastern flank, in 1935 he threw off the armament limitations imposed by the Versailles Treaty, and in 1936 ventured the military reoccupation of the Rhineland. That same year he craftily began 'camouflaged war' by supporting, in conjunction with Italy, General Franco's bid to overthrow the Spanish Republican Government. This was an indirect approach to the strategic rear of France and Britain that created a grand-strategic distraction. Having thus weakened their position in the west, and having also covered himself in the west by refortifying the Rhineland, he was able to turn eastwards—to make moves that were further indirect strokes at the strategic foundations of the Western Powers.

In March 1938 he marched into Austria, and thus laid bare the flank of Czechoslovakia, while breaking the girdle which France had woven round Germany after the last war. In September 1938 he secured, by the Munich agreement, not merely the return of the Sudetenland but the strategic paralysis of Czechoslovakia. In March 1939 he occupied the country he had already paralysed, and thereby enveloped the flank of Poland.

By this series of practically bloodless manœuvres, carried out by 'peace-marches' under cover of a smoke-screen of plausible propaganda, he had not only destroyed the former French domination of central Europe and strategic encirclement of Germany, but reversed it in his own favour. This process was the modern equivalent, on a wider scale and higher plane, of the classical art of manœuvring for position before offering battle. Throughout its course Germany's strength had been growing, both directly by the vast development of her armaments, and indirectly by subtraction from the strength of her potential main opponents—through lopping off their allies and loosening their strategic roots.

Thus by the spring of 1939 Hitler had decreasing cause to fear an open fight. And at this critical moment he was helped by a false move on Britain's part—the guarantee suddenly offered to Poland and Rumania, each of them strategically isolated, without first securing any assurance from Russia, the only power which could give them effective support. Such a blind step was the rashest reversal of a policy of appeasement and retreat that has ever been conceived. By their timing, these guarantees were bound to act as a provocation. By their placing, in parts of Europe inaccessible to the forces of Britain and France, they provided an almost irresistible temptation. Thereby the Western Powers undermined the essential basis of the only type of strategy which their now inferior strength made practicable tor them. For instead of being able to check aggression by presenting a strong front to any attack in the west, they gave Hitler an easy chance of breaking a weak front and thus gaining an initial triumph.

Hitler had always planned, as Rauschning shows, to direct his surprise strokes against weak or isolated countries while throwing on his opponents' shoulders the main burden of attack—the Germans had more real respect for the power of modern defence than any of the Allied soldiers or statesmen. Now he had been given an easy opportunity to do so. In such circumstances his principles of strategy obviously pointed to an immediate attempt to make a pact with Russia that would ensure her detachment. Once that was secured, Hitler was 'sitting pretty'. If the Allies declared war in fulfilment of their obligations they would automatically forfeit the advantages of defence and be committed to an inherently offensive strategy—without the necessary resources and under the most unfavourable conditions. If they merely tapped at the Siegfried Line they would manifest their impotence, and forfeit prestige. If they pressed the attack, they would only pile up their losses and weaken their own chance of subsequent resistance when Hitler was free to turn westwards.

The only way in which they might have extricated themselves from this awkward position, without allowing Hitler to have his way entirely, was by adopting the 'sanctions' policy of economic and diplomatic boycott, coupled with the supply of arms to the victim of aggression. This would have done Poland quite as much good, and done much less harm to their own prestige and prospects, than a declaration of war under such adverse conditions.

In the event, the deliberate offensive which the French attempted made no impression on the Siegfried Line, while the way it was 'boosted' meant that its failure was all the more damaging to the Allies' prestige. Coupled with the Germans' swift success in Poland, it had the effect of increasing the neutrals' fear of Germany while shaking practical confidence in the Allies even more than another compromise could have done.

Hitler was now able to consolidate his military gains and exploit his political advantages behind the cover of his Western defences that the would-be rescuers of Poland were palpably incapable of forcing. He might have maintained this secure defensive until the French and British peoples grew weary of war, as its farcical aspect became plainer. But the Allied statesmen were led to take the offensive in talk long before they had the means to translate it into effective action. All they succeeded in doing was to provoke consequences which they were unready to meet. For their line of talk gave Hitler a fresh opportunity, as well as an incentive, to forestall them in 'opening up' the war. While many people in Britain and France were dreaming of how the small neutral countries adjoining Germany might open a way to her flanks, Hitler turned the Allies' flanks by the invasion of no less than five of these countries —having an aggressor's characteristic freedom from scruples.

In the early months of the war Hitler had favoured the idea of preserving Norway's neutral position as cover for his flank and a covered route for Germany's shipments of Swedish iron-ore via the Norwegian Atlantic coast port of Narvik. It was only the palpable and increasing signs that the Allies were planning a move to secure control of Norway's waters and ports, to his disadvantage, which spurred him to undertake a forestalling occupation of the country.

It was, however, no new conception on his part. As far back as 1934 he had described to Rauschning and others how he might seize by surprise the chief ports of the Scandinavian peninsula through a simultaneous series of coups carried out by small seaborne expeditions, covered by the air force. The way would be prepared by his partisans on the spot, and the actual move would be made on the pretext of protecting these countries against invasion by other Powers. 'It would be a daring, but interesting undertaking, never before attempted in the history of the world'—there spoke the 'artist' of war. This striking conception was fulfilled in the plan that was executed on the 9th April 1940, and succeeded beyond expectation. Whereas he had reckoned that his coups might fail at several points, while counting for success on securing a majority of the strategic points, he gained every one without check—although he had audaciously stretched his fingers as far north as Narvik.

His amazingly easy success, sealed by the equally easy frustration of the Allies' attempted counter-invasion of Norway, naturally increased his eagerness to launch his next and bigger stroke, already planned. In earlier years, when discussing the circumstances in which he would risk a great war, he had expressed his intention to remain on the defensive in the West and leave the enemy to take the first offensive step, whereupon he would pounce upon Scandinavia and the Low Countries, improve his strategic position, and make a peace proposal to the Western Powers. 'If they don't like it, they can try to drive me out. In any case they will have to bear the main burden of attack.' But now the circumstances were different. He had made a peace proposal after the conquest of Poland, and it had been rejected by the Western Powers. Following that rebuff he had decided to force peace on France, and had switched his armies westward for an offensive against her that autumn. The doubts of his generals, who did not believe that they had sufficient strength to overthrow the Franco-British armies, combined with the weather to postpone his intention. But his impatience increased with the pause, while his triumph in Norway—where he had once again defied the cautionary advice of his generals—made it impossible for them to curb him any longer.

Long beforehand, when discussing the possibility of such an offensive, he had remarked—'I shall manœuvre France right out of her Maginot Line without losing a single soldier.' Granted the hyperbole—for his losses were small in comparison with his gains—that was what he accomplished in May 1940.

In the original plan the main effort was to have been on the right wing, by Bock's Army Group. But early in 1940 the plan was radically changed, and the centre of gravity shifted—following the arguments of General von Manstein (Chief of Staff to Rundstedt's Army Group) that a thrust through the Ardennes would have a much better chance of success, being the line of least expectation.

The most significant feature of the Western campaign was the

German Command's care to avoid any direct assault, and its continued use of the indirect approach—despite superiority in modern means of attack. It did not attempt to penetrate the Maginot Line. Instead, by a 'baited offensive' against the two small neutrals, Holland and Belgium, it managed to lure the Allies out of their defences on the Belgian frontier. Then, when they had advanced deep into Belgium, their march being deliberately unimpeded by the German air force, it struck in behind them—with a thrust at the uncovered hinge of the French advance.

This deadly thrust was delivered by a striking force that formed only a small fraction of the total German army, but was composed of armoured divisions. The German Command had been shrewd enough to realize that, for any chance of quick success, it must rely on mechanics rather than on mass. Even so, this spearhead was so small that the German generals were far from confident that the stroke would succeed. That it did was chiefly due to the recklessness, or perilous conventionality, of the French Command in concentrating almost the whole of their left wing for a massive advance to offer battle in Belgium, while leaving a few second-rate divisions to guard the pivotal sector facing the Ardennes—a wooded and hilly area which they assumed to be too difficult as a line of approach for mechanized divisions. The Germans, by contrast, in exploiting its possibilities for surprise, had shown their appreciation of the oft-taught lesson that natural obstacles are inherently less formidable than human resistance in strong defences.

It is clear, too, that the rapid progress of the German penetration beyond Sedan benefited much from the fact that it successively threatened alternative objectives, and kept the French in doubt as to its real direction—first, whether it was towards Paris or the rear of the forces in Belgium; then, when the German armoured divisions swung westwards, whether they were moving on Amiens or Lille. 'Selling the dummy' first one way and then the other, they swept on to the Channel coast.

The tactics of the German forces corresponded to their strategy—avoiding head-on assaults, and always seeking to find 'soft spots' through which they could infiltrate along the line of least resistance. While the Allied statesmen, vitally misunderstanding modern warfare, called on their armies to meet the invasion by 'furious unrelenting assault', the German tank-tide swept round and past their clumsy infantry-mops. (The Allied troops might perhaps have stemmed it if they had not been told to cast away the idea of defending barrier-lines: nothing could have been less effective than their attempts at counter-attack.) While the Allied commanders thought in terms of battle, the new German commanders sought to eliminate it by producing the strategic paralysis of their opponents, using their tanks, dive-bombers, and parachutists to spread confusion and dislocate communications. The outcome cast an ironical reflection on the comforting assumption of Field-Marshal Ironside that the opposing generals would be handicapped by the fact that none of them had been more than captains in the last war. Eight years earlier Hitler had criticized the German generals as 'blind to the new, the surprising things'; as imaginatively sterile; as being 'imprisoned in the coils of their technical knowledge'. Some of the later vintage, however, showed an exceptional capacity to appreciate new ideas.

But this exploitation of new weapons, tactics, and strategy does not cover all the factors in Germany's run of success. For in Hitler's warfare the indirect approach was carried into wider fields and deeper strata. Here he profited by studying the Bolshevik technique of revolution, just as the new German army had profited by applying the British-evolved technique of mechanized warfare—whether he knew it or not, the basic methods in both spheres could be traced back to the technique of Mongol warfare under Jenghiz Khan. To prepare the way for his offensive, he sought to find influential adherents in the other country who would undermine its resistance, make trouble in his interest, and be ready to form a new government compliant to his aims. Bribery was unnecessary—he counted on self-seeking ambition, authoritarian inclination, and party-spirit to provide him with willing and unwitting agents among the ruling classes. Then to open the way, at the chosen moment, he aimed to use an infiltration of storm-troopers who would cross the frontier while peace still prevailed, as commercial travellers or holiday-makers, and don the enemy's uniform when the word came; their role was to sabotage communications, spread false reports, and, if possible, kidnap the other country's leading men. This disguised vanguard would in turn be backed up by air-borne troops.

In the warfare he intended to stage, frontal advances would be either a bluff or a walking-on part. The leading role would always be played by the rear attack in one of its forms. He was contemptuous of assaults and bayonet-charges—the A B C of the traditional soldier. His way in warfare began with a double D—demoralization and disorganization. Above all, war would be waged by suggestion—by words instead of weapons, propaganda replacing the projectile. Just as an artillery bombardment was used in the last war to crush the enemy's defences before the infantry advanced, so a moral bombardment would be used in future. All types of ammunition would be used, but especially revolutionary propaganda. 'Generals, in spite of the lessons of the war, want to behave like chivalrous knights. They think war should be waged like the tourneys of the Middle Ages. I have no use for knights. I need revolutions.'

The object of war was to make the enemy capitulate. If his will to resist could be paralysed, killing was superfluous—besides being a clumsy and expensive way of attaining the object. The indirect way of injecting germs into the body of the opposing nation, to produce disease in its will, was likely to be far more effective.

Such was Hitler's theory of war with psychological weapons. Those who tried to check him should have taken care to understand it. The value of its application to the military sphere was proved. To paralyse the enemy's military nerve-system is a more economical form of operation than to pound his flesh. Its application to the political sphere was proved in effect, but not in content. It is open to question whether it would have succeeded in demoralizing resistance but for the paralysing effect of the new-type forces applying new methods of attack. Even in the case of France, the German superiority in military technique suffices to account for her collapse, apart from any decay or disorder of the national will.

Force can always crush force, given sufficient superiority in strength or skill. It cannot crush ideas. Being intangible they are invulnerable, save to psychological penetration, and their resilience has baffled innumerable believers in force. None of them perhaps were so aware of the power of ideas as Hitler. But the increasing extent to which he had to rely on the backing of force as his power extended, showed that he had over-estimated the value of his political technique in converting ideas to his purpose. For ideas that do not spring from the truth of experience have a relatively brief impetus—and a sharp recoil.

Hitler gave the art of offensive strategy a new development. He also mastered, better than any of his opponents, the first stage of grand strategy—that of developing and co-ordinating all forms of warlike activity, and all the possible instruments which may be used to operate against the enemy's will. But like Napoleon he had an inadequate grasp of the higher level of grand strategy—that of conducting war with a far-sighted regard to the state of the peace that will follow. To do this effectively, a man must be more than a strategist; he must be a leader and a philosopher combined. While strategy is the very opposite of morality, as it is largely concerned with the art of deception, grand strategy tends to coincide with morality: through having always to keep in view the ultimate goal of the efforts it is directing.

In trying to prove their irresistibility in attack the Germans had weakened their own defences in many ways—strategic, economic, and, above all, psychological. As their forces spread over Europe, bringing misery without securing peace, they scattered widespread the germs of resentment from which resistance to their ideas would develop. And to these germs even their own troops became more susceptible from being exposed to contact with the people of the occupied countries, and made sensitive to the feelings they inspire. This began to damp the martial enthusiasm which Hitler had so assiduously stimulated, and to deepen their longing for home. The sense of being friendless reinforces the effect of staleness, opening the way for the infiltration of war-weariness—as well as of counter-ideas.

By his offensive expansion Hitler had provided his remaining opponent with opportunity to wrest the advantage from him. It could have been developed more quickly by a fuller vision of grand strategy on her side. But even without that, the opportunity was likely to grow so long as Britain remained invincible. To impose his peace he needed complete victory—which he could not attain without conquering Britain—while the further he advanced elsewhere the more he enlarged his own problem in holding down the conquered peoples. Each step forward increased the dangers of a slip. Britain's problem was a simpler one, though a hard one. She had to hold out until he made an irreparable slip—as Napoleon had done. Fortunately for her he made this slip very soon, before the strain on her had become crippling. And the slip became irreparable because his flair for offensive strategy was not matched by a corresponding sense of defensive strategy. The immensity of his earlier successes led him, as Napoleon had been led, to believe that the offensive offered a solution of all problems.

CHAPTER XVI

HITLER'S RUN OF VICTORY

★

The German conquest of Poland in 1939 and the subsequent overrunning of western Europe in 1940 are landmarks in military history as decisive demonstrations of the theory of high-speed mechanized warfare—a theory which had been conceived in Britain but adopted in Germany, largely owing to the efforts of General Guderian, the creator of the German panzer forces. Although the senior German generals viewed the new technique with cautious doubt, and had allotted means for its development in more limited measure than its exponents desired, it sufficed to produce startling quick victories. The new technique not only revolutionized warfare but changed the course of world history. For the shattering effect of Hitler's victories on the position and outlook of western Europe could not be repaired by his ultimate defeat. Moreover the immense effort that America was led to make in turning the scales against Hitler resulted in the re-orientation of world-power to the Western hemisphere. The ascendency of Russia on the Eurasian Continent was another disturbing, and epoch-making, result.

The campaigns which produced the double revolution—in warfare and the balance of world-power—were also very significant examples of the strategy of indirect approach. In the second and greater case, particularly, analysis of the operations in the West makes it clear that the new type mechanized forces would hardly have succeeded without this accompaniment in strategy. But the effect was reciprocal. The mobility and flexibility of mechanized forces endowed the indirect approach with greater potentialities.

Poland, to her misfortune, provided an ideal demonstration site for the combination. Her frontier with Germany was 1,250 miles long, and had recently been extended a further 500 miles through the German occupation of Czechoslovakia. This had resulted in Poland's southern flank becoming as exposed to invasion as the northern flank facing East Prussia. Western Poland thus formed a vast salient between Germany's two jaws.

The risks were increased by the way that the Polish forces were deployed, the bulk of them being far forward in the salient. The natural desire to cover Poland's main industrial area, which lay west of the Vistula, was dangerously buttressed by national pride and military over-confidence.

The Polish army at peace strength was as large as the French and not much smaller than the German. It comprised 30 infantry divisions and 12 cavalry brigades. But Poland's industrial resources were insufficient to make full use of her man-power, or even furnish an adequate scale of equipment for her active forces. On mobilization she could only increase her number of divisions by a third, whereas Germany could more than double hers, except for the armoured and motorized ones—but this limitation on Germany's side was offset by Poland's almost complete lack of such modern type forces.

That was the more serious because the Polish plain offered flat and fairly easy going for a mobile invader—though not so easy as France would offer, because of the scarcity of good roads in Poland, the deep sand often met off the roads, and the frequency of lakes and forests in some areas. But the time chosen for the invasion minimized these drawbacks.

Poland's enveloped situation made it inviting, and easy, for the Germans to pursue a strategy of indirect approach in the physical form. But the effect was much enhanced by the way they pursued it.

In the north, the invasion was carried out by Bock's Army Group, which comprised the 3rd Army (under Küchler) and the 4th Army (under Kluge). The former thrust southward from its flanking position in East Prussia, while the latter pushed eastward across the Polish Corridor to join it in enveloping the Poles' right flank.

The greater role was given to Rundstedt's Army Group in the south. This was nearly twice as strong in infantry, and more in armour. It comprised the 8th Army (under Blaskowitz), the 10th (under Reichenau), and the 14th (under List). Blaskowitz, on the left wing, was to push towards the great manufacturing centre of Lodz, and help to isolate the Polish forces in the Poznan salient, while covering Reichenau's flank. On the right wing, List was to push for Cracow and simultaneously turn the Poles' Carpathian flank, using an armoured corps to drive through the mountain passes. The decisive stroke, however, was to be delivered by Reichenau, in the centre, and for that purpose he was given the bulk of the armoured forces.

The invasion was launched on the 1st September 1939, and by the 3rd—when Britain and France entered the war as required by their guarantee to Poland—Kluge's advance had cut the Corridor and reached the Lower Vistula, while Küchler's pressure from East Prussia towards the Narev was developing. What was more important, Reichenau's armoured forces had penetrated to the Warta, and forced the crossings there. Meanwhile List's army was converging from both flanks on Cracow. By the 4th Reichenau's spearheads had crossed the Pilica, fifty miles inside the frontier, and two days later his left wing was well beyond Tomaszow, while his right had driven into Kielce.

The Commander-in-Chief of the German army, Brauchitsch, ordered the drive to be continued straight ahead eastward to, and over, the Vistula. But Rundstedt and his Chief of Staff, Manstein, took the initiative in varying the plan when they gauged, correctly, that the main Polish armies were still west of the Vistula and might be trapped there. Reichenau's left wing, led by an armoured corps, was directed to swing northward on to the rear of the big Polish concentration around Lodz, and to establish a blocking position along the Bzura River between Lodz and Warsaw. This northward swerve met little opposition, being unexpected, and as a result of it this massed Polish force was cut off before it could withdraw over the Vistula.

The advantage which the Germans had gained by their deep strategic penetration—along the line of least expectation and the line of least resistance—was now reinforced by the advantage of tactical defence. To complete their victory they had merely to hold their ground—in face of the hurried assaults of an army which was fighting in reverse, cut off from its bases, with its supplies running short, and increasingly pressed from the flank and behind by the converging eastward advance of Blaskowitz's and Kluge's armies. Although the Poles fought fiercely, with a bravery that greatly impressed their opponents, only a small proportion ultimately managed to break out and join the garrison of Warsaw.

On the 10th the Polish Commander-in-Chief, Marshal Smigly-Rydz, ordered his remaining forces to make a general retreat into south-eastern Poland, in the hope of organizing a defence on a relatively narrow front for prolonged resistance. But this hope was frustrated. For while the ring west of the Vistula was being tightened, the Germans were already penetrating deeply into the region east of the Vistula, and carrying out a much wider pincer-manœuvre which outflanked the potential defence-lines of the San and the Bug.

The far-back line of the Bug was reached and turned by a remarkably indirect approach. At the opening of the invasion, Guderian's armoured corps had spearheaded Kluge's 4th Army in the thrust across the Corridor, in the north-west, to reach Germany's isolated province of East Prussia. It raced on through this German territory and came up on the extreme left, or eastern flank of Küchler's 3rd Army, facing south. Crossing the river-line of the Narev on the 9th September, Guderian drove southward, and by the 14th reached Brest-Litovsk on the Bug—a 100-mile drive down the baseline of the great Polish salient. His spearheads then thrust on a further forty miles to Vlodava, to meet the approaching southern pincer formed by Kleist's armoured corps. Thus the collapse of the Polish armies was ensured by the time that, on the 17th, the Russians crossed Poland's eastern frontier.

The Germans' triumphant campaign in the West nine months later was not so plainly an indirect approach in physical shape, but even more of an indirect approach psychologically. It was inspired by the idea of upsetting the opponent's balance in a compound way—through achieving the unexpected in direction, time, and method, preceded by the fullest possible distraction and followed by the quickest possible exploitation along the line of least resistance to the deepest possible range. Moreover it owed its success, above all, to a baited gambit and ju-jitsu effect.

Early in October 1939, after overrunning Poland, Hitler issued his first instructions for an offensive in the West. These stated that, if it became clear that Britain and France would not agree to end the war, he would take action at an early date—because 'a long waiting period' would 'strengthen the military power of our enemies to an increasing degree', while it was likely to result in the neutrals swinging to the Allied side. In his view, time was against Germany in every respect. He expressed the fear that if he waited, as his military advisers desired, the growth of the Allies' armament would overtake hers; that a long-drawn war would exhaust her existing, and limited, resources; and that it would leave her exposed to a fatal attack in the back from Russia—for he felt that his pact with Stalin would not ensure Russia's neutrality a moment longer than suited Stalin's purpose. Hitler's fear spurred him to force the French to make peace, by an early offensive, believing that once they dropped out of the war Britain would come to terms.

Hitler reckoned that for the moment he had the strength and equipment to beat France—because Germany possessed a superiority in the new arms that mattered most. 'The tank-arm and air force have, at the present time, attained technical heights—not only as weapons of attack but also for defence—that no other Power has reached. Their strategic potential for operations is ensured by their organization and well-practised leadership, which is better than in any other country.' While recognizing that the French had a superiority in the older weapons, particularly heavy artillery, he argued that 'these weapons are of no decisive significance whatsoever in mobile warfare'. With his technical superiority in the newer arms he could also discount the French superiority in the numbers of mobilizable soldiers.

The heads of the German army shared Hitler's long-term fears, but not his short-term hopes. Feeling that their forces were not strong enough to beat the French, they considered it wiser to stay on the defensive in order to see whether France and Britain became inclined for peace, or else attempted an advance that would offer an opening for crushing repulse and riposte.

But Hitler overruled their objections. The offensive was eventually fixed for the second week of November, but then deferred three days on account of unfavourable reports on the weather prospects and the railway transport situation. Similar short postponements—there were eleven in all—continued until the middle of January, after which there was a long interval until May, when the next warning order was issued—and this time confirmed. In the meantime, however, the plan had undergone a radical alteration.

The original plan, designed by the General Staff under Halder, had been to make the main attack through central Belgium—as in 1914. It was to be carried out by Army Group 'B' under Bock, while Army Group 'A' under Rundstedt delivered a secondary attack, on the left, through the hilly and wooded Ardennes. No big results were expected here, and all the armoured divisions were allotted to Bock, as the General Staff regarded the Ardennes as far too difficult country for a tank drive.

But Manstein, who was Rundstedt's Chief of Staff, considered that the plan was too obvious, and too close a repetition of the 1914 plan, thus being the line of attack that the Allies would expect, and be ready to meet. Another drawback, Manstein argued, was that it would strike the British army, which was likely to be a tougher opponent than the French. A third drawback, in his view, was that even if it succeeded it would only push the Allies back and gain the Flanders coast. It would not lead to a decisive result, as an indirect approach could—by cutting the communications and cutting off the retreat of the Allied armies in Belgium.

Manstein proposed that the centre of gravity should be shifted from the right to the centre, and that the principal thrust should be made through the Ardennes, as the line of least expectation. He considered that the armoured forces could be effectively used in that area, despite the apparent difficulties of the ground, and his view was reinforced by Guderian's expert judgement.

The boldness of the new conception appealed to Hitler. But the definite decision to change the original plan was produced by an extraordinary accident when, on 10th January, a staff officer who was carrying papers about the plan lost his way in a snowstorm when flying from Munster to Bonn, and landed by mistake in Belgian territory. The German High Command naturally feared that he might have been unable to destroy the papers (and, in fact, his attempt to burn them was a partial failure). Even then the Commander-in-Chief and the Chief of the General Staff hesitated to turn the plan round so completely as Manstein had proposed. Their resistance was only overcome after Manstein, going behind the backs of his superiors, had seen Hitler personally and gained his decisive support for the unconventional project.

During the interval, false alarms had led the Allies to show their hand, and their intention of advancing in force deep into Belgium. That disclosure, too, strengthened the case for changing the German plan in the way Manstein advocated.

Examining the course of events, it becomes clear that the old plan would almost certainly have failed to produce any such decisive result as the fall of France. For the direct German advance would have run head-on into the strongest and best-equipped portion of the Franco-British forces, and would have had to fight its way forward through a stretch of country filled with obstacles—rivers, canals and large towns. The Ardennes might seem more difficult still, but if the Germans could race through that wooded hill-belt of southern Belgium before the French High Command awoke to the danger, the rolling plains of France would lie open to them—ideal country for a great tank drive.

Manstein had also reckoned with the likelihood of the Allies advancing into Belgium, and he counted on gaining an increased advantage from such a move on their part. His calculations were shrewd. Under the plan framed by General Gamelin, the Commander-in-Chief, the reinforced left wing of the Allied armies was to rush into Belgium immediately a German invasion opened, and to push eastward to the line of the Dyle, or beyond if possible. That Plan 'D' proved as fatal as the Plan XVII of the French in 1914. It played straight into the Germans' hands, by giving their offensive the form and effect of a flank counter-stroke. The further the Allies pushed into Belgium the easier it became for the Germans' Ardennes drive to reach the Allies' rear and cut off their left wing.

The fatal outcome was made all the more certain because Gamelin employed the bulk of his mobile forces in the dash into Belgium and left only a thin screen of lower-grade divisions to guard the hinge of his advance—facing the exits from the supposedly impassable Ardennes. When the hinge was pierced he was not only thrown off his balance, but had all the less chance of recovering it because the forces best fitted for switching to close such a breach were deeply committed in Belgium. In rushing them forward he had largely cast away his strategic flexibility.

The danger to the hinge was obscured for the moment by the Germans' opening strokes in the Low Countries—so startling that they acted as a supremely effective distraction. The Dutch army was thrown into confusion by an airborne swoop on its rear combined with a violent assault on its front, and capitulated on the fifth day. The Belgian army had its forward position pierced on the second day, and then fell back to the Antwerp-Namur line as arranged, where it was joined by the British and French.

In Holland, early on the 10th May, German airborne forces made a surprise swoop upon both the capital, The Hague, and the hub of the country's communications, Rotterdam—simultaneously with the assault on its frontier defences 100 miles to the east. The confusion and alarm created by this double blow, in front and rear, were increased by the widespread menace of the Luftwaffe. Exploiting the disorder, a German armoured division raced through a gap in the southern flank and joined up with the airborne forces at Rotterdam on the third day. The Dutch, although strategically on the defence, were forced to become the attackers in a tactical sense—and were baffled in delivering assaults which they were not equipped to drive home. On the fifth day Holland surrendered, although her main front was still unbroken.

The physically direct invasion of Belgium also had a psychological indirectness of approach in the startling initial coup that opened the path for the invaders. The ground attack was carried out by the powerful 6th Army under Reichenau. It had to overcome a formidable barrier before it could effectively deploy, and only 500 airborne troops were left to help this attack. They were used to capture the two bridges over the Albert Canal together with Eben Emael, Belgium's most modern fort, which flanked this waterline-frontier. That tiny detachment, however, made all the difference to the issue. For the approach to the Belgian frontier here lay across the southerly projection of Dutch territory known as the 'Maastricht Appendix', and once the German army crossed the Dutch frontier the Belgian frontier guards on the Albert Canal would have had ample warning to blow the bridges before any invading ground forces could cross that fifteen-mile strip.

Airborne troops dropping silently out of the night sky offered a new way, and the only way, of securing the key-bridges intact. Fort Eben Emael was paralysed by a glider detachment of less than eighty men who descended on top of it, and bottled up the garrison of 1,200 men for twenty-four hours, until the German ground troops came up to capture the fort and drive across the captured bridges into the open plains beyond. The menace caused the Belgian forces to retreat towards the Dyle line where the French and British forces were just arriving.

These airborne coups in Belgium and Holland were conceived by Hitler himself, although their brilliantly successful execution was directed by the audacious General Student.

Meantime the armoured forces of Rundstedt's Army Group had been driving through Luxemburg and Belgium Luxemburg towards the French frontier. The bulk of them—5 armoured and 4 motorized divisions—were grouped under the command of General von Kleist, while the principal spearhead was Guderian's corps, of 3 armoured divisions. After traversing that seventy-mile stretch of the Ardennes, and brushing aside weak opposition, they crossed the French frontier and emerged on the banks of the Meuse—early on the fourth day of the offensive.

It had been a bold venture to send a mass of tanks and motor vehicles through such difficult country, which had long been regarded by conventional strategists as 'impassable' for a large-scale offensive, let alone for a tank operation. But that increased the chances of surprise, while the thick woods helped to cloak the advance and conceal the strength of the blow.

Yet, for all the surprise effect of this onrush of armour, it had still to cross the barrier-line of the Meuse. Much depended on the time of the crossing. General Doumenc, the French Chief of Staff, later ruefully said: 'Crediting our enemies with our own procedure, we had imagined that they would not attempt the passage of the Meuse until after they had brought up ample artillery: the five or six days necessary for that would have given us ample time to reinforce our dispositions.'

It is remarkable how closely these French time-calculations corresponded to those of the German higher command. The French chiefs had based their plans on the assumption that no assault on the Meuse was to be expected before the ninth day. That was the same timing that the German chiefs originally had in mind. At a war game in February, Guderian had proposed that the armoured forces should attack the Meuse as early as possible without waiting for the mass of the infantry and artillery to come up, but his proposal had been severely criticized by Halder, who considered that the ninth or tenth day was the earliest time practicable for such an attack. At a conference in March, Hitler asked Guderian what course he would propose taking after the capture of a bridgehead. Guderian answered that it should be exploited immediately by driving west towards Amiens and the Channel ports. His answer made heads shake disapprovingly at such rashness. But Hitler's nod was as good as a wink to Guderian.

When Guderian's corps reached the Meuse near Sedan on the 13th May, its assault on the river-line was delivered that same afternoon, and by evening a crossing was gained. One of the smaller spearheads, Rommel's 7th Panzer Division, likewise achieved a crossing on the 13th at Dinant, forty miles to the west, and thus created a fresh distraction to the French Command as well as a potential combination of dislocating penetrations.

By the afternoon of the 14th all three of Guderian's panzer divisions had crossed the Meuse, and after repelling a belated French counter-stroke he made a sudden turn westward. By the next evening he had broken through the last defence line behind the

Meuse, and the roads to the west—leading to the Channel coast, 160 miles—lay open to the panzer forces.

That night, the 15th, Guderian was ordered by the more cautious Kleist to halt the advance and keep the bridgehead secure until the infantry arrived to take it over. After a heated argument the order was modified to the limited extent of allowing Guderian to widen the bridgehead. Taking the fullest possible advantage of

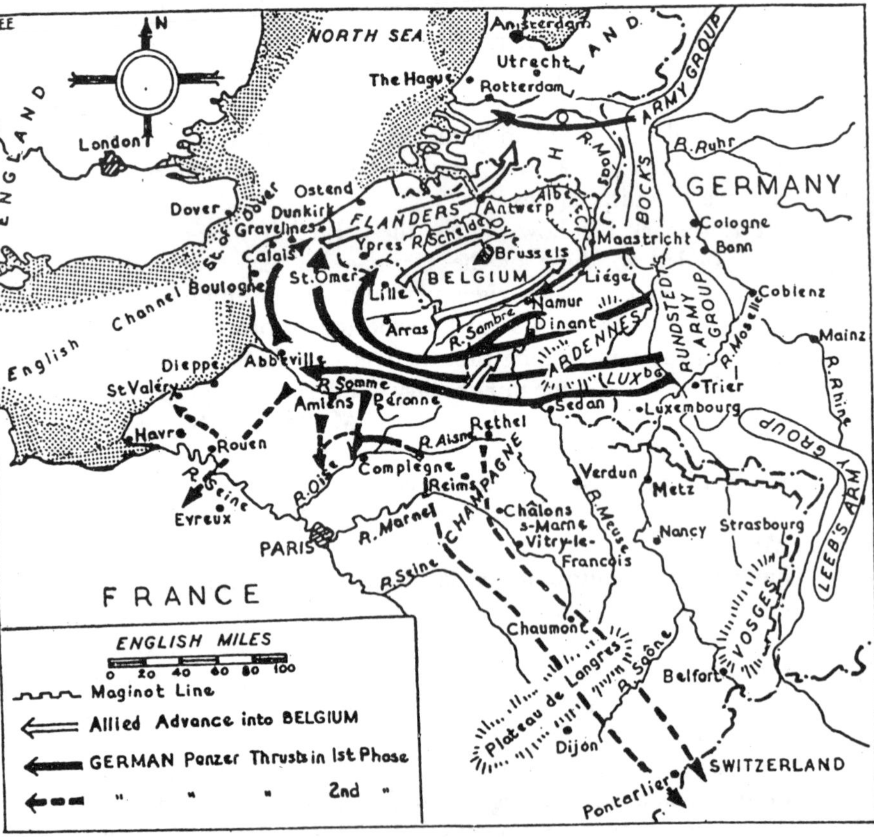

this permission he drove fifty miles westward next day to the Oise! The rest of the panzer forces joined in the westward surge, expanding the breach to a sixty-mile width and swelling the tank torrent that was pouring along the roads that ran across the back of the Allied armies in Belgium.

The torrent had its path made easier because the French Command was puzzled as to the course it was likely to take. A special advantage of the break-through at Sedan was that, being on a central axis, it could swing in any direction and threaten alternative objectives. Was it aiming at the Channel coast, or at Paris? While its advance seemed to be extending westward, it looked at first as if this might equally portend an early southwards turn towards Paris—and French imagination easily flew to such a possibility. The strategic flexibility of the German plan was increased by the mobility of the instrument, and the combination impaled the opponent on the horns of a dilemma.

The issue turned on the time-factor at stage after stage. French counter-movements were repeatedly thrown out of gear because their timing was too slow to catch up with the changing situations, and that was due to the fact that the German van kept on moving faster than the French—or the German higher command—had contemplated. The French, trained in the slow-motion methods of World War I, were mentally unfitted to cope with the new tempo, and it caused a spreading paralysis among them. The vital weakness of the French lay, not in quantity nor in quality of equipment, but in their *theory*. Their ideas had advanced less than their opponents beyond the methods of the First World War. As has happened so often in history, victory had bred a complacency and fostered an orthodoxy which led to defeat in the next war.

On the German side, the higher commanders remained apprehensive about the risks of such a deep strategic penetration by a handful of armoured divisions. Hitler himself showed much nervousness, and in his anxiety about the southern flank put a two-day brake on the westward drive, so that the 12th Army could come up and form a flank shield along the river-line of the Aisne.

That delay jeopardized the German prospects, and might have spoilt them if the French had not been by now in such a paralytic state. Hitler's hesitation foreshadowed a more costly one in the following week. But so much time had been gained in the preceding stages, and so much dislocation had been caused on the opposing side, that the pause on the Oise had no serious effect on the German prospects. Even so, it revealed a significant difference of time-sense on the German side. The gap between the new school and the old school there was greater than that between the Germans and the French.

In protest at the halt ordered on the 17th, Guderian had asked to be relieved of his command. But later in the day he was reinstated and told that he could continue 'strong reconnaissance'.

His interpretation of this was to push on with the whole of his force almost as hard as previously. When the brake was released, his pace became even faster and on the 20th May he swept into Amiens and reached the sea beyond Abbeville—having cut the communications of the Allied armies in Belgium.

On the 22nd, after fretting over a further day's pause imposed from above, he drove northward for the Channel ports and the rear of the British army—which was still in Belgium, facing the frontal advance of Bock's infantry forces. On Guderian's right in this northward drive was Reinhardt's panzer corps, also part of Kleist's group. On the 22nd, Boulogne was isolated by Guderian's advance, and on the next day Calais. This stride brought him to Gravelines, barely ten miles from Dunkirk. Reinhardt's tanks also arrived on the canal line Aire-St. Omer-Gravelines and seized bridgeheads across it. But the continuation of the drive for Dunkirk—the last escape-port left for the British—was stopped next day by Hitler's order. This saved the British army, when nothing else could have done, from sharing the fate that befell the Belgian and a large part of the three French armies on the left wing. After two days the order was cancelled, and the advance resumed, but by that time the defence had been strengthened and the establishment of this back-shield held off the Germans long enough for the evacuation by sea of 224,000 British troops and 114,000 Allied troops, mainly French. Even so, the Germans had taken a million prisoners—at a cost to themselves of only 60,000 casualties—as a result of their great indirect approach.

The cause of Hitler's fateful halt order will never be completely clear. One motive, which he mentioned, was his fear lest his armoured arm might become bogged—the marshy state of Flanders had been deeply impressed on him by his personal experience there, as a corporal, in World War I. Another motive was his anxiety to maintain his armour intact for his next, and knock-out, blow against the French. A third was the belief, fostered by Goering, that the German air force would suffice to prevent any large-scale escape by sea, from Dunkirk, of the trapped British forces. But investigation has shown that the most immediate cause was the psychological effect of a small British counter-stroke with two tank battalions, that had been launched, at Arras on the 21st May, against the flank of the German drive to the sea. It played on the fears that Hitler and several of the German higher commanders had felt during this audaciously deep strategic penetration, and shook their nerve at a crucial moment. Kleist repeatedly put a brake on Guderian's drive. Kluge, the army commander directly above Kleist, was inclined to stop any further advance until the situation at Arras was cleared up. Rundstedt was naturally influenced by their anxiety. Thus, when Hitler visited Rundstedt on the morning of the 24th, he received a reinforcement of his own nervous doubts—and issued his halt order immediately after the conference. On this occasion Brauchitsch and Halder were for pursuing the panzer drive, but on the level between Guderian and them Hitler found ample backing for his fit of caution.

The next, and final, stage of the campaign started on the 5th June—the day after the Germans entered Dunkirk. The prelude to the new German offensive was itself astonishing—in the way that the German panzer forces, which had just previously been striking north-westward, were so quickly switched southward for a fresh stroke. Such rapidity of re-concentration in another direction was fresh evidence of how mechanized mobility had revolutionized strategy.

The new offensive was delivered against the new front, held by the remaining French armies, along the Somme and the Aisne. It was longer than the original front, while the forces available to hold it were much fewer. For the French had lost 30 of their divisions, besides the aid of their Allies, except for 2 British divisions. Weygand, who had replaced Gamelin, had collected in all 66 divisions, of which 17 were in the heavily fortified Maginot Line, with which the improvised Somme-Aisne line linked up.

In this second act, Rundstedt's Army Group again played the decisive part, though it was not cast for this in the plan. Six of the ten German panzer divisions were allotted to Bock at the outset. But the planning was flexible and the battle took a different shape as it developed, so that Bock's strokes created the distraction which helped Rundstedt's to become decisive. The change of shape was a further proof of the capacity for *alternative* courses newly provided by armoured forces.

Bock's armies struck on the 5th June, but Rundstedt's not until four days later, owing to the longer time taken in re-deployment on that wing. In Bock's attack the principal effort was not so quickly or deeply successful as on the extreme right—where Rommel's panzer division broke right through the French defence by the third morning.

This quick penetration owed much to a piece of audacity on Rommel's part that no orthodox opponent would have expected—what he tried, and achieved, would hardly have been considered a practical possibility in any staff college exercise. On his sector, the French had blown up all the road bridges over the Somme, but had left intact a pair of rail bridges, with a view to the maintenance of the counter-offensive which they had dreamed of delivering. There can have seemed little risk in preserving these bridges as the single line rail-tracks were laid along two narrow embankments which ran for nearly a mile through marshy riverside meadows. Even for infantry to advance along these would be like 'running the gauntlet' on a tight-rope. Yet Rommel, having captured the bridges before dawn and gained a foothold on the plateau beyond the river, pulled up the rails and sleepers, and then ran his tanks and transport along the 'tight-ropes' under shell-fire, suffering only one check, of half an hour, when a tank was disabled in approaching one of the bridges.

By the first evening he had penetrated 8 miles deep, by the second 20 miles, and next day swept forward a further 30 miles, gaining quicker progress by advancing across country and thus by-passing the defended road-junctions. This deep thrust split the French 10th Army. Other German divisions were now pouring through the widening gap. On the night of the 8th, the fourth day, Rommel reached the Seine south of Rouen, after a 40 miles swerving drive through a dislocated and confused defence which had been hastily strung across the approaches to Rouen and the Seine. Crossings were gained before the French had begun to rally and establish a defence of that broad river-barrier. Rommel's division switched round on the 10th for a 50-mile thrust to the coast, which he reached that evening, cutting off the retreat of the left wing of the 10th Army—5 divisions (including the 51st Highland). These, surrounded, were forced to surrender at St. Valéry on the 12th.

Meanwhile the main right wing attack from the Somme had found the going more sticky. It was a pincer-stroke, by two panzer corps under Kleist, from the bridgeheads already gained across the Somme at Amiens and Péronne. The right pincer, at Amiens, eventually broke through the French defence on the 8th and then wheeled south towards the lower reaches of the Oise, but the left pincer became hung up by tough opposition north of Compiègne.

As Rundstedt's Army Group, attacking the Aisne line on the

9th, had there quickly broken through the French defence, the German Supreme Command decided to pull back to Kleist's two panzer corps and switch them east, pass them through the wide breach along the Aisne, and use them to help in exploiting the French collapse in Champagne. This rapid switch was a fresh example of the flexibility of mobile armoured forces.

The decisive thrust was again made by Guderian—and it was once more a striking demonstration of deep strategic penetration combined with indirect approach. He had now been promoted to command Rundstedt's panzer group, and his two corps concentrated on the Aisne near Rethel after a circuitous 200-mile move from the Pas de Calais. After the infantry of the 12th Army had gained three small footholds over the river around Château-Porcien, Guderian moved his leading panzer divisions into the bridgeheads during the night. They broke out next morning, the 10th, and drove forward with quickening pace, by-passing the villages and woods held by the French. Then French armour came into action, and a series of tank battles took place, but a penetration of nearly 20 miles was achieved in the first two days. On the third day Guderian's right wing reached Chalons-sur-Marne, and on the fourth Vitry-le-François, nearly 60 miles from the start. His left wing had now come up level after beating off flank counter-attacks. Guderian then drove on at increasing speed to, and over, the Plateau de Langres—far behind the back of the Maginot Line—and raced south-eastward for the Swiss frontier. Chaumont was reached in a 50-mile bound on the fifth day, the 14th June; the River Saône on the 15th, by a similar bound; and early on the 17th the leading division swept into Pontarlier on the Swiss frontier, 60 miles beyond the Saône. That stroke cut the communications of the large French forces still clinging to the Maginot Line. Guderian's other divisions were already wheeling north to the Moselle to bar their retreat. A few hours previously, the French Government, with its armies in collapse, had decided to capitulate and appealed for an armistice.

Yet this decisive strategic victory on the Continent was rendered indecisive on the higher strategic plane by Hitler's subsequent failure to conquer the island of Britain. Here he paid the penalty for his halt order at Dunkirk. If he had prevented the British forces escaping through this one remaining bolt-hole, Britain herself would have been so defenceless that he might have conquered her even by hastily improvised invasion. But having missed his supreme chance of trapping the British army at Dunkirk, he could not hope to subdue her without a well-organized invasion in strength, and for that he had made neither plans nor preparations. His belated steps were too late, while his peace moves were too weak. When the attempt to gain control of the air over the sea approach was defeated in the 'Battle of Britain' the invasion project was foredoomed.

The insular obstacle continued to defy him—covered by the grand anti-tank ditch provided by the English Channel—and developed into an increasing threat to his schemes of continental control. This frustration had fatal consequences for him.

His run of victory continued in the following year—first at the expense of the Balkan countries, and then at Russia's—before it was checked in the depths of Russia. But he lacked the resources to make sure of the results at which he was aiming. For all the brilliance of his 1941 successes his decline can be dated from his failure in the 'Battle of Britain'—and this, in turn, can be traced back to his hesitating halt when Dunkirk was within his grasp.

CHAPTER XVII

HITLER'S DECLINE

★

Before the end of June 1940, Germany bestrode the continent of Europe like a Colossus. She dominated the whole of western, central and south-eastern Europe—except for the small island of Britain on the western fringe. Apart from that 'off-shore' check, the only serious limitation on her supremacy was the existence of Soviet Russia, a looming shadow on her north-eastern flank. Hitler had enjoyed a run of success that seemed to promise him the complete domination of Europe, if not of the world. Five years later that midsummer night's dream had turned into a nightmare.

It was on the plane of *grand strategy* that his decline began. There lay his fatal flaw. If he had known how to allay the fears that his progress created, and to reassure the neighbouring peoples that his 'New Order' was beneficent, he might have succeeded where Napoleon failed, and achieved the union of Europe under German leadership—a union too strong for outside forces to break. But the end was frustrated by the means. His political approach had been too direct. It was subtle enough to cause dissension in the threatened countries, but not to disarm opposition. In his gospel of National Socialism, nationalistic emphasis marred the effect of the socialistic appeal that might otherwise have attracted the masses in other countries. The iron hand was poorly concealed by a threadbare velvet glove. Likewise, following his conquests, his attempts at conciliation were clumsy and ill-sustained. These mistakes piled up an accumulating debit as his further ventures miscarried.

The first check, and a continuing check, came with his failure either to subdue or to make peace with Britain after the collapse of the other countries in the West. So long as she stood out, Hitler's grip on the West could never become secure, and his position would be subject to ceaseless disturbance. At the same time,

Britain alone could not do more than prevent him reaping the fruits of his success. Her combination of resistance and interference might have succeeded in bending his will and leading him to bid for peace by increasing concessions. It could never have sufficed to shatter his power and eject him forcibly from his conquests. Such a possibility only arose when a baffled and apprehensive Hitler was driven—in June 1941—to turn eastward and strike at Soviet Russia.

That decision, which turned out fatally for him, marked his abandonment of the indirect approach in grand strategy. Before long, in his impatience or anxiety for victory, he was led on to discard the indirect approach even in strategy. The change was the more significant because of the care which he had shown in applying it previously, even in dealing with such a relatively minor obstacle as that presented by Greece.

The German Conquest of the Balkans

When the Germans invaded Greece in April 1941, following the landing of a small British army of reinforcement at Salonika, the Greek army was mainly aligned to cover the passages through the mountains from Bulgaria, where the German forces had assembled. But the expected advance down the Struma Valley masked a less direct move. German mechanized columns swerved westward from the Struma up to Strumitza Valley parallel with the frontier, and over the mountain passes into the Yugo-Slav end of the Vardar Valley. Thereby they pierced the joint between the Greek and Yugo-Slav armies, and exploited the penetration by a rapid thrust down the Vardar to Salonika. This cut off a large part of the Greek army, anchored in Thrace.

The Germans followed up this stroke, not by a direct advance southward from Salonika past Mount Olympus, where the British army had taken up its position, but by another swerving thrust down through the Monastir Gap, farther west. The exploitation of this advance towards the west cost of Greece cut off the Greek divisions in Albania, turned the flank of the British, and, by its threatened swerve back onto the line of retreat of the surviving Allied forces, produced the speedy collapse of all resistance in Greece.

HITLER'S DECLINE

The German Invasion of Russia

At the outset of the invasion of Russia, the Germans operationally exploited the indirect approach with striking success, aided by the geographical conditions. The 1,800 mile breadth of that front, and the scarcity of natural obstacles, offered the attacker immense scope for infiltration and manœuvre. Despite the great size of the Red army, the ratio of force to space was so low that the German mechanized forces could easily find openings for indirect advance onto their opponent's rear. At the same time the widely spaced cities where road and railways converged provided the attacker with alternative objectives that he could exploit to confuse the defending armies as to his direction, and impale them on the 'horns of a dilemma' in trying to meet his thrusts.

But after gaining great opening successes in this way, the Germans forfeited the advantage through a failure to decide in which direction the advantage should be pursued. Hitler and the Army Command had different ideas from the start of the planning, and never properly reconciled them.

Hitler wished to secure Leningrad as a primary objective, thus clearing his Baltic flank and linking up with the Finns, and tended to disparage the importance of Moscow. But, with a keen sense of economic factors, he also wanted to secure the agricultural wealth of the Ukraine and the industrial area on the Lower Dnieper. The two objectives were extremely wide apart, and thus entailed entirely separate lines of operation. That was essentially different from the flexibility inherent in operating on a single and central line of operation that threatens alternative objectives.

Brauchitsch and Halder wanted to concentrate on the Moscow line of advance—not for the sake of capturing the capital but because they felt that this line offered the best chance of destroying the mass of Russia's forces which they 'expected to find on the way to Moscow'. In Hitler's view that course carried the risk of driving the Russians into a general retreat eastward, out of reach. As Brauchitsch and Halder agreed with him about the importance of avoiding this risk, and as he agreed with them about the importance of destroying the enemy's main forces by an early 'Kesselschlacht' (battle of encirclement), they shelved a decision on further aims until the first phase of the invasion was completed.

Brauchitsch, by his tendency to avoid 'meeting trouble half-

THE RUSSIAN THEATRE, 1941–42

way' in dealing with Hitler, was apt to run into worse trouble in the end. In this case, by putting off the issue he ran into trouble midway in the campaign.

In the first phase, however, it was agreed that the centre of gravity should be in the sector of Bock's Army Group just north of the Pripet Marshes, and along the route from the Minsk and Moscow. Here the major part of the armoured forces were employed. At the outset the advance of Leeb's Army Group from its advanced left flank position in East Prussia, and on through the Baltic States, helped to mask the more dangerous thrust of its neighbour, Bock's Army Group. Moreover, the thrust of Rundstedt's Army Group on the other flank, south of the Pripet Marshes, kept the Russian Command in uncertainty as to the invader's main line of operation.

On Bock's sector the plan was to trap the mass of the opposing forces by a twofold encircling manœuvre—with the panzer groups of Guderian and Hoth advancing from either flank and converging on Minsk before driving on, while the infantry corps of the 4th and 9th Armies executed an inner pincer-stroke around and behind Bialystok.

The invasion began on the 22nd June—a day ahead of Napoleon's date. The panzer pincers of Guderian and Hoth quickly made two deep incisions, and on the sixth day met at Minsk, 200 miles inside the frontier. Behind them the infantry pincers closed in at Slonim, but not quite in time to catch the bulk of the Russians in their retreat from the Bialystok pocket. A second attempt, aimed to surround them near Minsk, was more successful, and nearly 300,000 were captured—although large fractions had managed to escape before the encirclement was sealed. The size of the bag gave rise to a wave of optimism, even among the generals, who had been apprehensive about Hitler's decision to invade Russia. Halder remarked on 3rd July: 'It is probably not an exaggeration when I contend that the campaign against Russia has been won in fourteen days.'

But the operations had already suffered an ominous hitch. For the panzer forces had been ordered to pause until the encirclement battle was complete, whereas in the original plan they were to have driven on beyond Minsk without delay, leaving only minimum detachments there to help the infantry armies in closing the ring.

Time was regained, however, by Guderian's bold action in attempting a crossing of the broad Dnieper without waiting for the foot-marching mass of the 4th Army to come up—*and* before the Russians could bring up reinforcements. His calculations was justified by the result. Concentrating his forces under cover of night, and behind a wide screen, he achieved crossings at three unguarded points on the 10th July. He then drove for Smolensk, which he reached on the 16th. The invaders had now penetrated over 400 miles into Russian territory, and Moscow lay only 200 miles ahead. For such a deep advance the pace had been very rapid.

With Hoth's arrival north of Smolensk, a fresh encircling move was undertaken to cut off the large Russian forces between the Dnieper and the Desna that had been by-passed in the panzer drives. The trap was almost closed, but difficult country and muddy going hampered the movement, and the Russians succeeded in extricating a large part of their forces. Even so, a total of 180,000 were captured in the Smolensk area.

Guderian urged the importance of keeping the Russians on the run, and allowing them no time to rally. He was convinced that he could get there if no time was wasted, and that such a thrust at the nerve-centre of Stalin's power might paralyse Russia's resistance. Hoth shared his views and Bock endorsed them.

But Hitler considered that the time had come to carry out his original conception of taking Leningrad and the Ukraine as primary objectives. While rating their importance higher than that of Moscow, he was not only thinking of the economic and political effect, as most of his critics among the generals tended to assume. He seems to have visualized a Cannae-like operation of super-large dimensions, in which the already created threat to Moscow would draw the Russian reserves to that sector of the front, thus making it easier for the German wings to gain their flank objectives, Leningrad and the Ukraine. And from these flank positions his forces could then converge on Moscow, which might fall like a ripe plum into their hands. It was a subtle as well as a vast conception. In the event it broke down on the time-factor—because Russian resistance proved tougher and the weather worse than had been expected. The prospects were not improved by the differences of opinion that were prevalent among the generals. Each tended, all too naturally, to focus his thought on his own sector and to press its claims for receiving preference. That tendency accentuated the risks of the very wide strategic divergence involved in the second stage of Hitler's concept.

On the 19th July Hitler issued his directive for this second stage —to begin as soon as the immediate mopping-up operations between the Dnieper and the Desna had been completed. Part of Bock's mobile forces was to wheel southward to help Rundstedt in destroying the Russian armies facing him, while the other part was to wheel northward to help Leeb's attack on Leningrad by cutting the communications between that city and Moscow. Bock would be left only with foot-marching forces to continue the frontal advance on Moscow as best he could.

Once again Brauchitsch temporized, instead of at once pressing for a different plan. He argued that before any further operations were started, the panzer forces must have a rest to overhaul their machines and get up replacements. Hitler agreed as to the necessity for such a pause. Meanwhile the high-level discussion about the course to be followed went on, and it continued even after the panzer forces could have resumed their drive. On the 21st August, turning down the arguments of Brauchitsch and Halder for taking the Moscow direction, Hitler issued a fresh directive. This repeated the lines of the one he had issued a month before, except that rather less emphasis was given to Leningrad and more emphasis was placed on an annihilating envelopment of the enemy forces in the Kiev area, on Rundstedt's front. After that Bock might resume the advance on Moscow, while Rundstedt was to push on in the south to cut off the Russians' oil supplies from the Caucasus.

During this prolonged period of discussion, various developments in the situation had tended to confirm Hitler in his decision. Reichenau's 6th Army on Rundstedt's left wing had been blocked in front of Kiev, and the strong Russian forces that were sheltered behind the eastern end of the Pripet marshes had continued to threaten his left flank, as well as threatening Bock's right flank. On the other hand, Kleist's panzer group had achieved brilliant success in an oblique move. Following a local break-through at Belaya-Tserkov, south of Kiev, at the end of July, Kleist swerved southward down the river-corridor between the Bug and the Dnieper. This indirect thrust not only opened the way into the Ukraine but threatened the rear of the Russian armies which were facing the Rumanians near the Black Sea. By the middle of August the Germans reached the ports of Nikolaiev and Kherson, at the mouths of the two great rivers. Although part of the endangered

Russian armies escaped before the trap closed, the deep penetration achieved by Kleist produced a widespread dislocation of the Russian resistance in the south.

This combination of events emphasized the possibility, if Kleist turned northwards and a strong force from Bock's front was sent southward, of bringing off a double flank stroke that would not only loosen the stubborn resistance of the Russian armies around and above Kiev but also put them in the bag—and thereby eliminate the danger that a drive for Moscow might be upset by a counter-offensive from the south of the Dnieper. The sum of these prospective benefits proved decisive in making Hitler settle on the Kiev operation, as a preliminary to the Moscow advance.

Nor was he alone in favouring it. It was natural that Rundstedt should welcome a reinforcement from the north to help him in solving the tough problem with which he was faced on his own front, and natural, too, that he should appreciate the prospect of achieving a great encirclement victory—the soldier's dream.

Strategically, too, there was much to be said for freeing the southern wing and removing the menace of a counter-stroke from that flank before pressing on to Moscow. Moreover, the relative immobility of the Russian masses increased the advantages of a strategy of switching the concentrated power of the German mobile forces successively from one sector to another, to produce a decisive effect on each in turn. But time for such a procedure was running short, especially as the German army was unprepared for a winter campaign.

The Kiev 'Kesselschlacht' itself proved a great success—much the greatest yet attained by the Germans. While Reichenau's and Weichs's infantry armies engaged the Russian armies in front of them, Guderian thrust downward across their rear while Kleist thrust upward from the Dnieper Bend. The two panzer groups met 150 miles east of Kiev, closing the trap behind the backs of the Russians. This time few escaped, and the total bag of prisoners amounted to over 600,000. But it was late in September before the battle ended—poor roads and bad weather had slowed down the pace of encircling manœuvre, though failing to prevent its completion.

Meanwhile the decision to concentrate on gaining victory in the Ukraine had resulted in Hitler's 'primary objective', Leningrad, becoming a secondary one—although it was pursued simultaneously. Sufficient strength and effort were used in this divergent direction to bring about the envelopment of Leningrad, but not sufficient to produce a decisive defeat of the Russian forces in that sector. The German strength there had also suffered subtraction because Hitler, when overruling Brauchitsch's and Bock's desire for an early continuation of the drive for Moscow, had met them to the extent of agreeing that the Moscow axis should again be made the centre of gravity as soon as the Kiev battle of encirclement had been completed.

The triumphant outcome of this battle had a too exhilarating effect on both Hitler and his topmost generals, uniting them in optimism while inducing fresh divergence of effort. Hitler's decision to embark on an autumn bid for Moscow was accompanied by another one which involved further complications and a loss of concentration—for he could not resist the temptation to exploit the victory in the south at the same time as he pursued the aim of capturing Moscow. He assigned Rundstedt the extremely ambitious fresh task of clearing the Black Sea coast, capturing the Donetz industrial area, and reaching the Caucasus.

The belated bid for Moscow was made with three infantry armies and three panzer groups—one of which, Guderian's, was now constituted as a panzer army. On the 2nd October the offensive was at last launched again on a pincer-plan. This time the circle was completed and 600,000 Russians were caught in the trap around Vyasma. But by the time they were rounded up winter had set in, and the belated exploitation of the victory was bogged in the mud on the way to Moscow.

Most of the executive commanders were now anxious to halt and take up a suitable advance line for the winter. They remembered what had happened to Napoleon's army, and many of them began to re-read Caulaincourt's grim account of 1812. But on the higher levels—more remote from the battle zone and its mud—a different view prevailed. Moscow exercised a magnetic attraction that induced excessive optimism about the practical possibility of attaining this goal. Contrary to what has been commonly assumed, Hitler himself was not the impelling cause of the continued effort. From the outset he had regarded Moscow as less important than other objectives, and although he had sanctioned the belated October drive in this direction, he came to have renewed doubts about it. But Bock's eyes were focused on Moscow, and his mind filled with the ambition of capturing that famed city. He was insistent on pursuing the offensive, arguing that, where both sides were nearing exhaustion, superior will-power would decide the issue. Brauchitsch and Halder were the more inclined to share Bock's view because they had been thwarted earlier in concentrating upon this objective. Having brought Hitler round to making the attempt, they were reluctant to admit, or tell him, that it could no longer succeed. Although Rundstedt and Leeb both argued that the offensive should be broken off—and Rundstedt even advocated a withdrawal to the original frontier in Poland—their views on the immediate issue had less influence, as they were not directly concerned with the Moscow offensive.

So another great effort was mounted by the Germans in November. But the obviousness of their aim and the convergence of the thrusts simplified the Russians' problem in concentrating reserves to check each dangerous development. Early in December, the German offensive subsided, and was followed by an enforced withdrawal under pressure of counter-attacks. Hitler thereupon dismissed Brauchitsch, and himself assumed direct control of the German army. By that move he attained an alternative objective of a personal kind, and in a double way—for he provided himself with a scapegoat for the past while seizing more power for the future.

In the south the German tide of invasion attained its high-water mark on the 23rd November, when it penetrated into the city of Rostov, on the Lower Don, the gateway to the Caucasus. But it had exhausted its fuel in the mud, and within a week the advanced troops in Rostov were led to withdraw by a deep flanking counter-stroke against their communication.

In an inquest on the Germans' failure in the 1941 campaign, the appropriate verdict would be 'defeat from natural causes'. Their strength became split in diverging directions—due partly to divided minds at the top, but also, ironically, to dazzling initial success in all directions. Instead of keeping a single line of operation that threatened alternative objectives, they were led to pursue several lines of operation each too obviously aiming at a single objective, which thus became easier for the defender to cover. Moreover, in each case the attacker's direction became obvious at the same time that his drive was becoming a precarious stretch of his own supply line.

HITLER'S DECLINE

The Russian Campaign of 1942

In 1942 the Germans no longer had the resources for an offensive on the previous year's scale, but Hitler was unwilling to stay on the defensive and consolidate his gains as a number of his generals advised, or withdraw to Poland as Rundstedt and Leeb had advocated—a course which, however wise strategically, would be a palpable admission that he had 'bitten off more than he could chew'. Driven on by the spur of insatiable appetite, by the haunting spectre of lost prestige, and by the instinctive feeling that attack was the only way of dealing with problems, Hitler searched for an offensive solution that with limited means might promise more than a limited result.

Lacking sufficient strength for a renewed offensive on the whole front, he decided to concentrate his effort in the southern sector, with the aim of securing the Caucasus oil and, still more important, shutting the Russians off from its supplies. If this, perforce, meant discarding a continued attempt to overthrow the enemy's main armed forces, Hitler hoped that he might succeed in undermining their power of resistance indirectly, because of their dependence on the Caucasus source of oil supply. It was a shrewd calculation, and came closer to being fulfilled than has commonly been realized—in the after light of its ultimately disastrous failure.

It had a brilliant start, and gained great advantage from the way it distracted the Russian forces by operating on a line that repeatedly threatened alternative objectives. But later it suffered badly from becoming split in seeking to reach two divergent objectives simultaneously. That fatally dual trend was largely due to the split mind of the German command. Halder, the Chief of the General Staff, planned the operation primarily with the aim of gaining a hold on the Volga round Stalingrad, and there establishing a strategic barrage between the main Russian armies and their oil supplies. Hitler, without revealing his mind to Halder, was primarily intent on driving direct into the Caucasus as quickly as possible, and encouraged the commanders of that drive to regard it as the main aim. The effort to gain the Stalingrad strategic position suffered in consequence. Then, at a later stage, the aggravation of being frustrated at Stalin's name-place altered the bent of Hitler's mind, and everything else was sacrificed for a too direct concentration, too directly aimed, against that untaken city.

The start of the Germans' 1942 offensive was helped by the way that the Russians played into its hands by their spring offensive towards Kharkov. This became so direct that it carried its own check, and so prolonged that it used up the Russian reserves, while the deep bulge it created gave the German command the chance of catching the Russians at a disadvantage. Thereby the subsequent German offensive, at the end of June, had the effect of a counter-offensive—against opponents who were deeply committed and awkwardly placed.

The original axis of the German drive was parallel to that of the Russian push, but in the opposite direction. Launched from the Kursk sector, north of Kharkov, it cut past the flank of the bulge which the Russians had made, and quickly traversed the 120-mile stretch to the Upper Don near Voronezh, an important junction on the main line from Moscow to the Caucasus. The Russians' concentration on blocking the path near Voronezh eased the way for the Germans to swing their weight south-eastward and force an entry into the corridor between the Don and the Donetz. This manœuvre was assisted by the leverage which the Germans were able to develop indirectly from the wedge which they had previously driven into the southern flank of the Russians' Kharkov bulge.

Under the combined pincer-pressure the Russian resistance broke down and the German mechanized forces gained an increasingly clear run through the Don-Donetz corridor, with their own flanks covered by two rivers. Within less than a month they had reached the farther end of the corridor and crossed the Lower Don north of Rostov. This opened the road to the Caucasus oilfields, and brought the campaign to a crisis. It looked as if Russia might be paralysed, by being cut off from her oil supplies, while the Germans' mobility would be assured. The way they had 'sold the dummy' in their swerving advance had been brilliantly successful.

But in their further advance, beyond the Don, the Germans forfeited the strategic advantages which they had hitherto enjoyed. Previously, they had been moving strategically concentrated—flexibly grouped—along an axis which threatened alternative objectives, so that their opponents were kept on the horns of a dilemma, while they themselves could swing their weight wherever a weakness developed in the enemy's front. After crossing the Don, however the Germans were led to divide their strength along divergent lines, one part pushing southward through the Caucasus, while the other part pushed eastward on Stalingrad.

So widespread was the Russians' collapse in the Don-Donetz corridor that Stalingrad and control of the Volga could have been gained with ease in July if the 4th Panzer Army, advancing in that direction, had not been diverted southward to help the 1st Panzer Army in crossing the Lower Don on its way to the Caucasus. That help was not needed, whereas by the time that the 4th Panzer Army turned northward again the Russian forces on the Stalingrad sector had begun to rally. It was easier for the Russians to reinforce this sector than the Caucasus, since it was nearer the central front and more accessible from the rail and road movement of reserves. The successive checks which the Germans met there then began to give Stalingrad a moral importance—enhanced by its name—which came to outweigh its strategic value. The Germans' attention and efforts became increasingly focused on its capture, to the forfeit of their chances of completing the capture of the Caucasus oil-fields—as the 1st Panzer Army there was increasingly drawn on for the reinforcement of the attack on Stalingrad. Yet this subtraction was without compensation.

After the first advance on Stalingrad had narrowly failed, the strengthening of the German forces was offset by the strengthening of the Russians, in face of such a direct approach. Thus the Germans' own offensive concentration became a proportionately less forceful concentration. That was the strategic price they paid for forfeiting their former power of distraction. And the more closely they converged on the city, the narrower became their scope for tactical manœuvre, as a lever in loosening resistance.

By contrast, the narrowing of the frontage made it easier for the defender to switch his local reserves to any threatened point on the defensive arc. Several times the Germans succeeded in piercing the defences round Stalingrad, but each time the gap was closed. The sum of experience suggests the axiom that a narrowing of the front always favours the defence.

The attackers' losses naturally began to mount higher as their scope for manœuvre diminished. Each step forward cost more and gained less. This process of attrition soon brought evidence that the Germans were running on a narrower margin of material strength than they had enjoyed in 1941. The first shortage that became apparent was in their armoured strength; the number of tanks that they could provide for each blow became smaller and smaller. Then their advantage in the air began to disappear. Their decline in these two master-weapons threw a heavier burden on their infantry. Naturally the price of any partial success gained by massed infantry assaults was exorbitant, and more became frayed.

The effect of this tactical overstrain was the more dangerous because of the way the invaders were strategically overstretched. Yet when Halder, the Chief of the General Staff, urged the wisdom of cutting their loss and making a timely halt to take up a good winter defence-line, his advice was rejected by Hitler, and merely led to his own replacement by Zeitzler, who was younger and more ardent. The lure of Stalingrad was too strong for Hitler, as the lure of Moscow had been the previous autumn, and he again found soldiers who were ready to encourage his hopes. This time the consequences were worse. The armies attacking Stalingrad had pushed forward so far, and on so narrow a front, that they had exposed themselves to encirclement.

This risk matured when the Russian counter-offensive was launched in November. The attackers were ripe for defeat both in the moral and in the strategical sense. The riposte itself, while shrewdly indirect in physical approach, gained deadliness from the recoil-spring effect which the counter-offensive form of action naturally possesses. The Russians also profited from the way their thrusts were directed against sectors held by the Rumanian and Italian forces that Hitler had employed to cover the far-stretched flank of his advance. The outcome was that the Russians cut off a large part of the attacking armies and secured their first great bag of prisoners.

With their path partially cleared, the Russians exploited their success by a series of southward drives which threatened the rear and communications of the German armies in the Caucasus. The danger to which these were exposed is most simply expressed in the fact that they were over 400 miles east of Rostov at the time, in January 1943, when the Russian drive down the Don was barely forty miles from Rostov, the bottle-neck through which ran the communications of the German armies in the Caucasus. Although the Germans succeeded in holding open the jaws of the trap long enough to make a gradual withdrawal, without being cut off, they were not only compelled to abandon the Caucasus but were then in turn squeezed out of the industrial Donetz Basin by enveloping pressure.

In February the Germans' retreat became suddenly quicker, and the Russians, pressing on their heels, reached and passed the line from which the German summer offensive had started. They recaptured Kharkov and approached the Dnieper. But late in February the Germans retorted with a counter-stroke that again wrested Kharkov from the Russians' hands and momentarily threw the Russians off their balance. Like the Germans in the summer, the Russians had overstrained themselves in the pursuit, outrunning their supplies, while the Germans had gathered renewed strength in snowball-fashion by falling back on their bases and reinforcements.

This Kharkov counter-stroke was a most striking example of the defensive-offensive form of the strategy of indirect approach, the use of the baited gambit to lure the enemy into a trap—in this case a super-size trap. It was planned and executed by Field-Marshal von Manstein—who in the first winter of the war, when Chief of Staff to Rundstedt's army group, had evolved the Ardennes plan that produced the French collapse in May 1940. While regarded by most of his fellows as the ablest strategist among them, he was not viewed with favour by Hitler. But when Paulus's army was surrounded at Stalingrad in November 1942, Hitler had sent Manstein to take command of Army Group 'Don' in an attempt to avert disaster. Although it was too late to retrieve the situation at Stalingrad, Manstein managed to hold off the Russians from cutting the Rostov bottle-neck long enough to save the forces from the Caucasus, and re-established a defensive position along the Mius River, between the Sea of Azov and the Donetz River.

But the Russians had by now broken through the front north of the Donetz held by the Italian and Hungarian armies, making a breach 200 miles wide between the Donetz and Voronezh, and were sweeping westward past Manstein's flank. Crossing the Donetz far in rear, they not only captured Kharkov but thrust south-westward to the great bend of the Dnieper, the area on which Manstein depended for his supplies. On the 21st February an advanced force came within sight of Zaporozhe, on the bend, whither he had just moved his own headquarters. In this critical situation he showed an extraordinarily cool head and steady nerve. He had already refused to throw his scanty reserves into a direct effort to recapture Kharkov as Hitler demanded, and now withstood the temptation to use them for a direct defence of the Dnieper line. For he had seen in the Russians' south-westward advance a great opportunity for a dislocating indirect stroke, and wanted to let them push deeper—despite the peril to his base.

Meantime he was regrouping his forces and bringing his three depleted panzer corps from the Mius to form a reversed front facing north-west. On the 26th he was ready to strike, and drove forward against the flank and rear of the Russian armies. It thus became a thrust against the hinge of an enemy advance—as at Sedan in 1940. Within a week the Russian armies advancing south-west had fallen back in confusion across the Donetz, having lost over six hundred tanks and a thousand guns. Manstein then drove on, turning northward against the rear flank of the Russian armies that were pushing west from Kharkov and Bielgorod. They, in turn, were dislocated and forced to retreat, abandoning both these cities. The results of these successive indirect approaches were a staggering achievement on the part of a force that was faced with adverse odds of eight to one in divisions. But for the extreme disparity of strength it might have had a Sedan-like decisiveness. That disparity was ominous.

The German reserves were much more limited than those of the Russians, and had been seriously depleted in two years' offensive effort, whereas a mass of newly formed Russian divisions were becoming available. Although the Kharkov counter-stroke temporarily paralysed the Russian menace, the balance of power had now turned heavily against Germany.

The War in the Pacific

Since 1931 the Japanese had been expanding their footholds on the Asiatic mainland at the expense of the Chinese, who were weakened by internal conflict, and to the detriment of American and British interests in that sphere. In that year they had invaded Manchuria and converted it into a Japanese satellite state. In 1932 they invaded China itself, but in the effort to establish their control of that vast area they became enmeshed in the toils of guerrilla warfare, and sought a solution of the problem in further expansionist moves, southward, aimed to shut off the Chinese from outside supplies. Following Hitler's defeat of France, the Japanese took advantage of her helplessness by getting her to agree, under threat, to their 'protective' occupation of French Indo-China.

In reply President Roosevelt demanded, on the 24th July 1941, the withdrawal of Japanese troops from Indo-China—and to enforce his demand he issued orders on the 26th for freezing all Japanese assets in the U.S.A. and placing an embargo on oil supply. Mr. Churchill took simultaneous action, and two days later the refugee Dutch Government in London was induced to follow suit—which meant, as Mr. Churchill has remarked, that 'Japan was deprived at a stroke of her vital oil supplies'.

In early discussions it had always been recognized that such a paralysing stroke would force Japan to fight, as the only alternative to collapse or the abandonment of her policy. It is remarkable that she deferred striking for more than four months, while trying to negotiate a lifting of the oil embargo. The United States Government refused to lift it, unless Japan withdrew not only from Indo-China but also from China. No Government, least of all the Japanese, could be expected to swallow such humiliating conditions, and utter loss of face. So there was every reason to expect war in the Pacific at any moment, from the last week of July onwards. In these circumstances the Americans and British were lucky to be allowed four months' grace before the Japanese struck. But little advantage was taken of this interval for defensive preparation.

On the morning of the 7th December 1941, a Japanese naval force with six aircraft carriers delivered a shattering air attack on Pearl Harbour, the American naval base in the Hawaiian Islands. The stroke was made ahead of the declaration of war, following the precedent of Port Arthur, the Japanese opening stroke in the war against Russia.

Until early in 1941 the Japanese plan in case of war against the United States was to use their main fleet in the southern Pacific in conjunction with an attack on the Philippine Islands, to meet an American advance across the ocean to the relief of their garrison in the Philippines. That was the move that the Americans were expecting the Japanese to make, and their expectation had been reinforced by the recent Japanese move down to Indo-China. But Admiral Yamamoto had in the meantime conceived a new plan—of a surprise attack on Pearl Harbour. The striking force made a very roundabout approach via the Kurile Islands and came down from the north upon the Hawaiian Islands undetected, then launching its attack before sunrise, with 360 aircraft, from a position nearly three hundred miles from Pearl Harbour. Four of the eight American battleships were sunk and the others badly damaged. In little over an hour the Japanese had gained control of the Pacific.

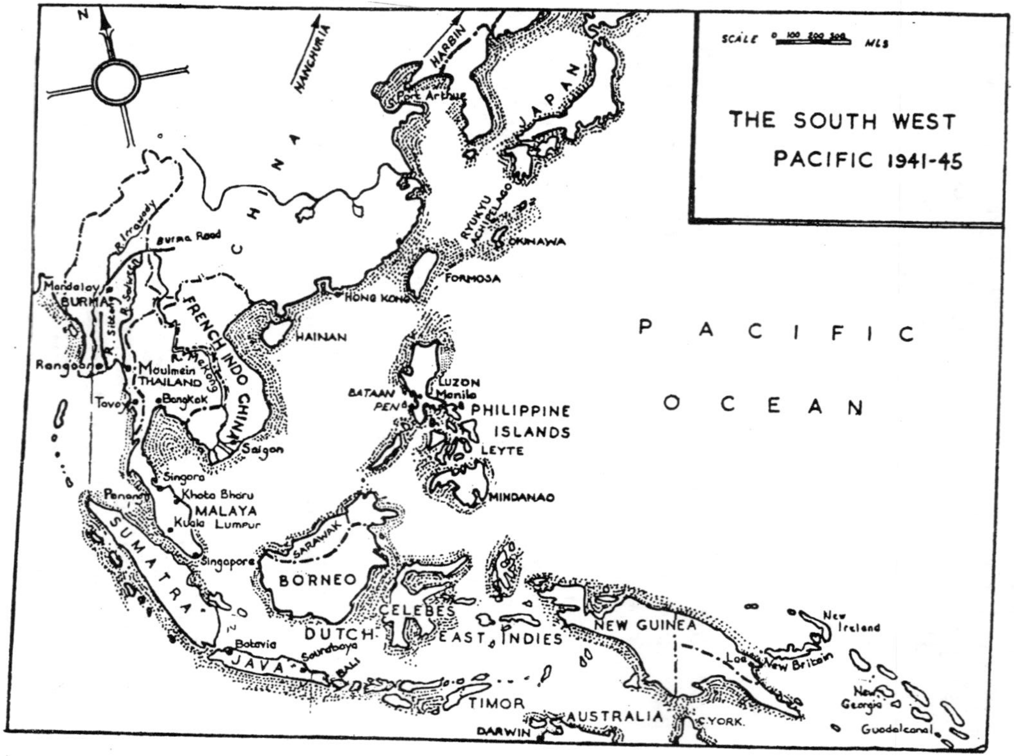
SCALE 0 100 200 300 MLS
THE SOUTH WEST
PACIFIC 1941-45
N
MANCHURIA
HARBIN
Port Arthur
JAPAN
CHINA
RYUKYU ARCHIPELAGO
OKINAWA
FORMOSA
HONG KONG
HAINAN
Burma Road
R. Irrawady
R. Salween
R. Sittang
Mandalay
BURMA
Rangoon
Moulmein
THAILAND
Bangkok
R. Mekong
FRENCH INDO CHINA
Saigon
Tavoy
Singora
Penang
Khota Bharu
MALAYA
Kuala Lumpur
Singapore
SUMATRA
Batavia
JAVA
Sourabaya
BALI
SARAWAK
BORNEO
CELEBES
DUTCH EAST INDIES
TIMOR
DARWIN
AUSTRALIA
C.YORK.
NEW GUINEA
Lae
New Britain
New Ireland
New Georgia
Guadalcanal
BATAAN PEN.
LUZON
Manila
PHILIPPINE ISLANDS
LEYTE
MINDANAO
PACIFIC
OCEAN

By that stroke the way was cleared for an uninterrupted sea-borne invasion of Malaya and the Malay Archipelago. While the main Japanese striking force had been steaming north-east towards the Hawaiian Islands, other naval forces had been escorting troopship convoys into the south-west Pacific. Almost simultaneously with the air attack on Pearl Harbour, landings began in the Malay Peninsula as well as in the Philippines. The former were aimed at the great British naval base at Singapore, but there was no attempt to attack it from the sea—the kind of attack which the defence had been primarily designed to meet. The approach was very indirect. While landings were made at two points on the east coast of the Malay Peninsula, to seize airfields and distract attention, the main forces were disembarked on the Siamese neck of the peninsula, some 500 miles north of Singapore. From these landing-places in the extreme north-east the Japanese forces poured down the *west* coast of the peninsula, successively outflanking the lines on which the British forces attempted to check them. The Japanese profited not only by their unexpected choice of such a difficult route but by the opportunities for unexpected infiltration which the thick vegetation often provided. After almost continuous retreat for six weeks the British forces were forced to withdraw from the mainland into the island of Singapore, at the end of January. On the night of the 8th February, the Japanese launched their attack across the mile-wide straits, got ashore at numerous points, and developed fresh infiltrations along a broad front.

The defending forces mustered more than double the attacker's numbers, but his were picked troops well trained for manœuvre in jungle and close country, whereas the defenders were a heterogeneous lot, mostly raw and unskilled, thus having little capacity for timely counter-manœuvre, while the course of the campaign had made them acutely susceptible to flank threats. These handicaps, heavy enough in themselves, were much increased by lack of air cover against the constant overhead menace of the Japanese air force. The defenders were soon thrown off their balance, and their attempts to recover it were hampered by confusion in rear. Far from having a secure base, they had at their back a crowded city of mixed population, threatened with the cutting of food and water supplies, and behind this an enemy-dominated sea. The background was made all the more unnerving by the sight of black smoke clouds billowing up from burning oil tanks—an aspect created by 'scorched-earth' orders, from the authorities at home, that showed a very dubious strategic psychology. On the 15th February, a second black Sunday in succession, the defending forces surrendered.

In the main Philippine island of Luzon, the initial landings north of Manila had been quickly followed by a landing in the rear of the capital. Under this dislocating leverage, and the converging threat, the American forces abandoned most of the island and fell back into the small Bataan Peninsula, before the end of December. There, by contrast, they were only open to frontal assault on a narrowly contracted front, and succeeded in holding out until April before they were overwhelmed.

Long before that, and even before the fall of Singapore, the Japanese tide of conquest was spreading through the Malay Archipelago. On the 24th January, different Japanese forces landed in Borneo, Celebes and New Guinea. Three weeks later they launched an attack on Java, the core of the Dutch East Indies, after the island had been isolated by flanking moves. Within a further three weeks, the whole of Java had fallen into their hands like a ripe plum.

But the apparently imminent threat to Australia did not develop. The main Japanese effort was now directed in the opposite direction, westwards, towards the conquest of Burma. The direct but wide-fronted advance from Thailand upon Rangoon was an indirect approach to their major object on the Asiatic mainland as a whole, the paralysis of China's power of resistance. For Rangoon was the port of entry for Anglo-American supplies of equipment to China, by way of the Burma Road. At the same time, this move was shrewdly designed to complete the conquest of the western gateway to the Pacific, and there establish a firm barrier across the main routes by which any overland Anglo-American offensive might subsequently be attempted. On the 8th March, Rangoon fell, and within a further two months the British forces were driven out of Burma, over the mountains, back into India. The Japanese had thus secured a covering position so strong by nature that any attempt at reconquest would be badly handicapped and bound to be a very slow process.

A long time passed before the Allies built up forces sufficient to attempt the recovery of Japan's conquests—beginning at the eastern end. Here they benefited from the preservation of Australia, which provided them with a large-scale base close to the chain of Japanese outposts.

In August 1942, General MacArthur's opening move was made against Guadalcanal—the most southerly, and nearest, of the Solomon Islands. The reconquest of Guadalcanal took six months. The next considerable island of the group, New Georgia, was not tackled until late in June 1943, and its reconquest took over three months.

Meanwhile, the Australian forces had started an offensive from the foothold they had retained in the south-eastern corner of the great island of New Guinea. But operations proceeded slowly and painfully, under conditions of appalling difficulty and in face of the most stubborn opposition. Nearly a year passed before the reconquest of the south-eastern end of New Guinea was completed, with the capture of Lae in September 1943.

It looked as if the long road back to the Philippines, and thence to Japan itself, would be an interminable journey. But in the autumn of 1943 the pace improved with the adoption of a by-passing method that was a variant of the strategy of indirect approach. The seaborne advance successively skipped past a number of islands in the outpost chain, leaving their Japanese garrisons isolated from supplies and in a state of strategic internment.

In October 1944, a greater leap carried the Americans back into the Philippines. It was preceded by heavy air attacks against the ports and airfields of Luzon and Mindanao, the main northern and southern islands of the Philippine group. These strokes naturally tended to make the Japanese anticipate a landing in either of these quarters, while leaving them uncertain which of them might be the objective. Then General MacArthur's seaborne armada appeared off the island of Leyte, midway between the two major islands, and there disembarked its forces. That stroke not only drove a wedge into the midst of the Philippines, but drove a wider strategic wedge between Japan and the larger part of her Pacific conquests, in the Dutch East Indies.

Inevitably, there was another interval before the Americans could build up their strength sufficiently to expand their offensive and complete the conquest of the Philippines. But ultimate success was assured by their combination of the 'log-splitting' method with an enveloping sea-air net that isolated the islands while their conquest was proceeding. Moreover, the Americans had now gained a position close enough to Japan itself for the development of a powerful and sustained air offensive. The next big leap, by-passing Formosa, carried them into the island of Okinawa in the Ryukyu Archipelago, midway between Formosa and Japan.

A notable feature throughout these later operations was the way that each by-passing move utilized the choice of alternative objectives to keep the enemy baffled as to the specific aim, and exploit the weakness inherent in his disposition. Thus the strategic indirectness of each move was multiplied in effect.

The Japanese tide of conquest had spread too far for permanence. It had resulted in Japan's forces becoming dangerously widespread, and thinly spread, so that they were susceptible to isolation in detail as soon as a change in the balance of sea-power and air-power enabled the Americans to profit by this scope for seaborne manœuvre. Aggression recoiled on to the aggressor. The recoil refuted the militaristic belief that 'attack is the best defence'. Instead, the result of too successful attack at the outset was to overstretch Japan's subsequent power of defence beyond the safety limit. The same fatal consequence followed Germany's offensive tide.

The War in the Mediterranean

The earlier campaigns in the Mediterranean centred on Italo-German attempts to gain control of Egypt and the Suez Canal. The course of those campaigns provided a most striking illustration of the effects of strategic overstretching, either longitudinally or laterally. They also brought many lessons in the value of the indirect approach.

Marshal Graziani's advance from Libya upon Egypt opened in September 1940. On any numerical calculation its success was a certainty, so large was the size of the invading army compared with the British force available to defend Egypt. But its mobility was low, and the handicap that limited mechanization imposed on manœuvre—for surprise—was increased by administrative inefficiency. After a seventy-mile advance through the Western Desert, the Italians halted at Sidi Barrani, and there stuck for a couple of months.

The British Commander-in-Chief in the Middle East, General Wavell, decided to try the effect of an upsetting stroke by the Western Desert Force—the embryo of the Eighth Army—under General O'Connor. It was visualized as in the nature of a powerful raid rather than an offensive: not tip-and-run but hit-and-withdraw. There were only two divisions available, the 7th Armoured and the 4th Indian; after this stroke the latter was to be brought back to the Nile and sent down to the Sudan, to help in dealing with the threat of the Italian army in Eritrea and Abyssinia.

The 'raid', however, turned into a decisive victory, thanks to the paralysis and dislocation produced by General O'Connor's surprise move through the desert on to the enemy's rear—an indirect approach both physically and psychologically. This sudden blow was delivered on the 9th December. A large part of Graziani's army was cut off and 35,000 captured, while the remainder only regained the shelter of their own frontier after a panic retreat that reduced them to a disorderly rabble. That fortified frontier was overrun by the 7th Armoured Division in its pursuit, and the surviving Italian forces, which had fallen back into Bardia, were momentarily cut off by its further encircling sweep.

The whole campaign might have ended at this point if the higher command had not insisted on the 4th Indian Division being withdrawn in accordance with the original plan. Deprived of its backing, the 7th Armoured Division was naturally unable to penetrate the Bardia defences, and several weeks elapsed before a fresh infantry division, the 6th Australian, could be brought from Palestine to act as a 'tin-opener'. Then Bardia was captured, on the 3rd January, with 40,000 prisoners. Tobruk fell on the 22nd, with a further 25,000.

The surviving part of Graziani's army retreated past Benghazi towards Tripoli, but was intercepted by an indirect approach in pursuit that proved one of the most brilliant and daring strokes of the war. The 7th Armoured Division made a dash through the desert interior to reach the sea south of Benghazi; on the 5th February. Its leading elements covered 170 miles in thirty-six hours over difficult and unknown country. While one fraction under Colonel Combe established a block across the enemy's line of retreat at Beda Fomm, another fraction—the 4th Armoured Brigade under Brigadier Caunter—pummelled his forces until they surrendered. The two fractions combined amounted to only 3,000 men, yet by their audacity in thrusting across the path of a vastly superior enemy they secured a bag of 21,000 prisoners.

Slender as were the forces which had achieved this astonishing conquest of Cyrenaica there was at that moment little to stop them driving on to Tripoli. Such Italian troops as remained, besides being ill-equipped to meet a tank thrust, were badly shaken by the fate of their main army. O'Connor was eager to exploit

N
GERMANY
POLAND
RUSSIA
Paris
Prague
Cracow
CZECHOSLOVAKIA
Stuttgart
Nantes
Vienna
Munich
AUSTRIA
Budapest
Odessa
Caucasus
Crimea
FRANCE
SWITZLD
HUNGARY
RUMANIA
BAY of BISCAY
Lyons
Trieste
Sevastopol
Bordeaux
Turin
Milan
Venice
YUGOSLAVIA
Bucharest
BLACK SEA
R. PO
Genoa
Belgrade
R. DANUBE
Toulouse
Nice
ARNO
Pesaro
Marseille
Pisa
Florence
Sofia
BULGARIA
Toulon
Adriatic Sea
Istanbul
PORTUGAL
Madrid
Corsica
ITALY
ALBANIA
Barcelona
Rome
Foggia
Macedonia
AnKara
SPAIN
ANZIO
R. VOLTURNO
Bari
BRINDISI
Salonika
Valencia
Naples
OLYMPUS
TURKEY
Sardinia
Salerno
GREECE
Aegean
Taranto
Sea
MEDITERRANEAN SEA
Messina
Palermo
Gibraltar
Bizerta
Athens
Algiers
C. Serrat
SICILY
Catania
Melos
Oran
C. Bon
Syracuse
Rhodes
SYRIA
SP. MOROCCO
Tunis
Thala
Malta
CYPRUS
Beirut
Damascus
Fondouk
Tebessa
Sbeitla
CRETE
Kasserine
Faid Pass
Haifa
Sfax
Gafsa
MOROCCO
El Guettar
GULF of GABES
Jerusalem
El Hamma
Mareth
Derna
El Alamein
Alexandria
Port Said
ALGERIA
Tripoli
Gazala
Tobruk
Bardia
Sidi Barrani
Matruh
Palestine
Homs
TUNISIA
Benghazi
El Mechili
Suez
ENGLISH MILES
0 100 200 300 400
El Agheila
Cairo
German Thrusts in Balkans (1941)
and into Egypt (1942)
CYRENAICA
EGYPT
Allied Thrusts in North Africa (1942-43)
Italy (1943-45), France (1944-45)
LIBYA
R. NILE
Red Sea

his shattering victory at Beda Fomm, and was convinced that he could carry out the fresh bound with little delay for the replenishment of supplies. But a halt was called by the British Government in order to provide the means of despatching the ill-starred expedition to Greece. Wavell was instructed to leave only a minimum to hold Cyrenaica. O'Connor also went back to Egypt, and the control was left in less capable hands. At this juncture also the leading part of the German *Afrika Korps*, under Rommel, arrived in Tripoli. Too late to save the Italians from disaster, this German help came in time to prolong the North African campaign for over two years, during which Britain's position in Egypt was brought into imminent danger.

With a force barely equal to one division in strength, Rommel launched a counter-stroke at the end of March. By swift night moves round his opponents' flank and on to their rear, he disrupted their advanced dispositions, and then by an encircling bluff produced the surrender of their main body at Mekili. The unexpectedness of his advance made the indirectness of his actual approach at successive stages all the more upsetting. Within a fortnight he had swept the British out of the whole of Cyrenaica, save for an isolated portion which withdrew into Tobruk—and there remained as a thorn in his side. By the time he reached the frontier, however, he had overstretched his supply lines and was thus compelled to halt.

In June the British, having received reinforcements, attempted a fresh offensive—archaically called 'Battleaxe'—against the Libyan frontier. Their offensive was largely a frontal push; Rommel dislocated it, and turned the tables, with a well-judged armoured counter-stroke wide round their desert flank.

In November the British mounted a bigger offensive. By this time Wavell had been replaced by General Auchinleck as Commander-in-Chief, while the forces on the Libyan frontier had been constituted as the Eighth Army, under General Cunningham. The offensive opened on the 18th, with a desert flank advance which placed the British close to Rommel's rear. But they forfeited the strategical advantage, gained through this indirect approach, by the too direct tactics of trying to smash the enemy's armour in head-on battles wherever they met it. Thereby they played into Rommel's hands.

In meeting the superior numbers and mobility of the British mechanized forces, the Germans skilfully applied an indirect approach in tactics which lured the British tanks into traps that were lined with their own concealed tanks and deadly 88 mm. guns. Rommel thus strikingly demonstrated, as already in Operation Battleaxe, the defensive-offensive method and baited gambit in modern mechanized warfare—blunting the edge of his opponent's 'sword' on his own 'shield', preparatory to the delivery of his thrust. As a result the British lost not only their strategic advantage but much of their numerical superiority in tanks. The Eighth Army was thrown off its balance, psychologically as well as physically, and on the 23rd Cunningham was inclined to break off the offensive and withdraw over the frontier to reorganize.

Next day Rommel, judging the situation to be ripe for bolder action, launched the mobile part of his forces on a daring swoop round the Eighth Army's desert flank and over the frontier on to its communications. As it burst through into the British rear areas it spread confusion and panic. The effect might have settled the issue of the battle if the decision to persist or retreat had remained with Cunningham. But Auchinleck, who flew up at this crucial moment, insisted on a continuance of the battle, and then on returning to Cairo two days later appointed Ritchie to command in place of Cunningham. Auchinleck's intervention brought victory out of defeat—yet it was basically more of a gamble than Rommel's strategic raid, because it staked the Eighth Army's survival on the maintenance of its far advanced position. It was very fortunate for the British that Rommel in his drive for the frontier had missed seeing, and thus missed the opportunity to capture, two huge supply dumps on which the whole British advance depended for its maintenance. They were preserved from discovery thanks mainly to British control of the air.

While Rommel's deep thrust failed in its aim only by a narrow margin, the penalty of failure was large. For while he and his three armoured divisions (two German and one Italian) were operating over the frontier, far away from the remainder, the split up British forces which he had left behind were able to recover their balance, resume their offensive pressure, and link up with the garrison of Tobruk, before he returned to the relief of his non-mobile formations. That exemplified the risks of the strategic-raid type of operation, by part of an army, where the pivot is not itself strong enough for lengthy resistance. Although he succeeded in regaining the advantage temporarily after several days hard fighting and close-quarter manœuvring, it was a barren success. His losses were much heavier than in the opening phase, and a bigger subtraction from his limited tank strength than he could withstand, particularly in view of the bigger reinforcements available to the British. On the 6th December Rommel was forced to break off the battle around Tobruk and retreat, first to Gazala, and then back to the frontier of Tripolitania.

Here he again resorted to the defensive-offensive method with striking success. When the British launched their attack on the 27th December, he checked their armoured force, outflanking it, forced it to fight on a reversed front, and finally surrounded it. The depletion of the British balance of tank strength in this battle was followed next week by the arrival of a convoy that brought the first considerable reinforcement of his own since mid-November. Thereupon he promptly planned to take advantage of the way that the British had become overstretched in their advance. By a surprise counter-stroke, when they imagined him as still exhausted, he dislocated their front, then exploited their disorder by an indirect thrust from the desert flank against their Benghazi base, and tumbled them back to Gazala—recapturing more than half their gains.

For three months the front was stabilized on the Gazala position, but the Eighth Army's linear dispositions were more suited to be the springboard of a fresh offensive than to provide a well-balanced defence. In May, Rommel moved first, and by a wide flanking manœuvre with his armour, in the night of the 26th, threw the Eighth Army off its balance. He was checked, however, before he could reach the coast and cut off the British forces holding the Gazala Line. Thereupon he took up a defensive position with his back against the British minefields—which led the British to feel that he was cornered, and bound to surrender. But their counter-moves were too direct and they fell into the defensive traps which Rommel had quickly improvised when he was checked. With its reserves entangled and expended, the Eighth Army was unable to meet Rommel's next flanking move, and was beaten piecemeal. While one portion was falling back to the frontier, another portion withdrew into Tobruk. Rommel's armoured forces swept past Tobruk, as if heading for the frontier, then suddenly switched round and struck at Tobruk in reverse, before the forces there had settled down. It was a masterpiece of indirect approach, physically and psychologically. Penetrating the defences at a weak point, the Germans overran the garrison and captured almost the whole of it—together with such an abundance of supplies and transport as to provide the means for a prolonged advance on their own part.

Rommel then chased the remains of the Eighth Army helter-skelter through the Western Desert, and came dangerously close to reaching the Nile Valley, the main artery of Egypt. If that had been secured, and with it the Suez Canal, Britain's whole position in the Middle East would have been wrecked. At this crisis Auchinleck intervened by taking over personal charge of the battered Eighth Army, and rallied it for a stand on the El Alamein position, in the desert bottle-neck which led to the Nile. Rommel's forces, weak in numbers and tired by their long pursuit, were checked by the unexpectedly tough resistance they met—a defence designed on fresh lines. When Rommel sought to break through by thrusts at different points Auchinleck replied with indirect ripostes which, though failing to overthrow him, shook him sufficiently to spoil his aim.

Soon, reinforcements arrived from England. Mr. Churchill wanted the British to take the offensive without delay, but Auchinleck, more wisely, insisted on waiting until the fresh troops had become tactically acclimatized to desert conditions. In the sequel, Auchinleck was replaced by Alexander as Commander-in-Chief, Middle East, and Montgomery took over command of the Eighth Army.

Rommel, however, struck first—at the end of August—but was again foiled by the new defensive tactics of the British. His armoured forces were encouraged to push through the minefields covering the southern half of the British front—a sector that was otherwise undefended, while the bulk of the British infantry were posted in strong positions in the northern sector. Then he was drawn to attack the main body of British armour on its own chosen ground in rear. He lost many tanks in these abortive assaults. While he was immobilized between this rear-flank position and the minefields, another armoured division, the 7th, enveloped his southern flank. The net was not drawn tight in time to prevent his withdrawal, but the initiative had changed sides.

The change became definite with the growth of Montgomery's forces and resources. After a long pause for thorough preparation —a longer pause than Auchinleck had contemplated—the Eighth Army launched its offensive in the last week of October. It was now backed by a tremendous superiority in air-power, gun-power and tank-power. Even then, the struggle was tough for a whole week, as the confined front allowed no scope for wide manœuvre to exert a leverage. But Rommel's forces, besides being badly overstrained, were vitally crippled by the submarine sinkings of most of their oil tankers, in crossing the Mediterranean. Their consequent immobility decided the issue, and once they began to collapse at their extreme forward point they were not capable of making another serious stand until they had coiled up their supply lines.

At the opening of the battle, Rommel had been away sick in Vienna, but flew back at once. Weighing up the situation, he planned to withdraw his army to the Fuka, a position sixty miles west of El Alamein. That step would have thrown Montgomery's battle-machine out of gear. But Rommel's intention was overruled by Hitler's insistence that no ground must be yielded. So retreat was deferred until after defeat. Then Rommel executed it with his usual celerity and ruthless calculation—abandoning his less mobile and less expert troops, including the bulk of the Italians, in order to bring away his picked troops in the motor transport available.

The chance of cutting him off was lost because the pursuit was not sufficiently indirect or extensive in its circling sweep. In the first place, it turned in too soon to catch the bulk of the forces retreating along the coast road. Then a longer-range turn-in at 'Charing Cross', near Mersa Matruh (120 miles west of El Alamein), failed to cut them off through running short of petrol after being impeded by heavy rain. A wider move through the desert, farther inland, would have avoided the rainy belt. But the main factor in the forfeited opportunity was that most of the transport in the three armoured divisions had been devoted to ammunition for the battle, at the expense of having adequate petrol supplies immediately available on wheels, ready for the pursuit.

Once Rommel had slipped through the jaws of his armoured pursuers, he did not pause until he had reached his favourite backstop position near El Agheila at the far end of Cyrenaica—700 miles back from El Alamein. In a fortnight's swift retreat he had outstripped the pursuit, and left few prisoners or supplies behind. There might have been a chance of disrupting his forces by air attack as they retreated round the Benghazi bend, but this could only have been done by using forward airfields before they were protected by the British army's advance, and although the air commanders were willing to take the risk, the army command was not. The staggering counter-strokes that Rommel had formerly staged had left a deep impression. But this time the odds against him were too heavy to permit any such riposte, or even a long-sustained stand at El Agheila.

A pause of three weeks occurred before the Eighth Army could bring up its strength and mount an offensive against the El Agheila position. Just as the offensive developed, Rommel began to slip off, and although a flanking manœuvre succeeded in cutting off his rearguard, this managed to break through and get away before the 'strategic barrage' was properly cemented. Rommel halted again on the Buerat position, a further 200 miles back. He stayed there three weeks, but when the Eighth Army closed up and launched its next offensive, in the middle of January, he fell back again. This time he made an almost continuous withdrawal for 350 miles, past Tripoli, to the Mareth Line inside the frontier of Tunisia. His decision was the consequence not merely of his weakness of force and the sinking of the majority of his supply-ships, but of the new situation produced by the Anglo-American invasion of Morocco and Algeria in November.

That move had closely followed the El Alamein offensive, some 2,500 miles distant at the other end of North Africa. It was a long-range indirect approach to Rommel's hold on Libya and his threatening position near the Nile Delta. In its own strategic sphere, its success was proportionate to its indirectness. As originally conceived, the Allied landings were to have taken place only on the Atlantic coast of Morocco. This would have meant a purely frontal advance, giving the French forces the fullest chance of effective resistance. The advance would have started 1,200 miles distant from Bizerta, the key to the whole North African theatre of war, so that the Germans would have had time and opportunity to stiffen the French resistance to the Allied invasion. Fortunately for the Allied prospects, landings on the Mediterranean coast, near Oran and Algiers, were added to the plan. American diplomacy smoothed the path of these landings by securing the acquiescence or quiescence of numerous Frenchmen in authority. Once lodgements were achieved at these points they created a decisive leverage on the backs of the French forces on the west coast, where the initial resistance threatened to be more stubborn.

The landings near Algiers reduced the distance from Bizerta to barely 400 miles. At that moment, a mere handful of motorized troops could have run through to Bizerta and Tunis without hindrance except from the mountain roads. Alternatively, either seaborne or airborne landings nearby would have met scarcely any opposition. But the naval authorities were chary of attempting even small-scale landings so far ahead of air cover, and the overland advance was too cautious. Meantime, the Germans' reaction was swift, though the landings had taken them by surprise. From the third day onwards they began to rush troops to Tunis in all available troop-carrying aircraft as well as in small coasting vessels. Although the total was still small, it was just sufficient to check the leading troops of the Allied First Army when these reached the immediate approaches to Tunis two and a half weeks after the initial landings.

The result of this check was a five months' deadlock in the mountainous arc covering Bizerta and Tunis. Nevertheless, this failure worked out to the Allies' advantage in the long run. For it encouraged the enemy to continue pouring reinforcements across the sea to Tunisia, where the Allies could cut off their supplies through developing the stranglehold of superior sea-power, and then cut off their retreat. Ironically, Hitler was led to stake larger forces on the retention of Tunisia than he had ever devoted to the capture of Egypt. By drawing so many of the German and Italian reserves across the Mediterranean and putting them 'in the bag' there, the way was eased for the Allies' subsequent invasion of Europe. North Africa thus became as fatal a strategic bait to Hitler as Spain had been to Napoleon, in conjunction with their respective invasions of Russia. Hitler became so stretched between Africa and Russia that these two original points of aim turned into the two horns of a dilemma, and the strain precipitated his collapse in a way similar to Napoleon's.

The 1943 campaign in Tunisia had opened, however, with a German counter-stroke that gave the Allies a bad shock. It came just when their two armies—the First from the west, and the Eighth from the east—seemed about to crunch the Axis forces between their jaws. The Axis command aimed to forestall that danger by dislocating both jaws, and for such an aim the conditions had become more favourable than was apparent on the surface of the situation. By now the reinforcements sent to Tunis had been built up into an army, under General von Arnim, while at the same time the remnant of Rommel's army was acquiring fresh strength, and equipment, as it came nearer to the supply ports in its westward retreat. Profiting by this temporarily favourable turn in the situation, Rommel's design was to exploit the 'interior lines' in Napoleonic style—utilizing his central position between the two converging Allied armies to strike, and cripple, them separately and successively. If he could crumple up the Anglo-American First Army that threatened him from behind he would have both hands free to tackle the British Eighth Army, which had become thinned out as its lines of supply had stretched out.

The design had brilliant promise, but its execution suffered a heavy handicap in being largely dependent on forces which were not under Rommel's control. For when the operation was launched Arnim's army was independent, and even the veteran 21st Panzer Division, which was to deliver the main thrust, had passed to Arnim's command when it had been sent back to help in holding open Rommel's line of retreat and supply.

The American 2nd Corps (which included a French division) was the immediate target of the counter-stroke. Its front covered 90 miles, but was focused on the three routes through the mountains to the sea, with spearheads at the passes near Gafsa, Faid and Fondouk. These passage-ways were so narrow that the occupiers felt secure.

But at the end of January, the 21st Panzer Division made a sudden spring at the Faid Pass, overwhelmed the French garrison before American support arrived, and thus gained a sally-port. This coup led the Allied commanders to expect a further and bigger attack, but they expected that it would come elsewhere. Regarding the Faid stroke as a diversion, they believed that the next stroke would come at Fondouk. As General Bradley remarked in his memoirs: 'This belief came to be a near-fatal assumption.'

On the 14th February the real blow came, starting with a fresh spring forward from the Faid Pass. Arnim's deputy, Ziegler, was in charge here. Opening out as the American armour came forward to meet it, the 21st Panzer Division pinned the Americans in front, turned their left flank, and drove round their right flank to catch them in the rear. More than a hundred of their tanks were destroyed in this trap. Rommel urged Ziegler to drive on during the night and exploit the success to the full, but Ziegler waited for forty-eight hours until he received Arnim's authorization before pushing on twenty-five miles to Sbeitla, where the Americans had rallied. Even then he was able to throw them back again, although the fight was harder and they rallied again at the Kasserine Pass. Meantime Rommel had brought a panzer detachment from the Mareth Line to deliver a more southerly thrust, through Gafsa; this had driven on fifty miles by the 17th and captured the American airfields at Thelepte, well to the west of Kasserine.

Alexander, who had just been placed in charge of both the Allied armies, and now arrived on the scene, said in his despatch: 'I found the position even more critical than I had expected, and a visit to the Kasserine area showed that in the confusion of the retreat American, French and British troops had been inextricably mingled, there was no co-ordinated plan of defence and definite uncertainty as to command.' Alexander went on to say that if Rommel 'could break through our weak screening position on the Western Dorsale'—the next mountain range—'he would find few natural obstacles to an advance northwards. . . . This would disrupt our front in Tunisia and bring on a withdrawal if not a disaster.'

On the other side, Rommel wanted to exploit the confusion and panic by a combined drive with all available mechanized forces through Tebessa (forty miles beyond the Western Dorsale) towards the Allies' main communications with their Algerian bases. Air reconnaissances had reported that Allied supply depots at Tebessa were already burning. But he found that Arnim was unwilling to embark on such a venture, so in desperation he appealed to Mussolini. The hours slipped by, and it was not until early on the 19th that a signal came from Rome authorizing a continuation of the thrust, and Rommel to conduct it—but ordering that it should be made due *northward* to Thala, instead of *north-westward* to Tebessa as Rommel had proposed. In Rommel's view that change was 'an appalling and incredible piece of shortsightedness', since it meant that the thrust was 'far too close to the front and bound to bring us up against strong enemy reserves'.

The outcome amply justified Rommel. For the thrust came along the line which Alexander had expected, and where he was best prepared to meet it. He had ordered the army commander to 'concentrate his armour for the defence of Thala', and British reserves from the north were being rushed down to that sector. It is thus evident that the Allies would again have been caught off balance if Rommel had been allowed to drive the way he wished.

The Americans, too, had collected in strength on the line of approach to Thala, and held on so stubbornly to the Kasserine

Pass that the Germans did not break through it until the evening of the 20th. Next day they drove into Thala, exhausted, and were pushed out by the British reserves that had now arrived there. So on the 22nd Rommel, realizing that his chance had passed, broke off the attack and began a gradual withdrawal. One day later, but much too late, a fresh order came from Rome placing all the Axis forces in Africa under Rommel's command.

This counter-offensive is, in analysis, a very significant lesson in the study of the indirect approach, since it brings out so clearly how loss of time can forfeit its advantages, and also the importance, if it is physically indirect, of moving wide enough to ensure unexpectedness.

A further penalty of the belated combination of the Axis armies under Rommel was that it came too late for him to cancel an attack that Arnim had mounted in the north against the Allied positions facing Tunis. This too direct approach not only proved an expensive failure itself but caused delay in releasing the divisions needed for Rommel's intended second stroke—against Montgomery.

The delay made a vital difference to its prospects. Until the 26th February Montgomery had got only one division forward facing the Mareth Line. For once he was worried, and his staff worked feverishly to redress the balance before the blow came. By the 6th March, when Rommel struck, Montgomery had quadrupled his strength—besides 400 tanks he had now over 500 anti-tank guns in position. Thus in the interval Rommel's chance of striking with superior force had vanished. The attack was brought to a standstill by the afternoon and the Germans' loss of fifty tanks was a serious handicap in the next phase of the campaign. By then they had also lost Rommel, who had gone back to Europe, sick and frustrated.

On the 17th March the Allied offensive opened with an attack by the American 2nd Corps, now under General Patton. This was aimed at the *Afrika Korps*' line of retreat to Tunis, and was intended to draw off resources from its front. But the advance was first cautiously slow and was then definitely checked in the mountain passes that covered the approach to the coastal strip. This defensive success encouraged the Germans to try another offensive stroke, which failed to pierce the American defence. The loss of some forty tanks not only blunted the edge of the attack but accentuated the Germans' handicap in armoured force, weakening their capacity to resist Montgomery's advance.

For their ultimate victory, the Allies owed more to the enemy's misjudged offensive efforts than to the effect of their own assaults. The Allies' chance to turn the tables only came after the Germans had overstretched themselves in the offensive. Later, the Germans might have protracted the issue, but for the way they used up their remaining strength in abortive retorts.

The Eighth Army's attack on the Mareth Line was launched on the night of the 20th March. The main blow was a frontal one, intended to break through the defence near the sea and make a gap through which the armoured divisions could sweep. At the same time, the New Zealand corps made a wide outflanking march towards El Hamma in the enemy's rear, with the aim of pinning down the enemy's reserves that were placed there. The frontal attack failed to make an adequate breach. So, after three days' effort, Montgomery changed his plan, side-stepping inland and sending the 1st Armoured Division to follow up the New Zealanders' threat to the enemy's rear. The sudden switch of his 'cavalry' from right to left reproduced, on a wider scale, Marlborough's manœuvre at Ramillies, an historic masterpiece of tactical flexibility. But the armoured charge ran through a valley lined with anti-tank guns on either flank, which might have proved a deadly trap if a dust-storm had not been blowing at the time. Even then, the British attacks were checked by the German back-stop defences at El Hamma. Thus although the threatened cut-off led the enemy to abandon the Mareth Line, he was able to hold the gate open and draw off his forces without much loss.

He stopped again barely ten miles behind El Hamma, along the Wadi Akarit which spanned the Gabes Gap—a very narrow-fronted position between the sea and the hills. The Americans, swinging south past El Guettar, had already tried to forestall the enemy on this position and to fall on his back while he was gripped by the Eighth Army, but they had again been checked before they could debouch from the hills. Then, in the early hours of the 6th April, the Eighth Army attacked the Wadi Akarit under cover of pitch darkness. That tactical innovation resulted in a penetration, though the exploitation was checked by the Germans when daylight came. But two of their three attenuated panzer divisions were now absorbed in holding off the American push, which left them without sufficient resources to maintain their resistance. So on the next night they broke away and retired rapidly up the coast towards Tunis.

A fresh attempt was made to cut off this retreat by the 9th Corps' effort to break through the Fondouk Pass on the 8th April and reach the sea in their rear. After the infantry attack had failed to open a clear passage for the tanks, the latter succeeded next day in a daring charge across a minefield, at heavy cost, but the break-through came just too late to intercept the enemy forces retreating up the coast. Within a few days the enemy's two armies had joined hands, to offer a united defence along the mountain arc covering Tunis, and it looked as though they might there maintain a prolonged resistance. Alternatively, they might utilize the breathing space, gained by the swift withdrawal, to evacuate their forces to Sicily.

The 2,000-mile retreat of Rommel's *Panzer Armee Afrika* from El Alamein to Tunis was one of the outstanding performances of its kind in military history, especially in the course of its first and last stages. From the Mareth Line back to Tunis it had to be carried out through a long corridor lined by hostile forces, and was thus exposed to a continuously imminent threat of fatal interruption. While there has been no parallel for this Xenophon-like feat in recent ages, the same winter witnessed a retreat comparable in danger, though not in pure length, and carried out under even worse conditions—the withdrawal of Kleist's army group from the depths of the Caucasus back through the Rostov bottle-neck, under continuous flanking menace from the Russian armies that were pressing down from the Don.

Such a 'double' provided impressive proof of the great resisting power inherent in modern defence, when skilfully handled. Moreover, this evidence of the limitations of the rear attack freshly emphasized the lesson of past experience that something more than a geographical indirectness of approach is required for offensive success. In each of these cases, an important part of the attacker's forces overhung the rear of the retreating forces from the outset, yet it could not close the trap. The line of danger was always obvious enough to enable the defending side to make effective use of its defensive assets and provide an adequate insurance. There must be a psychological indirectness of approach to upset the opponent's balance and create the conditions for a decisive issue.

The rapidity of the retreat from the Wadi Akarit, and its success in evading the Allied attempts at interruption, gave the German Supreme Command a chance to evacuate its forces to Sicily, if it had chosen that course. At least a fortnight's pause was inevitable before the Allies' armies could mount a serious offensive against the enemy's new defensive arc from Enfidaville, south of Tunis, to Cape Serrat, west of Bizerta. During that time there was a spell of misty weather which would have helped to screen the process of embarkation and transportation, so that a large proportion of the forces in Tunisia might have succeeded in getting away by sea and air.

The German Supreme Command, however, was led to attempt a prolongation of the campaign in Africa, rather than draw in its horns and base its defence of Europe upon the southern shores of Europe. Even in Tunisia it tried to hold too extensive a front for its resources—a 100-mile perimeter—in the endeavour to preserve both Tunis and Bizerta. Stretched between those two 'horns of a dilemma', it provided the Allies with an ideal opportunity to exploit the advantage of having alternative objectives.

Before playing his hand, Alexander reshuffled his cards. He brought the American 2nd Corps up from the south to the northern coast—from the right wing to the left wing, facing Bizerta. He also switched the 9th Corps northward and inserted it in the centre between the 5th Corps and the French 19th Corps, which now adjoined the Eighth Army on the Allied right wing.

On the 20th April the offensive was opened by the Eighth Army with an attack on the enemy's left flank. But the coastal corridor became very narrow beyond Enfidaville, and the advance soon slowed down, coming to a halt on the 23rd. On the 21st April the 5th Corps attacked from the left centre, through the hills leading to Tunis. Next day the 9th Corps struck from the right centre near Goubellat, with the aim of achieving an armoured break-through. But the effort failed to pierce the enemy's defences, though it strained them severely and further weakened the enemy's remaining tank strength. A pause of nearly a fortnight followed on most of the front, but in the north the Americans and a corps of French African troops continued to make a gradual penetration, which brought them within twenty miles of Bizerta.

Meantime Alexander again reshuffled his hand. Leaving only a screening force in the right centre near Goubellat, he moved the bulk of the 9th Corps over to the left centre, concentrated it behind the 5th Corps, and reinforced it with two picked divisions from the Eighth Army—the 7th Armoured and 4th Indian. At the same time an elaborate deception-plan was carried out to conceal the switching moves and persuade the enemy command that the next attack was coming in the south. The effect of the deception-plan was reinforced by the reputation of the Eighth Army, and of Montgomery, so that General von Arnim kept a disproportionate part of his strength in the south. But Arnim had little chance of perceiving the deception, or of readjusting his dispositions after the blow fell, because of the Allies' command of the air. They used this tremendous air superiority to drive the enemy's remaining aircraft out of the sky, and then to paralyse all movement of troops and supplies on the roads.

The highly concentrated assault of the 9th Corps, now under General Horrocks, was launched in the starlight but moonless early hours of the 6th May. It was preceded and covered by an intense artillery bombardment from over 600 guns, upon a sector less than two miles wide, in the Medjerda Valley leading to Tunis. After daylight, the air force extended the blast with a terrific storm of bombs. The stunned defenders of the gateway were soon overrun by the infantry of the 4th Indian and 4th British Divisions. The overstretched defence was not only thin but had little depth. Then the concentrated tanks of the 6th and 7th Armoured Divisions drove through the breach. But they lost time in dealing with various small pockets of German resistance. By nightfall they had only advanced a few miles beyond the breach and were still some fifteen miles from Tunis.

Next morning, however, it became clear that the opposing army as a whole was still paralysed by the combined air shock and strategic shock to such an extent that it could not develop any tactical counter-measures. By the afternoon the leading troops of the British armoured divisions had swept into Tunis. The 6th then turned south, while the 7th turned north, to spread dislocation. Almost simultaneously, the Americans and French poured into Bizerta. Enemy resistance dramatically collapsed on the northern half of the front.

In the south, the enemy might still have been able to withdraw into the Cape Bon Peninsula and there make a prolonged stand. But this possibility was frustrated by the rapidity with which the 6th Armoured Division drove down in the enemy's rear and cut across the neck of the peninsula. The collapse became general, and over quarter of a million prisoners were taken.

The enemy command had been caught off its balance, and then its machine was thrown out of gear by the combination of air pressure overhead and tank impact on its back. Dislocation of control was the primary cause of collapse, while the breakdown of communications accentuated the demoralizing effect of lack of reserves and disruption of supplies.

Another factor was the closeness of the enemy's bases to the broken front. The rapid penetration into the bases was as dislocating to morale as it was to the administrative system. It not only created immediate panic among the base personnel—always more susceptible to demoralization than the fighting troops—but naturally produced an outspreading wave. The loss of their bases deepened the depressing sensation of fighting with their backs to the sea—a sea now dominated by the Allies' sea-power and air-power.

It is remarkable how closely Alexander's plan of operations coincided with the classic pattern of the Napoleonic battle, just as the Battle of the Marne did in 1914—though without intention. The characteristics of that pattern were that after the enemy had been pinned and pressed in front, a manœuvre was directed against one of his flanks. This manœuvre was not decisive in itself but created the opportunity for a decisive stroke. For the threat of envelopment caused a stretching of the enemy's front in the attempt to meet it, and so produced a weak joint, on which the decisive stroke then fell.

Although handicapped by the want of an open flank, Alexander achieved victory by giving the pattern a greater internal development, combining flexibility and subtlety. As we have seen, he first drew the enemy's attention and resources to their left flank; then pressed hard on their right and right centre; following these attacks with his main punch at their left centre. When they managed to check his attempted break-through here, he turned this frustration to ultimate advantage by a pretence of swinging his weight farther to their left, while actually swinging it to the right of their centre—where his earlier push had given them reason to assume that they were adequately strong. The multiple process of *distraction* gave his final concentration the most concentrated possible effect, while exploiting the choice of alternative objectives that the situation offered.

It has seemed worth while to discuss the later phases of the

African campaign in more detail than others because they bring out so many points on both the logistical and psychological side of strategy. In particular, they furnish an object-lesson in the subtlety and variety of the indirect approach.

CHAPTER XVIII

HITLER'S FALL

★

After the disaster at Stalingrad and the retreat from the Caucasus, no real hope remained for the Germans of achieving decisive victory over Russia. The experience of 1941 and 1942 had shown the limitations of pursuing an offensive strategy with limited strength in unlimited space. Now, in 1943, the Germans' strength was scantier while the Russians' was increasing. But while the adverse ratio of force made an offensive strategy hopeless for the Germans, the ratio of force to lateral space was bound to make static defence very precarious. If the Germans were to change over to the defensive in such circumstances it would call for an extensive sacrifice of the territory they had gained in order to practise elastic defence—by a series of withdrawing manœuvres—with the aim of drawing the sting out of the enemy's attack. The same necessity of yielding ground would apply with a defensive-offensive strategy that aimed to create opportunity for riposte.

Even in 1943 there was good reason to reckon on a favourable prospect from a change-over to defence in a mobile form. Experience had shown that, on the defensive, the Germans could count on inflicting losses on the attacking Russians out of all proportion to their own casualties. While the Russian commanders had become skilful in manœuvre, and the wider spaces gave them opportunity, other circumstances tended to draw them into expensive efforts. Because of the Russians' instinctive urge to expel the invaders, and the Russian commanders' natural desire to prove their determination in Stalin's eyes, it was not difficult to lead them into direct assaults, and into repeating them. The consensus of opinion among German strategists was that, by carrying out a well-designed plan of elastic defence, they could wear down Russia's strength and her will to continue the war. It might even be possible to gain opportunity for a counter-stroke that would radically change the situation.

But Hitler was too offensive-minded to pay due heed to those counsels. He fervently believed that attack was the best form of defence, and that rigid resistance was the next best. Under this obsession he even rejected every plea for developing the scale of fighter aircraft for Germany's defence to meet the multiplying Allied bombing offensive, and did not alter this decision until as late as June 1944. In the same way, when his advisers dwelt on the shortage of German reserves, and pointed out the dangers of holding onto the awkward line where the winter campaign in Russia had ended, Hitler answered their arguments for a withdrawal to the line of the Dnieper by insisting that the problem could, and would, be solved by taking the offensive again in the summer of 1943. It was a new version of the cock crowing three times.

Here it is worth note that, in March, after Manstein's very indirect Kharkov counter-stroke had broken the Russians' post-Stalingrad advance, he proposed to Hitler a plan to repeat it in a more calculated way with a baited gambit. The Mius River sector, between the Donetz and the Sea of Azov, was now a very deep salient, jutting out from the German front. It was thus highly probable that the Russians' spring offensive would take it as a target. Manstein therefore suggested that the defending force there should be thinned out, and should fall back when the Russians attacked, drawing them on prior to a counter-stroke, with all possible strength, that should be delivered from the Kiev region against their northern flank with the aim of rolling up the Russians' whole front in the south and trapping their forces.

But this was too bold a plan for Hitler's stomach, while he was unwilling to give up the Donetz Basin with its industrial and mineral resources. So the alternative plan was adopted of trying to distract and dislocate the Russians, before they launched their expected spring offensive, by pinching off their large salient around Kursk which jutted into the German front between Bielgorod and Orel. The 4th Panzer Army of Manstein's Army Group 'South' (formerly 'Don') was to form the right pincer-arm while the 9th Army of Kluge's Army Group 'Centre' formed the left pincer-arm. Manstein insisted that if such a plan was adopted the stroke must be delivered early in May immediately the spring mud dried, and before the Russians could regroup their forces. But Model, the commander of the 9th Army, urged that the offensive should be delayed until larger tank reinforcements had arrived, and Hitler accepted his argument, postponing the offensive until June, and then until the 5th July. It was a very significant example of how *time* and *force* are apt to be conflicting factors, and the outcome was a lesson in the way that increased force may really prove less weighty than early timing that carries a greater measure of surprise.

As time passed, Hitler himself became dubious about the prospects, but could not bring himself to swallow the necessity of a strategic retreat as an alternative, and so yielded half-heartedly to the pro-offensive arguments of Zeitzler, Halder's successor—who was filled with the idea that it was essential to take the lead in attacking in order to forestall the Russians' attack.

This time the Russian command, with shrewder judgement, withheld their own offensive until the Germans had moved—thus giving a wider extension to the baited method which had so often proved profitable in the tactical field. Detecting the German preparations, and diagnosing the intention, the Russians filled the threatened salient with a deep layer of minefields and withdrew the bulk of their forces in rear of it. In consequence the German offensive not only failed to put the Russians 'in the bag' but itself became bogged. The right pincer-arm made moderate progress, penetrating the first two enemy positions and breaking up a large part of the enemy's armour on that sector, but the left pincer-arm, Model's, was checked at the outset. The frustrated effort had taken the Germans out of their defences and left them in a much more awkward position than before, highly susceptible to the powerful riposte which the Russians then delivered. This dislocated the Germans' front, north of Orel, and momentarily produced a crisis. Manstein was ordered to call off his own attack and send several of his panzer divisions to Kluge's aid. As a result the Russians then broke through a weak part of his own front. The whole sequence of operations bore a remarkable likeness to Pétain's elastic defence and counter-stroke in the Second Battle of the Marne which gave the decisive turn to the First World War.

Although the Germans rallied in time to put a check on the follow-through—just as they had done beyond the Marne in 1918—the Russians offset this rally by widening their leverage. The pattern and rhythm of their operations increasingly came to resemble those of the Allies' 1918 counter-offensive in the West—an alternating series of strokes at different points, each temporarily suspended when its impetus waned in face of stiffening resistance, each so aimed as to pave the way for the next, and all close enough in time and space to have a mutual reaction. It led the German command, as in 1918, to scurry their scanty reserves to the points that were struck, while simultaneously restricting their power to move reserves in time to the points that were threatened and about to be struck. The effect was to paralyse their freedom of action, while progressively decreasing their balance of reserves. It was a strategic form of 'creeping paralysis'.

This is the natural method for an army that possesses a general superiority of force—as the Allied armies in the West had in 1918, and the Red Army had in 1943. It is all the more suitable when and where the lateral communications are not ample enough to provide the attacker with the power of switching reserves to follow up a particular success, very quickly from one sector to another. Since it means breaking into a fresh front each time, the cost of the 'broad' method is apt to be higher than with the 'deep' method, and its effect less quickly decisive. But the effect is cumulative, provided that the side which operates it has an adequate balance of strength to maintain the process.

In the autumn of 1943 the Russian advance came to bear an increasing likeness to an incoming tide—along a 1,000-mile 'beach'. In September it reached the Dnieper at various points along a wide stretch of the river between the great bend and Kiev. The Germans evacuated the bridgehead they had retained in the Kuban, the western end of the Caucasus, and brought that part of their forces back, through the Crimea, in a belated attempt to strengthen the southern sector of their main front, between the Dnieper bend and the sea. But the Russians broke into this front before the reinforcements arrived, and in the resulting confusion reached the lower end of the Dnieper and isolated the Crimea. In October, also, the Russians succeeded in crossing the Dnieper, just north of the bend, and drove a massive wedge into this salient position. The Germans managed to avert the breakdown which the Allied reports prematurely announced, but their position as a whole was seriously weakened.

Hitler's reason for clinging on to the southern part of the Dnieper salient was to preserve the Nikopol area, an important source of manganese ore for Germany's armament industry. Economic necessity was here in conflict with strategy, developing a dangerous tug of war. The Germans paid a heavy price for Hitler's efforts to retain the manganese ore. For when any defence suffers such a persistent strain and stretch as theirs was now undergoing, there is always an increasing risk that some local effort may result in a widespread crack.

Each time the Germans were tied to the defence of a fixed point by Hitler's orders, an eventual collapse was the costly penalty. The weaker the defending side, the more essential it becomes to adopt mobile defence. For otherwise the stronger side can make space its ally and gain a decisive advantage through outflanking manœuvre.

Early in October the Russians had gained two other bridgeheads across the Dnieper, one north and one south of Kiev. The former was gradually extended until it provided a wide jumping-off position for an attack that was launched a month later. This produced the capture of Kiev and a rapid exploitation westwards. In barely a week, General Vatutin's advance reached the junctions of Zhitomir and Korosten, some eighty miles beyond the Dnieper.

Manstein, however, managed to retrieve the dangerous situation, although he had no reserves left. His rapid retreat, by luring on the Russians, created the opportunity for a flank counter-stroke and for its execution Manteuffel, one of the most dynamic younger generals, scraped up such armoured fragments as could be found. Slight in strength as was the stroke, it gained weight in effect from the Russians' overstretch and its own indirectness, so that it tumbled the Russians out of both the pivotal points they had reached.

Manstein then tried to develop the opportunity by organizing a larger counter-offensive when reinforcements arrived from the west. But the time-factor impaired its prospects, for by then Vatutin's forces had recovered their balance. Although Manstein's menacing flank pressure made them fall back and abandon more of the ground they had gained west of the Dnieper, this counter-offensive was never so dangerous as it appeared on the surface, and early in December it faded out in the mud. Moreover, by using up such reinforcements as Manstein had received, it left him without the means to meet the Russians' next moves, since Hitler again rejected his arguments for making a long step-back.

On Christmas Eve, Vatutin broke out again from his compressed, but still large, Kiev salient. Delivering his new stroke under the cloak of an early morning fog, Vatutin recaptured Zhitomir and Korosten within a week, and on the 4th January crossed the pre-war Polish frontier. A left-handed thrust reached the line of the Bug near Vinnitsa, thus threatening the main lateral railway from

Odessa to Warsaw. Here Manstein staged another counter-stroke, but Vatutin had sufficient strength to parry it. Moreover, the Russians then profited by Hitler's insistence on clinging to the Dnieper line below Kiev. Vatutin, in combination with Koniev from the other flank, now cut off this Korsun salient by a pincer-stroke, and surrounded ten enemy divisions—although part of them managed to break-out despite Hitler's order to stand fast.

This coup created a gap in the German front, thus easing the way for fresh Russian progress. The other Russian armies in the Ukraine now took up the rhythm of alternating strokes and levering advances. On the northern flank the Germans were now forced to abandon Luck and Rovno, and on the southern flank the Nikopol salient—along with its supplies of manganese ore.

On the 4th March, a new combined movement was opened by Marshal Zhukov, who had taken over command of Vatutin's armies when the latter fell ill. Striking from Shepetovka, Zhukov penetrated thirty miles in the first twenty-four hours, and got astride the Odessa–Warsaw railway two days later. This move outflanked the defensive line of the Bug. Near the Black Sea, Malinovsky drove forward and reached Nikolayev. Between these two horns, Koniev struck from Uman, reached the Bug on the 12th March, the Dniester on the 18th—and was over it next day. The rapidity with which these broad rivers were crossed was a new feature in the history of the war. Zhukov then thrust forward again, from the Tarnopol area, into the foothills of the Carpathian Mountains.

In immediate reaction to this threat, the Germans occupied Hungary. It was obvious that this step was taken in order to secure the mountain-line of the Carpathians. They needed to maintain this barrier, not only to check a Russian irruption into the central European plains, but as the pivot of any continued defence of the Balkans.

The Carpathians, prolonged southward by the Transylvanian Alps, constituted a line of defence of great natural strength. Its apparent length was diminished, in a strategical measurement, by the small number of the passes across it—thus facilitating economy of force. Between the Black Sea and the corner of the mountains near Focsani there was a flat stretch of 120 miles, but the eastern half of this was filled by the Danube Delta and a chain of lakes, so that the 'danger area' was reduced to the sixty-mile Galatz Gap.

Early in April it looked as if the Germans would soon fall back on this rearward line. Koniev's forces pushed across the Pruth into Rumania, while farther south the Germans were squeezed out of Odessa. The Crimea was also recaptured by two converging sweeps, and the enemy forces which had been left there were overrun. But the Germans managed to check the Russian drive beyond the Pruth and prevent it penetrating deeper into Rumania, thus preserving its oilfield supplies for the moment. That success became their undoing five months later. For it induced Hitler to maintain his forces in an exposed position, well to the east of the mountains and the Galatz Gap.

Farther north, the Germans also succeeded in stemming Zhukov's effort to rush the Carpathian passes, south-west of Tarnopol, though their counter-stroke was soon held.

Still farther north, near the Baltic, a Russian offensive in the middle of January, had freed Leningrad from the enemy's encircling grip, and was then exploited westward. But the Germans achieved an orderly withdrawal to a shorter and straighter line running from Narva past Pskov. It was only 120 miles long, and ninety of these were filled by two great lakes. Between Pskov and the Pripet Marshes, the enemy's front still hinged on the bastion-towns of Vitebsk and Orsha. The Russians had closed in upon them at the end of September, but the enemy's position here had withstood both direct assaults and outflanking moves. It continued to form an effective block for a further nine months—until July 1944.

Thus, in sum, the Russian front was temporarily stabilized by the end of April. The Red Army had made big gains of ground, especially in the south, but the Germans had usually managed to slip out of the traps produced by the Russian pincer manœuvre, and to stave off the disaster that so often appeared to be imminent. The total bag of prisoners was not large in comparison with the extent of the Russian advances, but the German forces had suffered a cumulative attrition that carried delayed effects of a more serious nature. Yet Hitler showed his decreasing sense of reality by removing Manstein from command, with the remark that yard by yard resistance was now more needed than skilful manœuvre.

The strain had been increased for nine months past by the Anglo-American invasion of Europe from the south. In that quarter the conquest of Sicily had been followed by the capitulation of Italy early in September 1942. The collapse of Germany's partner had created a hole in the southern wall of her 'Fortress of Europe' which, though restricted by the peninsular shape of Italy, was big enough to cause a serious diversion of her strength in filling the hole. Beyond this, she had also to increase her insurance-cover in the Balkans.

The Italian collapse had a further ill-effect on Germany by exposing her to a widened range of air attack from the Allied bombing forces, now rapidly swelling with the growth of the American forces.

The air offensive against Germany's industrial resources might be termed an indirect approach on the plane of grand strategy, for it undermined the balance of her war-making power as a whole. If the Allies' bombing strategy had been better designed—to dislocate supplies rather than to devastate populated areas—it could have produced a quicker paralysis of German resistance; but though much of the effort was misdirected, it did spread a creeping paralysis. Moreover, in the military field, the dislocation of communications was a major factor in immobilizing the German armies' power to counter the Allied armies' advance.

The success of the Allied invasion of Sicily, in July, owed much to the complete 'bag' they secured of the enemy forces in Tunisia. This removed most of the forces that were immediately available to stiffen the defence of Sicily. The moral impression that it made went far to demoralize the Italian forces in Sicily, and shook the foundations of Mussolini's regime in Italy. The Germans' fear that Italy would collapse or capitulate, and that any forces they sent south would be engulfed, hindered them from sending adequate forces to strengthen Sicily's defences. Save for these factors, the Allies might have had cause to regret that they did not make a move against Sicily while the enemy's attention was absorbed in the effort to bolster up their position across the sea in Tunisia. For, even with so many favourable conditions, the conquest of Sicily did not prove easy. There the Germans, although weak in strength, were no longer fighting in outlying territory that could be isolated by sea-power, in its new sea-air form.

The Allies, however, still enjoyed an inherent power of distraction owing to their amphibious power and the broad strategic situation—the immense stretch of the Germans' hold on southern

Europe, from the Pyrenees to Macedonia. The Allies' chief strategic asset lay in their possible choice of alternative objectives. Their concentration in French North Africa presented an almost equal threat to Sicily and Sardinia. If their main move were to be made on the western side of Italy, it could develop into an alternative, and therefore dual, threat to the industrial north of Italy or to the Germans' hold on southern France. If it were to be made along the Adriatic line, it might have either northern Italy or the western Balkans as its objective, and so would threaten both. If it developed along the Aegean line it would threaten the German hold on Greece and Yugo-Slavia or on Bulgaria and Rumania.

Later information confirmed that this axial strategic advantage of the Allies, coupled with their deception plans, produced a divided mind in the Axis command—which was led to expect an invasion of Sardinia or Greece as an alternative to Sicily, and even thought it might come on the mainland of Italy or southern France. Their apprehensions were increased by the fact that air reconnaissance reported the appearance of Allied ships at many points along the Mediterranean.

The actual landings in Sicily—on the 10th July—also profited from their wide distribution, along seventy miles of coastline. Like the widespread—though less widespread—landings on the Gallipoli Peninsula in 1915, they tended to keep the opponent in doubt as to the main point of danger, and then to delay his counter-moves during the most critical time. This state of doubt eased the way for the Eighth Army's disconcertingly rapid advance up the east coast, which helped to throw the opponent off his balance. The upsetting effect was increased because his dispositions were based on the mistaken assumption that the main Allied landings would be attempted at the western end of Sicily, since it was nearest to the Allied bases in North Africa and offered more numerous ports. The fact that the move was directed against the south-eastern corner of Sicily gave it the effect of a strategically indirect approach. Within four days Montgomery's forces had advanced forty miles up the east coast, almost half-way to the vital Straits of Messina, before they were checked on the outskirts of Catania.

The same effect was repeated when General Patton's American Seventh Army, after securing its foothold on Montgomery's left, suddenly swung its weight westward, and then swerved northward across the island to Palermo. This was like 'selling the dummy' in football. The general dislocation was increased because the Allied moves simultaneously menaced the alternative objectives of Palermo and Messina.

The resistance of the Italian forces collapsed at an early stage. The repercussion produced the fall of Mussolini's regime in Italy.

This collapse threw the whole burden of Sicily's defence upon the nucleus of German troops—two scratch divisions, made up from drafts, to which a third was added at a later stage. They were left to meet an invasion that had been launched with over seven divisions abreast, and soon rose to more than a dozen. Yet this small core of resistance, though devoid of air support, succeeded in delaying the Allied conquest of Sicily for over a month, and then slipped away across the Straits of Messina, under a canopy of *flak*, to the Italian mainland. Apart from the stubborn fighting qualities of the German troops, the explanation clearly lay in the increasing directness of the Allies' advance and the lie of the country.

After the capture of Palermo, and the clearance of western Sicily, Patton's army had turned eastward to combine with Montgomery's in a converging drive upon Messina. That north-eastern end of the island formed a triangle which was filled with mountains. The enemy could there profit, not only by the way the ground favoured defence, but also by the way the process of withdrawal towards the apex brought a shortening of his front. Thus his defensive density of force increased at each successive step-back, while the Allied armies were increasingly cramped in deploying their full superiority of force. It was an important negative lesson in the problem of the strategic approach. Further lessons were brought out in the next stage.

The Invasion of Italy

In occupying Sicily the Allies secured a European foothold that could easily be converted into a springboard. Its possession enabled them to bring their threat closer to the mainland of Europe, and to intensify their concentration, while still menacing a diversity of points on the enemy's side. They were offered a choice of courses. Besides the most obvious, direct, course up the toe of Italy, they had the possibility of a short jump on to the shin of Italy, or on to Sardinia, or on to the heel of Italy. The last was outside the reach of fighter cover from air interference, but for that very reason would, as one suggested at the time, be the course of least expectation. For all the Allied moves hitherto had been carefully confined within the limits of such cover, so that a departure from the rule would come as a surprise to the enemy. Once landings were achieved there, the heel offered the most favourable route for the rapid advance of mechanized forces. Moreover, it would open up a threat to the Balkans as well as to central Italy, thus creating a fresh dilemma for the German Supreme Command. Strategically, the heel of Italy was capable of being turned, with deadly effect, into a German 'Achilles' heel'.

The Allied Command, however, decided to make their main effort with the fighter-cover limits, though at the last moment they improvised a subsidiary landing on the heel. The main effort comprised a landing on the toe by the Eighth Army, and then a bigger landing at Salerno, just south of Naples, by the mixed American and British Fifth Army, newly formed for the purpose, under General Mark Clark.

The prospects were marred not only by the directness of the strategic approach but by the Allied statesmen's rigid insistence previously on 'unconditional surrender' by Italy. Most of the Italian leaders were desperately anxious for peace, but hesitated to bow their necks to such humiliation and take responsibility for a peace without any safeguards. Only the Sicilian disaster and the immediate exposure of the Italian mainland drove them to overthrow Mussolini and initiate negotiations for peace—which took time to arrange. The delay allowed the Germans more than a month's grace to prepare their counter-moves in readiness for the emergency.

The crossing of the Straits of Messina took place on the 3rd September, and the landing on the toe was preceded by a tremendous but superfluous bombardment—the only German division in the neighbourhood having moved north several days earlier. Even when the invading forces penetrated deeper they met with little opposition, but their rate of advance was slowed down by the cramping nature of the country and by their own excessive caution. The move was thus of little help in easing the way for the major landing at Salerno. This was made on the 9th September, and the announcement of the arranged capitulation of Italy was timed to take place the previous afternoon. It did not shake the German forces which were posted there, and, following their counter-stroke, the situation was critical until the sixth day.

The root of the matter was contained in General Mark Clark's subsequent explanation:

'The Germans could see that in the nature of the problem another landing was probably on the way. They could also calculate that it *would have to* come within the limits of air cover. At that time, operating from Sicily, the maximum limit was approximately Naples. *Therefore*, they concentrated in the Salerno–Naples area, and we met their full force.'

The words italicized have an underlying significance. For they make it clear that the enemy profited by the probability that the Allied plans would be governed by conformity to an accepted limitation. The outcome showed the limited results of choosing the course of 'most expectation'. By arriving where they were expected the Allies suffered a costly check, both in life and time, and courted a disaster—which was only avoided by a narrow margin. Salerno provided one more demonstration of the lesson of history that nothing can be more hazardous for an army than to concentrate its effort at the point where the enemy can calculate on its coming, and can thus concentrate his forces to meet it. At that time the German commander, Field-Marshal Kesselring, had only seven divisions to defend the whole south and centre of the Italian peninsula, besides having to quell and disarm forces of his ex-ally.

By contrast with the main landing at Salerno, the subsidiary landing on the heel of Italy met with no opposition, and quickly secured two fine ports, Taranto and Brindisi. It opened up good avenues of approach up the coast towards the focal rail junction of Foggia and the important cluster of airfields near there. At that time, the hostile forces in the whole area between Taranto and Foggia comprised only one low-strength German parachute division.

But the landing force consisted only of the British 1st Airborne Division, 'dismounted' for the task. It had been hurriedly collected from rest-camps in Tunisia and rushed across in such few ships as were available at short notice. It arrived without any tanks, without any artillery except for one howitzer, and with scarcely any motor transport. In brief, it lacked the very things it needed to exploit the opportunity it had gained.

After nearly a fortnight had passed, another small force, including an armoured brigade, was landed at Bari, the next port up the east coast. It pushed north without meeting opposition and occupied Foggia. The German forces facing the Fifth Army in the mountains, astride the direct route to Naples, began to fall back as soon as this indirect advance from the 'heel' had gone far enough to carry a potential threat to their rear flank. On the 1st October the Allies entered Naples—three weeks after the landing. But in the meantime the Germans, reacting to the threat far more quickly than the Allies anticipated, had established a firm grip on the rest of Italy, dispersed the Italian forces, and nullified most of the effects of Italy's surrender.

Henceforth the Allied armies were reduced to pushing their way up the Italian peninsula like a sticky piston-rod in a stickier cylinder against increasingly strong compression. For the Germans had originally hoped to do no more than impose a short delay on the Allied advance to Rome, and had intended to await the Allies in the north. But they were emboldened to push reinforcements southwards to Kesselring's aid as they came to realize how badly the Allies were cramped by the narrowness of the front and the difficulty of the country, and the extent to which the Allies had lost the power of amphibious flexibility in committing their strength to this restricted effort.

The Fifth Army's advance was temporarily checked on the line of the Volturno River, twenty miles beyond Naples, and then more definitely on the line of the Garigliano, in front of Cassino. Successive assaults in November and December failed to pierce this barrier. Meanwhile, the advance of the Eighth Army up the east coast had been checked on the Sangro, and then blocked soon after crossing it. By the end of the year, the Allies had advanced only seventy miles beyond Salerno—in four months. Most of that ground had been gained during September, and thereafter the rate of progress became so gradual as to be generally described by the term 'inching'. The invasion had been slowed down to a process of gnawing and grinding.

In the light of long experience, such tactics sometimes succeed, but far more often result in disappointment. This campaign was no exception to the rule. It repeatedly demonstrated that direct attack on narrow fronts commonly leads to negative results. Even a big superiority of force rarely suffices unless there is room for manœuvre—which requires a relatively wider front. The Italian peninsula was barely a hundred miles wide, and most of that space was filled by a mountain spine and its ribs. Once the German Supreme Command decided to double their stake in the south, the establishment of a reasonable defensive density was bound to produce strategic cramp in the Allied advance up the leg of Italy.

Early in 1944, the Allies attempted a fresh seaborne manœuvre against the long coastline in the enemy's rear. On the 22nd January a flanking force was landed near Anzio, twenty-five miles south of Rome. Only two German battalions were present in the area, and a swift dash inland could have seized the Alban Hills, covering the immediate approach to Rome—or even Rome itself. But the Allies' plan had been based on the calculation that the enemy would immediately counter the landing, so that they were primarily concerned to consolidate the lodgement, while the main forces in the south took advantage of the anticipated weakening of the enemy's resistance there. But the enemy did not react in the way expected.

When the lack of opposition near Anzio became clear, Alexander wished to quicken the move inland, but the local executive commander proved a brake in himself. Under his cautious handling, no serious advance was attempted for over a week. Kesselring was thus allowed time to switch reserves to the scene, while he also held in check the forward drive of the main Allied forces on the Cassino sector. On the 3rd February, the thirteenth day after the landing, the Germans developed a powerful counter-offensive against the Anzio bridgehead. This in turn was checked, but the Allied force was left in an awkwardly shallow and narrow bridgehead. It looked uncomfortably like a large-scale 'internment camp'—as the Germans had called the Allies' Salonika bridgehead in the last war. But those who remembered how that joke had ultimately turned out in 1918, when the break-out from Salonika started the process of Germany's collapse, could find comfort in the proverb, 'He laughs best who laughs last'.

The offensive in Italy was renewed in May on a large scale. This time it was also part of a larger plan. For it formed the opening stroke in the Allies' 'Grand Design' for a decisive offensive against Germany. Less than a month later came the cross-Channel invasion of France by the Allied armies assembled in southern England. Both strokes were preceded and accompanied by a terrific air offensive to strangle the enemy's lines of supply.

The first phase of General Alexander's plan comprised a fresh attack on either side of Cassino, where previous offensives had been blocked. To intensify its effect, General Leese's Eighth Army extended its frontage and shifted its weight over from the Adriatic sector to join with General Clark's Fifth Army in a combined blow against the western sector of the Gustav Line. The attack was launched at 11 p.m. on the 11th May, just before moonrise, and was particularly aimed to seize the mountain gate-posts that supported the enemy's fortified barrier across the narrow entrance to the Liri Valley.

The attack on the easterly gate-post, Monte Cairo, made little progress in several days of tough fighting, but between Cassino and the sea wedges were driven into the Gustav Line at a number of points. The most significant penetration was made by General Juin's French Colonial Corps, which exploited its specialized skill in mountain-warfare to pursue a difficult route across the Aurunci Mountains, and thus gained the advantage of unexpectedness. Its six-mile thrust, in three days, past Monte Majo to the heights overlooking the Liri Valley, created a leverage that loosened the enemy's hold on the Gustav Line. The threat eased the way for British troops of the Eighth Army to press up the valley and outflank Cassino, which fell on the 18th, Ascension Day. It also eased the way for an American push up the coast.

Then, on the 23rd, the Allied force at Anzio chimed in with a stroke from the bridgehead. Here, the investing force had been whittled down in order to send reinforcements south, and the Allied move was neatly timed to exploit the weakening. On the third day the German defence cracked under the pressure. Once the break-out was achieved, the Germans were caught short of reserves with which to meet the Allied follow-through, towards the Alban Hills and the communications of the enemy's main forces in the south.

Simultaneously with the Anzio stroke, the Eighth Army launched an assault on the Germans' final position in the Liri Valley. The Canadian Corps penetrated this on the first day, and next day it became clear that the Germans were falling back everywhere. Their retreat was soon accelerated, as the menace from Anzio developed. Within a few days the direct line of retreat on Rome up Highway 6 was blocked, and the Germans were compelled to fork north-eastward up difficult mountain roads, where their withdrawing columns were more exposed to a hammering from the air.

Although a considerable part of the imperilled army managed to escape from the trap by this branching move, it forfeited the Germans' chance of covering Rome. General Alexander switched all possible strength to his left wing against the other German army, and in a week of tough fighting loosened its grip on the Alban Hills. Once this strategic breakwater collapsed, the Allied

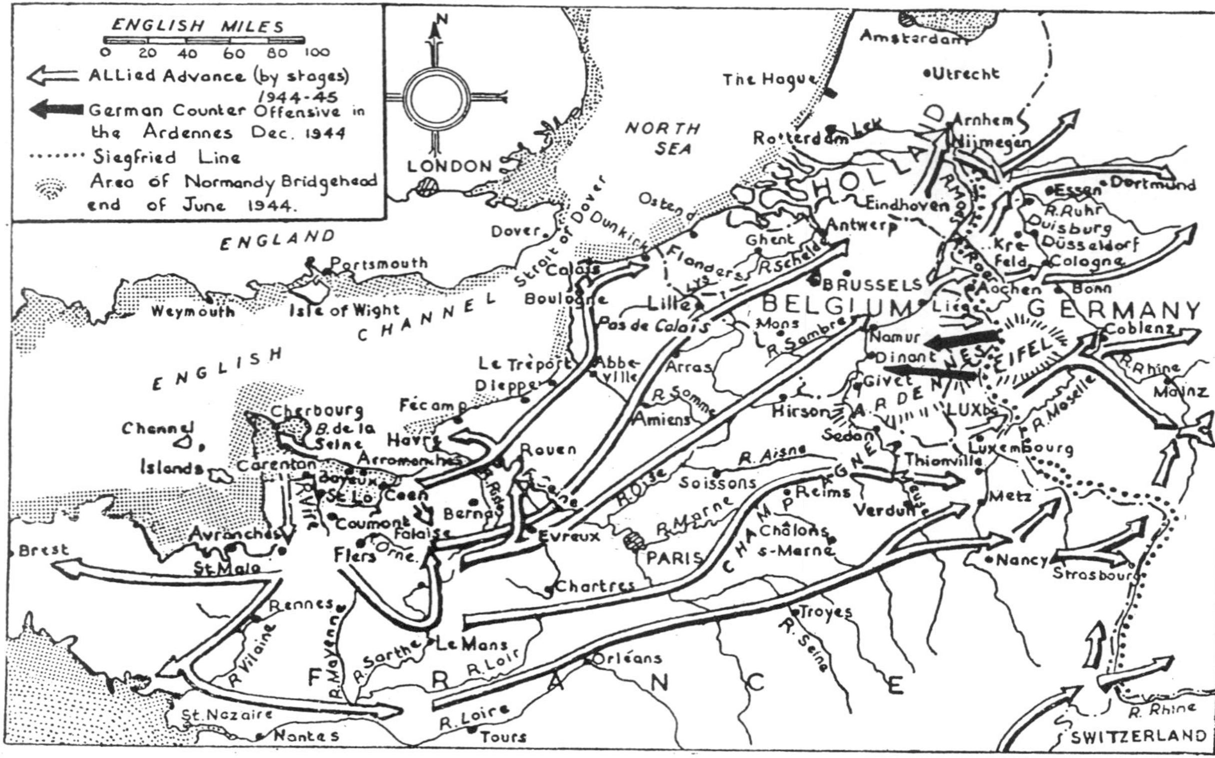
ENGLISH MILES
0 20 40 60 80 100
ALLied Advance (by stages) 1944-45
German Counter Offensive in the Ardennes Dec. 1944
Siegfried Line
Area of Normandy Bridgehead end of June 1944.
N
LONDON
ENGLAND
Portsmouth
Weymouth
Isle of Wight
ENGLISH CHANNEL
Dover
Strait of Dover
NORTH SEA
The Hague
Amsterdam
Utrecht
Rotterdam
Lek
HOLLAND
Arnhem
Nijmegen
Eindhoven
R.Maas
Antwerp
Ostend
Dunkirk
Calais
Boulogne
Flanders
R.Scheldt
Ghent
Lys
Lille
Pas de Calais
BRUSSELS
BELGIUM
Mons
R.Sambre
Namur
Dinant
Givet
ARDENNES
LUXbg
EIFEL
Liège
Aachen
R.Roer
Krefeld
Duisburg
Düsseldorf
Cologne
Bonn
R.Ruhr
Essen
Dortmund
GERMANY
Coblenz
R.Rhine
Mainz
R.Moselle
Luxembourg
Thionville
Metz
Nancy
Strasbourg
R.Rhine
SWITZERLAND
Le Trèport
Abbeville
Dieppe
Arras
R.Somme
Amiens
Fécamp
Havre
Rouen
Cherbourg
B.de la Seine
Arromanches
Channel Islands
Carentan
Bayeux
St.Lo
Caen
R.Vire
Coumont
Falaise
Bernay
Orne
Flers
Avranches
St.Malo
Brest
Rennes
R.Vilaine
R.Mayenne
R.Sarthe
Le Mans
R.Loir
Evreux
Seine
Chartres
PARIS
R.Marne
R.Oise
Soissons
R.Aisne
Hirson
Sedan
Reims
Verdun
Meuse
CHAMPAGNE
Châlons s-Marne
Troyes
R.Seine
Orléans
FRANCE
R.Loire
Tours
St.Nazaire
Nantes

forces quickly flooded the flat country around Rome, capturing the city early on the 5th June. They had gained the prize which had been so nearly within their grasp nine months earlier, when the Italian Government capitulated.

The Invasion of France

The day after the capture of Rome came the landing in Normandy—the most dramatic, and decisive, event of the war. The cross-sea move of the Anglo-American expeditionary force, based on England, had been delayed by bad weather. It was launched when the wind was still strong enough to make the move hazardous—but also unlikely. General Eisenhower's decision to take the risk was not only justified by the outcome but contributed to its surprise effect.

The Allied landings were made on the morning of the 6th June, in the Bay of the Seine between Caen and Cherbourg, and immediately preceded by the moonlight dropping of strong airborne forces near the two flanks.

The invasion was prepared by a sustained air offensive of unparalleled intensity, which had been particularly directed against the enemy's communications, with the aim of paralysing his power of moving reserves to the crucial area.

Although many factors had pointed to this sector as the probable scene, the Germans were caught off their balance—with most of their reserves posted east of the Seine. That was due partly to the ingenuity of the plans for misleading them, and partly to an obstinate preconception that the Allies would come not only direct across the Channel but by the shortest route. The Allies' cautious desire for the maximum possible air cover had been a hindrance to their aim and progress in their Italian campaign, but now brought an unsought profit through its effect in making their opponents reckon that they would always take this cautious course. The effect of this miscalculation was made fatal by the action of the Allied air forces in breaking the bridges over the Seine.

By deductions drawn from the lay-out of the Anglo-American forces in England prior to the invasion, and contrary to the views of his military staff, Hitler had, in March, begun to suspect the Allies would land in Normandy. Rommel, who was put in charge of the forces on the north coast, came to the same view. But Rundstedt, who was Commander-in-Chief in the West, counted on the

Allies landing in the narrower part of the Channel between Dieppe and Calais. That conviction was due not only to the Allies' past fondness for maximum air cover, and the effect of their present deception plans, but even more to his reasoning that such a line was theoretically the right line since it was the shortest line to their objective. That was a characteristic calculation of strategic orthodoxy. Significantly, it did not credit the Allied Command with a preference for the unexpected, nor even with an inclination to avoid the most strongly defended approach.

The invaders' actual plan secured more than the avoidance of the best-prepared defences. In choosing the Normandy route, the Allied Command operated on a line which alternatively threatened the important ports of Havre and Cherbourg, and was able to keep the Germans in doubt until the last moment as to which was the objective—thus fixing them on the horns of a dilemma. When they came to realize that Cherbourg was the main objective, the Seine had become a partition wall dividing their forces, and they could only move their reserves to the critical point by a wide detour. The movement was lengthened by the continued interference of the Allied air forces. Moreover, when the reinforcements reached the battle-area, they tended to arrive in the sector farthest from Cherbourg—the Caen sector. The British lodgement here became, not only a menace in itself, but a shield for the development of the American operations farther west, in the Cherbourg Peninsula. That double effect and alternative threat had a vital influence on the success of the invasion as a whole.

The vast armada achieved the sea-passage without interference, and the beaches were captured more easily than had been expected, except where the American left wing landed, east of the Vire Estuary. Much was due to the excellence of the planning and equipment, which included many new devices. Even so, the margin between success and frustration, in driving the bridgehead deep enough, was narrower than appeared. The invaders did not succeed in gaining control of the keys to Caen and Cherbourg. Fortunately, the wide frontage of attack became a vital factor in redeeming the chances. The Germans' natural concentration on preserving these keys on either flank left them weak in the space between them. A quick exploitation of the intermediate landings near Arromanches carried the British into Bayeux, and by the end of the week the expansion of this penetration gave the Allies a bridgehead nearly forty miles broad and five to twelve miles deep between the Orne and Vire. They had also secured another, though smaller, bridgehead on the east side of the Cherbourg Peninsula. On the 12th, the Americans pinched out the intermediate key-point of Carentan, so that a continuous bridgehead of over sixty miles span was secured.

General Montgomery, who was in executive command of the invading forces as a whole, under Eisenhower, could now develop his offensive moves more fully.

The second week brought a marked expansion of the bridgehead on the western flank. Here the American First Army developed a drive across the waist of the Cherbourg peninsula, while the British Second Army on the eastern flank continued to absorb the bulk of the German reinforcements, especially the panzer divisions, by its pressure around Caen. On the strategic plane, this British threat of an easterly break-out was an indirect approach in aid of Montgomery's plan to break-out at the western end of the bridgehead.

In the third week, having cut off Cherbourg, the Americans wheeled up the peninsula and drove into the port from the rear. Cherbourg was captured on the 27th June, though not before the port itself had been made temporarily unusable. Around Caen, British thrusts were baffled by the enemy's skilful defensive tactics in country favourable to a flexible defence, but their threat continued to be a distraction to the German Command's free use of its reserves.

Under cover of this pressure, the build-up of the invading forces proceeded at a remarkably rapid rate. It was aided by the development of artificial harbours, which mitigated the interference of the weather, and also contributed to surprise—by upsetting the enemy's calculations.

The Russian Surge into Poland

Following a preliminary offensive on the Finnish front, the summer campaign of the Red Army opened on the 23rd June—the day after the third anniversary of Hitler's invasion of Russia. The offensive was launched in White Russia, north of the Pripet Marshes. This sector had proved in 1943 the toughest of all, and the Germans had felt justified in giving it less reinforcement than the more open sector between the Pripet Marshes and the Carpathians, where it was expected that the Red Army would renew its spring push. Thus the defenders were again caught off their balance.

The German situation was made worse because Hitler had vetoed the local army commanders' arguments for a withdrawal to the line of Beresina, ninety miles behind the existing front. Such a step-back, if made in time, would have thrown the Russian offensive out of gear.

Once the German crust was pierced, Russian progress became startlingly swift. Vitebsk fell on the fourth day to the converging thrusts of Bagramyan's and Chernyakovsky's army groups, thus tearing a hole in the front of the 3rd Panzer Army. This opened the way for a drive southward across the Moscow–Minsk highway, and onto the rear of the German 4th Army (Tippelskirch) which had partially damped the shock of the Russian offensive on its own front by a short step-back to the line of the Dnieper. Meantime Rokossovsky's army group had delivered an upper-cut against the other flank of the great German salient. Breaking through just north of the Pripet Marshes, it bounded forward in twenty-mile-a-day strides to get across the communications behind Minsk, isolating this focal centre, which fell on the 3rd July.

These multiple indirect thrusts produced a general breakdown of the German defence, and the immediate bag of prisoners was the largest taken in any Russian break-through up to that time. After the first few weeks these captures dwindled, however, though the pace of the advance did not slacken. That combination of facts was significant. On the one hand, it was testimony to the skill of the German commanders in extricating their forces once Hitler had at last been forced by events to accept the necessity of a large-scale retreat. On the other hand, the speed and extent of the retreat, as well as the large number of important centres that was abandoned without a fight, indicated the growing skill of the Russian commanders in undercutting resistance by indirect approach.

Examining the course of operations, it can be seen how time after time the Russian advances appeared to be carrying an alternative threat to one or other of a couple of big centres, and would then avoid both—instead, cutting through the lightly guarded space between them, and penetrating so far in their rear as to produce the abandonment of both. Significantly, also, the two main advances suffered their first severe check when they converged on Warsaw and Insterburg respectively, where in either case the advance became canalized into a direct approach.

In less than a fortnight the Red Army swept the enemy out of White Russia. By the middle of July it had overrun more than half of north-eastern Poland, come close to Brest-Litovsk and Bialystok, enveloped Vilna, crossed the Niemen, and was approaching the borders of East Prussia. Here its advancing wave was over 200 miles beyond the flank of the German army group under Lindemann that was still covering the Baltic States, along the front between Narva and Pskov—an ominous back-to-front situation.

On the 14th July the Russians launched their long-expected offensive south of the Pripet Marshes, on the front between Kovel and Tarnopol, where the Germans had already begun to withdraw. Within ten days they had reached Lwow and Lublin, 100 miles south-east of Warsaw. The fortress-cities of Przemysl, Brest-Litovsk and Bialystok fell in the same week. On the northern flank the Russians thrust past Dvinsk towards the Baltic coast behind Riga, thus threatening to cut off Lindemann's forces, who had been strangely slow to withdraw. By the end of July the Russians had reached the Gulf of Riga, while in the centre they penetrated to the outskirts of Warsaw.

But events now showed that the Germans were recovering from the shock and regaining control of their situation as their retreat went far enough to carry them out of immediate danger—to a line where they might benefit from the measure in which the pursuers were outrunning their supplies. On the other side, the natural law of strategic overstretch began to operate. It soon became clear that the Germans were still capable of imposing a check on the advance, and that the Russians would need time to repair communications, through the vast tract they had overrun, before they could renew their momentum.

Early in August, German counter-strokes reopened the line of retreat in the north and also pushed the Russians back from Warsaw, where the Germans also proved strong enough to deal with a Polish rising that had started when the Russians drew near the city. South of Warsaw, the Russians succeeded in establishing bridgeheads across the Vistula, but were then checked. The remainder of August passed without any important change in the situation.

The temporary deadlock was broken by a change of direction—a new Russian move in the south, on the Rumanian front. Almost simultaneously with its launching, Rumania announced on the

23rd August that she had arranged to make peace. This cleared the way for a rapid Russian advance past Jassy, down the corridor between the Pruth and the Sereth, towards the Galatz Gap. It also helped the Red Army to encircle the German forces that had remained in their exposed coastal salient east of Pruth. Behind their backs, the Russian sweep continued, capturing Galatz and Focsani on the 27th, the Ploesti oilfields on the 30th, and entering Bucharest next day. The tanks had covered 250 miles in twelve days' driving.

The Russian armies then fanned out northward, westward, and southward. They pushed through the Transylvanian Alps towards Hungary, reached the borders of Yugo-Slavia in a drive to cut off the German divisions garrisoned in Greece, and thrust south over the Danube into Bulgaria—on whom the Soviet Government now declared war.

The Deadlock in Italy

The fall of Rome was not followed by any such rapid collapse of German resistance as had been anticipated. Kesselring extricated his forces from their badly entangled situation, conducted the retreat with a masterly hand, and succeeded in imposing a fresh series of checks on the Allied advance northward. Seven weeks passed before the Allied armies reached the outskirts of Pisa and Florence, on the Arno, 160 miles north of Rome. It was three weeks longer before Kesselring yielded Florence and fell back from the Arno to his main defensive position in the mountains behind—the Gothic Line.

Recognizing the formidable nature of this barrier, General Alexander now planned a fresh side-stepping manœuvre. Switching the weight of the Eighth Army back to the Adriatic flank, he struck at the east coast sector of the Gothic Line near Pesaro, at the end of August, and broke through towards Rimini.

But Kesselring managed to parry the threat and close the door, and Alexander had to revert to a process of trying to prise it open by levering attacks. Although the continued effort gradually forced a way into the eastern end of the Po Valley, that flat country was filled with vineyards and had a clay soil which quickly turned into a quagmire under rain, so that it was bad country for a rapid follow-through. The autumn rains came to rescue the battered and exhausted German forces, when they were dangerously near collapse, and a fresh deadlock ensued. It lasted until the spring.

Part of Alexander's forces had been taken away to carry out the invasion of southern France in August. In the event, that diversion had little effect on the main battle in northern France, where the issue had been decided a fortnight before the landing in the south was made. At the same time it deprived Alexander of the extra margin of strength which would probably have been decisive towards winning the battle in Italy. Yet, as so often before, the disadvantage carried compensating advantages. For in the measure that Alexander's autumn offensive fell short of locally decisive pressure, it hindered the Germans from retreating to the foothills of the Alps while they were still strong enough to make an effective stand there, and at a time when their withdrawal would have been favoured by the weather conditions.

Early in 1945, four of Kesselring's divisions were taken away to stiffen the defence in the West, while Hitler continued to forbid any immediate retreat to the Alps. Meanwhile the poverty of the Germans' material resources became even more marked. By the spring they were desperately short of aircraft, tanks, transport and petrol—of all the requirements for a rapid retreat to the shelter of the Alps. When the Allied armies took the offensive in April, and burst through the thin German front, they were able to drive swiftly to the enemy's rear and there fan out to block all the bolt-holes, while the German forces were floundering in confusion or trudging back on foot.

That final triumph came to the Allied armies in Italy as a fitting reward for prolonged effort, wiping out the memory of many frustrations. In the way the enemy's collapse in Italy preceded that in the main theatre, it bore a striking parallel to the way that the break-out of the strategically 'interned' Allied army in Macedonia had started the ending of the last war. But this time the enemy's general collapse had been more definitely due to the operations in the main theatre. There the most decisive phase had developed in August 1944, following the break-out from Normandy.

The Break-out from Normandy

July was a month of tough fighting in Normandy, with little to show for the effort except heavy casualties. But the Germans could not afford such a drain as well as the Allies could, while behind the almost static battle-front the Allied resources were continually growing.

On the 3rd July the American First Army, having regrouped after the capture of Cherbourg, began an attempted break-out push southward towards the base-line of the peninsula. But the attackers were still cramped in room for manœuvre, and progress was slow. On the 8th General Dempsey's British Second Army penetrated into Caen, but was blocked at the crossings of the Orne. Successive flanking thrusts were also parried. On the 18th a more ambitious stroke, 'Operation Goodwood', was attempted—when a phalanx of three armoured divisions one behind the other, was launched from a bridgehead north-east of Caen, through a narrow gap created by a terrific air bombardment on a three-mile frontage, and drove across the rear of the Caen defences. A break-through was momentarily in sight, but the pace was too slow, and subordinate leaders too hesitant in by-passing defended villages, while the Germans were quick in swinging a screen of tanks and anti-tank guns across the path. After that missed opportunity, fresh British and Canadian attacks made little headway. But they served to keep the enemy's attention, and his best troops, fixed in the Caen sector. Seven of his nine panzer divisions were drawn there.

At the western end of the Normandy bridgehead, the American forces under General Bradley advanced their front five to eight miles during the first three weeks of July. Meantime, General Patton's Third American Army had been transported over from England to Normandy, in readiness for a bigger thrust.

This 'Operation Cobra' was launched on the 25th July, initially by six divisions on a four-mile frontage, and was preceded by an air bombardment even heavier than in 'Goodwood'. The ground was so thickly cratered that it aided the sparse and dazed defenders in putting a brake on the American drive. On the first two days only five miles was covered, but then the breach was widened, and progress quickened—towards the south-west corner of the peninsula. The decisive break-out took place on the 31st July. It was helped by a sudden switch of the weight of the British Second Army from east of the Orne to the central sector south of Bayeux, for an attack near Caumont the previous day. While the enemy were reinforcing this danger-point with such troops as they could spare from Caen the Americans forced the lock of the door at

Avranches, near the west coast of the Cherbourg peninsula.

Pouring through the gap, Patton's tanks surged southward and then westward, quickly flooding most of Brittany. Then they turned eastward and swept through the country north of the Loire, towards Le Mans and Chartres. The cramped 70-mile front of the bridgehead had been immediately converted into a potential 400-mile front. Space was too wide for the enemy's available forces to impose any effective check on the advance, which repeatedly by-passed any of the road-centres where they attempted a stand.

The one danger to this expanding torrent was that the enemy might bring off a counter-thrust to cut the Avranches bottle-neck, through which its supplies had to be maintained. On Hitler's insistence, the Germans attempted such a stroke on the night of the 6th August, switching four panzer divisions westwards for the purpose. The approach, chosen by Hitler on the map at his remote headquarters in the East, was too direct, and thus ran head-on into the Americans' flank shield—as Bradley remarked: 'Had the enemy side-slipped his panzers several thousand yards south he might have broken through to Avranches that very first day.' Once checked, the attack was disrupted by the swift intervention of the Allied air forces. And when the thrust failed, it turned in a fatal way for the Germans—by drawing their weight westward just as the American armoured forces were sweeping eastward behind their rear. The American left wing wheeled north to Argentan, to combine in a pincer move with General Crerar's First Canadian Army, pushing down from Caen upon Falaise. Although the pincers did not close in time to cut off completely the two armies within their embrace, 50,000 prisoners were taken and 10,000 corpses found on the battlefield, while all the divisions which got away were badly mauled. Their vehicles were even worse hit than their men by the continuous air-bombing they suffered in an ever-narrowing space. The Germans' losses in the 'Falaise Pocket' left them without the forces or movement resources to meet the Allies' continued easterly sweep to the Seine, and past the Seine.

Each time the enemy wriggled out of a trap he found himself caught in a bigger one. All the time his inland flank was being turned, and his rear increasingly menaced, by Patton's armoured drive on the Allied right wing. While repeatedly by-passing resistance on its own path, the speed of its progress produced a continuous strategic by-passing of the main body of the German forces.[1]

Space and speed had formed the dual key by which the Allied armies had unlocked the gates of the West. Manœuvre had triumphed where assault had been repeatedly baffled. Once unlimited room for manœuvre was secured, mechanized mobility had been able to exploit the Allies' tremendous superiority of force.

The rapidity of this wide flanking manœuvre, and its speedy effect in causing a general collapse of the German position in France, forestalled the need of the further lever that was inserted by the landing of General Patch's American (and French) Seventh Army in southern France on the 15th August. The invasion was a 'walk-in', as the Germans had been forced to denude the Riviera coast of all but a mere four divisions, of inferior quality. The subsequent advance inland and up the Rhône Valley was mainly a supply problem, rather than a tactical problem. Marseilles was occupied on the 23rd, while a drive through the mountains reached Grenoble the same day.

On the 19th the French Forces of the Interior had started a rising in Paris, and although their situation was critical for some days, the scales were turned in their favour by the arrival of Allied armoured forces in the city on the 25th. Meantime Patton's army was racing towards the Marne, north-east of Paris.

The next important development was an exploiting thrust by the British Second Army, which crossed the Seine east of Rouen, to trap the remnants of the German Seventh Army, which were still opposing the First Canadian Army west of Rouen. A large proportion of the enemy succeeded in slipping back over the Seine in time—only to find that the British armoured columns were travelling on a wider and deeper 'by-pass', to cut off their retreat farther back. Dempsey's spearheads reached Amiens early on the 31st, having covered seventy miles from the Seine in two days and a night. Crossing the Somme, they then drove on swiftly past Arras and Lille to the Belgian frontier—behind the back of the German 15th Army on the Pas de Calais coast. To the east, Hodges's First

[1] As he was racing on across the Seine, above Paris, General Wood, who commanded Patton's leading armoured division, the 4th, sent me an outline of his course since breaking out from Avranches, remarking that it 'shows what can be done by following the principles . . . (1) De l'audace; (2) indirect approach'.

American Army had also leapt forward to the Belgian frontier near Hirson.

Farther east, Patton's army made an even more dazzling drive through Champagne, and past Verdun, to the Moselle between Metz and Thionville, close to the frontier of Germany. But it had begun to lose weight through the difficulty of maintaining petrol supplies on an adequate scale, and then its armoured spearheads were brought to a halt by running out of petrol—though the strategic prospect was becoming greater day by day. For they were hardly eighty miles from the Rhine. When they received sufficient fuel to resume their advance, opposition was stiffening. Patton's thrust had produced a decisive issue in the Battle of France, but the supply position checked it from deciding the Battle for Germany in the same breath. The strategic law of overstretch reasserted itself, to impose a postponement. On this sector it proved a long one, as Patton became drawn into a direct approach to Metz, and then into a protracted close-quarter battle for that famous fortress-city, to the forfeit of the prospects of a by-passing manœuvre.

In the early days of September the pace grew fastest on the left wing, and it was thither that a bid for early victory was now transferred. British armoured columns entered Brussels on the 3rd, Antwerp on the 4th, and then penetrated into Holland. By this great manœuvre, Montgomery had cut off the Germans' remaining troops in Normandy and the Pas de Calais—their principal force in the West. The First American Army occupied Namur and crossed the Meuse at Dinant and Givet.

At this crisis the executive command of the German forces in the West was taken over by General Model, who had gained the reputation on the Russian front of being able 'to scrape up reserves from nowhere'. He now performed that miracle on a bigger scale. On any normal calculation it appeared that the Germans, of whom more than half a million had been captured in the drive through France, had no chance of scraping up reserves to hold their own frontier—in any degree of density that could suffice for an effective defence of the 500-mile-wide stretch between Switzerland and the North Sea. But in the event they achieved an amazing rally, which prolonged the war for eight months.

In this recovery they were greatly helped by the Allies' supply difficulties, which reduced the first onset to a lightweight charge that could be checked by a hastily improvised defence, and then curtailed the build-up of the Allied armies for a powerful attack. In part, the supply difficulties were due to the length of the Allies' own advance. In part, they were due to the Germans' strategy in leaving garrisons behind to hold the French ports. The fact that the Allies were thus denied the use of Dunkirk, Calais, Boulogne and Havre, as well as the big ports in Brittany, became a powerful indirect brake on the Allies' offensive. Although they had captured the still greater port of Antwerp in good condition, the enemy kept a tenacious grip on the estuary of the Scheldt, and thus prevented the Allies making use of the port.

Before the break-out from Normandy, their supplies had to be carried less than twenty miles from the base in order to replenish the striking forces. They now had to be carried nearly 300 miles. The burden was thrown almost entirely on the Allies' motor transport, as the French railway network had been destroyed by previous air attacks. The bombing that had been so useful in paralysing the German counter-measures against the invasion became a boomerang when the Allies needed to maintain the momentum of their pursuit.

In mid-September a bold attempt was made to loosen the stiffening resistance by dropping three airborne divisions behind the army's right flank in Holland, to clear the way for a fresh drive by the British Second Army up to and over the Lower Rhine. By dropping the airborne forces in successive layers over a sixty-mile belt of country behind the German front a foothold was gained on all four of the strategic stepping-stones needed to cross the interval—the passage of the Wilhelmina Canal at Eindhoven, of the Maas (Meuse) at Grave, of the Waal and Lek (the two branches of the Rhine) at Nijmegen and Arnhem respectively. Three of these four stepping-stones were secured and passed. But a stumble at the third forfeited the chance of securing the fourth, in face of the Germans' speedy reaction.

This check led to the frustration of the overland thrust and the sacrifice of the 1st Airborne Division at Arnhem. But the possibility of outflanking the Rhine defence-line was a strategic prize that justified the stake and the exceptional boldness of dropping airborne forces so far behind the front. The 1st Airborne Division maintained its isolated position at Arnhem for ten days instead of the two that were reckoned as the maximum to be expected. But the chances were lessened by the way that the descent of the airborne forces at these four successive points, in a straight line, sign-posted all too clearly the direction of the Second Army's thrust.

The obviousness of the aim simplified the opponent's problem in concentrating his available reserves to hold the final stepping-stone, and to overthrow the British airborne forces there, before the leading troops of the Second Army arrived to relieve them. The nature of the Dutch country, with its 'canalized' routes, also helped the defenders in obstructing the advance, while there was a lack of wider moves to mask the directness of the approach and distract the defender.

The Fight for the Rhine

After the failure of the Arnhem gamble, the prospect of early victory faded. The Allies were thrown back on the necessity of building up their resources along the frontiers of Germany for a massive offensive of a deliberate kind. The build-up was bound to take time, but the Allied Command increased its own handicap by concentrating, first, on an attempt to force the Aachen gateway into Germany, rather than on clearing the shores of the Scheldt to open up a fresh supply route. The American advance on Aachen developed into a too direct approach, and its progress was repeatedly checked.

Along the rest of the Western Front the efforts of the Allied armies during September and October amounted to little more than a process of nibbling. Meantime the German defence was being continuously reinforced—with such reserves as could be scraped from elsewhere, and with freshly raised forces, beyond the troops which had managed to make their way back from France. The German build-up along the front was progressing faster than that of the Allies, despite Germany's great inferiority of material resources. The Scheldt Estuary was not cleared of the enemy until early in November.

In mid-November a general offensive was launched by all six Allied armies on the Western Front. It brought disappointingly small results, at heavy cost; and continued efforts merely exhausted the attacking troops.

There had been a difference of view between the American and British commanders as to the basic pattern of this offensive. The British advocated a concentrated blow, whereas the Americans chose to test the German defences over a very wide front. After the offensive had ended in failure, the British naturally criticized the plan for its dispersion of effort. But closer analysis of the operations suggests that a more fundamental fault was its obviousness. Although the offensive was wide in the sense of being distributed among several armies, it was narrowly concentrated within each army's sector. In each case the offensive effort travelled along the line where the defender would be inclined to expect it. For the attacks were directed against the natural gateways into Germany. Moreover, the main attacks were made in flat country that easily became waterlogged in winter.

In mid-December the Germans gave the Allied armies, and peoples, a shock by launching a counter-offensive. They had been able to hold the Allied offensive and slow it down to a crawl, without having to engage their own mobile reserves. Thus from the time when the chances of an American break-through waned, the risk of a serious German riposte might have become apparent—and the more so, in view of the knowledge that the Germans had withdrawn many of their panzer divisions from the line during the October lull, to re-equip them with fresh tanks. But the Allies' expectations of victory tended to blind them to the possibility of any counter-stroke, so that this profited by unexpectedness in that respect.

The best moment for a major counter-offensive, as for a minor counter-attack, is usually when the attacking opponent has fully committed his own strength without having gained his objective. At that moment, his troops will be suffering from the natural reaction due to a prolonged effort, while the Command will have relatively few reserves of its own ready to meet a counter-stroke—especially if this comes from a different direction.

The German Command also profited by treating the problem of suitable ground in a way very different from their opponents. They chose for the site of their counter-offensive the hilly and wooded country of the Ardennes. Being generally regarded as difficult country, a large-scale offensive there was likely to be unexpected by orthodox opponents. At the same time, the woods provided concealment for the massing of forces, while the high ground offered drier ground for the manœuvre of tanks. Thus the Germans might hope to score both ways.

Their chief danger was from the speedy interference of Allied air-power. Model summed up the problem thus: 'Enemy No. 1 is the hostile air force which, because of its absolute superiority, tries to destroy our spearheads of attack and our artillery through fighter-bomber attacks and bomb carpets, and to render movement in the rear impossible.' So the Germans launched their stroke when the meteorological forecast promised them a natural cloak, and for the first three days mist and rain kept the Allied air forces on the ground. Thus even bad weather was converted into an advantage.

The Germans needed all the advantage that they could possibly secure. They were playing for high stakes on very limited funds. They knew it was a desperate gamble, and that they were playing their last trump. The striking force comprised the 5th and 6th Panzer Armies, to which had been given the bulk of the tanks that could be scraped together.

An awkward feature of the Ardennes from an offensive point of view was the way that the high ground was intersected with deep valleys where the through roads became bottle-necks. At these points a tank advance was liable to be blocked. The German Command might have forestalled this risk by using parachute troops to seize these strategic defiles. But they had allowed this specialist arm to dwindle, and its technique to become rusty, since the coup that captured Crete in May 1941. Only a few handfuls were used.

The aim of the counter-offensive was far-reaching—to break through to Antwerp by an indirect approach, cut off the British army group from the American as well as from its supplies, and then crush the former while isolated. The 5th Panzer Army, now led by Manteuffel, was to break through the American front in the Ardennes, swerve westward, then wheel north across the Meuse, past Namur to Antwerp. As it advanced, it was to build up a defensive flank-barricade to shut off interference from the American armies farther south. The 6th Panzer Army, under an S.S. commander, Sepp Dietrich, was to thrust north-west on an oblique line, past Liége to Antwerp, creating a strategic barrage astride the rear of the British and the more northerly American armies.

Aided by its surprise, the German counter-offensive made menacing progress in the opening days, creating alarm and confusion on the Allied side. The deepest thrust was made by Manteuffel's 5th Panzer Army. But time and opportunities were lost through petrol shortages, resulting from Allied air-pressure, and the drive fell short of the Meuse, though it came ominously close to it at some points. In that frustration much was due to the indomitable way in which outflanked American detachments held on to several of the most important bottle-necks in the Ardennes, as well as to the speed with which Montgomery, who had taken charge of the situation on the northern flank, swung his reserves southward to forestall the enemy at the crossings of the Meuse.

In the next phase, when the Allied armies had concentrated their strength and attempted to pinch off the great wedge driven into their front, the Germans carried out a skilful withdrawal that brought them out of the potential trap. Judged on its own account, the German counter-offensive had been a profitable operation, for even though it fell short of the objectives it had upset the Allies' preparations, and inflicted much damage, at a cost that was not excessive for the effect—except in the later phase, when Hitler hindered the withdrawal.

But viewed in relation to the whole situation, this counter-offensive had been a fatal operation. During the course of it the Germans had expended more of their strength than they could afford in their straitened circumstances. That expenditure forfeited the chance of maintaining any prolonged resistance to a resumed Allied offensive. It brought home to the German troops their incapacity to turn the scales, and thereby undermined such hopes as they had retained. In brief, it was Germany's declaration of military bankruptcy. Henceforth it was impossible to disguise from the German army and people that they were reaching the end of their resources, and merely sacrificing themselves in a forlorn fight.

The Final Phase

From August until the end of the year the main Russian front had been static—astride the middle of Poland—while the Russian armies were repairing communications through the territory over which their summer tidal wave had swept, and building up their strength forward. An autumn effort to force the narrow gateway into East Prussia failed to crack the defence.

Meanwhile the Russian left-wing armies, moving on from Rumania and Bulgaria, had been gradually pushing round through Hungary and Yugo-Slavia in a vast flanking movement. This was a movement in grand strategy—with long-term objects—as well as in strategy. It was slowed down by the burden of establishing control in the countries it traversed, and by the paucity of communications through that region. But as the circuit continued it naturally developed an increasing strategic convergence on the common objective, while the extent of the German forces that were absorbed in opposing this side-door approach was an important distraction from the Germans' capacity to maintain their main Eastern and Western fronts.

In mid-January Koniev's armies launched a great offensive against the German front in southern Poland, starting from their bridgehead over the Vistula near Sandomierz. After it had pierced the enemy's defences, and produced a flanking menace to the central sector, Zhukov's armies bounded forward from their bridgeheads nearer Warsaw. During the first week the offensive swept forward nearly as far under winter conditions as the summer offensive had done in the same time.

Behind the front in western Poland most of the country was so open as to be awkward for defence—as the Germans had found in their 1939 attack. By nature it gave a mobile attacker the balance of advantage, especially when he possessed the superiority of strength to exploit the opportunity for manœuvre provided by the wide spaces. Now the Germans, themselves on the defensive, were short of strength and mobility.

During the second week the Russians' pace was maintained while the scale of prisoners increased, which showed that the Russian spearheads were outstripping a belated attempt by the German command to carry out a general withdrawal. The hasty evacuation of the civil population from various big towns inside Germany's borders was a sign that the speed and power of the Russian advance had once again upset the German command's calculations, and hustled them out of intermediate positions they had reckoned on holding.

Driving through the wide space between the cities of Cracow and Lodz, Koniev's armies swept over the western Polish frontier into Silesia. Both Cracow and Lodz fell on the 19th January, the latter to Zhukov's flanking advance. On the 23rd Koniev reached the Oder above Breslau on a forty-mile front, and then gained several crossings over this barrier-river. In this swift drive he overran the important industrial areas in Upper Silesia, thus impoverishing Germany's war-production. But the Germans then rallied strongly behind the Oder, and succeeded in curbing the extension of his bridgeheads beyond the river.

On the Russian right wing, Rokossovsky's armies sprang forward from the Narev River, north-east of Warsaw, and delivered an upper-cut against East Prussia. Piercing that frontier at its western end, they thrust past the famous battlefield of Tannenberg —scene of the great Russian disaster in 1914—and reached the Baltic east of Danzig on the 26th. Most of the German forces in East Prussia were cut off, and were then invested at Koenigsberg.

Meanwhile Zhukov, in the Russian centre, had been driving north-westward towards Torun and Poznan, a pair of pivotal communication centres. By-passing each of them, he swept on to the German frontier, leaving them isolated like islets standing out above the incoming tide. The frontier was crossed on the 29th, and Zhukov then thrust on towards the Oder, which there runs farther west than in Silesia. As his objective was obviously Berlin, which lies barely fifty miles beyond the Oder, he naturally met stiffening resistance. Although his tanks reached the Oder near Kustrin on the 31st, some time passed before he was able to push up to the river on a broad front, and then successive attempts to force a crossing were parried by the Germans.

Koniev's forces endeavoured to create a flanking leverage by pushing north-west down the far bank of the Oder, but they in turn were stopped along the Neisse, which provided a defensive switch-line for the Germans.

The law of overstretch came into play once again, and the Russians were held up in the East until the issue had been finally decided in the West.

While the Russians were battling for the Oder, Eisenhower's armies launched another great offensive early in February, aimed to trap and destroy the German armies west of the Rhine before they could withdraw across it. The opening attack was made by the First Canadian (and British) Army on the left wing, wheeling up the west bank of the Rhine to develop a flanking leverage on the German forces that faced the American Ninth and First Armies west of Cologne. But the delay caused by the enemy's Ardennes stroke had the effect that the attack was not delivered until the frozen ground had been softened by a thaw. This helped the Germans' resistance. They improved their dangerous situation by blowing up the dams on the River Roer, thus delaying the American attack over that waterline until a fortnight later. Even then it met tough opposition. As a result, the Americans did not enter Cologne until the 5th March. The Germans had gained time to evacuate their depleted forces, and much of their equipment, over the Rhine crossings.

But the Germans had been led to throw a high proportion of their strength into the effort to check the Allied left wing. The consequent weakness of their own left wing created an opportunity for the American First and Third Armies. The right of the First Army broke through to the Rhine at Bonn, and a detachment was able to seize by surprise an intact bridge over the Rhine at Remagen. Eisenhower did not immediately exploit this unexpected opening, which would have involved a switch of his reserves and a considerable readjustment of his plans for the next, and decisive, stage. But the Remagen threat served as a useful distraction to the Germans' scanty reserve.

A bigger advantage was gained by the Third Army's break-through in the Eifel (the German continuation of the Ardennes). The 4th Armoured Division—once again Patton's spearhead as in the break-out from Normandy—dashed through to the Rhine at Coblenz. Patton then wheeled his forces southward, over the Lower Moselle into the Palatinate, and swept up the west bank of the Rhine across the rear of the forces that were opposing Patch's seventh Army. By this stroke he cut them off from the Rhine, and secured a huge bag of prisoners, while gaining for himself an unopposed crossing of the Rhine when he turned eastward again. This crossing was achieved on the night of the 22nd, between Mainz and Worms, and was quickly exploited by a deep advance into northern Bavaria. That unhinged the Germans' whole front, and forestalled the much-discussed possibility that the enemy might attempt a general withdrawal into their reputed mountain stronghold in the south.

On the night of the 23rd the planned assault on the Rhine was carried out, far downstream near the Dutch frontier, by Montgomery's army group. The great river was crossed at four points during the night, and in the morning two airborne divisions were dropped beyond it, to loosen the opposition facing the newly gained bridgeheads. The Germans' resistance began to crumble everywhere, and the crumbling developed into a general collapse.

Even then the end was postponed for more than a month. That was due not to serious opposition from the splintered German army—except at a few points in the extreme north and south—but to the Allied armies' own supply problem as their advance extended beyond the Rhine, to the obstruction created by their air forces' way of blocking the roads with heaps of rubble, and to the complication of political factors.

The military issue was finally settled when the Rhine was crossed, and long before that it had become merely a question of the exact time when the overstrained German army would snap like an overstretched piece of elastic.

Although its formerly immense frontage had been contracted as it was pressed back on all sides towards the centre, its own size had shrunk even more in proportion to the area of pressure—owing to excessive losses incurred through the inelastic defence strategy on which Hitler had insisted. His crass inflexibility when on the defensive was in striking contrast to the shrewd flexibility of his offensive methods earlier, before the fumes of victory intoxicated him.

When account is taken of the shrinkage of the German forces, and of their material resources, it appears almost a miracle that their resistance lasted as long as it did, when stretched over so wide a circumference. It was partly due to an extraordinary capacity for endurance, and greatly helped by the forbidding nature of the Allies' demand for 'unconditional surrender'—which might be classified as a too direct approach in the field of grand strategy. But it was, above all, proof of the immense inherent strength of modern defence. On any orthodox military calculation the German forces were inadequate to resist for even a week the weight of attacking power which they withstood for many months. When they could hold frontages of reasonable proportion to their strength, they frequently beat off attacks delivered with a superiority of a force of over six to one, and sometimes over twelve to one. It was space that beat them.

If Germany's opponents had recognized that condition in advance, and had themselves prepared to meet aggression in a way suited to make the most of the defensive advantage, the world could have been saved immense trouble and tragedy.

Long ago, that famous pugilist, Jem Mace, summed up all his experience of the ring in the maxim: 'Let 'em come to ye, and they'll beat theirselves.' Kid McCoy later expressed the same idea in his teaching: 'Draw your man into attack—and get him so that he has both hands out of business and you have one hand free.'

The truth of Jem Mace's maxim became the outstanding tactical lesson of the battlefields in Africa, Russia, and western Europe. With growing experience all skilful commanders sought to profit by the power of the defensive, even when on the offensive.

It was also the main underlying lesson of the war as a whole. Germany went far to beat herself. Without what she did in that way her opponents would have found it much harder to beat her. Her too direct approach to the problem of victory became the indirect solution of their problem. Her frustration and distension, together, were of immense help to them in shortening the war. But if the Allied nations had understood the basic conditions of warfare, in the first place, instead of preparing to fight in a conventional way, the length and devastation of the war might have been much less.

PART IV

★

FUNDAMENTALS OF STRATEGY AND GRAND STRATEGY

CHAPTER XIX

THE THEORY OF STRATEGY

★

Having drawn our conclusions from an analysis of history it seems advantageous to construct on the fresh foundation a new dwelling-house for strategic thought.

Let us first be clear as to what is strategy. Clausewitz, in his monumental work, *On War,* defined it as 'the art of the employment of battles as a means to gain the object of war. In other words strategy forms the plan of the war, maps out the proposed course of the different campaigns which compose the war, and regulates the battles to be fought in each.'

One defect of this definition is that it intrudes on the sphere of policy, or the higher conduct of the war, which must necessarily be the responsibility of the government and not of the military leaders it employs as its agents in the executive control of operations. Another defect is that it narrows the meaning of 'strategy' to the pure utilization of battle, thus conveying the idea that battle is the only means to the strategical end. It was an easy step for Clausewitz's less profound disciples to confuse the means with the end, and to reach the conclusion that in war every other consideration should be subordinated to the aim of fighting a decisive battle.

Relation to Policy

To break down the distinction between strategy and policy would not matter much if the two functions were normally combined in the same person, as with a Frederick or a Napoleon. But as such autocratic soldier-rulers have been rare in modern times and became temporarily extinct in the nineteenth century, the effect was insidiously harmful. For it encouraged soldiers to make the preposterous claim that policy should be subservient to their conduct of operations, and, especially in democratic countries, it drew the statesman on to overstep the definite border of his sphere and interfere with his military employees in the actual use of their tools.

Moltke reached a clearer, and wiser, definition in terming strategy 'the practical adaptation of the means placed at a general's disposal to the attainment of the object in view'.

This definition fixes the responsibility of a military commander to the government by which he is employed. His responsibility is that of applying most profitably to the interest of the higher war policy the force allotted to him within the theatre of operations assigned to him. If he considers that the force allotted is inadequate for the task indicated he is justified in pointing this out, and if his opinion is overruled he can refuse or resign the command; but he exceeds his rightful sphere if he attempts to dictate to the government what measure of force should be placed at his disposal.

On the other hand, the government, which formulates war policy, and has to adapt it to conditions which often change as a war progresses, can rightly intervene in the strategy of a campaign not merely by replacing a commander in whom it has lost confidence, but by modifying his object according to the needs of its war policy. While it should not interfere with him in the handling of his tools, it should indicate clearly the nature of his task. Thus strategy has not necessarily the simple object of seeking to overthrow the enemy's military power. When a government appreciates that the enemy has the military superiority, either in general or in a particular theatre, it may wisely enjoin a strategy of limited aim.

It may desire to wait until the balance of force can be changed by the intervention of allies or by the transfer of forces from another theatre. It may desire to wait, or even to limit its military effort permanently, while economic or naval action decides the issue. It may calculate that the overthrow of the enemy's military power is a task definitely beyond its capacity, or not worth the effort—and that the object of its war policy can be assured by seizing territory which it can either retain or use as bargaining counters when peace is negotiated.

Such a policy has more support from history than military opinion hitherto has recognized, and is less inherently a policy of weakness than some apologists imply. It is, indeed, bound up with the history of the British Empire, and repeatedly proved a lifebuoy to Britain's allies as well as of permanent benefit to herself. However unconsciously followed, there is ground for inquiry whether this 'conservative' military policy does not deserve to be accorded a place in the theory of the conduct of war.

The more usual reason for adopting a strategy of limited aim is that of awaiting a change in the balance of force—a change often sought and achieved by draining the enemy's force, weakening him by pricks instead of risking blows. The essential condition of such a strategy is that the drain on him should be disproportionately greater than on oneself. The object may be sought by raiding his supplies; by local attacks which annihilate or inflict disproportionate loss on parts of his force; by luring him into unprofitable attacks; by causing an excessively wide distribution of his force; and, not least, by exhausting his moral and physical energy.

This closer definition sheds light on the question, previously raised, of a general's independence in carrying out his own strategy inside his theatre of operations. For if the government has decided upon a limited aim or 'Fabian' grand strategy the general who, even within his strategic sphere, seeks to overthrow the enemy's military power may do more harm than good to the government's war policy. Usually, a war policy of limited aim imposes a strategy of limited aim, and a decisive aim should only be adopted with the approval of the government which alone can decide whether it is 'worth the candle'.

We can now arrive at a shorter definition of strategy as—'the art of distributing and applying military means to fulfil the ends of policy'. For strategy is concerned not merely with the movement of forces—as its role is often defined—but with the effect. When the application of the military instrument merges into actual fighting, the dispositions for and control of such direct action are termed 'tactics'. The two categories, although convenient for discussion, can never be truly divided into separate compartments because each not only influences but merges into the other.

Higher, or Grand Strategy

As tactics is an application of strategy on a lower plane, so strategy is an application on a lower plane of 'grand strategy'. While practically synonymous with the policy which guides the conduct of war, as distinct from the more fundamental policy which should govern its object, the term 'grand strategy' serves to bring out the sense of 'policy in execution'. For the role of grand strategy—higher strategy—is to co-ordinate and direct all the resources of a nation, or band of nations, towards the attainment of the political object of the war—the goal defined by fundamental policy.

Grand strategy should both calculate and develop the economic resources and man-power of nations in order to sustain the fighting services. Also the moral resources—for to foster the people's willing spirit is often as important as to possess the more concrete forms of power. Grand strategy, too, should regulate the distribution of power between the several services, and between the services and industry. Moreover, fighting power is but one of the instruments of grand strategy—which should take account of and apply the power of financial pressure, of diplomatic pressure, of commercial pressure, and, not least of ethical pressure, to weaken the opponent's will. A good cause is a sword as well as armour. Likewise, chivalry in war can be a most effective weapon in weakening the opponent's will to resist, as well as augmenting moral strength.

Furthermore, while the horizon of strategy is bounded by the war, grand strategy looks beyond the war to the subsequent peace. It should not only combine the various instruments, but so regulate their use as to avoid damage to the future state of peace—for its security and prosperity. The sorry state of peace, for both sides, that has followed most wars can be traced to the fact that, unlike strategy, the realm of grand strategy is for the most part *terra incognita*—still awaiting exploration, and understanding.

Pure, or Military, Strategy

Having cleared the ground, we can build up our conception of strategy on its proper plane and original basis—that of 'the art of the general'.

Strategy depends for success, first and most, on a sound *calculation and co-ordination of the end and the means*. The end must be proportioned to the total means, and the means used in gaining each intermediate end which contributes to the ultimate must be proportioned to the value and needs of that intermediate end—whether it be to gain an objective or to fulfil a contributory purpose. An excess may be as harmful as a deficiency.

A true adjustment would establish a perfect *economy of force*, in the deeper sense of that oft-distorted military term. But, because of the nature and uncertainty of war, an uncertainty increased by lack of scientific study, even the greatest military ability could not achieve a true adjustment, and success lies in the closest approximation to truth.

This relativity is inherent because, however far our knowledge of the science of war be extended, it will depend on art for its application. Art can not only bring the end nearer to the means, but by giving a higher value to the means, enable the end to be extended.

This complicates calculation, because no man can exactly calculate the capacity of human genius and stupidity, nor the incapacity of will.

Elements and Conditions

In strategy, however, calculation is simpler and a closer approximation to truth possible than in tactics. For in war the chief incalculable is the human will, which manifests itself in resistance, which in turn lies in the province of tactics. Strategy has not to overcome resistance, except from nature. *Its purpose is to diminish the possibility of resistance*, and it seeks to fulfil this purpose by exploiting the elements of *movement* and *surprise.*

Movement lies in the physical sphere, and depends on a calculation of the conditions of time, topography, and transport capacity. (By transport capacity is meant both the means by which, and the measure in which, force can be moved and maintained.)

Surprise lies in the psychological sphere and depends on a calculation, far more difficult than in the physical sphere, of the manifold conditions, varying in each case, which are likely to affect the will of the opponent.

Although strategy may aim more at exploiting movement than at exploiting surprise, or conversely, the two elements react on each other. Movement generates surprise, and surprise gives impetus to movement. For a movement which is accelerated or changes its direction inevitably carries with it a degree of surprise, even though it be unconcealed; while surprise smoothes the path of movement by hindering the enemy's counter-measures and counter-movements.

As regards the relation of strategy to tactics, while in execution the borderline is often shadowy, and it is difficult to decide exactly where a strategical movement ends and a tactical movement begins, yet in conception the two are distinct. Tactics lies in and fills the province of fighting. Strategy not only stops on the frontier, but has for its purpose the reduction of fighting to the slenderest possible proportions.

Aim of Strategy

This statement may be disputed by those who conceive the destruction of the enemy's armed force as the only sound aim in war, who hold that the only goal of strategy is battle, and who are obsessed with the Clausewitzian saying that 'blood is the price of victory'. Yet if one should concede this point and meet its advocates on their own ground, the statement would remain unshaken. For even if a decisive battle be the goal, the aim of strategy must be to bring about this battle under the most advantageous circumstances. And the more advantageous the circumstances, the less, proportionately, will be the fighting.

The perfection of strategy would be, therefore, to produce a decision without any serious fighting. History, as we have seen, provides examples where strategy, helped by favourable conditions, has virtually produced such a result—among the examples being Caesar's Ilerda campaign, Cromwell's Preston campaign, Napoleon's Ulm campaign, Moltke's encirclement of MacMahon's army at Sedan in 1870, and Allenby's 1918 encirclement of the Turks in the hills of Samaria. The most striking and catastrophic of recent examples was the way that, in 1940, the Germans cut off and trapped the Allies' left wing in Belgium, following Guderian's surprise break-through in the centre at Sedan, and thereby ensured the general collapse of the Allied armies on the Continent.

While these were cases where the destruction of the enemy's armed forces was economically achieved through their disarming by surrender, such 'destruction' may not be essential for a decision, and for the fulfilment of the war-aim. In the case of a state that is seeking, not conquest, but the maintenance of its security, the aim is fulfilled if the threat be removed—if the enemy is led to abandon his purpose.

The defeat which Belisarius incurred at Sura through giving rein to his troops' desire for a 'decisive victory'—after the Persians had already given up their attempted invasion of Syria—was a clear example of unnecessary effort and risk. By contrast, the way that he defeated their more dangerous later invasion and cleared them out of Syria, is perhaps the most striking example on record of achieving a decision—in the real sense, of fulfilling the national object—by pure strategy. For in this case, the psychological action was so effective that the enemy surrendered his purpose without any physical action at all being required.

While such bloodless victories have been exceptional, their rarity enhances rather than detracts from their value—as an indication of latent potentialities, in strategy and grand strategy. Despite many centuries' experience of war, we have hardly begun to explore the field of psychological warfare.

From deep study of war, Clausewitz was led to the conclusion that—'All military action is permeated by intelligent forces and their effects.' Nevertheless, nations at war have always striven, or been driven by their passions, to disregard the implications of such a conclusion. Instead of applying intelligence, they have chosen to batter their heads against the nearest wall.

It rests normally with the government, responsible for the grand strategy of a war, to decide whether strategy should make its contribution by achieving a military decision or otherwise. Just as the military means is only one of the means to the end of grand strategy—one of the instruments in the surgeon's case—so battle is only one of the means to the end of strategy. If the conditions are suitable, it is usually the quickest in effect, but if the conditions are unfavourable it is folly to use it.

Let us assume that a strategist is empowered to seek a military decision. His responsibility is to seek it under the most advantageous circumstances in order to produce the most profitable result. Hence *his true aim is not so much to seek battle as to seek a strategic situation so advantageous that if it does not of itself produce the decision, its continuation by a battle is sure to achieve this*. In other words, dislocation is the aim of strategy; its sequel may be either the enemy's dissolution or his easier disruption in battle. Dissolution may involve some partial measure of fighting, but this has not the character of a battle.

Action of Strategy

How is the strategic dislocation produced? In the physical, or 'logistical', sphere it is the result of a move which (*a*) upsets the enemy's dispositions and, by compelling a sudden 'change of front', dislocates the distribution and organization of his forces; (*b*) separates his forces; (*c*) endangers his supplies; (*d*) menaces the route or routes by which he could retreat in case of need and re-establish himself in his base or homeland.

A dislocation may be produced by one of these effects, but is more often the consequence of several. Differentiation, indeed, is difficult because a move directed towards the enemy's rear tends to combine these effects. Their respective influence, however, varies and has varied throughout history according to the size of armies and the complexity of their organization. With armies which 'live on the country', drawing their supplies locally by plunder or requisition, the line of communication has negligible importance. Even in a higher stage of military development, the smaller a force the less dependent it is on the line of communication for supplies. The larger an army, and the more complex its organization, the more prompt and serious in effect is a menace to its line of communication.

Where armies have not been so dependent, strategy has been correspondingly handicapped, and the tactical issue of battle has played a greater part. Nevertheless, even thus handicapped, able strategists have frequently gained a decisive advantage previous to battle by menacing the enemy's line of retreat, the equilibrium of his dispositions, or his local supplies.

To be effective, such a menace must usually be applied at a point closer, in time and space, to the enemy's army than a menace to his communications; and thus in early warfare it is often difficult to distinguish between the strategical and tactical manœuvre.

In the psychological sphere, dislocation is the result of the impression on the commander's mind of the physical effects which we have listed. The impression is strongly accentuated if his realization of his being at a disadvantage is *sudden*, and if he feels that he is unable to counter the enemy's move. *Psychological dislocation fundamentally springs from this sense of being trapped.*

This is the reason why it has most frequently followed a physical move on to the enemy's rear. An army, like a man, cannot properly defend its back from a blow without turning round to use its arms in the new direction. 'Turning' temporarily unbalances an army as it does a man, and with the former the period of instability is inevitably much longer. In consequence, the brain is much more sensitive to any menace to its back.

In contrast, to move directly on an opponent consolidates his balance, physical and psychological, and by consolidating it increases his resisting power. For in the case of an army it rolls the enemy back towards their reserves, supplies, and reinforcements, so that as the original front is driven back and worn thin, new layers are added to the back. At the most, it imposes a strain rather than producing a shock.

Thus a move round the enemy's front against his rear has the aim not only of avoiding resistance on its way but in its issue. In the profoundest sense, it takes the *line of least resistance*. The equivalent in the psychological sphere is the *line of least expectation*. They are the two faces of the same coin, and to appreciate this is to widen our understanding of strategy. For if we merely take what obviously appears the line of least resistance, its obviousness will appeal to the opponent also; and this line may no longer be that of least resistance.

In studying the physical aspect we must never lose sight of the psychological, and only when both are combined is the strategy truly an indirect approach, calculated to dislocate the opponent's balance.

The mere action of marching indirectly towards the enemy and on to the rear of his dispositions does not constitute a strategic indirect approach. Strategic art is not so simple. Such an approach may start by being indirect in relation to the enemy's front, but by the very directness of its progress towards his rear may allow him to change his dispositions, so that it soon becomes a direct approach to his new front.

Because of the risk that the enemy may achieve such a change of front, it is usually necessary for the dislocating move to be preceded by a move, or moves, which can best be defined by the term 'distract' in its literal sense of 'to draw asunder'. The purpose of this 'distraction' is to *deprive the enemy of his freedom of action*, and it should operate in both the physical and psychological spheres. In the physical, it should cause a distension of his forces or their diversion to unprofitable ends, so that they are too widely distributed, and too committed elsewhere, to have the power of interfering with one's own decisively intended move. In the psychological sphere, the same effect is sought by playing upon the fears of, and by deceiving, the opposing command. 'Stonewall' Jackson aptly expressed this in his strategical motto—'Mystify, mislead, and surprise'. For to mystify and to mislead constitutes 'distraction', while surprise is the essential cause of 'dislocation'. It is through the 'distraction' of the commander's mind that the distraction of his forces follows. The loss of his freedom of action is the sequel to the loss of his freedom of conception.

A more profound appreciation of how the psychological permeates and dominates the physical sphere has an indirect value. For it warns us of the fallacy and shallowness of attempting to analyse and theorize about strategy in terms of mathematics. To treat it quantitatively, as if the issue turned merely on a superior concentration of force at a selected place, is as faulty as to treat it geometrically: as a matter of lines and angles.

Even more remote from truth—because in practice it usually leads to a dead end—is the tendency of text-books to treat war as mainly a matter of concentrating superior force. In his celebrated definition of economy of force Foch termed this—'The art of pouring out *all* one's resources at a given moment on one spot; of making use there of *all* troops, and, to make such a thing possible, of making those troops permanently communicate with each other, instead of dividing them and attaching to each fraction some fixed and invariable function; its second part, a result having been attained, is the art of again so disposing the troops as to converge upon, and act against, a new single objective.'

It would have been more exact, and more lucid, to say that an army should always be so distributed that its parts can aid each other and combine to produce the maximum *possible* concentration of force at one place, while the minimum force *necessary* is used elsewhere to prepare the success of the concentration.

To concentrate *all* is an unrealizable ideal, and dangerous even as a hyperbole. Moreover, in practice the 'minimum necessary' may form a far larger proportion of the total than the 'maximum possible'. It would even be true to say that the larger the force that is effectively used for *distraction* of the enemy, the greater is the chance of the concentration succeeding in its aim. For otherwise it may strike an object too solid to be shattered.

Superior weight at the intended decisive point does not suffice unless that point cannot be reinforced *in time* by the opponent. It rarely suffices unless that point is not merely weaker numerically but has been weakened morally. Napoleon suffered some of his worst checks because he neglected this guarantee—and the need for distraction has grown with the delaying power of weapons.

Basis of Strategy

A deeper truth to which Foch and other disciples of Clausewitz did not penetrate fully is that in war every problem, and every principle, is a duality. Like a coin, it has two faces. Hence the need for a well-calculated compromise as a means to reconciliation. This is the inevitable consequence of the fact that war is a two-party affair, so imposing the need that while hitting one must guard. Its corollary is that, in order to hit with effect, the enemy must be taken off his guard. Effective concentration can only be obtained when the opposing forces are dispersed; and, usually, in order to ensure this, one's own forces must be widely distributed. Thus, by an outward paradox, true concentration is the product of dispersion.

A further consequence of the two-party condition is that to ensure reaching an objective one should have *alternative objectives.* Herein lies a vital contrast to the single-minded nineteenth century doctrine of Foch and his fellows—a contrast of the practical to the theoretical. For if the enemy is certain as to your point of aim he has the best possible chance of guarding himself—and blunting your weapon. If, on the other hand, you take a line that threatens alternative objectives, you distract his mind and forces. This, moreover, is the most economic method of *distraction*, for it allows you to keep the largest proportion of your force available on your real line of operation—thus reconciling the greatest possible concentration with the necessity of dispersion.

The absence of an alternative is contrary to the very nature of war. It sins against the light which Bourcet shed in the eighteenth century by his most penetrating dictum that 'every plan of campaign ought to have several branches and to have been so well thought out that one or other of the said branches cannot fail of success'. This was the light that his military heir, the young Napoleon Bonaparte, followed in seeking always, as he said, to '*faire son thème en deux façons*'. Seventy years later Sherman was to re-learn the lesson from experience, by reflection, and to coin his famous maxim about 'putting the enemy on the horns of a dilemma'. In any problem where an opposing force exists, and cannot be regulated, one must foresee and provide for alternative courses. Adaptability is the law which governs survival in war as in life—war being but a concentrated form of the human struggle against environment.

To be practical, any plan must take account of the enemy's

power to frustrate it; the best chance of overcoming such obstruction is to have a plan that can be easily varied to fit the circumstances met; to keep such adaptability, while still keeping the initiative, the best way is to operate along a line which offers alternative objectives. For thereby you put your opponent on the horns of a dilemma, which goes far to assure the gaining of at least one objective—whichever is least guarded—and may enable you to gain one after the other.

In the tactical field, where the enemy's dispositions are likely to be based on the nature of the ground, it may be more difficult to find a choice of dilemma-producing objectives than it is in the strategical field, where the enemy will have obvious industrial and railway centres to cover. But you can gain a similar advantage by adapting your line of effort to the degree of resistance that is met, and exploiting any weakness that is found. A plan, like a tree, must have branches—if it is to bear fruit. A plan with a single aim is apt to prove a barren pole.

Cutting Communications

In the planning of any stroke at the enemy's communications, either by manœuvre round his flank or by rapid penetration of a breach in his front, the question will arise as to the most effective point of aim—whether it should be directed against the immediate rear of the opposing force, or further back.

When studying this question at the time that experimental mechanized forces were first created, and their strategic use was under consideration, I sought guidance on it by an analysis of cavalry raids carried out in the past, especially in the more recent wars since railways came into use. While such cavalry raids had more limited potentialities than a deep strategic penetration of mechanized forces seemed to me to promise, this difference emphasized rather than detracted from the significance of the evidence which they provided. Making the necessary adjustment, the following deductions could be drawn:

> In general, the nearer to the force that the cut is made, the *more immediate* the effect; the nearer to the base, the *greater* the effect. In either case, the effect becomes much greater and more quickly felt if made against a force that is in motion, and in course of carrying out an operation, than against a force that is stationary.

In deciding the direction of a mobile stroke, much depends on the strategic position and supply conditions of the enemy forces, i.e. the number of their lines of supply, the possibility of adopting alternative lines of supply, the amount of supplies likely to be accumulated in advanced depots close behind their front. After these factors have been considered, they should be reconsidered in the light of the *accessibility* of the various possible objectives, i.e. the distance, the natural obstacles, and the opposition likely to be met. In general, the longer the distance that has to be covered, the greater the ratio of natural obstacles, but the less the ratio of opposition.

Thus, unless the natural obstacles are very severe, or the enemy has unusual independence of supplies from base, more success and more effect is to be expected from cutting his communications as far back as possible.

A further consideration is that while a stroke close in rear of the enemy force may have more effect on the minds of the enemy troops, a stroke far back tends to have more effect on the mind of the enemy commander.

Cavalry raids in the past had often forfeited their effect by lack of care in carrying out the demolition side of their task. As a result the propective value of mobile raids on communications had been unduly discounted. It should be realized, too, that the flow of supplies may be interrupted not only by demolitions on the route, but by actual or threatened interception of trains and lorry convoys. This form of interruption was increased in potentiality by the development of mechanized forces—because of their flexibility and power of cross-country manœuvre.

These deductions were confirmed by the experience of the Second World War—above all by the catastrophically paralysing effect, physically and psychologically, that was produced when Guderian's panzer forces, racing far ahead of the main German armies, severed the Allied armies' communications where these crossed the far back line of the Somme, at Amiens and Abbeville.

The Method of Advance

Until the end of the eighteenth century, a physically concentrated advance, both strategic (*to* the battlefield) and tactical (*on* the battlefield) was the rule. Then Napoleon, exploiting Bourcet's ideas and the new divisional system, introduced a *distributed* strategic advance—the army moving in independent fractions. But the tactical advance was still, in general, a concentrated one.

Towards the end of the nineteenth century, with the development of fire weapons, the tactical advance became dispersed, i.e. in particles, to diminish the effect of fire. But the strategic advance had again become concentrated—this was due partly to the influence of railways and the growth of masses, partly to the misunderstanding of the Napoleonic method.

A revival of the distributed strategic advance was required in order to revive the art and effect of strategy. Moreover, new conditions—air power and motor power—point to its further development into a *dispersed strategic advance*. The danger of air attack, the aim of mystification, and the need of drawing full value from mechanized mobility, suggest that advancing forces should not only be distributed as widely as is compatible with combined action, but be dispersed as much as is compatible with cohesion. This becomes essential in face of atomic weapons. The development of radio is a timely aid towards reconciling dispersion with control.

Instead of the simple idea of a concentrated stroke by a concentrated force, we should choose according to circumstance between these variants:

(i) Dispersed advance with concentrated single aim, i.e. against one objective.

(ii) Dispersed advance with concentrated serial aim, i.e. against successive objectives.

(These will each demand preliminary moves to distract the enemy's attention and forces, unless the possibility of taking alternative objectives enables us to rely on such distracting effect being produced already by the enemy's perplexity.)

(iii) Dispersed advance with distributed aim, i.e. against a number of objectives simultaneously.

(Under the new conditions of warfare, the *cumulative* effect of partial success, or even mere threat, at a number of points may be greater than the effect of complete success at one point.)

The effectiveness of armies depends on the development of such new methods—methods which aim at permeating and dominating areas rather than capturing lines; at the practicable object of paralysing the enemy's action rather than the theoretical object of crushing his forces. Fluidity of force may succeed where concentration of force merely entails a perilous rigidity.

CHAPTER XX

THE CONCENTRATED ESSENCE OF STRATEGY AND TACTICS

★

This brief chapter is an attempt to epitomize, from the history of war, a few truths of experience which seem so universal, and so fundamental, as to be termed axioms.

They are practical guides, not abstract principles. Napoleon realized that only the practical is useful when he gave us his maxims. But the modern tendency has been to search for principles which can each be expressed in a single word—and then need several thousand words to explain them. Even so, these 'principles' are so abstract that they mean different things to different men, and, for any value, depend on the individual's own understanding of war. The longer one continues the search for such omnipotent abstractions, the more do they appear a mirage, neither attainable nor useful—except as an intellectual exercise.

The principles of war, not merely one principle, can be condensed into a single word—'concentration'. But for truth this needs to be amplified as the 'concentration of strength against weakness'. And for any real value it needs to be explained that the concentration of strength against weakness depends on the dispersion of your opponent's strength, which in turn is produced by a distribution of your own that gives the appearance, and partial effect of dispersion. Your dispersion, his dispersion, your concentration—such is the sequence, and each is a sequel. True concentration is the fruit of calculated dispersion.

Here we have a fundamental principle whose understanding may prevent a fundamental error (and the most common)—that of giving your opponent freedom and time to concentrate to meet your concentration. But to state the principle is not of much practical aid for execution.

The above-mentioned axioms (here expressed as maxims) cannot be condensed into a single word; but they can be put into the fewest words necessary to be practical. Eight in all, so far—six are positive and two negative. They apply to tactics as well as strategy, unless otherwise indicated.

Positive

1. *Adjust your end to your means.* In determining your object, clear sight and cool calculation should prevail. It is folly 'to bite off more than you can chew', and the beginning of military wisdom is a sense of what is possible. So learn to face facts while still preserving faith: there will be ample need for faith—the faith that can achieve the apparently impossible—when action begins. Confidence is like the current in a battery: avoid exhausting it in vain effort—and remember that your own continued confidence will be of no avail if the cells of your battery, the men upon whom you depend, have been run down.

2. *Keep your object always in mind,* while adapting your plan to circumstances. Realize that there are more ways than one of gaining an object, but take heed that every objective should bear on the object. And in considering possible objectives weigh their possibility of attainment with their service to the object if attained—to wander down a side-track is bad, but to reach a dead end is worse.

3. *Choose the line (or course) of least expectation.* Try to put yourself in the enemy's shoes, and think what course it is least probable he will foresee or forestall.

4. *Exploit the line of least resistance*—so long as it can lead you to any objective which would contribute to your underlying object. (In tactics this maxim applies to the use of your reserves; and in strategy, to the exploitation of any tactical success.)

5. *Take a line of operation which offers alternative objectives.* For you will thus put your opponent on the horns of a dilemma, which goes far to assure the chance of gaining one objective at least—whichever he guards least—and may enable you to gain one after the other.

Alternative objectives allow you to keep the opportunity of gaining *an* objective; whereas a single objective, unless the enemy is helplessly inferior, means the certainty that you will not gain it—once the enemy is no longer uncertain as to your aim. There is no more common mistake than to confuse a single line of operation, which is usually wise, with a single objective, which is usually futile. (If this maxim applies mainly to strategy, it should be applied where possible to tactics, and does, in effect, form the basis of infiltration tactics.)

6. *Ensure that both plan and dispositions are flexible—adaptable to circimstances.* Your plan should foresee and provide for a next step in case of success or failure, or partial success—which is the most common case in war. Your dispositions (or formation) should be such as to allow this exploitation or adaptation in the shortest possible time.

Negative

7. *Do not throw your weight into a stroke whilst your opponent is on guard*—whilst he is well placed to parry or evade it. The experience of history shows that, save against a much inferior opponent, no effective stroke is possible until his power of resistance or evasion is paralysed. Hence no commander should launch a real attack upon an enemy in position until satisfied that such paralysis has developed. It is produced by *disorganization*, and its moral equivalent, *demoralization*, of the enemy.

8. *Do not renew an attack along the same line (or in the same form) after it has once failed.* A mere reinforcement of weight is not sufficient change, for it is probable that the enemy also will have strengthened himself in the interval. It is even more probable that his success in repulsing you will have strengthened him morally.

The essential truth underlying these maxims is that, for success, two major problems must be solved—*dislocation* and *exploitation*. One precedes and one follows the actual blow—which in comparison is a simple act. You cannot hit the enemy with effect unless you have first created the opportunity; you cannot make that effect decisive unless you exploit the second opportunity that comes before he can recover.

The importance of these two problems has never been adequately recognized—a fact which goes far to explain the common indecisiveness of warfare. The training of armies is primarily devoted to developing efficiency in the detailed execution of the *attack*. This concentration on tactical technique tends to obscure the psychological element. It fosters a cult of soundness, rather than of surprise. It breeds commanders who are so intent not to do anything wrong, according to 'the book', that they forget the necessity of making the enemy do something wrong. The result is that their plans have no result. For, in war, it is by compelling mistakes that the scales are most often turned.

Here and there a commander has eschewed the obvious, and has found in the unexpected the key to a decision—unless fortune has proved foul. For luck can never be divorced from war, since war is part of life. Hence the unexpected cannot guarantee success. But it guarantees the best chance of success.

CHAPTER XXI

NATIONAL OBJECT AND MILITARY AIM

★

In discussing the subject of 'the objective' in war it is essential to be clear about, and to keep clear in our minds, the distinction between the political and the military objective. The two are different but not separate. For nations do not wage war for war's sake, but in pursuance of policy. The military objective is only the means to a political end. Hence the military objective should be governed by the political objective, subject to the basic condition that policy does not demand what is militarily—that, is practically—impossible.

Thus any study of the problem ought to begin and end with the question of policy.

The term 'objective', although common usage, is not really a good one. It has a physical and geographical sense—and thus tends to confuse thought. It would be better to speak of '*the object*' when dealing with the purpose of policy, and of '*the military aim*' when dealing with the way that forces are directed in the service of policy.

The object in war is a better state of peace—even if only from your own point of view. Hence it is essential to conduct war with constant regard to the peace you desire. That applies both to aggressor nations who seek expansion and to peaceful nations who only fight for self-preservation—although their views of what is meant by a better state of peace are very different.

History shows that gaining military victory is not in itself equivalent to gaining the object of policy. But as most of the thinking about war has been done by men of the military profession there has been a very natural tendency to lose sight of the basic national object, and identify it with the military aim. In consequence, whenever war has broken out, policy has too often been governed by the military aim—and this has been regarded as an end in itself, instead of as merely a means to the end.

The ill effects have gone further. For by losing sight of the proper relationship between the object and the military aim—between policy and strategy—the military aim became distorted, and over-simplified.

For a true understanding of the problem, essentially complex, it is necessary to know the background of military thought on this subject during the past two centuries, and to realize how conceptions have evolved.

For more than a century the prime canon of military doctrine has been that 'the destruction of the enemy's main forces on the battlefield' constituted the only true aim in war. That was universally accepted, engraved in all military manuals, and taught in all staff colleges. If any statesman ventured to doubt whether it fitted the national object in all circumstances, he was regarded as blasphemously violating holy writ—as can be seen in studying the official records and the memoirs of the military heads of the warring nations, particularly in and after World War I.

So absolute a rule would have astonished the great commanders and teachers of war-theory in ages prior to the nineteenth century. For they had recognized the practical necessity and wisdom of adapting aims to limitations of strength and policy.

Clausewitz's Influence

The rule acquired its dogmatic rigidity largely through the posthumous influence of Clausewitz and his books upon the minds of Prussian soldiers, particularly Moltke—and thence more widely through the impact that their victories in 1866 and 1870 made upon the armies of the world, which copied so many features of the Prussian system. Thus it is of vital importance to examine his theories.

As so often happens, Clausewitz's disciples carried his teaching to an extreme which their master had not intended.

Misinterpretation has been the common fate of most prophets and thinkers in every sphere. Devout but uncomprehending disciples have been more damaging to the original conception than even its prejudiced and purblind opponents. It must be admitted, however, that Clausewitz invited misinterpretation more than most. A student of Kant at second-hand, he had acquired a philosophical mode of expression without developing a truly philosophical mind. His theory of war was expounded in a way too abstract and involved for ordinary soldier-minds, essentially concrete, to follow the course of his argument—which often turned back from the direction in which it was apparently leading. Impressed yet befogged, they gasped at his vivid leading phrases, seeing only their surface meaning, and missing the deeper current of his thought.

Clausewitz's greatest contribution to the theory of war was in emphasizing the psychological factors. Raising his voice against the geometrical school of strategy, then fashionable, he showed that the human spirit was infinitely more important than operational lines and angles. He discussed the effect of danger and fatigue, the value of boldness and determination, with deep understanding.

It was his errors, however, which had the greater effect on the subsequent course of history.

He was too continental in outlook to understand the meaning of sea-power. And his vision was short—on the very threshold of the mechanical era he declared his 'conviction that superiority in numbers becomes every day more decisive'. Such a 'commandment' gave reinforcement to the instinctive conservatism of soldiers in resisting the possibilities of the new form of superiority which mechanical invention increasingly offered. It also gave a powerful impulse to the universal extension and permanent establishment of the method of conscription—as a simple way of providing the greatest possible numbers. This, by its disregard for psychological suitability, meant that armies became much more liable to panic, and sudden collapse. The earlier method, however unsystematic, had at least tended to ensure that the forces were composed of good 'fighting animals'.

Clausewitz contributed no new or strikingly progressive ideas to tactics or strategy. He was a *codifying* thinker, rather than a *creative* or *dynamic* one. He had no such revolutionary effect on warfare as the theory of the 'divisional system' produced in the eighteenth century or the theory of armoured mobility in the twentieth.

But in seeking to formulate the experience of the Napoleonic wars, the emphasis he put on certain retrograde features helped to cause what might be termed a '*revolution in reverse*'—back towards *tribal* warfare.

Clausewitz's Theory of the Military Aim

In defining the military aim, Clausewitz was carried away by his passion for pure logic:

'The aim of all action in war is to disarm the enemy, and we shall now show that this, in *theory at least*, is indispensable. If our opponent is to be made to comply with our will, we must place him in a situation which is more oppressive to him than the sacrifice we demand; but the disadvantages of this position must naturally not be of a transitory nature, at least in appearance, otherwise the enemy, instead of yielding, will hold out in the hope of a change for the better. Every change in this position which is produced by a continuation of the war must, therefore, be a change for the worse.

'The worst condition in which a belligerent can be placed is that of being completely disarmed. If, therefore, the enemy is to be reduced to submission . . . he must either be positively disarmed or placed in such a position that he is threatened with it. From this it follows that the complete disarming or overthrow of the enemy . . . must always be the aim of warfare.'

The influence of Kant can be perceived in Clausewitz's dualism of thought—he believed in a perfect (military) world of ideals while recognizing a temporal world in which these could only be imperfectly fulfilled. For he was capable of distinguishing between what was militarily ideal and what he described as 'a modification in the reality'. Thus he wrote:

'Reasoning in the abstract, the mind cannot stop short of an extreme. . . . But everything takes a different shape when we pass from abstractions to reality.' 'This object of war in the abstract . . . the disarming of the enemy, is rarely attained in practice and is not a condition necessary to peace.'

Clausewitz's tendency to the extreme is shown, again, in his discussion of battle as a means to the end of war. He opened with the startling assertion—'There is only one single means, it is the fight.' He justified this by a long argument, to show that in every form of military activity 'the idea of fighting must necessarily be at the foundation'. Having elaborately proved what most people would be ready to accept without argument, Clausewitz said 'the object of a combat is not always the destruction of the enemy's forces . . . its object can often be attained as well without the combat taking place at all'.

Moreover, Clausewitz recognized that 'the waste of our own military forces must, *ceteris paribus*, always be greater the more our aim is directed upon the destruction of the enemy's power. The danger lies in this—that the greater efficacy which we seek recoils on ourselves, and therefore has worse consequences in case we fail of success.'

Out of his own mouth, Clausewitz here gave a prophetic verdict upon the consequences of following his own gospel in World Wars I and II. For it was the ideal, and not the practical, aspect of his teaching on battle which survived. He contributed to the distortion by arguing that it was only to avoid the risks of battle that 'any other means are taken'. And he fixed the distortion in the minds of his pupils by hammering on the abstract ideal.

Not one reader in a hundred was likely to follow the subtlety of his logic or to preserve a true balance amid such philosophical jugglery. But every one could catch such ringing phrases as:

'We have only one means in war—the battle.'

'The bloody solution of the crisis, the effort for the destruction of the enemy's forces, is the first-born son of war.'

'Only great and general battles can produce great results.'

'Let us not hear of generals who conquer without bloodshed.'

By the reiteration of such phrases Clausewitz blurred the outlines of his philosophy, already indistinct, and made it into a mere marching refrain—a Prussian *Marseillaise* which inflamed the blood and intoxicated the mind. In transfusion it became a doctrine fit to form corporals, not generals. For by making battle appear the only 'real warlike activity', his gospel deprived strategy of its laurels, and reduced the art of war to the mechanics of mass-slaughter. Moreover, it incited generals to seek battle at the *first* opportunity, instead of creating an *advantageous* opportunity.

Clausewitz contributed to the subsequent decay of generalship when in an oft-quoted passage he wrote:

'Philanthropists may easily imagine that there is a skilful method of disarming and overcoming the enemy without great bloodshed, and that this is the proper tendency of the Art of War. . . . That is an error which must be extirpated.'

It is obvious that when he wrote this he did not pause to reflect that what he decried had been regarded as the proper aim of generalship by all the masters of the art of war—including Napoleon himself.

Clausewitz's phrase would henceforth be used by countless blunderers to excuse, and even to justify, their futile squandering of life in bull-headed assaults.

The danger was increased because of the way he constantly dwelt on the decisive importance of a *numerical* superiority. With deeper penetration, he pointed out in one passage that *surprise* lies 'at the foundation of all undertakings, for without it the preponderance at the decisive point is not properly conceivable'. But his disciples, struck by his more frequent emphasis on 'numbers', came to regard mere mass as the simple recipe for victory.

Clausewitz's Theory of the Object

Even worse was the effect of his theoretical exposition, and exaltation, of the idea of 'absolute' warfare—in proclaiming that the road to success was through the unlimited application of force. Thereby a doctrine which began by defining war as only 'a continuation of state policy by other means' led to the contradictory end of making policy the slave of strategy—and bad strategy at that.

The trend was fostered, above all, by his dictum that—'To introduce into the philosophy of war a principle of moderation would be an absurdity. War is an act of violence pushed to its utmost bounds.'

That declaration has served as a foundation for the extravagant absurdity of modern total warfare. His principle of force without limit and without calculation of cost fits, and is only fit for, a hate-maddened mob. It is the negation of statesmanship and of intelligent strategy—which seeks to serve the ends of policy.

If war be a continuation of policy, as Clausewitz had elsewhere declared, it must necessarily be conducted with a view to post-war benefit. A state which expends its strength to the point of exhaustion bankrupts its own policy.

Clausewitz himself had qualified his principle of 'utmost force' by the admission that 'the political object, as the original motive of the war, should be the standard for determining both the aim of the military force and also the amount of effort to be made'.

Still more significant was a reflective passage in which he remarked that to pursue the logical extreme entailed that 'the means would lose all relation to the end, and in most cases the aim at an extreme effort would be wrecked by the opposing weight of forces within itself'.

His classic work *On War* was the product of twelve years' intensive thought; if its author had lived to spend a longer time in thinking about war, he might have reached wiser and clearer conclusions. As his thinking progressed, he was being led towards a different view—penetrating deeper. Unhappily, the process was cut short by his death from cholera in 1830. It was only after his death that his writings on war were published, by his widow. They were found in a number of sealed packets, bearing the significant and prophetic note:

'Should the work be interrupted by my death, then what is found can only be called a mass of conceptions not brought into form . . . open to endless misconceptions.'

Much of the harm might have been avoided but for that fatal cholera germ. For there are significant indications that in the gradual evolution of his thought he had reached a point where he was about to drop his original concept of 'absolute 'war, and revise his whole theory on more common-sense lines—when death intervened.

In consequence, the way was left open to 'endless misconceptions' far in excess of his anticipation—for the universal adoption of the theory of unlimited war has gone far to wreck civilization. The teachings of Clausewitz, taken without understanding, largely influenced both the causation and the character of World War I. Thereby it led on, all too logically, to World War II.

Theory in Flux—After World War I

The course and effects of the First World War provided ample cause to doubt the validity of Clausewitz's theory, at least as interpreted by his successors. On land, innumerable battles were fought without ever producing the decisive results expected of them. But the responsible leaders were slow to adapt their aim to circumstances or develop new means to make the aim more possible. Instead of facing the problem, they pressed theory to a suicidal extreme, draining their own strength beyond the safety limit, in pursuit of an ideal of complete victory by battle which was never fulfilled.

That one side ultimately collapsed was due more to emptiness of stomach, produced by the economic pressure of sea-power, than to loss of blood—although the blood which was lost in the abortive German offensives of 1918, and the loss of spirit in consequence of their palpable failure to gain the victory, hastened the collapse. If this provided the opposing nations with the *semblance* of victory, their efforts to *win* it cost them such a price, in moral and physical exhaustion, that they, the seeming victors, were left incapable of consolidating their position.

It became evident there was something wrong with the theory, or at least with its application—alike on the planes of tactics, strategy, and policy. The appalling losses suffered in vain pursuit of the 'ideal' objective, and the post-war exhaustion of the nominal victors, showed that a thorough re-examination of the whole problem of the object and aim was needed.

Besides these negative factors there were also several positive reasons to prompt a fresh inquiry. One was the decisive part that sea-power had played, without any decisive battle at sea, in producing the enemy's collapse by economic pressure. That raised the question whether Britain in particular had not made a basic mistake in departing from her traditional strategy and devoting so much of her effort, at such terrific cost to herself, to the prolonged attempt to win a decisive victory on land.

Two other reasons arose from new factors. The development of air forces offered the possibility of striking at the enemy's economic and moral centres without having first to achieve 'the destruction of the enemy's main forces on the battlefield'. Air-power might attain a direct end by indirect means—hopping over opposition instead of overthrowing it.

At the same time, the combined development of the petrol motor and the caterpillar track opened up a prospect of developing mechanized land forces of high mobility. This, in turn, foreshadowed a newly enlarged possibility of producing the collapse of 'the enemy's main forces' without a serious battle—by cutting their supply lines, dislocating their control-system, or producing paralysis by the sheer nerve-shock of deep penetration into their rear. Mechanized land forces of this new kind might also provide—like air-power, though in a lesser degree—the possibility of striking direct at the heart and nerve-system of the opposing country.

While air-mobility could achieve such direct strokes by an overhead form of indirect approach, tank-mobility might achieve them by indirect approach on the ground avoiding the 'obstacle' of the opposing army. To illustrate the point by a board-game analogy, with chess—air-mobility introduced a knight's move, and tank-mobility a queen's move, into warfare. This analogy does not, of course, express their respective values. For an air force combined the vaulting power of the knight's move with the all-ways flexibility of the queen's move. On the other hand, a mechanized ground force, though it lacked vaulting power, could remain in occupation of the 'square' it gained.

These new air and land developments were bound to have a profound influence on the *military aim*, and choice of *objectives* in future war.

They increased the capacity of applying military action against civil objectives, economic and moral, while making it more powerful in effect. They also increased the 'range' of military action against military objectives, making it easier to overthrow an opposing 'body'—such as an army—by paralysing some of its vital organs instead of having to destroy it physically and as a whole by hard fighting. To nullify opposition by paralysing the power to oppose is far better economy of force than actual destruction of opposition, which is always a more prolonged process and more costly to the victor. Air-power promised new scope for producing such paralysis of armed opposition—besides its capacity to evade opposition and strike at civil objectives in the enemy country.

The sum effect of the advent of this multiplied mobility, both on the ground and in the air, was to increase the power and importance of strategy relatively to tactics. The higher commanders of the future would have the prospect of achieving decisive results much more by movement than by fighting compared with their predecessors.

While the value of winning a decisive battle would not disappear, and the chances of doing so would actually be increased by the new powers of mobility, even such a battle would have less of the traditional battle form. It would become more like the natural completion of a strategic manœuvre. 'Battle' is really a misnomer for such a *consecutive* operation.

Unfortunately, those who were at the head of the armies after the World War I were slow to recognize the need of a fresh definition of the military aim in the light of changed conditions and war instruments.

Unfortunately, also, those who were at the head of the air forces were too exclusively concerned to assert their independence, and thus concentrated too narrowly on exploiting the possibilities of striking at civil objectives—without regard either to its limitations or to its detrimental results. Filled with a natural enthusiasm for the new service to which they belonged, they were excessively confident that it could produce either the speedy moral collapse of the opposing people or the economic stranglehold of sea-power in an intensified form and with much more quickly decisive effect.

Practice in World War II

When the next war came, the handful of new land forces of a mechanized kind that had been created amply fulfilled the claims that had been made for them, and for their decisive effect if employed for long-range strokes at strategic objectives.

A mere six divisions of this kind were largely instrumental in producing the collapse of Poland within a few weeks. A mere ten such divisions virtually decided the so-called 'Battle of France' before the infantry mass of the German army had even come into action—and made the collapse of all the Western countries an almost inevitable sequel. This conquest of the West was completed in barely a month's campaign, with amazingly small cost to the victor. Indeed, the 'bloodshed' all round was very slight, and in the decisive phase trifling, by any Clausewitzian standard.

While this sweeping victory was attained by action against objectives of a military nature, it was mainly through action of a *manœuvre* form—strategic more than tactical.

Moreover, the effect of cutting the opposing armies' communications, and dislocating their control-system, in the deeply penetrating drive is hard to distinguish from its accompanying effect in shaking the people's morale *and* disrupting civic organization. So it could be termed as, at least in part, a proof of the new effectiveness of operating against civil objectives.

Similar reflections apply to the even swifter conquest of the Balkans in April 1941—which once again demonstrated the paralysing effect of the new instruments and their strategic application. 'Battle' was insignificant in comparison, and 'destruction' palpably an inappropriate term for the way that the decision was achieved.

When it came to the invasion of Russia a somewhat different method was tried. Many of the German generals—particularly Halder, the Chief of the General Staff—complain of Hitler's tendency to aim at economic rather than military objectives. But analysis of the operational orders and of their own evidence does not bear out the charge. While Hitler was inclined to think that the economic aim would be more effective, it is clear that in the crucial period of the 1941 campaign he conformed to the General Staff's preference for fighting battles. The pursuit of this aim did not prove decisive, although it produced several great victories in which immense forces of the enemy were destroyed.

Whether concentration on economic objectives would have been more decisive remains an open question. But in reflection some of the ablest of the German generals consider that the best chance of defeating Soviet Russia was lost by aiming to win battles in the 'classical' way, instead of driving through as fast as possible to the moral-cum-economic objectives offered by Moscow and Leningrad—as Guderian, the leading exponent of the new school of mechanical mobile warfare, wished to do. On this key question Hitler had sided with the orthodox school.

In the series of swift German conquests, the air force combined with the mechanized elements of the land forces in producing the paralysis and moral disintegration of the opposing forces and of the nations behind. Its effect was terrific, and must be reckoned fully as important as that of the panzer forces. The two are inseparable in any valuation of the elements that created the new style of lightning warfare—the *blitzkrieg*.

Even greater was the contribution that the British and American air forces made, later in the war, to the success of the Allied armies and navies. It was due to the air forces, above all, that the Allied invasion of the Continent became possible in the first place, and then an assured advance to victory. By their action against military objectives—particularly communications—they had a decisively crippling effect on the ability of the German armies to counter the Allied moves.

The Air Staffs, however, never showed the same eagerness to conduct operations of this kind as they did to pursue independent operations against 'civil' objectives—the attack on the industrial centres of the opposing country. Its purpose, as conceived, was to combine a direct economic and moral effect on the opposing nation, in the belief that it would prove more decisive, and more quickly decisive, than co-operative action against the enemy's armed forces.

Although the Air Staffs termed this 'strategic bombing' the term was really a misnomer, for such an aim and action lies in the sphere of grand strategy. It would be more correctly defined as 'grand strategic bombing', or, if that seems too cumbrous a term, as 'industrial bombing', a term which covers moral as well as economic effect.

The actual effect which this kind of bombing achieved as a contribution to victory is very difficult to assess despite much detailed investigation. The estimation of the data is confused by partisan assessments—both by those who favoured industrial bombing, and by those who opposed it on various grounds. Apart from the fog thus created, a correct assessment is handicapped and made almost impossible by the amount of *imponderabilia* in the data—even more than in the evidence about any other form of military action.

But it seems fairly certain, even on a reasonably favourable view of its effects, that they were less decisive than the action of air forces against strategic objectives—in the military sphere. In any case, they were much less clearly decisive. It is also clear that, stage by stage throughout the war, the results fell far short of what was being claimed for this kind of action by those who were conducting it.

Still clearer is the extremely detrimental effect of industrial bombing on the post-war situation. Beyond the immense scale of devastation, hard to repair, are the less obvious but probably more lasting social and moral effects. This kind of action inevitably produces a deepening danger to the relatively shallow foundations of civilized life. That common danger is now immensely increased by the advent of the atomic bomb.

Here we are brought to the fundamental difference between strategy and grand strategy. Whereas strategy is only concerned with the problem of winning military victory, grand strategy must take the longer view—for its problem is the winning of the peace. Such an order of thought is not a matter of 'putting the cart before the horse', but of being clear where the horse and cart are going.

Air action against an object that is primarily 'civil' is action on the plane of grand strategy. It is called into question on that very account. By the test of its own nature, it is seen to be an unsound objective. It would be an unwise choice as a military aim even if its ability to decide a war were more conclusively proved, or at least more clearly demonstrated, than it actually has been.

Further Revision of Theory

In trying to revise any theory and readjust it for better balance, it is a help to have a background of study in the subject—as long as one is willing to modify one's conclusions. I was, so far as I know, the first student of war after 1914–18 to make a re-examination of the prevailing doctrines, derived from Clausewitz, about the objective in war. After calling it in question in a number of articles in the military journals, I dealt with it more fully in *Paris, or the Future of War*, 1925.

This little book began with a criticism of the way that the orthodox aim, 'the destruction of the enemy's main forces on the battlefield', had been pursued in World War I—pointing out its indecisive and exhausting results. It then went on to argue the advantages of the 'moral objective', showing (i) how armoured forces might deliver a decisive blow against 'the Achilles' heel of the enemy army—the communications and command centres which form its nerve system'; (ii) how air forces, besides co-operating in this strategic action, might also strike with decisive effect direct at 'a nation's nerve system', its 'static civil centres' of industry.

The General Staff prescribed the book for the study of the officers of the first Experimental Mechanized Force when this was formed two years later. The Air Staff, less surprisingly, made still fuller use of it—there was then a lack of text-books on air strategy, and it fitted the developing trend of their views on the subject. The Chief of the Air Staff distributed copies of it to his fellow Chiefs of Staff!

What I have said now is thus a revision, after prolonged reflection, of what I wrote a quarter of a century ago—and an avowal of error over part of the thesis. It shows how in correcting the balance one is apt to tilt it too far the other way. T. E. Lawrence observed in a letter he wrote me in 1928:

'The logical system of Clausewitz is too complete. It leads astray his disciples—those of them, at least, who would rather fight with their arms than with their legs. . . . You, at present, are trying (with very little help from those whose business it is to think upon their profession) to put the balance straight after the orgy of the last war. When you succeed (about 1945) your sheep will pass your bounds of discretion, and have to be chivvied back by some later strategist. Back and forward we go.'

In 1925, I myself went too far in arguing the advantages of the air stroke at civil objectives—though I did qualify this by emphasizing the importance of executing it in such a way as to inflict 'the least possible permanent injury, for the enemy of to-day is the customer of the morrow and the ally of the future'. My belief then was that 'a decisive air attack would inflict less total damage and constitute less of a drain on the defeated country's recuperative power than a prolonged war of the existing type'.

In further study I came to realise that an air attack on industrial centres was unlikely to have an immediately decisive effect, and more likely to produce another prolonged war of attrition in a fresh form—with perhaps less killing but more devastation than the 1914–18 form. But when one began to point this out, one soon found that the Air Staff was far less receptive to the revised conclusion than to the original conclusion! They continued to cherish faith in a speedy decision, and when war experience compelled them to relinquish it, they pinned their faith instead to industrial attrition—as fervently as the General Staff of the last war had done to man-power attrition.

Nevertheless, a realization of the drawbacks and evils of taking the civil fabric as the objective does not mean the restoration of 'battle' in the old sense as the objective. The drawbacks of that Clausewitzian formula were amply shown in World War I. In contrast, World War II demonstrated the advantages and new potentialities of indirect, or strategic, action against a military objective—amply confirming what had been forecast in that respect. Even in the past such action had been effectively exploited by some of the Great Captains, despite the limitations of their instruments. But now, with the help of new instruments, it proved still more decisive—despite the increased strength of tactical resistance. *The new mobility produced a flexibility, in varying the direction of thrust and threat, which 'disarmed' such resistance.*

The time has come for a fresh revision of the doctrine of the objective, or military aim, in the light of recent experience and present conditions. It is much to be desired that it should be undertaken on a Combined Service basis, to produce an agreed solution—for there is a dangerous discordance of doctrine at present.

The outlines of a revised theory fitted to present conditions and knowledge have emerged, I hope, in the course of this discussion of the subject. The key idea is 'strategic operation' rather than 'battle' —an old term that has outlived its suitability and utility. Battles may still occur, but should not be regarded as the aim itself. To repeat an earlier conclusion that was strikingly vindicated in

World War II—'the true aim is not so much to seek battle as to seek a strategic situation so advantageous that if it does not of itself produce the decision, its continuation by a battle is sure to achieve this'.

CHAPTER XXII

GRAND STRATEGY

★

This book is concerned with strategy, rather than with grand strategy—or war policy. To deal adequately with this wider subject would require not only a much larger volume, but a separate volume—for while grand strategy should control strategy, its principles often run counter to those which prevail in the field of strategy. For that very reason, however, it is desirable to include here some indication of the deeper conclusions to which a study of grand strategy leads.

The object in war is to attain a better peace—even if only from your own point of view. Hence it is essential to conduct war with constant regard to the peace you desire. This is the truth underlying Clausewitz's definition of war as a 'continuation of policy by other means'—the prolongation of that policy through the war into the subsequent peace must always be borne in mind. A State which expends its strength to the point of exhaustion bankrupts its own policy, and future.

If you concentrate exclusively on victory, with no thought for the after-effect, you may be too exhausted to profit by the peace, while it is almost certain that the peace will be a bad one, containing the germs of another war. This is a lesson supported by abundant experience.

The risks become greater still in any war that is waged by a coalition. For in such a case a too complete victory inevitably complicates the problem of making a just and wise peace settlement. Where there is no longer the counter-balance of an opposing force to control the appetites of the victors, there is no check on the conflict of views and interests between the parties to the alliance. The divergence is then apt to become so acute as to turn the comradeship of common danger into the hostility of mutual dissatisfaction—so that the ally of one war becomes the enemy in the next.

This raises a further and wider question. The friction that commonly develops in any alliance system, especially when it has no balancing force, has been one of the factors that have fostered the numerous attempts throughout history to find a solution in fusion. But history teaches us that in practice this is apt to mean domination by one of the constituent elements. And although there is a natural tendency towards the fusion of small groups in larger ones, the usual result of forcing the pace is the confusion of the plans to establish such a comprehensive political unit.

Moreover, regrettable as it may seem to the idealist, the experience of history provides little warrant for the belief that real progress, and the freedom that makes progress possible, lies in unification. For where unification has been able to establish unity of ideas it has usually ended in uniformity, paralysing the growth of new ideas. And where the unification has merely brought about an artificial or imposed unity, its irksomeness has led through discord to disruption.

Vitality springs from diversity—which makes for real progress so long as there is mutual toleration, based on the recognition that worse may come from an attempt to suppress differences than from acceptance of them. For this reason, the kind of peace that makes progress possible is best assured by the mutual checks created by a balance of forces—alike in the sphere of internal politics and of international relations.

In the former sphere, the experience of the two-party system in English politics continued long enough to show its practical superiority, whatever its theoretical drawbacks, to any other system of government that has yet been tried. In the international sphere, the 'balance of power' was a sound theory so long as the balance was preserved. But the frequency with which the European 'balance of power' has become unbalanced, thereby precipitating war, has produced a growing urge to find a more stable solution—either by fusion or federation. Federation is the more hopeful method, since it embodies the life-giving principle of co-operation, whereas fusion encourages the monopolizing of power by a single political interest. And any monopoly of power leads to ever-repeated demonstration of the historical truth epitomized in Lord Acton's famous dictum—'All power corrupts, and absolute power corrupts absolutely.' From that danger even a federation is not immune, so that the greatest care should be taken to ensure the mutual checks and balancing factors necessary to correct the natural effect of constitutional unity.

Another conclusion which develops from the study of grand strategy against the background of history is the practical necessity of adapting the general theory of strategy to the nature of a nation's fundamental policy. There is an essential difference of aim, and must be a consequent difference of appropriate method between an 'acquisitive' and a 'conservative' State.

In the light of this difference it becomes clear that the pure theory of strategy, as outlined earlier in Chapter XIX, best fits the case of States that are primarily concerned with conquest. It has to be modified if it is to serve the true purpose of peoples that are content with their existing territorial bounds, and are primarily concerned to preserve their security and maintain their way of life. The acquisitive State, inherently unsatisfied, needs to gain victory in order to gain its object—and must therefore court greater risks in the attempt. The conservative State can achieve its object by merely inducing the aggressor to drop his attempt at conquest—by convincing him that 'the game is not worth the candle'. Its victory is, in a real sense, attained by foiling the other side's bid for victory. Indeed, in attempting more it may defeat its own purpose —by exhausting itself so much that it is unable to resist other enemies, or the internal effects of overstrain. Self-exhaustion in war has killed more States than any foreign assailant.

Weighing these factors of the problem, it can be seen that the problem of a conservative State is to find the type of strategy that is suited to fulfil its inherently more limited object in the most strength-conserving way—so as to insure its future as well as its present. At first glance, it might seem that pure defence would be the most economical method; but this implies static defence—and historical experience warns us that it is a dangerously brittle method on which to rely. Economy of force and deterrent effect are best combined in the defensive-offensive method, based on high mobility that carries the power of quick riposte.

The East Roman Empire was a case where such an actively 'conservative' strategy had been carefully thought out, as a basis of war-policy—a fact which goes far to explain this empire's unrivalled span of existence. Another example, more instinctive than reasoned, is provided by the strategy, based on sea-power, that England practised in her wars from the sixteenth to the nineteenth century. The value of it was shown by the way that her strength kept pace with her growth, while all her rivals broke down in turn through self-exhaustion in war—traceable to their immoderate desire for the immediate satisfaction of outright victory

A long series of mutually exhausting and devastating wars, above all the Thirty Years' War, had brought statesmen by the eighteenth century to realize the necessity, when engaged in war, of curbing both their ambitions and their passions in the interests of their purpose. On the one hand, this realization tended to produce a tacit limitation of warfare—an avoidance of excesses which might damage after-the-war prospects. On the other hand, it made them more ready to negotiate a peace if and when victory came to appear dubious of achievement. Their ambitions and passions frequently carried them too far, so that the return to peace found their countries weakened rather than strengthened, but they had learnt to stop short of national exhaustion. And the most satisfactory peace settlements, even for the stronger side, proved to be those which were made by negotiation rather than by a decisive military issue.

This gradual education in the inherent limitations of war was still in process when it was interrupted by the French Revolution, which brought to the top men who were novices in statesmanship. The Directory and its successor, Napoleon, pursued the vision of an enduring peace through war after war for twenty years. The pursuit never led to the goal, but only to spreading exhaustion and ultimate collapse.

The bankruptcy of the Napoleonic Empire renewed a lesson that had often been taught before. The impression, however, came to be obscured by the sunset haze of Napoleonic myth. The lesson had been forgotten by the time it was repeated in the war of 1914–18. Even after that bitter experience the statesmen of the Second World War were no wiser.

Although war is contrary to reason, since it is a means of deciding issues by force when discussion fails to produce an agreed solution, the conduct of war must be controlled by reason if its object is to be fulfilled. For—

(1) While fighting is a physical act, its direction is a mental process. The better your strategy, the easier you will gain the upper hand, and the less it will cost you.

(2) Conversely, the more strength you waste the more you increase the risk of the scales of war turning against you; and even if you succeed in winning the victory, the less strength you will have to profit by the peace.

(3) The more brutal your methods the more bitter you will make your opponents, with the natural result of hardening the resistance you are trying to overcome; thus, the more evenly the two sides are matched the wiser it will be to avoid extremes of violence which tend to consolidate the enemy's troops and people behind their leaders.

(4) These calculations extend further. The more intent you appear to impose a peace entirely of your own choosing, by conquest, the stiffer the obstacle you will raise in your path.

(5) Furthermore, if and when you reach your military goal, the more you ask of the defeated side the more trouble you will have, and the more cause you will provide for an ultimate attempt to reverse the settlement achieved by the war.

Force is a vicious circle—or rather, a spiral—unless its application is controlled by the most carefully reasoned calculation. Thus war, which begins by denying reason, comes to vindicate it—throughout all phases of the struggle.

The fighting instinct is necessary to success in the battlefield—although even here the combatant who can keep a cool head has an advantage over the man who 'sees red'—but should always be ridden on a tight rein. The statesman who gives that instinct its head loses his own; he is not fit to take charge of the fate of a nation.

Victory in the true sense implies that the state of peace, and of one's people, is better after the war than before. Victory in this sense is only possible if a quick result can be gained or if a long effort can be economically proportioned to the national resources. The end must be adjusted to the means. Failing a fair prospect of such a victory, wise statesmanship will miss no opportunity for negotiating peace. Peace through stalemate, based on a coincident recognition by each side of the opponent's strength, is at least preferable to peace through common exhaustion—and has often provided a better foundation for lasting peace.

It is wiser to run risks *of* war for the sake of preserving peace than to run risks of exhaustion *in* war for the sake of finishing with victory—a conclusion that runs counter to custom but is supported by experience. Perseverance in war is only justifiable if there is a good chance of a good end—the prospect of a peace that will balance the sum of human misery incurred in the struggle. Indeed, deepening study of past experience leads to the conclusion that nations might often have come nearer to their object by taking advantage of a lull in the struggle to discuss a settlement than by pursuing the war with the aim of 'victory'.

History reveals, also, that in many cases a beneficial peace could have been obtained if the statesmen of the warring nations had shown more understanding of the elements of psychology in their peace 'feelers'. Their attitude has commonly been too akin to that seen in the typical domestic quarrel; each party is afraid to appear yielding, with the result that when one of them shows any inclination towards conciliation this is usually expressed in language that is too stiff, while the other is apt to be slow to respond—partly from pride or obstinacy and partly from a tendency to interpret such a gesture as a sign of weakening when it may be a sign of returning common sense. Thus the fateful moment passes, and the conflict continues—to the common damage. Rarely does a continuation serve any good purpose where the two parties are bound to go on living under the same roof. This applies even more to modern war than to a domestic conflict, since the industrialization of nations has made their fortunes inseparable. It is the responsibility of statesmanship never to lose sight of the post-war prospect in chasing the 'mirage of victory'.

Where the two sides are too evenly matched to offer a reasonable chance of early success to either, the statesman is wise who can learn something from the psychology of strategy. It is an elementary principle of strategy that, if you find your opponent in a strong position costly to force, you should leave him a line of retreat—as the quickest way of loosening his resistance. It should, equally, be a principle of policy, especially in war, to provide your opponent with a ladder by which he can climb down.

The question may arise as to whether such conclusions, based on the history of war between so-called civilized States, apply to the conditions inherent in a renewal of the type of purely predatory war that was waged by the barbarian assailants of the Roman Empire, or the mixed religious and predatory war that was pursued by the fanatical followers of Mahomet. In such wars any negotiated peace tends to have in itself even less than the normal value (it is only too clear from history that States rarely keep faith with each other, save in so far, and so long, as their promises seem to them to combine with their interests). But the less that a nation has regard for moral obligations the more it tends to respect physical strength—the deterrent power of a force too strong to be challenged with impunity. In the same way, with individuals it is a matter of common experience that the bully-type and the robber-type hesitate to assail anyone who approaches their own strength —and are far more reluctant to attempt this than a peaceful type of individual is to tackle an assailant bigger than himself.

It is folly to imagine that the aggressive types, whether individuals or nations, can be bought off—or, in modern language, 'appeased'—since the payment of danegeld stimulates a demand for more danegeld. But they can be curbed. Their very belief in force makes them more susceptible to the deterrent effect of a formidable opposing force. This forms an adequate check except against pure fanaticism—a fanaticism that is unmixed with acquisitiveness.

While it is hard to make a real peace with the predatory types, it is easier to induce them to accept a state of truce—and far less exhausting than an attempt to crush them, whereby they are, like all types of mankind, infused with the courage of desperation.

The experience of history brings ample evidence that the downfall of civilized States tends to come not from the direct assaults of foes but from internal decay, combined with the consequences of exhaustion in war. A state of suspense is trying—it has often led nations as well as individuals to commit suicide because they were unable to bear it. But suspense is better than to reach exhaustion in pursuit of the mirage of victory. Moreover, a truce to actual hostilities enables a recovery and development of strength, while the need for vigilance helps to keep a nation 'on its toes'.

Peaceful nations are apt, however, to court unnecessary danger, because when once aroused they are more inclined to proceed to extremes than predatory nations. For the latter, making war as a means of gain, are usually more ready to call it off when they find an opponent too strong to be easily overcome. It is the reluctant fighter, impelled by emotion and not by calculation, who tends to press a fight to the bitter end. Thereby he too often defeats his own end, even if he does not produce his own direct defeat. For the spirit of barbarism can be weakened only during a cessation of hostilities; war strengthens it—pouring fuel on the flames.

APPENDIX I

THE STRATEGY OF INDIRECT APPROACH IN THE NORTH AFRICAN CAMPAIGN, 1940–42

An account by MAJOR-GENERAL ERIC DORMAN-SMITH,
Deputy Chief of the General Staff, Middle East, 1942
(*originally a letter, printed as foreword to the 1946 edition*)

★

MY DEAR BASIL,

I told you earlier that your ideas had influenced the course of events in Egypt in our favour at two crucial times between 1940 and 1942. For the plan of attack that led to the annihilation of Graziani's army at Sidi Barrani, and broke the first invasion of Egypt in 1940, was a perfect example of your strategy of indirect approach, while the defensive strategy and tactics that foiled Rommel's invasion at El Alamein in July 1942 was more immediately inspired by it. I was going to tell you the story in more detail, and here it is. From it you will see that whenever we neglected the principle we paid dearly for our neglect.

In September 1940 I was sent (from being Director of Military Training in India) to be Commandant of the newly created Middle East Staff College. Early in October, when Graziani's invading army was halted about Sidi Barrani, I went up to stay for two weeks with O'Connor's forces in the Western Desert. O'Connor was studying the possibilities of an offensive stroke, despite Graziani's numerical superiority by land and air. We discussed the faults in Graziani's dispositions and the possibilities of a wide approach manœuvre south of the escarpment, aimed at Sollum and Halfaya, there creating what you call a 'strategic barrage' behind the enemy's front; or, alternatively, a stroke nearer Sidi Barrani. Transport stringency eventually dictated the second course.

The diversion of part of the Middle East's scanty air force to Greece postponed the offensive, and on 21st November, Wavell ordered me to revisit the Western Desert headquarters. There O'Connor asked me to give him an independent opinion on the 4th Indian Division's rehearsal for an attack against a fortified desert encampment such as the Italians held in their chain of positions south of Sidi Barrani. This trial attack, as rehearsed, was entirely frontal and would have been delivered along 'the line of most expectation', straight over a minefield which at that time we had no means of lifting. It was timed so that our artillery could have four hours after daylight for registration—which was dangerous, for during that pause our assaulting troops would have lain under the menace of the enemy's very superior air force. In sum, the method conformed to the official pamphlet, and not to the tactical situation: it would certainly have failed. That evening O'Connor, Galloway and I evolved an unorthodox and very indirect manœuvre. We embodied our conclusions in a paper, 'Method of Attack on a Desert Camp', which served as the tactical directive for the operation, and worked like a charm. It applied your principle of the 'Indirect Approach'—in direction, in method, in timing, and psychologically.

The approach march started on the 8th, and that night our forces assembled in the area south of Nibeiwa, the southernmost camp in the enemy's front, and close to the gap between that and the group of camps at Sofafi which covered his landward flank. Immediately after first light on 9th December the Army Tank Battalion (the 7th R.T.R.) and some motorized infantry of the 4th Indian Division assaulted and captured the Nibeiwa camp *from the rear*, afterwards going on to take Tummar, also from the rear. The long pause for registration was eliminated, and the artillery support was entirely unregistered, seventy-two guns 'browned' the Italian encampment from the opposite direction to the tank assault, and we placated the gunners by calling it 'fire for demoralization', which it certainly was. Meantime the 7th Armoured Division had swept through the gap and gone westward into the rear of the enemy's whole forward area to cut him off from reinforcements, and block his retreat to Sollum. This compound of indirect tactical moves completely upset the enemy's balance. His resistance collapsed, and we rounded up the bulk of his army east of the escarpment at amazingly slight cost to our own forces, numerically much smaller, despite our marked air inferiority. As Wavell once wrote me: 'A little unorthodoxy is a dangerous thing, but without it one seldom wins battles.'

Not the least interesting feature of O'Connor's offensive was the fact that owing to acute transport stringency he was forced to dump water-supplies and ammunition for forty-eight hours' fighting, in the mobile outpost zone under Graziani's nose, and had his operation not succeeded within this time margin he would have had to retreat for lack of water, using his administrative transport to carry his infantry. No other British, and I think very few Continental commanders, except possibly the Russians, would have begun an offensive under this handicap. But O'Connor twice did this, the second time at Beda Fomm. He is a bold and calculating fighter, and a very dangerous opponent, who undertakes the indirect approach in thc administrative field.

After our advance into eastern Cyrenaica, I went up in January, to prepare a report on the operations leading to the capture of Bardia and Tobruk. O'Connor told me his future plans, and I had the luck to take part in evolving and accompanying the Beda Fomm flank march (by the 7th Armoured Division) which cut off the remainder of the enemy's forces south of Benghazi, before it could retreat into Tripolitania.

All this took place before the new edition of your *Strategy of Indirect Approach* was published. But you must remember that for a long time my mind has been steeped in the essence you have distilled from history, into which you have infused your own military philosophy, and it fascinated me to perceive how strikingly all these operations demonstrated your theory in practice.

Late in 1941 I received the copy of your republished classic that you had sent to me some time that summer. I read and re-read it in the next few months. My grasp of strategic principles was refreshed and aroused. The significance of your theory, checked with the facts of the North African campaign, became even clearer than before. Certainly O'Connor's operations from December 1940 to February 1941 were an outstanding example of strategical and tactical indirectness. From their brilliant beginning at Sidi Barrani to their dashing finale at Beda Fomm every masterly move was a direct testimony of the truth analysed and expounded in Chapters X to XII[1] of your book. But then O'Connor is a commander of the first order, and in fact the only leader of a British field force during this war to 'kill his fox in the open'.

In the spring of 1941, the dramatic advent of Rommel saw the weapon of the indirect approach turned against us, and our small

[1] Now Chapters X, XIX, XX.

and ill-equipped forces barely escaped disaster by a disorderly retreat to Tobruk. This was when, alas, we lost O'Connor. But the decision to halt within the 27½ miles of the Tobruk perimeter with a force of 4½ brigades—which, though absurdly small for the purpose, was practically all the fighting troops we had in Egypt—daringly wrested the weapon of indirectness from Rommel, and for all that summer and autumn the enemy had barely sufficient strength to contain us in Tobruk and to hold his positions about Sollum against our efforts to relieve Tobruk by land. The decision to hold Tobruk we owe to Churchill and Wavell. I flew up to Tobruk on the 10th April to give Morshead the order to stand there.

Our offensives in June 1941 on the Egyptian frontier, though the situation offered wide scope for 'obliquity', were frontal and obvious and dismally abortive. For that matter our very direct and frank advance into Syria from Palestine met with sharp checks, and might well have led to defeat had not our subsequent indirect advances from northern Iraq, then under Auchinleck's command, against the vulnerable eastern flank of Vichy-Syria, reaffirmed the correctness of the principle by taking the French in rear. So far in every operation your theory had been justified.

Command of the Middle East changed in June 1941, and it fell to Auchinleck from India to reorganize and re-inspire the somewhat dispirited forces in the Western Desert for the next onslaught on the Axis in Cyrenaica. At that stage the Western Desert Force became the Eighth Army. Tobruk was still invested, and Rommel was gradually collecting the means to deliver a decisive assualt on its weak defences. In November, before Rommel was ready to assault Tobruk, we launched the offensive known as 'Crusader'. It had a sound strategical background which gave the army commander, Cunningham, a well-placed line of operations northwards from a hidden desert supply area about Maddalena, and a two-pronged choice of objectives against the rear of the enemy investing Tobruk, or alternatively of those on the frontier defences. Rommel, on the other hand, was very awkwardly disposed with his back to the sea and, having to protect both the siege of Tobruk and his Halfaya positions, he had no depth. Our approach from Maddalena compelled him to engage at right angles to his communications. Despite these considerable advantages the operation failed to destroy Rommel's forces, because our tactical plan was designed to enable our armour to bring Rommel's armour to battle as a preliminary to any indirect moves against Tobruk or the frontier defences. Rommel, though partially surprised strategically, fought his technically superior armour in combination with his other arms and administered an initial tactical defeat, which was only retrieved after the operation had degenerated into a corps commanders' battle, from which Ritchie belatedly developed an indirect approach via Bir Gobi and El Adem. This caused Rommel to withdraw his main forces in fair order to El Agheila, sacrificing his troops on the frontier and in Bardia.

Thereafter the principle of indirect approach left our banners. Rommel's next sally from El Agheila found our forces over-dispersed and thrust them back in disorder. Once at Msus he had Ritchie on the horns of a dilemma, with its points at Benghazi and Mechili; from these Ritchie escaped by a precipitate retreat towards Tobruk which halted on the Gazala–Bir Hacheim line, having outstripped pursuit. From February 1942 to May 1942 the Eighth Army lay disposed in line between Gazala and Bir Hacheim much as it had come to rest after retreat, while Rommel, secure in the Jebel Akdar, planned its further discomfiture. During that period, having visited the Eighth Army front, I interested myself in thinking out a tactical layout for a modern army which would avoid the defects which were apparent in Graziani's dispositions at Sidi Barrani, and which had reappeared in Ritchie's dispositions at Gazala and Tobruk. For the dispositions of the Eighth Army in the period February to May 1942 bore a striking resemblance to the dispositions of the Italian army about Sidi Barrani in October and November 1940, in that they lacked depth and flexibility, and important detachments were exposed beyond tactical support.

Here we come up against the greatest problem of desert warfare: the ratio of frontage to depth, and forward troops to reserves. Mechanized mobility is so easy in the desert, particularly since administrative factors greatly reduce the size of the field armies, that the side which 'stays put' in defence is readily outflanked by its opponent. To counter this, the tendency is to over-extend the front in detriment to depth and reserves, and a surrender to this tendency has never proved the right answer. This tendency is particularly noticeable when the army is short of mobile troops or weak in offensive armour, and also where the command is ignorant of the fundamental nature of this type of warfare. Rommel himself succumbed to this in the autumn of 1942, when as a result of the

July fighting he over-extended his front to the Qattara depression, and so had little real depth of defence when Montgomery attacked.

The problem that defeated first Graziani, and then Ritchie, is clearly defined in your passages on the *Action of Strategy*, being: How to avoid the psychological dislocation which results from the enemy making a sudden move against one's rear or, conversely, how to dispose an army so that it can use its arms in a new direction without becoming unbalanced. The solution lies in so disposing one's own forces that 'the mere fact of one's enemy marching towards the rear of one's dispositions does not constitute a strategic indirect approach'. This implies that the defending army must be able to develop as powerful a defence to its flanks and rear as to the part originally nearest to the enemy, and in all warfare effective defensive action is the resultant of a check to the enemy's advance and a general counter-attack.

There are in fact only three possible dispositions for a defending army. One is linear with mobile reserves. The second is circular, i.e. linear but with a closed rear ('the hedgehog'); and the third is an open chequered square. This chequer square must have the centres of resistance as widely separated as is compatible with mutual artillery fire support and the capacity of reinforcing movement within its area, and the whole disposition must admit of at least 75 per cent of the mobile missile-throwing element of the whole being able to concentrate at the point of attack before the enemy can break the resistance of the threatened 'chequer localities'. This implies some abandonment of the rigid divisional area and divisional front idea laid down in *Field Service Regulations* which has produced a tendency in our commanders to think that if on any given frontage you deploy *x* divisions in line, each should concentrate solely on the defence of its own frontage and only assist its nearest neighbours in its own particular interest. In this idea it is the task of reserve formations to support any forward division which is heavily attacked or to protect the array from rear attack. The difficulty of defensive action by small forces in open country arises from the fact that the defender invariably over-extends his front, and so has little or no depth or reserves, unless he understands that we are now back to the Waterloo ratios of number, frontage and mobility—and adjusts accordingly.

The answer seemed to lie in a modernized form of the Legionary disposition in which the army on the defensive is disposed with its stable defensive element holding localities some 10,000 yards apart laterally and in depth, each containing a quota of artillery and infantry; while the remainder of the artillery, infantry and armour is free to move within this framework either to concentrate at any threatened point or to strike at the flank and rear of an enemy attempting to by-pass the array. In this way an army of, say, four infantry divisions and an armoured corps could be disposed in a rectangle of 24 miles by 18 miles and still be mutually supporting, while the armoured element could operate with this disposition as a pivot. The airfields must be covered by the ground layout, and in rear of it. Outside, on either flank of the rectangle of the chequer, there should be light mobile elements, with independent maintenance areas; and, slightly withdrawn but within gun-support from the 'legion' should be such heavy armour as one has—with the whole system flexible. In very open country the 'legionary pivots' occupy areas of observation—for thus they control, by commanding, the fields of movement. In close and roaded country, they would be placed at road centres. The whole should be mobile, flexible, yet well-defended. Compare this system with the paper on defence you gave me when I first came back from Egypt, and you will see that it is the same idea.

A disposition of the Eighth Army south of Tobruk on these lines would have defeated Rommel. But the actual dispositions of the Eighth Army were, as I have said, linear, and lay wide open to an attack in the classical oblique order. This Rommel undertook on the 27th May. His plan was for the bulk of the Italian element of *Panzer Armee Afrika* to contain Ritchie's front, while the relatively small German Afrika Korps, with a few of the better Italians, bypassed the Free French post at Bir Hacheim and struck at Ritchie's sensitive area between El Adem and Knightsbridge. Though the initial attack did not entirely succeed, this clever blow so paralysed Ritchie that Rommel was enabled, firstly, to destroy an isolated brigade of the 50th Division, and also capture the even more isolated Free French position at Bir Hacheim, thus clearing his rear; and secondly, after defeating several frontal counter-attacks with heavy loss, to develop a new advance against El Adem which again placed Ritchie on the horns of a dilemma, because this advance equally threatened the rear of our forces holding the Gazala sector, or the ground immediately east of Tobruk where lay our railhead and dumps. This threat so impressed the army commander that he withdrew something more than half the Eighth Army to the Egyptian frontier, leaving the remainder in Tobruk without fighter cover, doomed to inevitable destruction.

In these operations, Rommel gave a masterly exposition of the principle of indirect approach—with a small German body approximating to two brigades of armour, and four of mechanized infantry, he attacked and defeated in detail the whole of Ritchie's Eighth Army, most of which he immobilized by means of a frontal threat from the numerous but otherwise quite useless Italian element.

On the 25th June, Auchinleck, superseding Ritchie, took direct command of operations in the Western Desert, and I accompanied Auchinleck to Headquarters Eighth Army. By this time what remained of the Eighth Army was retreating to the vicinity of Mersa Matruh, Ritchie having evaded Rommel's effort to cut it off at the Egyptian frontier. Auchinleck's arrival brought a new factor into the struggle, for he disposed of what remained of the military forces between Matruh and Persia, and as Commander-in-Chief was able to make the wider strategical decisions necessary to produce the maximum concentration of effort in this crisis. His first problem was whether to give battle near Matruh or to withdraw farther east. In view of the mythical prestige which attached to the defended areas about Matruh it would seem at first sight a good place to fight, but Mersa Matruh could only be held if the defending army had an armoured force large enough to prevent the enemy from by-passing via the desert; without such a force, the Matruh and Baguish defences would have become waterless internment camps, past which the enemy would have swept to the Nile Delta.

Since the bulk of our armour had been lost during the earlier fighting, the Commander-in-Chief decided only to delay the enemy in mobile battle south of Matruh, and to make his main stand near El Alamein, where he would fight the 'Battle for Egypt'. But he made two other decisions which were to alter the whole technique of that later battle, and would automatically give it a quality of indirectness. The first decision was to centralize once more the higher control of the artillery of the army, which had been unsoundly fractionized by a permanent dispersal of the field regiments into the infantry brigade-groups. The second decision was to ignore the widely dispersed previously prepared defences between El Alamein and the Qattara depression, which were no longer suited to the type of battle he intended to fight. In the event this last decision considerably perplexed the enemy. He also thinned out his formations, which were carrying over-many vulnerable unmechanized infantry for this mobile warfare.

History will, I think, show that Auchinleck's handling of the Eighth Army in June and July 1942 not only saved the United Nations from very far-reaching defeat, but also provided students of war with a classical exposition of the application of the indirect approach. Though his strategy was necessarily defensive, every tactical action was offensive. Having got his remnants back to Alamein, his first concern was to smash Rommel's head-on rush on Alexandria via the coast. Between the 1st and the 3rd July the Axis forces attacked our positions south of El Alamein, only to meet intense artillery fire and air bombardment from an elastic and evasive front stretching from El Alamein to the dominating ground of the Rweisat ridge. The technique of this front itself was novel, for in it the infantry and artillery lay side by side. It was in fact a flexible 'front' of 25-pounders protected by closely disposed infantry, and supported by such tanks as we had left. Against this disposition the Afrika Korps wilted, and by 3rd July its attacks ceased.

Without delay Auchinleck took the offensive and struck with his left wing, under Gott, comprising the mobile element of the New Zealand Division and the 7th Motor Brigade, against Rommel's right flank guard, which was at that time about half-way between the coast and the Qattara depression. This attack, which seriously damaged the Italian Ariete Division, Rommel met by dispatching most of his German troops to extend his right to the Qattara depression, leaving his left by the coast to be held mainly by Italians. These, on 10th July, Morshead's 9th Australian Division attacked with such success that Rommel only saved the day with troops just arrived by air from Crete, and had to bring his tired Germans north again at full speed. No sooner had this happened than Auchinleck made his third attack, this time with the New Zealanders against the Italians at the centre of Rommel's front.

The effect of these three well-calculated attacks was to force Rommel to stiffen the demoralized Italians by dispersing the German Afrika Korps along the whole forty miles between the sea and the Qattara depression, so in effect immobilizing the offensive element of *Panzer Armee Afrika*.

Thus by mid-July the Axis invasion had been defeated; and from then onwards the enemy faced an increasing scale of loss by battle-casualty, and disease, as they lay on a forty-mile front in open desert, exposed to the pitiless bombardment of a powerful air force and the concentrated fire of more than three hundred field-guns. Rommel's offensive against the Delta had failed decisively, and since his arrival at El Alamein he had lost some 9,000 prisoners. But Rommel had considerable powers of recovery. It yet remained to destroy him, and meanwhile so to strengthen the general defences of Egypt and the position of the Eighth Army that if Rommel attacked again he would fail. It was also necessary to be prepared for pursuit in case circumstances compelled Rommel to withdraw from his exposed and over-extended front, though in view of his temperament this step appeared to be unlikely.

The most immediate task was to strengthen the position of the Eighth Army in the open country between the sea and the Rweisat ridge with one flank open to the south, for we have seen that twice in these campaigns had armies lying thus in open desert been attacked and destroyed by smaller forces. (The effect is fully described in Chapter XI[1] of your book.) Auchinleck's problem was how to secure the Eighth Army against a repetition by Rommel of the move round Ritchie's flank. His solution embodied the theoretical layout I have already described. Having abandoned the unsuitable positions prepared in 1941 he constructed immediately in rear of the front of the Eighth Army, which extended only slightly south of the Rweisat ridge, a distance of 20 miles, a chequer of localities each 10,000 yards apart laterally and in depth, and each garrisoned by two infantry battalions and one 25-pounder battery. Divisions with three infantry brigades had three such localities in their area. There were no isolated localities. But these localities were merely a skeleton framework for the defence plan of the whole army's area; as much of the army as was not required to hold this framework was free to operate, under Auchinleck's personal command, in the interval between the localities to either flank or to front and rear. Inside this great chequer board lay mine belts so disposed as to present no protection to an enemy and to facilitate one's own counter-manœuvre. An army so disposed could form front in any direction without loss of equilibrium. In consequence there was no danger of any part of the army fighting in isolation or its higher command experiencing that distraction from the rearward attack which was so fatal to Graziani and Ritchie. Auchinleck's headquarters lay within the chequer area. But more than this is necessary. Should the enemy operate

[1] Now Chapter XIX.

against one or other flank of the defended area he too must be attacked from outside as well as inside, and Auchinleck therefore arranged for a counter-stroke by armoured and motor elements from the south-east against any such movement. This plan embraced a three-way application of the indirect approach—the 'chequer' being designed to meet the enemy's advance in an essentially indirect way, while both the heavy armoured group and the light mobile group were so placed as to be capable of executing an indirect approach to the enemy's flank and rear in their varying ways.

But even had Rommel succeeded in compelling us to retreat from our Alamein–Rweisat chequer positions before the Eighth Army had absorbed its reinforcements just arriving from home, all would have by no means been over, for as soon as we got to Alamein preparations were made for a second defensive battle farther east if our first failed. To this end the defences of Alexandria were extended both into the desert beyond Amriya and east of the Nile. The obstacle of the Wadi Natrun was also made the basis of a defended area, while west of Cairo the defences in the Cultivation were extended towards the Fayum and preparations made to bridge the Nile near Maadi and farther south. This work ensured that should the Eighth Army have to withdraw from the El Alamein area because Rommel was too strong for it, its withdrawal would be in good order and intact, and so conducted as always to threaten the flank of the enemy's advance from two directions.

On 6th August 1942, when Wavell visited the Eighth Army, he said to me before leaving: 'You are very advantageously posted indeed. This is a form of defence which would justify a withdrawal of your front so as to lure the enemy into your network. Have you considered doing so?' We had, in fact, examined this possibility, and the idea seemed promising.

It is perhaps unfortunate for military science that this defensive layout was never properly tested in battle. For when Rommel next advanced in September, the reinforced and rested Eighth Army was superior to him in numbers, fire-power and armour, and his attack which came against the southern flank of the chequer layout met with such opposition from our powerful reserve formations that it never got anywhere and lost some sixty tanks. In fact, he never looked like getting anywhere. Even so, the general pattern of the battle developed on the late Commander-in-Chief's plan and not on Rommel's. It was Auchinleck's victory, other commanders profited by his foresight. This does not detract from the value of the idea, or from the merit of the commander who was prepared to use a whole sequence of new ideas even in a crisis. In effect Rommel was defeated in July, even if we had to wait till October for Montgomery's riposte to put the seal on Auchinleck's victory. The spirit of the indirect approach and the offensive-defensive which inspired this layout will be found in all your works.

Twice in this war have our forces in the Middle East passed through crises which, had events gone other than they did, might have sealed their fate. The offensive Battle of Sidi Barrani was the first occasion; the defensive Battle for Egypt was the second. Had O'Connor failed or had Rommel defeated the Eighth Army under Auchinleck, the Axis would have overrun Egypt and the Middle East. The history of the war would have been totally changed. Seldom has any general in Auchinleck's position faced such a crucial situation so coolly or so intelligently. Seldom has the art of war seen such a sequence of well-judged examples of the indirect approach, either in defence or in attack, as those which wrested victory from disaster in July 1942. It is almost as if the contents of Chapters X to XII[1] inspired them, and this is to some extent the case, as I have indicated. This is not to imply that O'Connor or the Auk or any good general makes war from any book, but their study and reflection were as continuous in war as in peace. One can conclude from this review of a series of campaigns in which victory uniformly followed the application of your principles of indirect approach, that except where one side has a crushing preponderance of land weapons, mobility and air-power, any commander is unwise to neglect those principles. It is, moreover, significant to note that neither Rommel at Gazala nor O'Connor at Sidi Barrani possessed air superiority. Air superiority, however powerful, will never compensate for bad generalship on the ground.

Critical readers of your book will find in it no ritual formulae for success—instead they will discover a key to a method of approach to the solution of the problems of war on all planes of action, and that key is 'obliquity'. It is a purely mental instrument, and only for the use of the critical and unorthodox—those open-minded soldiers who can say with Brian Boru before the battle of Clontarf, 'What sort of a war will it be to-day?' There is

[1] Now Chapters X, XIX, XX.

no readily discernible law about the business—the current factors of the situation correctly appraised in the search for the best means of indirect attack on the enemy's mental and physical freedom of action will dictate the appropriate obliquity of action. At one time this is logistical, at another ballistical. Attack and defence must be employed according to the dictates of obliquity. Strategic defence may dictate attack. Strategical attack may best derive from an initial tactical defensive. The attitude of mind is important. Obliquity is always offensive. A defensive *spirit* towards one's opponent, however powerful he may appear, is a defeated spirit. The object of obliquity is to find the chink in the armour, the mental armour at that. One's object is the psychological disruption of the opposing command, and the yardstick of success is the degree of freedom of action one enjoys at the end of the process. To this end one seeks all possible means of keeping the enemy guessing, hence the value of alternative objectives. But there are no tangible rules and there is no hope for the direct-minded 'bon general ordinaire' to whom the 'dust upon the shewbread is holy over all'.

There is little doubt that the true mental qualities for success on all the planes of military action are common sense, reason and obliquity; and the last quality becomes the more necessary as one ascends the scale to the plane of independent command. The way of the indirect approach is assuredly the way to win wars.

Yours ever,

ERIC

October 1942

APPENDIX II

Condensed translation of Article by General Yigael Yadin, published in *Bamachaneh* (The Israel Forces' Journal), September 1949.

'FOR BY WISE COUNSEL THOU SHALT MAKE THY WAR'

(Proverbs 24, 6)

A strategical analysis of last year's battles
by GENERAL Y. YADIN,
Chief of the General Staff, Israel Forces

★

The problem that faces strategical planning (and also tactical planning, though in a more restricted sense) is twofold. We must, on the one hand, strive by all means to prevent the enemy from acting on sound principles; on the other hand, a supreme planning effort must be made to enable our forces to exploit those principles, in order to facilitate the achievement of our aims and objectives. For this purpose every principle which the enemy is likely to apply must serve as a target for the ingenuity of those who plan the operations of our forces.

Let us examine what this requires: Against the principle of surprise—continuous activity by the various intelligence agencies. Against the principle of maintenance-of-aim—tactical diversionary attacks and strategical, psychological and political offensives. Against the principle of economy-of-force—attacks against lines of communications and stores in the rear, thereby pinning down the enemy's forces and dispersing them. Against the principle of co-ordination—strike against the channels of administration. Against the principle of concentration—diversionary attacks and air activity to split up the enemy's forces. Against the principles of security—sum total of the above activities and those that follow. Against the principle of offensive-spirit—offensive spirit. Against the principle of mobility—destruction of lines of communications.

As to planning our activity—designed to achieve the military-political aim determined by the Government at each stage—this must be co-ordinated with secondary and diversionary operations. But we should always bear in mind that its main object is to exploit the principles of war so fully, and in such manner, that the fate of the battle will be strategically determined even before the fighting begins—or, at least, ensure that the fighting will proceed with maximum advantage to ourselves. Indeed, this is the secret of perfect strategic planning. Clausewitz's famous saying that 'blood is the price of victory' is obsolete thinking.

The days of frontal tactical attacks are fast disappearing, and the art of tactics aims at achieving the main task by flank and rear attacks. There are still, however, debates among the captains-of-war whether this is also the method applicable to strategy. It certainly applies, but in a different manner, naturally. There is no doubt that the strategy of indirect approach is the only sound strategy; but the constitution of the indirect approach in strategy —as brilliantly defined, explained and elaborated by Captain Liddell Hart—is far wider and more complex than in the tactical field. To exploit the principles of war for our purpose and base ourselves upon strategic indirect approach, so as to determine the issue of the fighting even before fighting has begun, it is necessary to achieve the three following aims:

(*a*) to cut the enemy's lines of communication, thus paralysing his physical build-up;

(*b*) to seal him off from his lines of retreat, thus undermining the enemy's will and destroying his morale;

(*c*) to hit his centres of administration and disrupt his communications, thus severing the link between his brain and his limbs.

Reflection on these three aims proves the truth of Napoleon's saying: 'The whole secret of the art of war lies in the ability to become master of the lines of communication.'

The execution of these aims is the condition for the primary strategic mission, as so aptly defined by Captain Liddell Hart in analysing the aim of strategy and the responsibility of the strategist: 'The true aim is not so much to seek battle as to seek a strategic situation so advantageous that if it does not of itself produce a decision, its continuation by a battle is sure to achieve this.'

The determinant strategical situation is achieved mainly by dislocating the enemy's organization—and thus causing 'the enemy's dissolution or his disruption in battle'—by the three methods described above. On the other hand, in planning their execution one has often to take account of political factors that govern the form of execution. Thus, for example, it is well known that the quickness of the effect of cutting lines of communication and blocking routes of retreat is in inverse ratio to the distance of the location, where such operations are carried out, from the main force against which one fights. In other words, the nearer the cutting-off point lies to the main force of the enemy, the more *immediate* the effect; whereas the further back it takes place, and the nearer to the enemy's strategic base, the *greater* the effect. Plans have therefore to be framed in accordance with the time factor available for the operation. This time factor was sometimes determined in our battles by 'artificial' causes, because of the special character of the war last year—i.e. the intervention of the United Nations from time to time. It sometimes necessitated choosing plans that would achieve a more immediate effect and not necessarily the greatest effect, as we shall note further on when we analyse the battles of last year.

A few more words on maintenance-of-aim. The aim must be single, but the method of achieving it, if we want to be sure of maintaining it, must comprise alternatives—for otherwise the failure of one method will immediately bring about failure in achieving the aim. A plan must be based upon: 'If . . . such and such will happen . . . then . . .; if, on the other hand such will happen . . . then. . . .' See in this connection the very lucid considerations of Jacob in his preparations for battle with Esau in Genesis 32. Liddell Hart very aptly wrote: 'A plan, like a tree, must have branches if it is to bear fruit; a plan with a single aim is apt to prove a barren pole.'

My purpose is to enable our soldiers to study and analyse for themselves the battles in which they took part and make them try to apply it to strategic considerations and assumptions, and not be satisfied with tactical subjective descriptions in which our war literature so abounds. Nevertheless, let me say a few words in analysing some of last year's operations in the light of what was said before. The most important were:

(*a*) Operation Ten Plagues (against the Egyptians);
(*b*) Operation Ayin (against the Egyptians);
(*c*) Operation of consolidation in Elath (Gulf of Aqaba area);

(*d*) Operation 'Hiram' (liberation of Galilee);

and from a strategical point of view, as defined above, even the 'Rhodes Operations' (Armistice agreements). A survey will show that the planning of all these operations was prepared upon the strategical principles and methods that we have mentioned—indirect strategical approach, cutting off, sealing off, and maximum exploitation of cunning to achieve surprise directed at a basic and speedy dislocation of the enemy's deployment. Time factors, not least by reason of various interventions, have also influenced the choice of methods.

The Egyptian enemy invading the country hoped that its gateways would be open to him, and he therefore moved north up the coastal highway towards Isdud, and when he was halted he branched off towards Faluja in the direction of Jerusalem. His forces were very superior and compelled us to avoid frontal battles as far as possible, as he would have enjoyed superiority—being established as he was in a number of defensive localities and having a superior quantity of defensive weapons, On the other hand, his main weakness was in that very point above quoted from Napoleon: 'The whole secret of the art of war lies in the ability to become master of the communications'—for his lines of communication were extremely long.

'Operation Ten Plagues'—the aim of which was to open the way to the Negev and dislocate the enemy's deployment—exploited this weakness to the maximum. And the triple system I have mentioned—cutting off supplies, blocking routes of retreat, and striking at centres of administration—found a classical example in 'Operation Ten Plagues':

(1) The break-through east of Iraq el Manshiyah, cutting the enemy's eastern communications on the one side and taking Hill 113 on the other side, combined with numerous strokes by the various commando units, undermined the physical structure of the enemy's deployment.

(2) The conquest of Beth-Hanun—thus blocking the retreat route for his main force—confused the enemy, and in addition to the physical effect of cutting lines of communication, fundamentally undermined his will and morale, bringing about his decision to withdraw (this, incidentally, is an example of close-blocking, and the way it has an immediate effect).

(3) The repeated bombardment of Gaza, Majdal, Rafah and El-Arish hit the arteries and centres of the enemy's administration

and paralysed his entire nerve system—the system linking the brain with the limbs.

One should mention the fact that our forces operated both against the enemy's northern sector and against his western sector with large and independent formations, thus giving the command the flexibility for fruitful shifting of the centre of gravity in accordance with requirements.

'Operation Ayin', also against the Egyptians, in the Auja-El-Arish area, brought some very striking lessons in the art of war. At the outset the Egyptian enemy failed to exploit his two arms, western and eastern, in such a way as to gain a decisive strategical advantage. After 'Operation Ten Plagues', he belatedly tried to make use of the eastern arm to cut off and seal off the southern Negev. As remarked earlier, the most suitable answer to offensive spirit is offensive spirit, and this was, indeed, the origin of 'Operation Ayin'. (Our sages have long ago said: 'He who comes to kill thee, thou precede to kill him.') The weight of the offensive against the enemy's rear, the surprise in the route of approach (doing what the enemy regards as 'the impossible') through Haluzah towards Auja and the strategical diversion (combining tactical, psychological and political threat) against the western sector along the coast, all combined to produce victory.

'Operation Ayin' demonstrated clearly the truths mentioned above—that the aim of a strategical plan is to decide the issue of battle even before battle begins, or at least to create such conditions that the battle itself is sure to bring about a decision. The exploitation of 'Operation Ayin' by pursuit into Egypt also demonstrated in an apt way the other principle mentioned earlier, regarding the relationship between the location of the sealing-off and the speed and proportion of its effect. The break-through of our forces towards El-Arish, and the domination of the vital crossroads at Abu Aweiglia in the Sinai Desert, would have brought even more decisive results, but the time required for a decision was too long. On the other hand, the speedy switch of the sealing-off action to the neighbourhood of Rafah—although likely to be of a less decisive character by reason of its proximity to the enemy's main forces (thus placing him in a position of tactical superiority *vis-à-vis* our forces)—produced more immediate results, and promptly brought the Egyptian application for an armistice.

The various 'Rhodes operations' and the operation for our establishment in Elath as well as our expansion in the so-called near the 'junction'. Since it had failed, there was no choice but to assault these unassisted. The Egyptian defences there were based on a number of hills—some in its immediate vicinity, some up to a mile away—and on the police fortress of Iraq-Suweidan, some two miles to the east of the junction, dominating the country for scores of miles around. There was nothing indirect about the assault on these features. During the night of the 16th–17th, Hill 113 and a number of other hills were taken, after severe hand-to-hand fighting, which in some instances ended with teeth being used. The Egyptians proved that they knew not only how to organize a position for defence, but also how to defend it.

The attack opened that night against the Egyptian right flank in the hills of Judea to the south-west of Jerusalem. Although acting as a strategic diversion as intended, this attack could do little to assist the forces 'cracking' the junction, the toughest nut of all.

During the course of the 17th the Egyptians counter-attacked strongly, in order to restore their communications between the Majdal and Faluja areas. They failed, however, to retake any of the hills we had captured. The position now was such that, although the east-west road had been denied to the Egyptians, the south-north road had not yet been opened by us. That could be done either through the capture of the remaining Egyptian strongholds along the north-south road in the area of Huleiqat, or of other strongholds further east which would enable us to by-pass Huleiqat. The following two days were spent by us in this sector in seeking to achieve either of these two objectives, and by the Egyptians in stubborn defence and counter-attack. While the Egyptians managed to hold their ground in the east, from the police fortress of Iraq-Suweidan up to Iraq-el-Manshiyah—the area henceforth known as the Faluja pocket—Huleiqat fell on the night of the 19th–20th October. After an isolation lasting many months (practically since December 1947), a firm bridge had finally been established between the Negev and the rest of Israel.

The remainder of the operation can be briefly summarized. In the west the Egyptians, worried about their communications by the wedge of Beth Hanun, evacuated the area of Majdal almost without firing a shot—thereby evacuating among other points, the Jewish settlements of Yad Mordechai and Nitzanim, which had fallen into their hands in May, after some of the toughest fighting of the war. In the east they were driven from their positions in the mountains, by a swift offensive which brought our forces to the

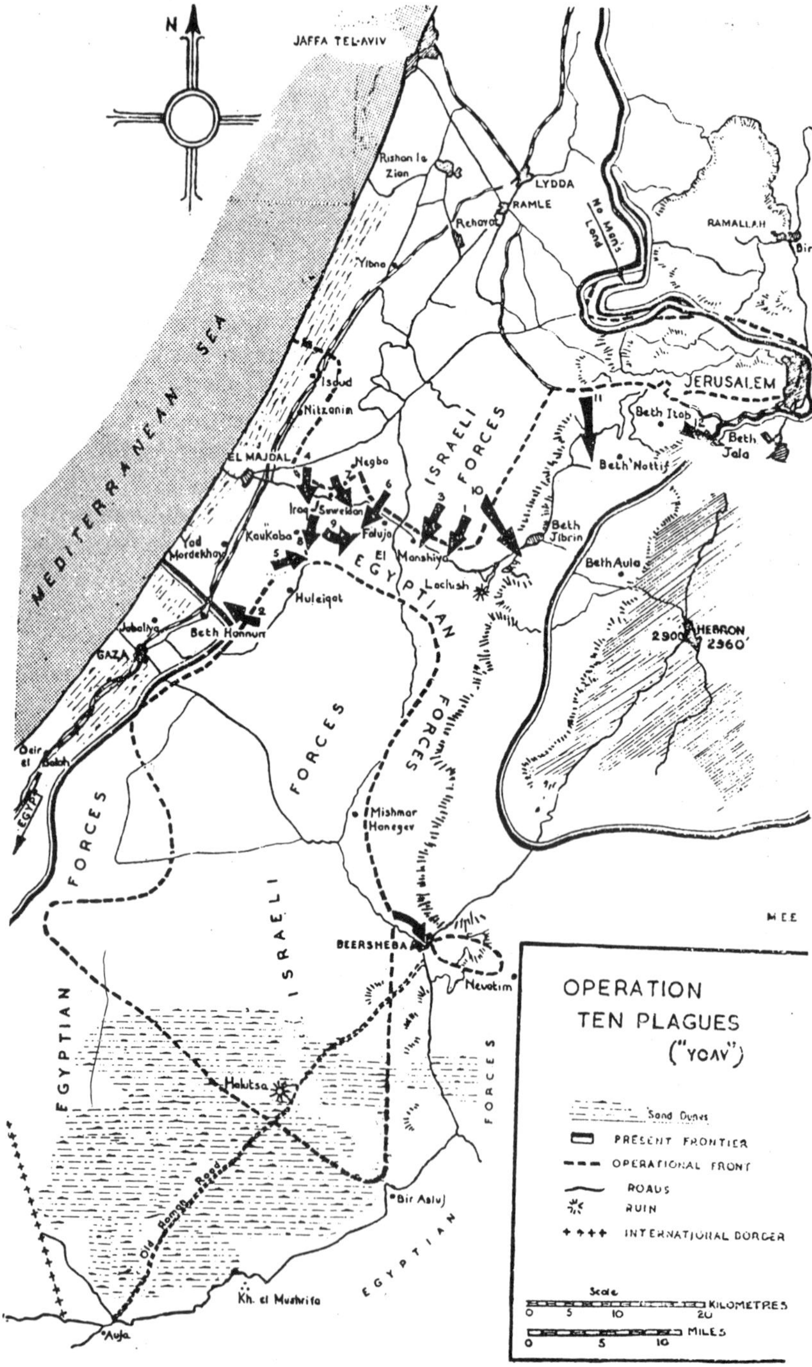

N
JAFFA TEL-AVIV
MEDITERRANEAN SEA
Rishon le Zion
LYDDA
RAMLE
Rehovot
No Man's Land
RAMALLAH
Bira
Yibna
Isdud
Nitzanim
JERUSALEM
Beth Itab
Beth Jala
EL MAJDAL
Negba
ISRAELI FORCES
Beth Nottif
Iraq Suweidan
Faluja
Beth Jibrin
Kaukaba
Yad Mordekhay
El Manshiya
EGYPTIAN
Beth Aula
Laclush
Huleiqat
Jabaliya
Beth Hannun
HEBRON
2900
2960'
GAZA
FORCES
Deir el Balah
EGYPT
Mishmar Hanegev
FORCES
ISRAELI
BEERSHEBA
Nevatim
EGYPTIAN
FORCES
Halutsa
Old Roman Road
Bir Aslu
EGYPTIAN
Kh. el Mushrifa
Auja
OPERATION TEN PLAGUES
("YOAV")
Sand Dunes
PRESENT FRONTIER
OPERATIONAL FRONT
ROADS
RUIN
INTERNATIONAL BORDER
Scale
KILOMETRES
MILES

of Arab settlements along the coastal road as far north as Isdud; those along the Auja-Asluj-Beersheba-Hebron-Bethlehem road; and along the Majdal-Beth Jibrin road, connecting the two laterally.

In spite of considerable exertions, only two Jewish settlements lying isolated astride the coastal road had been taken. A third one, after having successfully withstood a number of attacks, had been evacuated during the first truce. The main area of Jewish settlement in the Negev—the semi-arid area in the south of Palestine which had for the most part been allotted to the Jewish State by the United Nations' Resolution on Partition (November 1947)—was situated further away from the highways, and had remained intact. But its communications with the north—the centre of the State—had been severed by Egyptian positions on both sides of the above-mentioned Majdal-Beth Jibrin positions lateral road.

It was obvious that the resulting situation could only be transitory, even if the provisions of the truce—providing for the use by the Egyptians of the East-West road during certain hours of the day, and by the Israelis of the North-South road during different hours—had been scrupulously observed by the Egyptians, which they were not. Whereas the Egyptians could rest content for the time being, hoping to reduce the Jewish Negev at some future date, or starve it into surrender, the problem of supplies to the settlements forced Israel to take the initiative, particularly since there were indications that the present military situation was contemplated as a basis for a political solution, which would leave Israel without the Negev.

The problem facing the Israeli Command was a formidable one. Conditions in the area had been unsettled for some time. An Israeli convoy despatched south according to a United Nations decision, had been attacked, some of its vehicles set on fire, and the convoy had been compelled to withdraw. It was obvious, therefore, that any action that might be decided upon in retaliation would not achieve surprise. Secondly, it was clear that a way to Negev could only be secured by the capture of one or more of the strongholds on either side of the Majdal-Beth Jibrin road, all of which were well fortified. Furthermore, this had to be achieved early in the operation. In other words, not only did surprise in time have to be sacrificed, but a considerable amount of direct attack—at the very point which the Egyptians would expect us to attack—was unavoidable.

On the other hand, the Egyptian dispositions lacked depth. They consisted of a number of strips—the coastal strip (wedged between the sea and our forces in the Negev), the strip along the Majdal-Beth Jibrin road, and a third strip running north-east into the mountains of Judea. It was this weakness that was exploited by us during the operation, and it compensated to a large extent for the handicaps mentioned above. This, however, required larger forces in the south than we originally possessed. 'Operation Ten Plagues' was therefore preceded by a considerable air-lift into the isolated Negev, which culminated in the passage of a considerable mobile force through the Egyptians' lines, under their noses.

This accomplished, the signal for our offensive was given on the 15th October 1948. That same day, in the afternoon, the Israeli air force attacked the Egyptian airfield at El-Arish and several other targets, including Gaza, Beth Hanun, Majdal and Faluja, dealing a formidable blow to the Egyptian air force—which, though active during the rest of the operation, did not regain superiority in the air. On the following night, Israeli ground forces drove a deep wedge into the Egyptian lines near the village of Beth Hanun, on the coastal road. This threatened, and later on almost severed, the Egyptian communications—thereby preventing reinforcements and supplies from flowing freely towards Majdal, and forcing the Egyptians to divert considerable forces from the main scene of battle. The same motive underlay a series of raids further south, whose task was to blow up bridges and railway lines between El-Arish, Rafah and Han Unis.

At the same time the Majdal-Beth Jibrin lateral road was cut through the occupation of a number of hills hitherto unoccupied by the Egyptians, in the area of Beth Jibrin. Thus, on the morning of the 16th October, though hardly any fighting had as yet taken place, the Egyptian communications had been severed in the north and threatened in the west. The scene seemed to be set for an attempt to cut away through the Egyptian lines in the north. This took the shape of an attack by armour and infantry against the village of Iraq-el-Manshiyah and the ancient Tell, its dominant feature, at dawn on the 16th October. The attack, however, ran into well-ranged artillery defensive fire. A number of tanks were put out of action, and the infantry, now unsupported, was unable to assault. The order was given to retreat.

The capture of Iraq-el-Manshiyah had been intended, *inter alia*, to enable us to threaten from the rear the Egyptian dispositions triangle and Wadi Arah (Megiddo Pass) bring out the lesson that the tools employed in strategy often differ from the tools employed in tactics—in that strategy sometimes chooses political tools to achieve conditions favourable to tactical decision. These tools, when they succeed, save a great deal of blood and sweat.

Last, but not least, I would mention 'Operation Hiram'. This was a blitz operation of classical type, but also provided an apt illustration of a strategical decision—the importance of which is not less, and in this case proved even more effective, than a tactical decision. Kaukji wanted to force a tactical decision that would have ended in his favour if, after his pressure on Manarah, we had allowed ourselves to be drawn into further frontal attacks, when some of them had already failed. In 'Operation Hiram' we applied the strategy of indirect approach, with the fullest possible use of alternatives—co-ordinated in an overall plan and aim based, again, upon the 'triangle' combination of cutting off, sealing off, and striking at centres of administration. The two arms of our forces, the one moving from Safad northwards towards Sasa and the other from Kabri eastwards through Tarshiha, constituted a fine example of planned strategical encirclement in the 1948 campaign, as well as producing the quickest decision.

In conclusion, I would emphasize that it has not been my intention to describe the various actions in detail, but to throw a strategical searchlight upon them—thus providing a comprehensive approach to the understanding of their significance.

NARRATIVE

(by LIEUT.-COLONEL N. LORCH, Chief of the Historical Section, Israel General Staff)

Operation 'Ten Plagues'—15th–21st October 1948

Whereas on other fronts the ten days' fighting between the first and second truces (9th–19th July) had witnessed Isreali initiative and resulting gains, the situation on the Egyptian front had remained more or less static. The Egyptian army, having been disappointed in its original hope of a swift and decisive victory over the poorly equipped and battle-weary Israeli forces, had been concentrating ever since the first truce on consolidating its positions in the part of Palestine held by its forces—which consisted mainly outskirts of Bethlehem. In the north only the force in the Faluja pocket stood fast. This stand underlined a danger inherent in the indirect approach—by cutting his lines of communications an enemy who might otherwise have been inclined to retreat was forced to turn back and fight. But the periphery of the pocket was progressively curtailed, and when the fortress of Iraq-Suweidan finally fell on the 8th November, the pocket had lost its last vestige of potential offensive value. Incidentally, it is of interest that among the documents captured in the fortress was a copy of the *Strategy of Indirect Approach* belonging to the Egyptian commander. It is now cherished as a souvenir by the officer in command of the assault.[1]

In the meantime the operation had been crowned, further south, by the capture of Beersheba. Swiftly exploiting success, forces had been rushed south into the Negev along the road just opened, and together with others already in the Negev they captured the city during the night of the 20th–21st. Although probably not unaware of the fighting going on in the north, the commander of the garrison, not expecting the knock at his door so soon, was taken by surprise, and surrendered after only five hours of fighting. The surrender occurred thirty-one years, almost to a day, after the British had taken Beersheba in World War I, and in sight of the monument which commemorated the Commonwealth soldiers who had fallen in that attack. The capture of Beersheba sealed the fate of the Egyptian garrison in the Hebron area, which soon after was relieved by the Arab Legion, the Egyptians pulling back their right flank southward to Bir-Asluj, south-west of Beersheba.

Operation 'Ayin'—22nd December 1948–7th January 1949

The Egyptian dispositions at the opening of 'Operation Ayin' were similar to those prior to 'Operation Ten Plagues', though greatly reduced in extent. Again there were two wings: that on the left following the coastal road as far as Gaza; that on the right following the Auja-Hebron road up to Bir-Asluj, south-west of Beersheba. The two wings were connected laterally by the Rafah-Auja road, which ran partly in Egyptian territory, and further south by the road connecting El Arish with Abu Aweiglia. In

[1] But fortunately for us they did not grasp the essence of the book, and therefore were completely surprised by our strategical plan based on the principles of this book (*signed*) Y. Yadin.

addition there were still detached Egyptian forces in the Faluja pocket, and to a lesser degree in the Hebron area. Although unlikely to undertake any major offensive operation without the assistance of at least one of the other Arab armies, the Egyptian army had not been defeated. Still holding considerable areas of Palestine, it constituted a threat—and, unless finally defeated, would constitute a permanent danger—to the safety of the young State.

The Egyptians' dispositions were based mainly on two premises, of which one proved correct, whereas the second turned out to be erroneous, and led ultimately to their defeat. The first of these was that in an unpopulated area like the southern Negev, whoever was master of the lines of communication would be master of the whole area; the second, that lines of communication in this territory could be identified with the existing metalled roads. Consequently they once more based their defence on a series of strongholds lying astride the above-mentioned roads, with their main fields of fire towards the roads themselves.

The only lessons they had learnt from 'Operation Ten Plagues' were that the Israelis specialized in night attack, and that the Israel air force had now become a weapon to be considered. As a result, their positions were better camouflaged than before, and alertness during the night had been stepped up.

Our general plan of attack resembled that of Allenby for the third Gaza battle in the autumn of 1917, but carried out in the reverse direction—for whereas Allenby's drive pushed up from the south, ours came down from the north. The idea was to attract and pin down as large a proportion of the Egyptian forces as possible in the western sector and then, by a determined push, to roll up the eastern wing beyond the Egyptian border. That accomplished, our forces were to wheel north-west, and force an evacuation of the Gaza strip by threatening its communications with Egypt—if necessary accompanied by a direct attack on Gaza in the last stage of battle.

The operation opened with a concentrated attack by the Israeli air force on Egyptian airfields and troop concentrations at Rafah, Hans Yunis and Gaza, followed by artillery shelling of Egyptian strongholds along the whole front. During the same night our forces on the Western Front occupied a series of hills some eight miles south of Gaza, thus threatening to cut the Rafah-Gaza road. Following their previous experience, the Egyptians were not slow

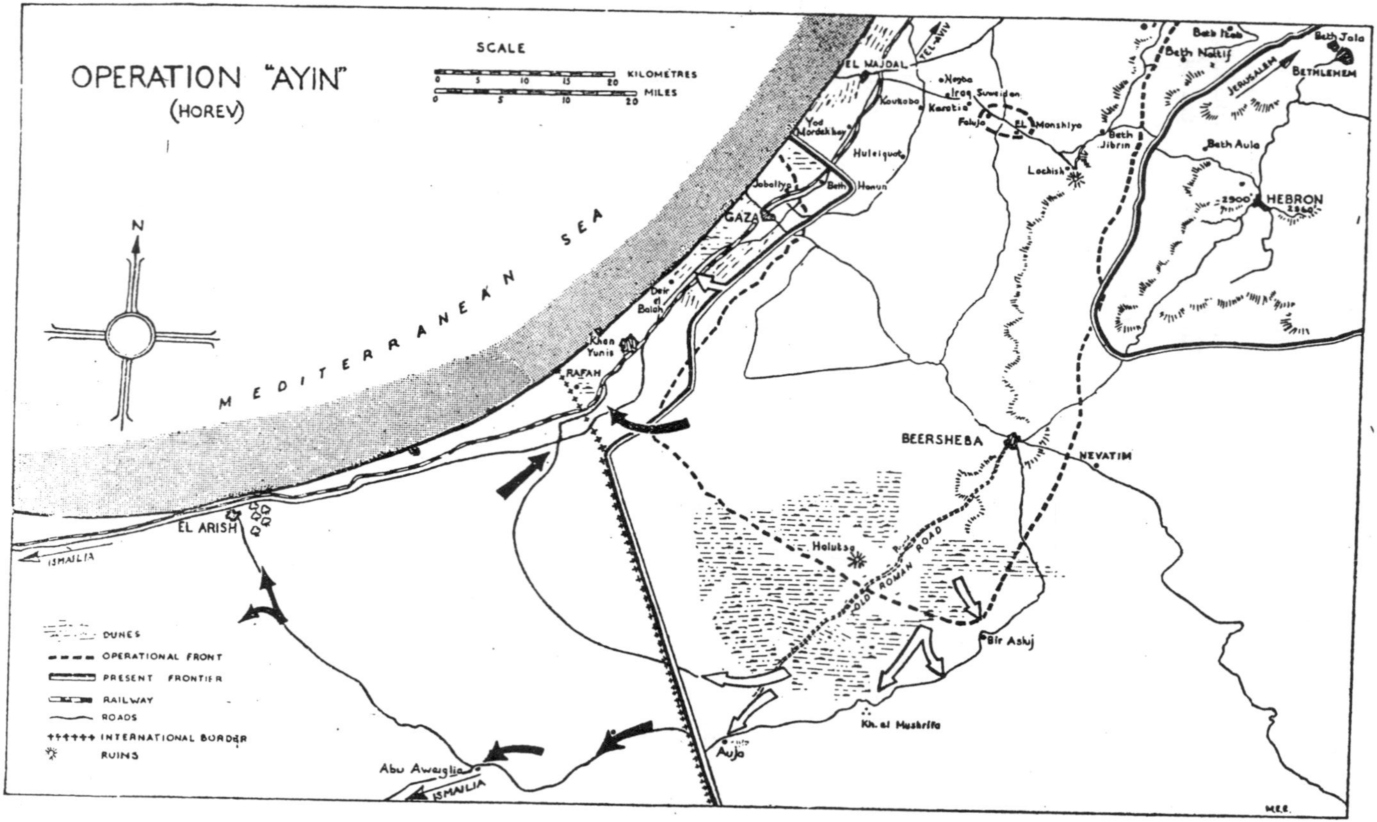

OPERATION "AYIN"
(HOREV)
SCALE
KILOMETRES
MILES
N
MEDITERRANEAN SEA
EL MAJDAL
TEL-AVIV
Kaukaba
Karatia
Iraq Suweidan
Faluja
EL Monshiya
Beth Jibrin
Lachish
Yad Mordekhay
Huleiquat
Jabaliya
Beth Hanun
GAZA
Deir el Balah
Khan Yunis
RAFAH
Beth Natif
JERUSALEM
BETHLEHEM
Beth Jala
Beth Aula
HEBRON
2900
BEERSHEBA
NEVATIM
Halutsa
OLD ROMAN ROAD
Bir Asluj
Kh. el Mushrifa
Auja
Abu Aweiglia
ISMAILIA
EL ARISH
DUNES
OPERATIONAL FRONT
PRESENT FRONTIER
RAILWAY
ROADS
INTERNATIONAL BORDER
RUINS

in swallowing the bait, and they concentrated a considerable force, including most of their armour, four counter-attack in that sector, while also strengthening their defences in the Gaza-Rafah area as a whole.

Although Hill 86 was retaken by the Egyptians after obstinate fighting, it served its purpose of a diversion. Thus when the attack started in the eastern sector, it achieved complete strategic surprise. The first objective was the clearing of the Beersheba-Auja road up to and including Auja itself. The Egyptians were, of course, prepared for such a move; they little expected, however, that our intelligence would rediscover an ancient Roman road running from Beersheba in an almost straight line to the rear of Auja. Even less did they expect that our engineers would be able, undetected, to prepare that road for the passage of vehicles as heavy as medium tanks. Yet that was what happened. While the Egyptian outposts at Bir-Asluj were eagerly watching the Beersheba road, expecting an attack from that direction, Israeli light mobile forces emerged from the desert, captured a series of strongholds further south, and blocked the Auja-Rafah road in two places. When Auja itself was attacked at dawn on the 25th December, it had already been cut off both from its northern outposts and from its bases in the west. The garrison of that locality did its utmost, but after all reinforcements had been repulsed by the blocking forces on the road to Rafah it retreated into the desert in the early hours of the 27th December. A few hours later Bir-Asluj, now completely isolated, was occupied, and the Beersheba-Auja road was opened to our traffic, thus completing the first phase of our plan.

Although our troops were tired by the fighting of the previous days, Phase II of the operation started after only the shortest possible interval for rest, and the bringing up of supplies, then pushing on into Egypt. Abu Aweiglia, an Egyptian base in Sinai on the road to Ismailya, was taken during the night of the 28th-29th December, and an armoured column was now pushed forward along the road to El-Arish, capturing an airfield south of the townlet, with some of its aircraft intact. Another push should have enabled us to take up positions astride the coastal road, and to reach the coast in the vicinity of El Arish. Here, however, political circumstances intervened in the military conduct of the offensive. Whereas the Egyptians had been suffered all along to operate undisturbed on Israeli territory, it was made clear that the presence

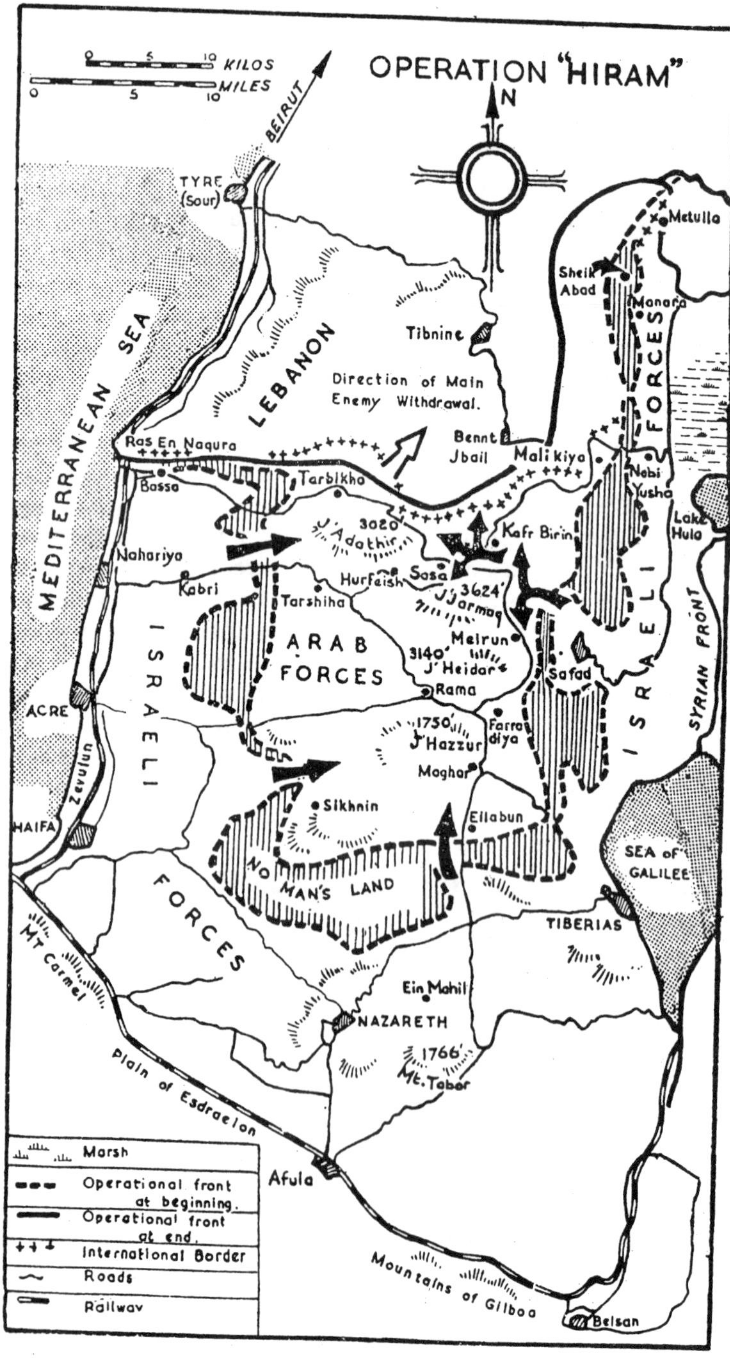

OPERATION "HIRAM"
KILOS
MILES
BEIRUT
N
TYRE (Sour)
MEDITERRANEAN SEA
LEBANON
Tibnine
Direction of Main Enemy Withdrawal.
Metulla
Sheik Abad
Manara
Ras En Naqura
Bennt Jbail
Mali kiya
Nebi Yusha
Bassa
Tarbikha
3020' J'Adathir
Kafr Birin
Lake Hula
Nahariya
Kabri
Hurfeish
Sasa
3624' J'Jarmaq
Tarshiha
ARAB FORCES
Meirun
3140' J'Heidar
Safad
Rama
ACRE
ISRAELI FORCES
SYRIAN FRONT
1750' J'Hazzur
Farradiya
Moghar
Sikhnin
Ellabun
HAIFA
Zevulun
NO MAN'S LAND
SEA of GALILEE
TIBERIAS
Mt Carmel
Ein Mahil
NAZARETH
1766' Mt. Tabor
Plain of Esdraelon
Afula
Mountains of Gilboa
Beisan
Marsh
Operational front at beginning
Operational front at end
International Border
Roads
Railway

of Israeli forces on Egyptian soil would not be tolerated. Under severe political pressure, and the threat of British military intervention, the armoured column was ordered to withdraw into Israel territory.

There was no choice but to attempt to achieve the same end north of the border line. To that end a number of brigades were hurriedly assembled for an attack on Rafah from the south-east and the south. They occupied a redoubt at the cemetery, within sight of the town and the large British-built camps near it, as well as a group of hills to the south of the El-Arish-Rafah-Auja roads. When the battle had thus reached this stage, on the afternoon of the 7th January, the Egyptians asked for an armistice.

Although the order to retreat from Egyptian territory had been received at the height of the offensive, when the fruits of this seemed in reach, Israel had good grounds for satisfaction when reviewing the results of the operation. Except for the Gaza strip, the Egyptians had been expelled from the whole of Palestine, and a major part of their army had been destroyed or disrupted, being put out of action for a considerable time to come. All this had been achieved by an attacking force barely superior to the defenders in number, and still inferior to them in equipment.

Operation 'Hiram'—28th–30th October 1948

When the regular Arab armies invaded Palestine, the Liberation army under command of Fawzi Kaukji, which had hitherto carried the brunt of the fighting, was withdrawn to reorganize—or rather, to be formed into a regular force. After the first truce Kaukji was left master of Galilee, flirting in turn with the Syrians, the Lebanese, the Iraqis, still nominally under direct command of the Arab League, and not under command of any of the regular armies.

The ten days' fighting between the two truces had cost him most of Lower Galilee, including Nazareth. However, he had succeeded in withdrawing most of his forces into Upper Galilee, where he occupied a rectangular area, about twenty miles by fifteen. Although unlikely to undertake any major offensive on his own in the near future, in view of the repulses he had suffered previously, he still constituted a potential danger in conjunction with one or more of the regular Arab armies. Operating on interior lines, from the vantage-point of the high ground of Galilee, the highest in western Palestine, he was able to undertake an offensive against any one of the three narrow strips held by Israel surrounding his territory—against the Valley of Zebulun in the west, in conjunction with the Lebanese; the Valley of Esdraelon to the south, with the Iraqis; or, most likely, against the Valley of the Hule, with the Syrians.

About the middle of October, Kaukji—counting on Israel having its hands full with fighting on the Egyptian front—decided the time had come in spite of the truce to score at least a partial success in order to re-establish his prestige. He therefore decided to attack the redoubt of Sheikj Abed overlooking the Jewish settlement of Manara (precariously perched on the edge of the mountain ridge, 2,500 feet above the Hule Valley). The redoubt was taken by a surprise attack, and Manara was cut off once more, placing Hule in danger.

However, Kaukji had miscalculated once more—this time fatally. In view of Kaukji's provocation and breach of the truce, and taking advantage of a lull in the fighting on the Egyptian front, which freed the Israeli air force for action elsewhere, the Israeli High Command decided to settle with Kaukji's Army of Liberation once and for all, and to expel it from Palestine—also, if possible, to destroy it completely. The former of these objectives was attained in full, and the latter to a considerable extent, in no more than sixty hours—by 'Operation Hiram'.[1]

The area held by Kaukji was ideally suited for guerrilla warfare, or for defensive action by any resourceful and resolute force. For a regular modern army—and Kaukji had acquired most of the handicaps, though few of the capabilities of such an army—it held one considerable disadvantage: the paucity of adequate roads. One north-south road and four east-west roads were all that could be used. For the rest, there were footpaths, most of them too difficult even for mules. The key to the whole system of communications was the village and road junction of Sasa, where the Bassa-Tarbika and Naharya-Tarshiha roads, coming from the coast, join up with the Farradiya road from the south, and with the Malikiya road running north into the Lebanon—Kaukji's base of supply.

Kaukji's forces were formed into three more or less equal parts, called 'Yarmuk' brigades. Calling them 'brigades' was rather pretentious, and so was their titular association with the Army of the

[1] The code name HIRAM was given after the name of one of the ancient Kings of the Lebanon: Hiram.

Yarmuk which took Palestine from the Byzantines, under command of Khalid-ibn-el-Walid. One of the brigades lay south of the Acre road, the second holding the north-eastern area, including Sasa, and the third the north-west, with headquarters at Tarshiha.

The outline of our plan ran as follows:

Two forces were detailed to pin down Kaukji's forces in the south by feint attacks from the south and south-west, and a third force was to take Tarshiha from the west. Meanwhile the main force—consisting of light armoured cars, half-tracks and infantry—was to push west from Safad to capture Sasa, while securing its flanks and rear against attack from the south and west. Once a junction had been achieved between the western and eastern arms of the pincer, success should be exploited—

(*a*) to wipe out the forces remaining in the bulge, now turned into a pocket;

(*b*) to push north-east and clear the area along the Malikiya-Metulla road, thereby making secure the area of Jewish settlement in the Hule valley below.

The air force was to bomb the main objectives—Tarshiha, Sasa, Malikiya, etc., on the afternoon preceding the zero hour, and subsequently be on call to give support to attacking ground forces where required. Artillery was scanty, being mainly attached to the main effort, but even there hardly amounted to the strength of one battery.

The task of armour in this plan is particularly deserving of note. At first sight its use in this area looked risky, for it would be tied down to the few roads, and at the mercy of an enemy occupying the high ground to either side. Nevertheless, it was decided not only to use it, but to use it as spearhead for the attack on the main objective, and to hold off or delay reinforcements which might be despatched. The dominant consideration was speed. The success of the whole operation depended, both for political and military reasons, on crushing Kaukji before any regular army had time to intervene, and before he himself had time to take stock and evaluate a situation which, even after the loss of Sasa, might have been retrieved. The use of armour under these circumstances was a gamble, but one which came off.

As to the execution of the plan, there is little to be added. Although the clearing of road-blocks and mines during the first night took up more time than anticipated—so that the attack on Meirun and Gish, originally planned for the night, was carried out at dawn —the eastern force was well on its way towards Sasa by the morning of the 29th, having captured two villages just south of it, and repulsed several counter-attacks. A regular Syrian battalion, which had been sent during the night, was attacked and largely destroyed—almost before it had time to take up its allotted positions. The enemy had been taken by surprise.

At the same time the two feint attacks from the south, and southwest, had both succeeded and failed. They succeeded in convincing Kaukji that here was the 'real' effort, but failed to pin down forces on that front, since he hastily ordered a retreat north of the Acre road, i.e. into the area which contained our main objective. The retreating units were, however, of little avail in that area.

The western force failed to capture Tarshiha during that night (28th–29th), with the result that some villages which had already surrendered now turned on the occupying forces, more as an alibi in case of Kaukji succeeding than for anything else.

In the early hours of the following night, the 29th–30th, Sasa was taken, whereupon Kaukji's forces evacuated Tarshiha, which was entered on the 30th early in the morning. A few hours later a junction was established between the forward elements of the east and west forces, though not effective enough to prevent a considerable number of Arab soldiers breaking through and crossing the border into the Lebanon. What followed was a rout—the pursuit not only cleared the whole of Upper Galilee as far as the mandatory boundaries of Palestine in the north, but brought some of our units into the Lebanon, to the Wadi Dubbe.

By 0600 hours on the 31st, less than sixty hours after the start, 'Operation Hiram' had been completed, with hardly any casualties to the attackers.

INDEX OF DEDUCTIONS

INDEX OF DEDUCTIONS

INDEX

INDEX

INDEX

INDEX

INDEX

INDEX

INDEX